Beginning C# Object-Oriented Programming

Dan Clark

Apress®

Beginning C# Object-Oriented Programming

ISBN-13 (pbk): 978-1-4302-3530-9

ISBN-13 (electronic): 978-1-4302-3531-6

President and Publisher: Paul Manning
Lead Editor: John Osborn
Technical Reviewer: Jeff Sanders
Editorial Board: Steve Anglin, Mark Beckner, Ewan Buckingham, Gary Cornell, Jonathan Gennick, Jonathan Hassell, Michelle Lowman, Matthew Moodie, Jeff Olson, Jeffrey Pepper, Frank Pohlmann, Douglas Pundick, Ben Renow-Clarke, Dominic Shakeshaft, Matt Wade, Tom Welsh
Coordinating Editor: Corbin Collins
Copy Editor: Mary Behr
Compositor: Richard Ables
Indexer: John Collin
Artist: April Milne
Cover Designer: Anna Ishchenko

Distributed to the book trade worldwide by Springer Science+Business Media, LLC., 233 Spring Street, 6th Floor, New York, NY 10013. Phone 1-800-SPRINGER, fax (201) 348-4505, e-mail orders-ny@springer-sbm.com, or visit www.springeronline.com.

For information on translations, please e-mail rights@apress.com, or visit www.apress.com.

Apress and friends of ED books may be purchased in bulk for academic, corporate, or promotional use. eBook versions and licenses are also available for most titles. For more information, reference our Special Bulk Sales–eBook Licensing web page at www.apress.com/bulk-sales.

The source code for this book is available to readers at www.apress.com. You will need to answer questions pertaining to this book in order to successfully download the code.

Contents at a Glance

Contents

About the Author

Dan Clark is a senior IT consultant specializing in .NET and SQL Server technology. He is particularly interested in C# programming and SQL Server Business Intelligence development. Dan is a Microsoft Certified Trainer and a Microsoft Certified Solution Developer. For over a decade, he has been developing applications and training others to develop applications using Microsoft technologies. Dan has published several books and numerous articles on .NET programming. He is a regular speaker at various developer conferences and user group meetings, and he conducts workshops in object-oriented programming and database development. He finds particular satisfaction in turning new developers on to the thrill of developing and designing object-oriented applications. You can reach Dan at `Clark.drc@gmail.com`.

About the Technical Reviewer

Jeff Sanders is a published author, technical reviewer, and an accomplished technologist. He is currently employed with Avanade in the capacity of Group Manager/Senior Architect.

Jeff has years of professional experience in the field of IT and strategic business consulting, leading both sales and delivery efforts. He regularly contributes to certification and product roadmap development with Microsoft and speaks publicly on Microsoft enterprise technologies. With roots in software development, Jeff's areas of expertise include operational intelligence, collaboration and content management solutions, digital marketing, distributed component-based application architectures, object-oriented analysis and design, and enterprise integration patterns and designs.

Jeff is also the CTO of DynamicShift, a client-focused organization specializing in Microsoft technologies, specifically SharePoint Server, StreamInsight, Windows Azure, AppFabric, Business Activity Monitoring, BizTalk Server, Commerce Server, and .NET. He is a Microsoft Certified Trainer, and he leads DynamicShift in both training and consulting efforts.

He enjoys non–work-related travel and spending time with his wife and daughter—and wishes he more time for both. He may be reached at `jeff.sanders@dynamicshift.com`.

Acknowledgments

A special thanks to the following people who made this book possible:

- Jonathan Hassell for once again leading the effort to get the project approval.
- Corbin Collins for keeping me on task and for managing the madness.
- Jeff Sanders for the helpful suggestions and making sure this book was technically accurate.
- John Osborn for clarifying my thoughts and increasing the readability of this book.
- The rest of the team at Apress for once again making the process of writing an enjoyable experience.
- And, last but not least, my family for their patience.

Introduction

It has been my experience as a .Net trainer and lead programmer that most people do not have trouble picking up the syntax of the language. What perplexes and frustrates many people are the higher-level concepts of object-oriented programming methodology and design. To compound the problem, most introductory programming books and training classes skim over these concepts or, worse, don't cover them at all. It is my hope that this book fills this void. My goal in writing this book is twofold. First, to provide you with the information you need to understand the fundamentals of programming in C#. Second and more importantly, to present you with the information required to master the higher-level concepts of object-oriented programming methodology and design.

This book provides the knowledge you need to architect an object-oriented programming solution aimed at solving a business problem. As you work your way through the book, you will learn first how to analyze the business requirements of an application. Next, you will model the objects and relationships involved in the solution design. Finally, you will implement the solution using C#. Along the way, you will learn about the fundamentals of software design, the Unified Modeling Language (UML), object-oriented programming, C#, and the .NET Framework.

Because this is an introductory book, it's meant to be a starting point for your study of the topics it presents. As such, this book is not designed to make you an expert in object-oriented programming and UML; nor is it an exhaustive discussion of C# and the .NET Framework; nor is it an in-depth study of Visual Studio. It takes considerable time and effort to become proficient in any one of these areas. It is my hope that by reading this book, your first experiences in object-oriented programming will be enjoyable and comprehensible—and that these experiences will instill a desire for further study.

Target Audience

The target audience for this book is the beginning C# programmer who wants to gain a foundation in object-oriented programming along with the C# language basics. Programmers transitioning from a procedural-oriented programming model to an object-oriented model will also benefit from this book. In addition, there are many Visual Basic (VB) programmers who want to transition to C#. Before transitioning to C#, it is imperative that you understand the fundamentals of object-oriented programming.

Because the experience level of a "beginner" can vary immensely, I have included a primer in Appendix A that discusses some basic programming concepts and how they are implemented in C#. I would suggest you review these concepts if you are new to programming.

Organization of the Book

This book is organized into three parts:

Part 1 delves into object-oriented programming methodology and design—concepts that transcend a particular programming language. The concepts presented are important to the success of an object-oriented programming solution regardless of the implementation language chosen. At the conclusion of this part, a case study walks you through the steps of modeling a real-world application.

Part 2 looks at how object-oriented programming is implemented in C#. You will look at creating class structures, creating hierarchies, and implementing interfaces. This part also introduces object interaction and collaboration. You will see how the object-oriented programming topics discussed in Part 1 are transformed into C# coding constructs.

Part 3 covers creating .NET applications. You will learn how to develop a data access layer using the classes that make up the ADO.NET set of namespaces. You will create a Windows-based user interface, a web-based user interface, and a service-based programmatic interface. At the end of Part 3, you will revisit the case study developed in Part 1 and transform the design into a fully functional C# application. This includes creating a graphical user interface, implementing the business logic, and integrating with a relational database to store data.

Activities and Software Requirements

One of the most important aspects of learning is doing. You can't learn to ride a bike without jumping on a bike, and you can't learn to program without cranking out code. Any successful training program needs to include both a theory component and a hands-on component.

I have included both components throughout this book. It is my hope that you will take seriously the Activities I have added to each chapter and work through them thoroughly—even repeatedly. Contrary to some students' perception that these activities are "exercises in typing," this is where you get a chance to make the theory concrete and where true simulation of the concepts occurs. I also encourage you to play as you work through an Activity. Don't be afraid to alter some of the code just to see what happens. Some of the best learning experiences occur when students "color outside the lines."

The UML modeling activities in Part 1 are for someone using UMLet. I chose this program because it's a good diagramming tool to learn on. It lets you create UML diagrams without adding a lot of advanced features associated with the high-end CASE tools. UMLet is a free open source tool and can be downloaded from `www.umlet.com`. You can also use another tool such as Visio to complete the activities. However, you don't even need a tool to complete these activities; paper and pencil will work just fine.

The activities in Part 2 require Visual Studio 2010 Express with C# installed. I encourage you to install the help files and make ample use of them while completing the activities. The activities in Part 3 require Microsoft SQL Server 2008 with the Pubs and Northwind databases installed. Appendix C includes instructions on downloading and installing the sample databases. You can find free Express editions of both Visual Studio 2010 and SQL Server 2008 at `www.msdn.microsoft.com`.

CHAPTER 1

Overview of Object-Oriented Programming

To set the stage for your study of object-oriented programming and C#, this chapter will briefly look at the history of object-oriented programming and the characteristics of an object-oriented programming language. You will look at why object-oriented programming has become so important in the development of industrial-strength distributed software systems. You will also examine how C# has evolved into one of the leading application programming languages.

After reading this chapter, you will be familiar with the following:

- What object-oriented programming is.
- Why object-oriented programming has become so important in the development of industrial-strength applications.
- The characteristics that make a programming language object-oriented.
- The history and evolution of C#.

The History of OOP

Object-oriented programming (OOP) is an approach to software development in which the structure of the software is based on objects interacting with each other to accomplish a task. This interaction takes the form of messages passing back and forth between the objects. In response to a message, an object can perform an action or method.

If you look at how you accomplish tasks in the world around you, you can see that you interact in an object-oriented world. If you want to go to the store, for example, you interact with a car object. A car object consists of other objects that interact with each other to accomplish the task of getting you to the store. You put the key in the ignition object and turn it. This in turn sends a message (through an electrical signal) to the starter object, which interacts with the engine object to start the car. As a driver, you are isolated from the logic of how the objects of the system work together to start the car. You just initiate the sequence of events by executing the start method of the ignition object with the key. You then wait for a response (message) of success or failure.

Similarly, users of software programs are isolated from the logic needed to accomplish a task. For example, when you print a page in your word processor, you initiate the action by clicking a print button. You are isolated from the internal processing that needs to occur; you just wait for a response telling you if it printed. Internally, the button object interacts with a printer object, which interacts with the printer to accomplish the task of printing the page.

OOP concepts started surfacing in the mid-1960s with a programming language called Simula and further evolved in the 70s with advent of Smalltalk. Although software developers did not overwhelmingly embrace these early advances in OOP languages, object-oriented methodologies continued to evolve. In the mid-80s there was a resurgence of interest in object-oriented methodologies. Specifically, OOP languages such as C++ and Eifle became popular with mainstream computer programmers. OOP continued to grow in popularity in the 90s, most notably with the advent of Java and the huge following it attracted. And in 2002, in conjunction with the release of the .NET Framework, Microsoft introduced a new OOP language, C# (pronounced C-sharp) and revamped Visual Basic so that it is truly an OOP language.

Why Use OOP?

Why has OOP developed into such a widely used paradigm for solving business problems today? During the 70s and 80s, procedural-oriented programming languages such as C, Pascal, and Fortran were widely used to develop business-oriented software systems. Procedural languages organize the program in a linear fashion—they run from top to bottom. In other words, the program is a series of steps that run one after another. This type of programming worked fine for small programs that consisted of a few hundred code lines, but as programs became larger they became hard to manage and debug.

In an attempt to manage the ever-increasing size of the programs, structured programming was introduced to break down the code into manageable segments called functions or procedures. This was an improvement, but as programs performed more complex business functionality and interacted with other systems, the following shortcomings of structural programming methodology began to surface:

- Programs became harder to maintain.
- Existing functionality was hard to alter without adversely affecting all of the system's functionality.
- New programs were essentially built from scratch. Consequently, there was little return on the investment of previous efforts.
- Programming was not conducive to team development. Programmers had to know every aspect of how a program worked and could not isolate their efforts on one aspect of a system.
- It was hard to translate business models into programming models.
- It worked well in isolation but did not integrate well with other systems.

In addition to these shortcomings, some evolutions of computing systems caused further strain on the structural program approach, such as:

- Nonprogrammers demanded and were given direct access to programs through the incorporation of graphical user interfaces and their desktop computers.
- Users demanded a more-intuitive, less-structured approach to interacting with programs.
- Computer systems evolved into a distributed model where the business logic, user interface, and backend database were loosely coupled and accessed over the Internet and intranets.

As a result, many business software developers turned to object-oriented methodologies and programming languages to solve these problems. The benefits included the following:

- A more intuitive transition from business analysis models to software implementation models.
- The ability to maintain and implement changes in the programs more efficiently and rapidly.
- The ability to more effectively create software systems using a team process, allowing specialists to work on parts of the system.
- The ability to reuse code components in other programs and purchase components written by third-party developers to increase the functionality of their programs with little effort.
- Better integration with loosely coupled distributed computing systems.
- Improved integration with modern operating systems.
- The ability to create a more intuitive graphical user interface for the users.

The Characteristics of OOP

In this section you are going to look at the some fundamental concepts and terms common to all OOP languages. Don't worry about how these concepts get implemented in any particular programming language; that will come later. My goal is to merely familiarize you with the concepts and relate them to your everyday experiences in such a way that they make more sense later when you look at OOP design and implementation.

Objects

As I noted earlier, we live in an object-oriented world. You are an object. You interact with other objects. In fact, you are an object with data such as height and hair color. You also have methods that you perform or are performed on you, such as eating and walking.

So what are objects? In OOP terms, an object is a structure for incorporating data and the procedures for working with that data. For example, if you were interested in tracking data associated with products in inventory, you would create a product object that is responsible for maintaining and working with the data pertaining to the products. If you wanted to have printing capabilities in your application, you would work with a printer object that is responsible for the data and methods used to interact with your printers.

Abstraction

When you interact with objects in the world, you are often only concerned with a subset of their properties. Without this ability to abstract or filter out the extraneous properties of objects, you would find it hard to process the plethora of information bombarding you and concentrate on the task at hand.

As a result of abstraction, when two different people interact with the same object, they often deal with a different subset of attributes. When I drive my car, for example, I need to know the speed of the car and the direction it is going. Because the car is an automatic, I do not need to know the RPMs of the engine, so I filter this information out. On the other hand, this information would be critical to a racecar driver, who would not filter it out.

When constructing objects in OOP applications, it is important to incorporate this concept of abstraction. If you were building a shipping application, you would construct a product object with attributes such as size and weight. The color of the item would be extraneous information and filtered out. On the other hand, when constructing an order-entry application, the color could be important and would be included as an attribute of the product object.

Encapsulation

Another important feature of OOP is encapsulation. Encapsulation is the process in which no direct access is granted to the data; instead, it is hidden. If you want to gain access to the data, you have to interact with the object responsible for the data. In the previous inventory example, if you wanted to view or update information on the products, you would have to work through the product object. To read the data, you would send the product object a message. The product object would then read the value and send back a message telling you what the value is. The product object defines what operations can be performed on the product data. If you send a message to modify the data and the product object determines it is a valid request, it will perform the operation for you and send a message back with the result.

You experience encapsulation in your daily life all the time. Think about a human resources department. They encapsulate (hide) the information about employees. They determine how this data can be used and manipulated. Any request for the employee data or request to update the data has to be routed through them. Another example is network security. Any request for the security information or a change to a security policy must be made through a network security administrator. The security data is encapsulated from the users of the network.

By encapsulating data you make the data of your system more secure and reliable. You know how the data is being accessed and what operations are being performed on the data. This makes program maintenance much easier and also greatly simplifies the debugging process. You can also modify the methods used to work on the data, and if you do not alter how the method is requested and the type of response sent back, then you do not have to alter the other objects using the method. Think about when you send a letter in the mail. You make a request to the post office to deliver the letter. How the post office accomplishes this is not exposed to you. If it changes the route it uses to mail the letter, it does not affect how you initiate the sending of the letter. You do not have to know the post office's internal procedures used to deliver the letter.

Polymorphism

Polymorphism is the ability of two different objects to respond to the same request message in their own unique way. For example, I could train my dog to respond to the command *bark* and my bird to respond to the command *chirp*. On the other hand, I could train them to both respond to the command *speak*. Through polymorphism I know that the dog will respond with a bark and the bird will respond with a chirp.

How does this relate to OOP? You can create objects that respond to the same message in their own unique implementations. For example, you could send a print message to a printer object that would print the text on a printer, and you could send the same message to a screen object that would print the text to a window on your computer screen.

Another good example of polymorphism is the use of words in the English language. Words have many different meanings, but through the context of the sentence you can deduce which meaning is intended. You know that someone who says "Give me a break!" is not asking you to break his leg!

In OOP you implement this type of polymorphism through a process called overloading. You can implement different methods of an object that have the same name. The object can then tell which method to implement depending on the context (in other words, the number and type of arguments passed) of the message. For example, you could create two methods of an inventory object to look up the price of a product. Both these methods would be named getPrice. Another object could call this method and either pass the name of the product or the product ID. The inventory object could tell which getPrice method to run by whether a string value or an integer value was passed with the request.

Inheritance

Most objects are classified according to hierarchies. For example, you can classify all dogs together as having certain common characteristics such as having four legs and fur. Their breeds further classify them into subgroups with common attributes such as size and demeanor. You also classify objects according to their function. For example, there are commercial vehicles and recreational vehicles. There are trucks and passenger cars. You classify cars according to their make and model. To make sense of the world, you need to use object hierarchies and classifications.

You use inheritance in OOP to classify the objects in your programs according to common characteristics and function. This makes working with the objects easier and more intuitive. It also makes programming easier because it enables you to combine general characteristics into a parent object and inherit these characteristics in the child objects. For example, you can define an employee object that defines all the general characteristics of employees in your company. You can then define a manager object that inherits the characteristics of the employee object but also adds characteristics unique to managers in your company. The manager object will automatically reflect any changes in the implementation of the employee object.

Aggregation

Aggregation is when an object consists of a composite of other objects that work together. For example, your lawn mower object is a composite of the wheel objects, the engine object, the blade object, and so on. In fact, the engine object is a composite of many other objects. There are many examples of aggregation in the world around us. The ability to use aggregation in OOP is a powerful feature that enables you to accurately model and implement business processes in your programs.

The History of C#

In the 1980s, most applications written to run on the Windows operating system were written in C++. Even though C++ is an OOP language, it's arguably a difficult language to master and the programmer is responsible for dealing with such housekeeping tasks such as memory management and security. These housekeeping tasks are difficult to implement and often neglected which results in buggy applications that are difficult to test and maintain.

In the 1990s, the Java programming language became popular. Because it's a managed programming language, it relieves the programmer from having to worry about the housekeeping code. Managed languages provide a generalized way (through a base set of common classes) to handle the housekeeping details such as memory management and garbage collection. This allows the programmer to concentrate on the business logic and frees them from having to worry about the error-prone housekeeping code. As a result, programs are more compact, reliable, and easier to debug.

Seeing the success of Java and the increased popularity of the Internet, Microsoft developed its own set of managed programming languages. Microsoft wanted to make it easier to develop both Windows- and Web-based applications. These managed languages rely on the .NET Framework to provide much of the functionality to perform the housekeeping code required in all applications. During the development of the .NET Framework, the class libraries were written in a new language called C#. The principal designer and lead architect of C# is Anders Hejlsberg. Hejlsberg was previously involved with the design of Turbo Pascal and Delphi. He leveraged this previous experience to design an OOP language that built on the successes of these languages and improved upon their shortcomings. Hejlsberg also incorporated syntax similar to C into the language in order to appeal to the C++ and Java developers. Some of the goals of creating the .NET Framework, the Common Language Runtime (CLR), and the C# language was to introduce modern concepts such as object orientation, type safety, garbage collection, and structured exception handling directly into the platform.

Another goal of Microsoft has always been increasing programmer productivity. Since its initial release in 2002, Microsoft has continued to improve and innovate the .NET Framework along with their core languages built on top of the framework – C# and Visual Basic. Microsoft is also committed to providing .NET developers the tools necessary to have a highly productive and intuitive programming experience. With the current release of C# 4.0 and Visual Studio 2010, Microsoft has greatly enhanced both the language and the design time developing experience for developers. As you work your way through this book, I think you will come to appreciate the power and productivity that Visual Studio and the C# language provides.

Summary

In this chapter, you were introduced to OOP and got a brief history of C#. Now that you have an understanding of what constitutes an OOP language and why OOP languages are so important to enterprise-level application development, your next step is to become familiar with how OOP applications are designed.

In order to meet the needs of the users, successful applications must be carefully planned and developed. The next chapter is the first in a series of three aimed at introducing you to some of the techniques used when designing object-oriented applications. You will look at the process of deciding which objects need to be included in an application and which attributes of these objects are important to the functionality of that application.

CHAPTER 2

Designing OOP Solutions: Identifying the Class Structure

Most software projects you will become involved with as a business software developer will be a team effort. As a programmer on the team, you will be asked to transform the design documents into the actual application code. Additionally, because the design of object-oriented programs is a recursive process, designers depend on the feedback of the software developers to refine and modify the program design. As you gain experience in developing object-oriented software systems, you may even be asked to sit in on the design sessions and contribute to the design process. Therefore, as a software developer, you should be familiar with the purpose and the structure of the various design documents, as well as have some knowledge of how these documents are developed.

This chapter introduces you to some of the common documents used to design the static aspects of the system. (You'll learn how the dynamic aspects of the system are modeled in the next chapter.) To help you understand these documents, this chapter includes some hands-on activities based on a limited case study. You'll find similar activities corresponding to the topics of discussion in most of the chapters in this book.

After reading this chapter, you will be familiar with the following:

- The goals of software design.
- The fundamentals of the Unified Modeling Language.
- The purpose of a software requirement specification.
- How use case diagrams model the services the system will provide.
- How class diagrams model the classes of objects that need to be developed.

Goals of Software Design

A well-organized approach to system design is essential when developing modern enterprise-level object-oriented programs. The design phase is one of the most important in the software development cycle. You can trace many of the problems associated with failed software projects to poor upfront design and inadequate communication between the system's developers and the system's consumers. Unfortunately, many programmers and program managers do not like getting involved in the design aspects of the system. They view any time not spent cranking out code as unproductive.

To make matters worse, with the advent of "Internet time," consumers expect increasingly shorter development cycles. So, to meet unrealistic timelines and project scope, developers tend to forgo or cut short the system design phase of development. This is truly counterproductive to the system's success. Investing time in the design process will achieve the following:

- Provide an opportunity to review the current business process and fix any inefficiencies or flaws uncovered.
- Educate the customers as to how the software development process occurs and incorporate them as partners in this process.
- Create realistic project scopes and timelines for completion.
- Provide a basis for determining the software testing requirements.
- Reduce the cost and time required to implement the software solution.

A good analogy to software design is the process of building a home. You would not expect the builder to start working on the house without detailed plans (blueprints) supplied by an architect. You would also expect the architect to talk to you about the home's design before creating the blueprints. It is the architect's job to talk to you about the design and functionality you want in the house and convert your requests to the plans that the builder uses to build the home. A good architect will also educate you as to what features are reasonable for your budget and projected timeline.

Understanding the Unified Modeling Language

To successfully design object-oriented software, you need to follow a proven design methodology. One of the most common design methodologies used in OOP today is the Unified Modeling Language (UML).

UML was developed in the early 80s as a response to the need for a standard, systematic way of modeling the design of object-oriented software. It consists of a series of textual and graphical models of the proposed solution. These models define the system scope, components of the system, user interaction with the system, and how the system components interact with each other to implement the system functionality.

Some common models used in UML are the following:

- *Software Requirement Specification (SRS)*: A textual description of the overall responsibilities and scope of the system.
- *Use Case*: A textual/graphical description of how the system will behave from the user's perspective. Users can be human or other systems.
- *Class Diagram*: A visual blueprint of the objects that will be used to construct the system.
- *Sequence Diagram*: A model of the sequence of object interaction as the program executes. Emphasis is placed on the order of the interactions and how they proceed over time.
- *Collaboration Diagram*: A view of how objects are organized to work together as the program executes. Emphasis is placed on the communications that occur between the objects.
- *Activity Diagram*: A visual representation of the flow of execution of a process or operation.

In this chapter, you'll look at the development of the SRS, use cases, and class diagrams. The next chapter covers the sequence, collaboration, and activity diagrams.

Developing a SRS

The purpose of the SRS is to do the following:

- Define the functional requirements of the system.
- Identify the boundaries of the system.
- Identify the users of the system.
- Describe the interactions between the system and the external users.
- Establish a common language between the client and the program team for describing the system.
- Provide the basis for modeling use cases.

To produce the SRS, you interview the business owners and the end users of the system. The goals of these interviews are to clearly document the business processes involved and establish the system's scope. The outcome of this process is a formal document (the SRS) detailing the functional requirements of the system. A formal document helps to ensure agreement between the customers and the software developers. The SRS also provides a basis for resolving any disagreements over perceived system scope as development proceeds.

As an example, suppose that the owners of a small commuter airline want customers to be able to view flight information and reserve tickets for flights using a web registration system. After interviewing the business managers and the ticketing agents, the software designers draft an SRS document that lists the system's functional requirements. The following are some of these requirements:

- Nonregistered web users can browse to the web site to view flight information, but they can't book flights.
- New customers wanting to book flights must complete a registration form providing their name, address, company name, phone number, fax number, and e-mail address.
- A customer is classified as either a corporate customer or a retail customer.
- Customers can search for flights based on destination and departure times.
- Customers can book flights indicating the flight number and the number of seats requested.
- The system sends customers a confirmation via e-mail when the flight is booked.
- Corporate customers receive frequent flier miles when their employees book flights.
- Frequent-flier miles are used to discount future purchases.
- Ticket reservations can be canceled up to one week in advance for an 80% refund.
- Ticketing agents can view and update flight information.

In this partial SRS document, you can see that several succinct statements define the system scope. They describe the functionality of the system as viewed by the system's users and identify the external entities that will use it. It is important to note that the SRS does not contain references to the technical requirements of the system.

Once the SRS is developed, the functional requirements it contains are transformed into a series of use case diagrams.

Introducing Use Cases

Use cases describe how external entities will use the system. These external entities can be either humans or other systems (called *actors* in UML terminology). The description emphasizes the users' view of the system and the interaction between the users and the system. Use cases help to further define system scope and boundaries. They are usually in the form of a diagram, along with a textual description of the interaction taking place. Figure 2-1 shows a generic diagram that consists of two actors represented by stick figures, the system represented by a rectangle, and use cases depicted by ovals inside the system boundaries.

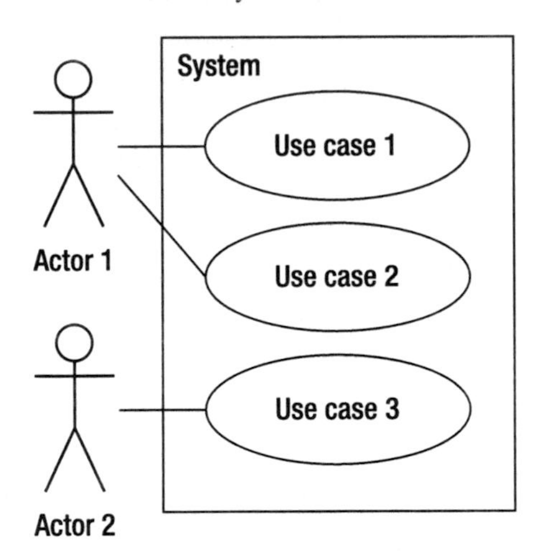

Figure 2-1. *Generic use case diagram with two actors and three use cases*

Use cases are developed from the SRS document. The actor is any outside entity that interacts with the system. An actor could be a human user (for instance, a rental agent), another software system (for instance, a software billing system), or an interface device (for instance, a temperature probe). Each interaction that occurs between an actor and the system is modeled as a use case.

The sample use case shown in Figure 2-2 was developed for the flight booking application introduced in the previous section. It shows the use case diagram for the requirement "Customers can search for flights based on destination and departure times."

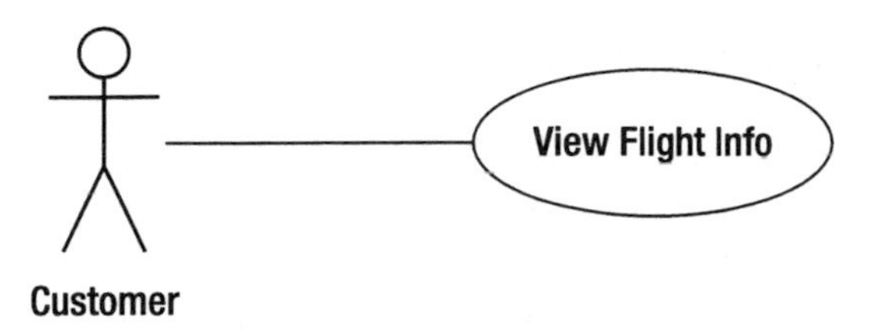

Figure 2-2. *View Flight Info use case*

Along with the graphical depiction of the use case, many designers and software developers find it helpful to provide a textual description of the use case. The textual description should be succinct and focused on what is happening and not on how it is occurring. Sometimes any preconditions or postconditions associated with the use case are also identified. The following text further describes the use case diagram shown in Figure 2-2:

- *Description*: A customer views the flight information page. The customer enters flight search information. After submitting the search request, the customer views a list of flights matching the search criteria.
- *Preconditions*: None.
- *Postconditions*: The customer has the opportunity to log in and proceed to the flight booking page.

As another example, take a look at the Reserve Seat use case shown in Figure 2-3.

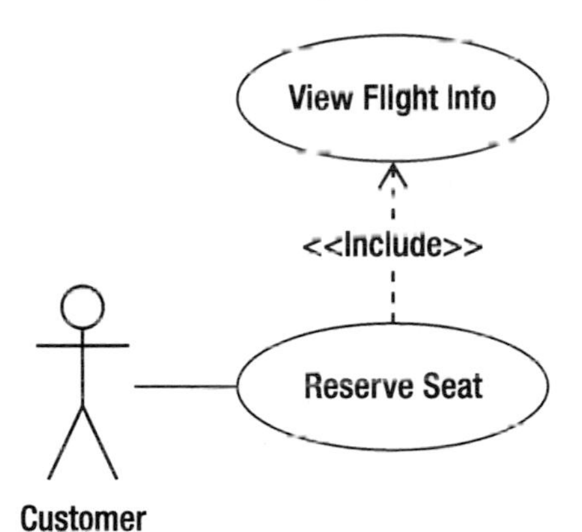

Figure 2-3. *Reserve Seat use case diagram*

The following text further describes the use case diagram shown in Figure 2-3:

- *Description*: The customer enters the flight number and indicates the seats being requested. After the customer submits the request, some confirmation information is displayed.
- *Preconditions*: The customer has looked up the flight information. The customer has logged in and is viewing the flight booking screen.

- *Postconditions*: The customer is sent a confirmation e-mail outlining the flight details and the cancellation policy.

As you can see from Figure 2-3, certain relationships can exist between use cases. The Reserve Seat use case includes the View Flight Info use case. This relationship is useful because you can use the View Flight Info use case independently of the Reserve Flight use case. This is called inclusion. You cannot use the Reserve Seat use case independently of the View Flight Info use case, however. This is important information that will affect how you model the solution.

Another way that use cases relate to each other is through extension. You might have a general use case that is the base for other use cases. The base use case is extended by other use cases. For example, you might have a Register Customer use case that describes the core process of registering customers. You could then develop Register Corporate Customer and Register Retail Customer use cases that extend the base use case. The difference between extension and inclusion is that in extension the base use case being extended is not used on its own. Figure 2-4 demonstrates how you model this in a use case diagram.

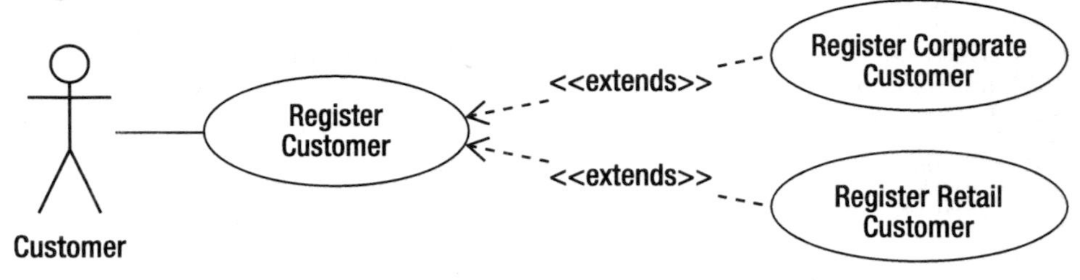

Figure 2-4. *Extending use cases*

A common mistake when developing use cases is to include actions initiated by the system itself. The emphasis of the use case is on the interaction between external entities and the system. Another common mistake is to include a description of the technical requirements of the system. Remember that use cases do not focus on how the system will perform the functions, but rather on what functions need to be incorporated in the system from the user's standpoint.

After you have developed the use cases of the system, you can begin to identify the internal system objects that will carry out the system's functional requirements. You do this through the use of a class diagram.

ACTIVITY 2-1. CREATING A USE CASE DIAGRAM

After completing this activity, you should be familiar with the following:

- Producing a use case diagram to define a system's scope.
- Using a UML modeling tool to create and document a use case diagram.

Examining the SRS

The software user group you belong to has decided to pool its resources and create a lending library. Lending items include books, movies, and video games. Your task is to develop the application that will keep track of the loan item inventory and the lending of items to the group members. After interviewing the group's members and officers, you have developed a SRS document that includes the following functional requirements:

- Only members of the user group can borrow items.
- Books can be borrowed for four weeks.
- Movies and games can be borrowed for one week.
- Items can be renewed if no one is waiting to borrow them.
- Members can only borrow up to four items at the same time.
- A reminder is e-mailed to members when an item becomes overdue.
- A fine is charged for overdue items.
- Members with outstanding overdue items or fines can't borrow new items.
- A secretary is in charge of maintaining item inventory and purchasing items to add to the inventory.
- A librarian has been appointed to track lending and send overdue notices.
- The librarian is also responsible for collecting fines and updating fine information.

The next steps are to analyze the SRS to identify the actors and use cases.

1. By examining the SRS document, identify which of the following will be among the principal actors interacting with the system:

   A. Member

   B. Librarian

   C. Book

   D. Treasurer

   E. Inventory

   F. E-mail

   G. Secretary

2. Once you have identified the principal actors, you need to identify the use cases for the actors. Identify the actor associated with the following use cases:

A. Request Item

B. Catalog Item

C. Lend Item

D. Process Fine

See the end of the chapter for Activity 2-1 answers.

Creating a Use Case Diagram

Although it is possible to create the UML diagrams by hand or on a whiteboard, most programmers will eventually turn to a diagramming tool or a Computer-Aided Software Engineering (CASE) tool. CASE tools help you construct professional-quality diagrams and enable team members to easily share and augment the diagrams. There are many CASE tools on the market, including Microsoft Visio. Before choosing a CASE tool, you should thoroughly evaluate if it meets your needs and is flexible enough. A lot of the advanced features associated with high-end CASE tools are difficult to work with, so you spend more time figuring out how the CASE tool works than documenting your design.

A good diagraming tool to learn on is UMLet. It enables you to create UML diagrams without adding a lot of advanced features associated with the high-end CASE tools. Best of all, UMLet is a free open source tool and can be downloaded from `www.umlet.com`.

■ Note These activities use the UMLet 10.4 stand-alone edition. This also requires Java 1.6 available at `www.java.com`.

After downloading and installing UMLet, you can complete the following steps (if you do not want to use a tool, you can create the following diagram by hand):

1. Start UMLet. You are presented with three windows. The main window is the design surface, the upper right window contains the UML object templates, and the lower right window is where you change or add properties to the objects.
2. Locate the actor template in the upper right window (see Figure 2-5). Double click the actor template. An actor will appear in the upper left corner of the design surface.

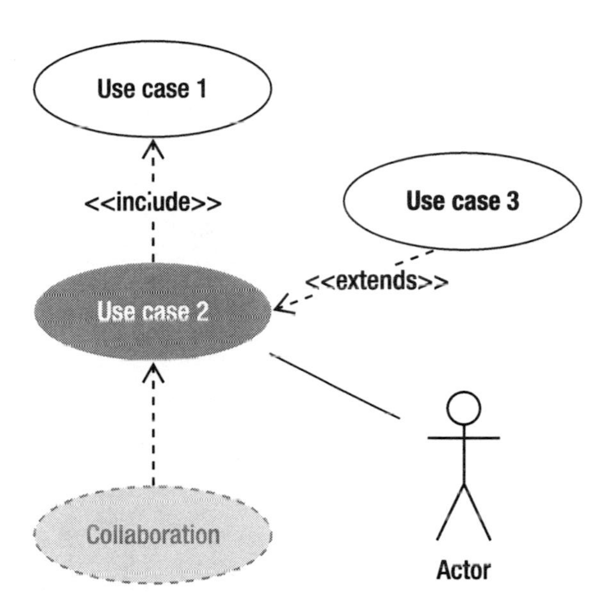

Figure 2-5. *Locating the actor template*

3. If not already selected, select the actor shape on the design surface. In the lower left window, change the name of the actor shape to Member.
4. Repeat the procedures to add a Secretary and a Librarian actor.
5. From the Template window, double click the Use case 1 shape to add it to the design surface. Change the name of the use case to Request Item.
6. Repeat step 5 for two more use cases. Include a Catalog Item use case that will occur when the Secretary adds new items to the library inventory database. Add a Lend Item use case that will occur when the Librarian processes a request for an item.
7. From the Template window, double click the Empty Package shape and change the name to Library Loan System. Right click on the shape in the design surface and change the background color to white. Move the use case shapes inside the Library Loan System shape (see Figure 2-6).

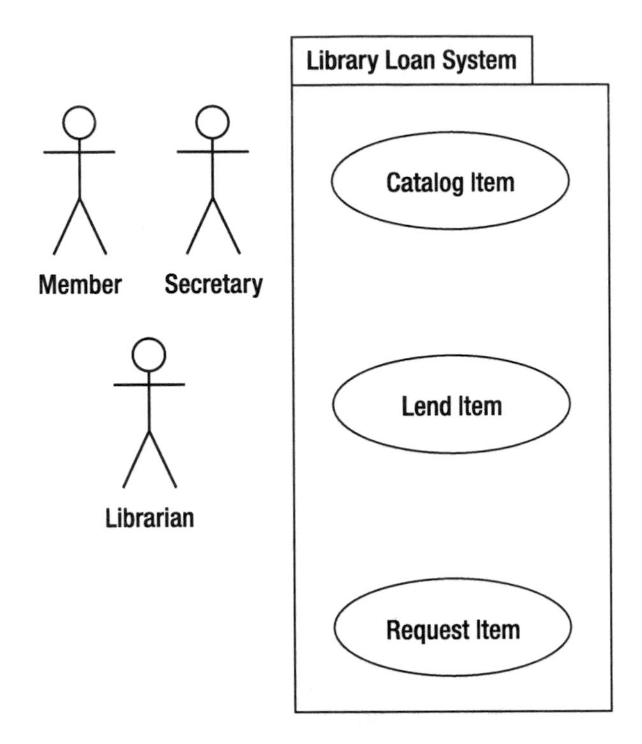

Figure 2-6. *Placing the use cases inside the system boundary*

8. From the Template window, double click on the Communications Link shape. It is the line with no arrow heads (see Figure 2-7). On the design surface, attach one end to the Member shape and the other end to the Request Item shape.

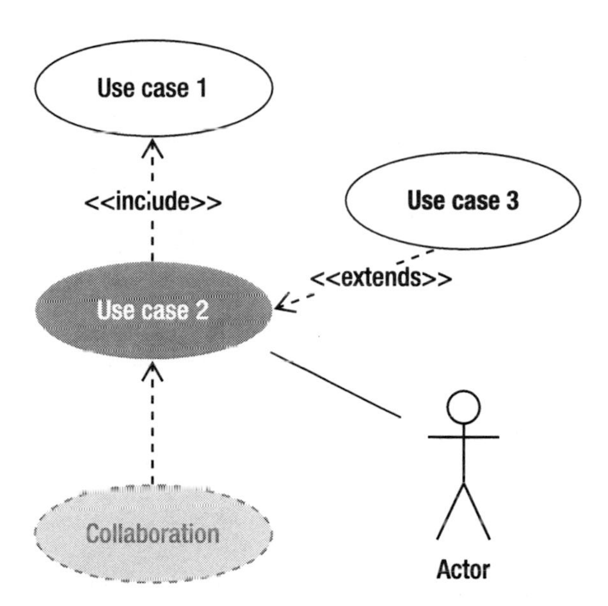

Figure 2-7. *Locating the Communications Link shape*

9. Repeat step 8 two times to create a Communication Link shape between the Librarian and the Lend Item shapes as well as a Communication Link shape between the Secretary and the Catalog Item shapes.

10. From the Templates widow, double click the Extends Relationship arrow. Attach the tail end of the Extends arrow to the Lend Item use case and attach the head of the arrow to the Request Item use case.

11. Your completed diagram should be similar to the one shown in Figure 2-8. Save the file as UMLAct2_1 and exit UMLet.

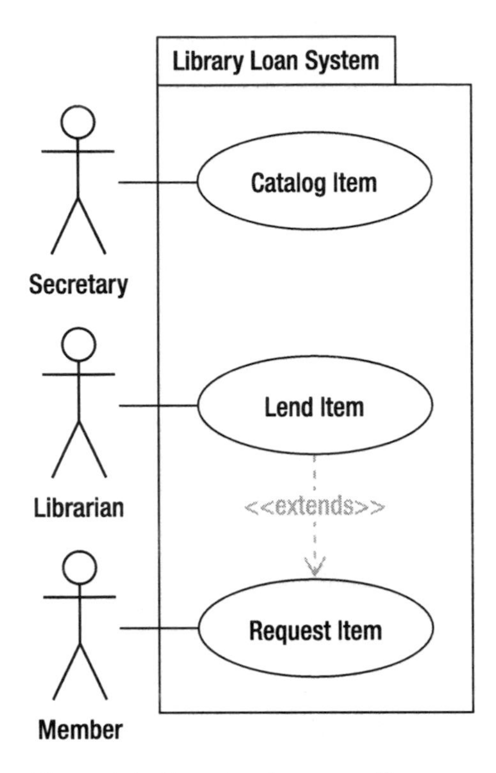

Figure 2-8. *Completed use case diagram*

Understanding Class Diagrams

The concepts of classes and objects are fundamental to OOP. An object is a structure for incorporating data and the procedures for working with the data. These objects implement the functionality of an object-oriented program. Think of a class as a blueprint for the object. A class defines the structure and the methods that objects based on the class type will contain.

Designers identify a potential list of classes that they will need to develop from the SRS and the use case diagrams. One way you identify the classes is by looking at the noun phrases in the SRS document and the use case descriptions. If you look at the documentation developed thus far for the airline booking application, you can begin to identify the classes that will make up the system. For example, you can develop a Customer class to work with the customer data and a Flight class to work with the flight data.

A class is responsible for managing data. When defining the class structure, you must determine what data the class is responsible for maintaining. The class attributes define this information. For example, the Flight class will have attributes for identifying the flight number, departure time and date, flight duration, destination, capacity, and seats available. The class structure must also define any operations that will be performed on the data. An example of an operation the Flight class is responsible for is updating the seats available when a seat is reserved.

A class diagram can help you visualize the attributes and operations of a class. Figure 2-9 is an example of the class diagram for the Flight class used in the flight booking system example. A rectangle divided into three sections represents the class. The top section of the rectangle shows the name of the class, the middle section lists the attributes of the class, and the bottom section lists the operations performed by the class.

Flight
flightId date origin destination departureTime arrivalTime seatingCapacity
reserveSeat() unreserveSeat()

Figure 2-9. *Flight class diagram*

Modeling Object Relationships

In OOP, when the program executes, the various objects work together to accomplish the programming tasks. For example, in the flight booking application, in order to reserve a seat on the flight, a Reservation object must interact with the Flight object. A relationship exists between the two objects, and this relationship must be modeled in the class structure of the program. The relationships among the classes that make up the program are modeled in the class diagram. Analyzing the verb phrases in the SRS often reveals these relationships (this is discussed in more detail in Chapter 3). The following sections examine some of the common relationships that can occur between classes and how the class diagram represents them.

Association

When one class refers to or uses another class, the classes form an association. You draw a line between the two classes to represent the association and add a label to indicate the name of the association. For example, a Seat is associated with a Flight in the flight booking application, as shown in Figure 2-10.

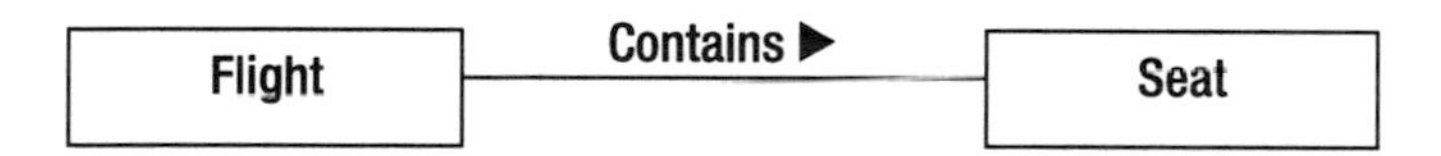

Figure 2-10. *Class associations*

Sometimes a single instance of one class associates with multiple instances of another class. This is indicated on the line connecting the two classes. For example, when a customer makes a reservation, there is an association between the Customer class and the Reservation class. A single instance of the Customer class may be associated with multiple instances of the Reservation class. The *n* placed near the Reservation class indicates this multiplicity, as shown in Figure 2-11.

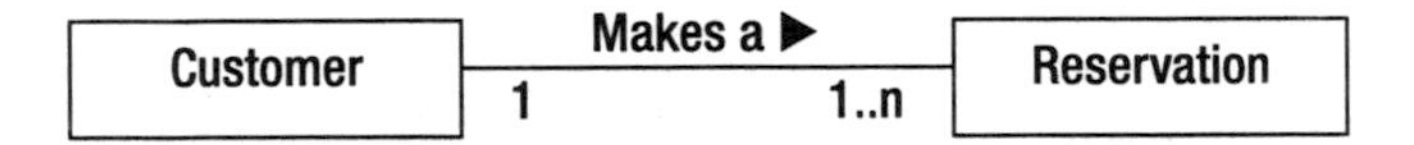

Figure 2-11. *Indicating multiplicity in a class diagram*

A situation may also exist where an instance of a class may be associated with multiple instances of the same class. For example, an instance of the Pilot class represents the captain while another instance of the Pilot class represents the co-pilot. The pilot manages the co-pilot. This scenario is referred to as a self-association and is modeled by drawing the association line from the class back to itself, as shown in Figure 2-12.

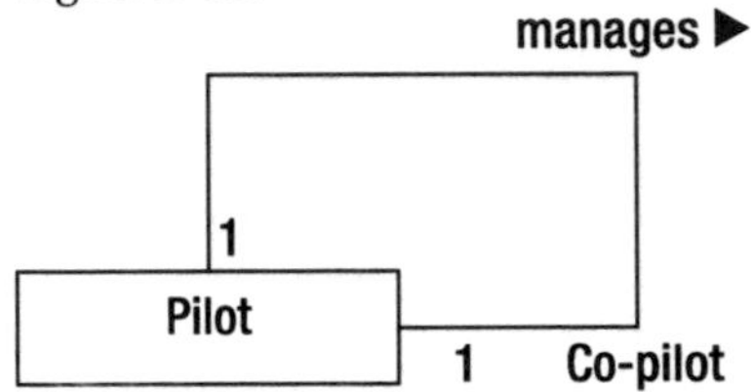

Figure 2-12. *A self-associating class*

Inheritance

When multiple classes share some of the same operations and attributes, a base class can encapsulate the commonality. The child class then inherits from the base class. This is represented in the class diagram by a solid line with an open arrowhead pointing to the base class. For example, a CorporateCustomer class and a RetailCustomer class could inherit common attributes and operations from a base Customer class, as shown in Figure 2-13.

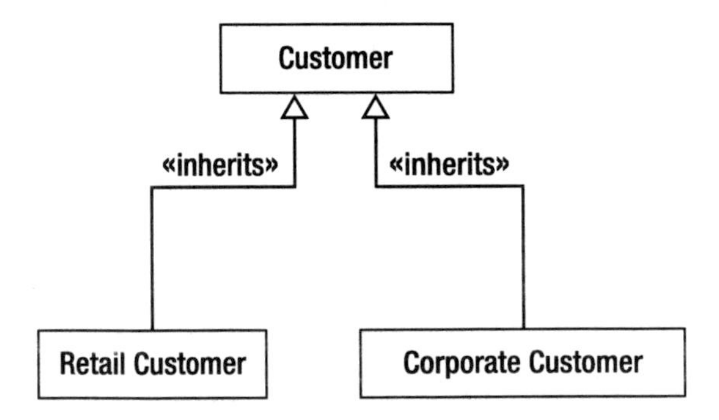

Figure 2-13. *Documenting inheritance*

Aggregation

When a class is formed by a composition of other classes, they are classified as an aggregation. This is represented with a solid line connecting the classes in a hierarchical structure. Placing a diamond on the line next to a class in the diagram indicates the top level of the hierarchy. For example, an inventory application designed to track plane parts for the plane maintenance department could contain a Plane class that is a composite of various Part classes, as shown in Figure 2-14.

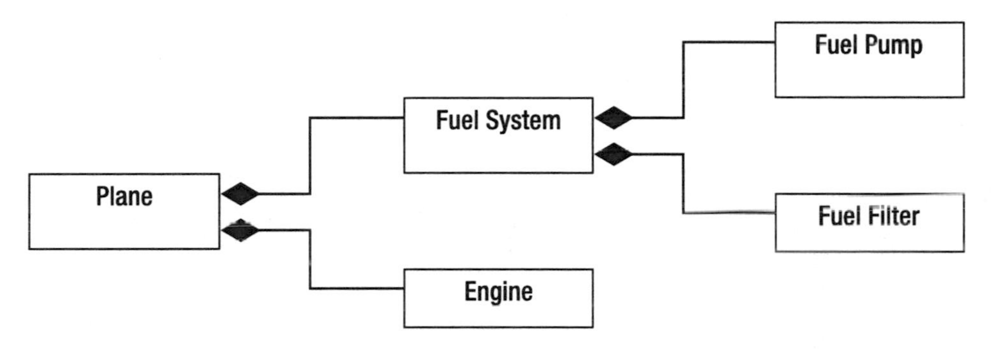

Figure 2-14. *Depciting aggregations*

Association Classes

As the classes and the associations for a program are developed, there may be a situation where an attribute can't be assigned to any one class but is a result of an association between classes. For example, the parts inventory application mentioned previously may have a Part class and a Supplier class. Because a part can have more than one supplier and the supplier supplies more than one part, where should the price attribute be located? It does not fit nicely as an attribute for either class, and it should not be duplicated in both classes. The solution is to develop an association class that manages the data that is a product of the association. In this case, you would develop a Part Price class. The relationship is modeled with a dashed line drawn between the association and the association class, as shown in Figure 2-15.

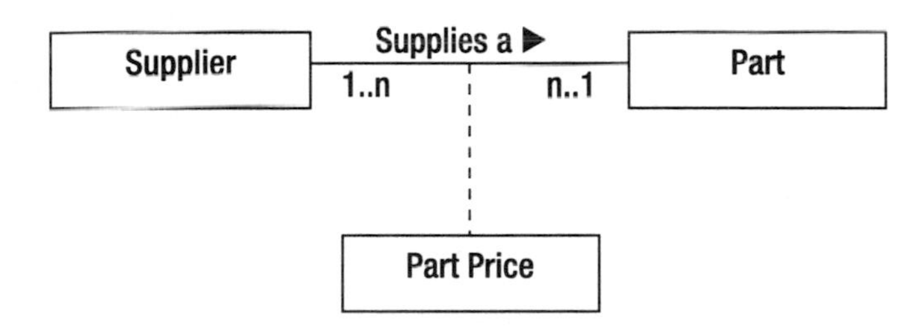

Figure 2-15. *An association class*

Figure 2-16 shows the evolving class diagram for the flight booking application. It includes the classes, attributes, and relationships that have been identified for the system. The operations associated with the classes will be developed in Chapter 3.

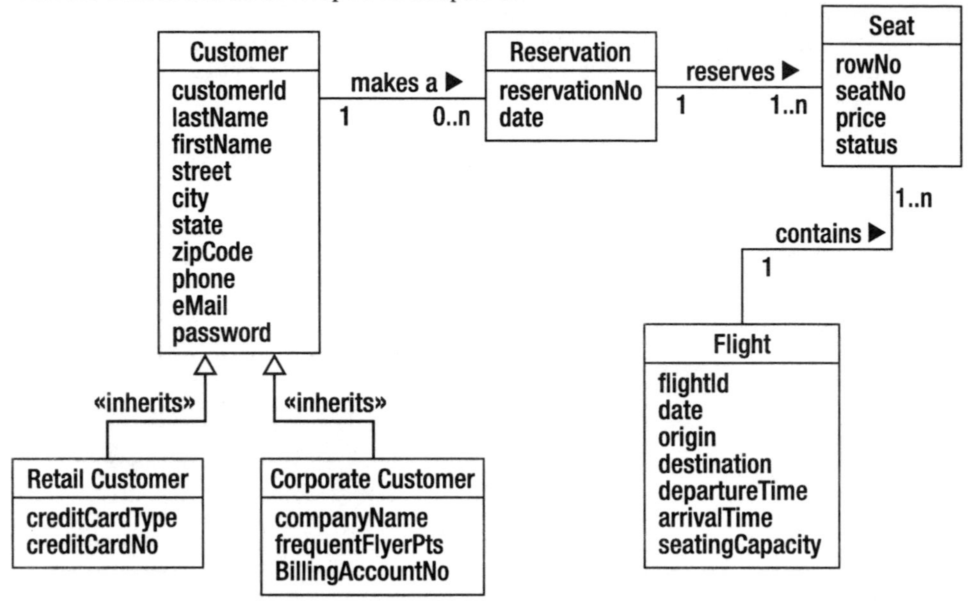

Figure 2-16. *Flight booking class diagram*

ACTIVITY 2-2. CREATING A CLASS DIAGRAM

After completing this activity, you should be familiar with the following:

- Determining the classes that need to be constructed by examining the use case and the system scope documentation.
- Using a UML modeling tool to create a class diagram.

Identifying Classes and Attributes

Examine the following scenario developed for a use case from the user group library application:

After viewing the list of available loan items, members request an item to check out on loan. The librarian enters the member number and retrieves information about outstanding loans and any unpaid fines. If the member has fewer than four outstanding loans and does not have any outstanding fines, the loan is processed. The librarian retrieves information about the loan item to determine if it is currently on loan. If the item is available, it is checked out to the member.

1. By identifying the nouns and noun phrases in the use case scenario, you can get an idea of what classes you must include in the system to perform the tasks. Which of the following items would make good candidate classes for the system?

   A. Member

   B. Item

   C. Librarian

   D. Number

   E. Fine

   F. Checkout

   G. Loan

2. At this point, you can start identifying attributes associated with the classes being developed. A Loan class will be developed to encapsulate data associated with an item out on loan. Which of the following would be possible attributes for the Loan class?

   A. MemberNumber

   B. MemberPhone

   C. ItemNumber

   D. ReturnDate

   E. ItemCost

   F. ItemType

See the end of the chapter for Activity 2-2 answers.

Creating a Class Diagram

To create a class diagram using UML Modeler, follow these steps (you can also create it by hand):

1. Start UMLet. You are presented with three windows. The main window is the design surface, the upper right window contains the UML object templates, and the lower right window is where you change or add properties to the objects.

2. Locate the SimpleClass template in the upper right window (see Figure 2-17). Double click the SimpleClass template. A SimpleClass will appear in the upper left corner of the design surface.

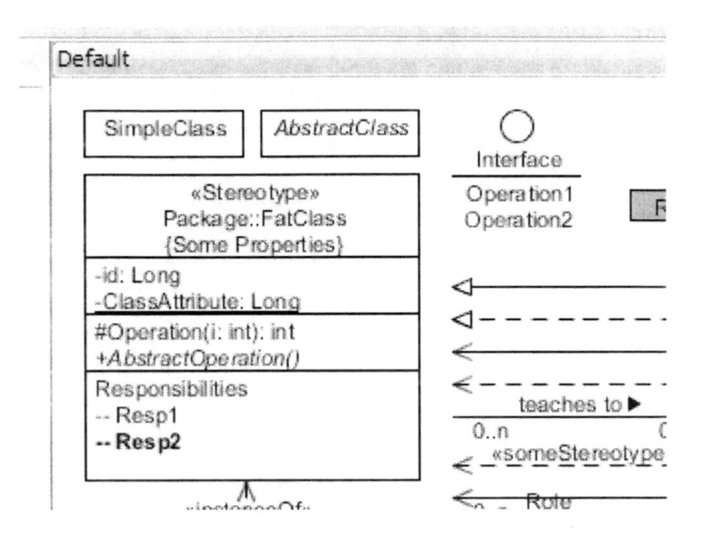

Figure 2-17. *Adding a class shape*

3. In the lower left properties window, change the class name to Member.
4. Repeat the procedure for a Loan, Item, Book, and Movie class.
5. Locate the association template in the upper right window (see Figure 2-18). Double click the association template. An association will appear in the upper left corner of the design surface.

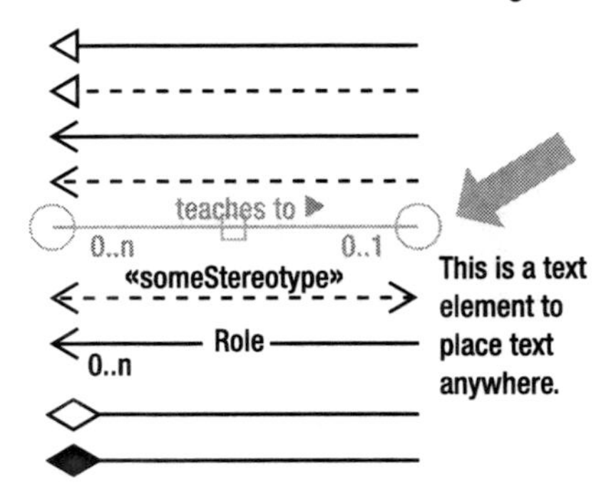

Figure 2-18. *Adding an association shape*

6. Attach the left end of the association shape to the Member class and the right end to the Loan class shape. Select the association shape and update the properties in the properties widow so that they match Figure 2-19.

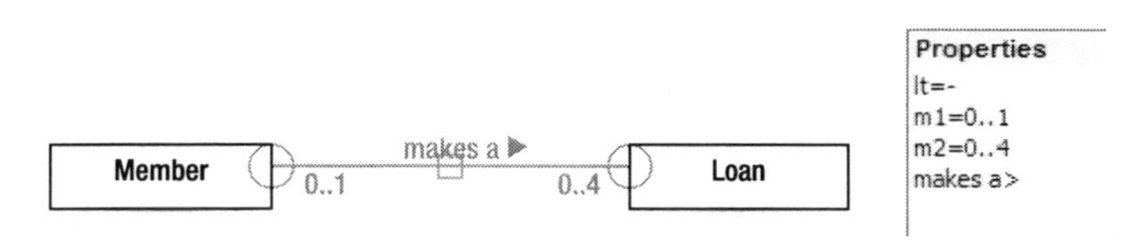

Figure 2-19. *Updating association properties*

7. Repeat steps 5 and 6 to create a "Contains a" association shape between the Loan class and the Item class. This should be a one-to-one association.

8. Locate the generalization shape template in the upper right window (see Figure 2-20). Double click the generalization shape. A generalization shape will appear in the upper left corner of the design surface.

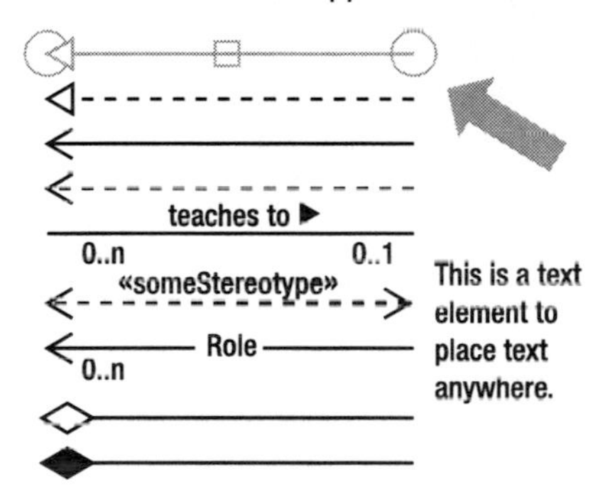

Figure 2-20. *Adding a generalization shape*

9. Attach the tail end of the generalization shape to the Book class and the head end to the Item class shape. Select the generalization shape and update the properties in the properties widow so that they match Figure 2-21.

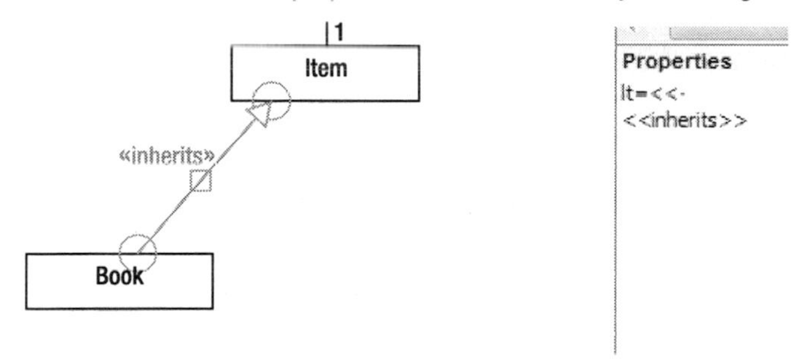

Figure 2-21. *Updating generalization properties*

10. Repeat steps 8 and 9 to show that the Movie class inherits from the Item class.

11. Click on the Member class in the design window. In the properties window, add the MemberNumber, FirstName, LastName, and Email attributes as shown in Figure 2-22.

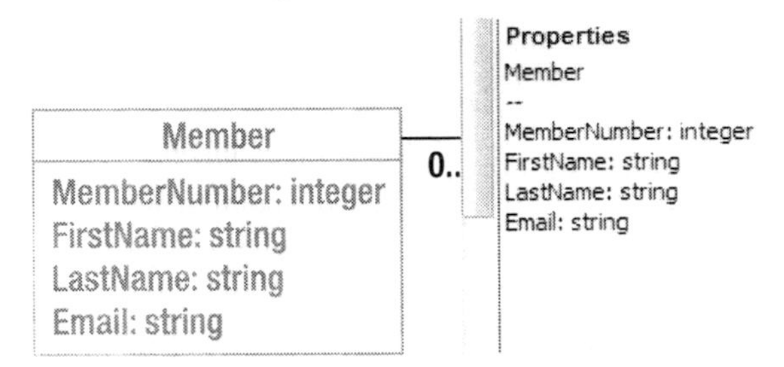

Figure 2-22. *Adding class attributes*

12. Your completed diagram should be similar to Figure 2-23. Save the file as UMLAct2_2.

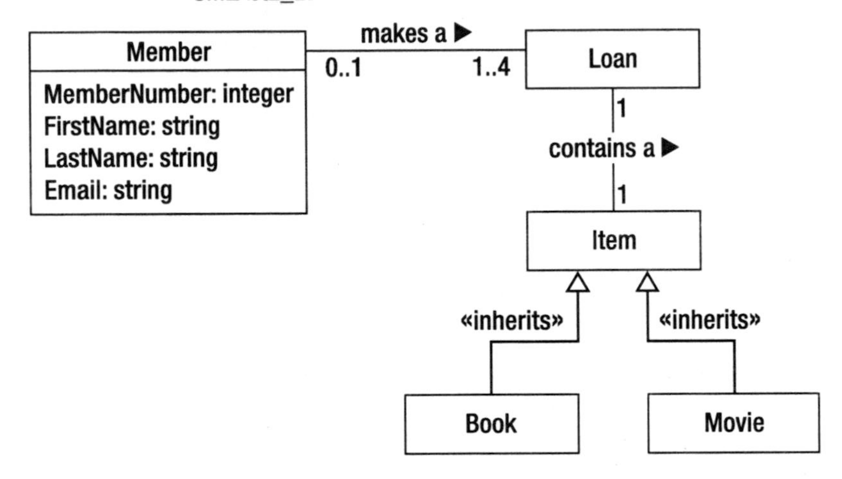

Figure 2-23. *Completed class diagram*

Summary

In this chapter, you were introduced to the goals of the object-oriented design process and UML. You learned about some of the design documents and diagrams produced using UML. These include the SRS, which defines the scope of the system; use case diagrams, which define the system boundaries and identify the external entities that will use the system; and class diagrams, which model the structure of the classes that will be developed to implement the system.

You saw how modeling the class structure of your applications includes identifying the necessary classes, identifying the attributes of these classes, and establishing the structural relationships required among the classes. In the next chapter, you will continue your study of object-oriented design. In particular, you will look at modeling how the objects in your applications will collaborate to carry out the functionality of the application.

ACTIVITY ANSWERS

Activity 2-1 Answers

1. A, B, G. The actors are Member, Librarian, and Secretary.
2. A. Member, B. Secretary, C. Librarian, D. Librarian. The Request Item use case goes with Member, the Catalog Item use case goes with Secretary, the Lend Item use case goes with Librarian, and the Process Fine use case goes with Librarian.

Activity 2-2 Answers

1. A, B, C, E, G. The candidate classes are Member, Item, Librarian, Fine, and Loan.
2. A, C, D. The attributes associated with the Loan class are MemberNumber, ItemNumber, and ReturnDate.

CHAPTER 3

Designing OOP Solutions: Modeling the Object Interaction

The previous chapter focused on modeling the static (organizational) aspects of an OOP solution. It introduced and discussed the methodologies of the UML. It also looked at the purpose and structure of use case diagrams and class diagrams. This chapter continues the discussion of UML modeling techniques and focuses on modeling the dynamic (behavioral) aspects of an OOP solution. The focus in this chapter is on how the objects in the system must interact with each other and what activities must occur to implement the solution.

After reading this chapter, you should be familiar with the following:

- The purpose of scenarios and how they extend the use case models.
- How sequence diagrams model the time-dependent interaction of the objects in the system.
- How activity diagrams map the flow of activities during application processing.
- The importance of graphical user interface design and how it fits into the object-oriented design process.

Understanding Scenarios

Scenarios help determine the dynamic interactions that will take place between the objects (class instances) of the system. A scenario is a textual description of the internal processing needed to implement the functionality documented by a use case. Remember that a use case describes the functionality of the system from the viewpoint of the system's external users. A scenario details the execution of the use case. In other words, its purpose is to describe the steps that must be carried out internally by the objects making up the system.

Figure 3-1 shows a Process Movie Rental use case for a video rental application. The following text describes the use case:

- Preconditions: The customer makes a request to rent a movie from the rental clerk. The customer has a membership in the video club and supplies the rental clerk with her membership card and personal identification number (PIN). The customer's membership is verified. The customer information is displayed, and the customer's account is verified to be in good standing.

- Description: The movie is confirmed to be in stock. Rental information is recorded, and the customer is informed of the due date.
- Post conditions: None.

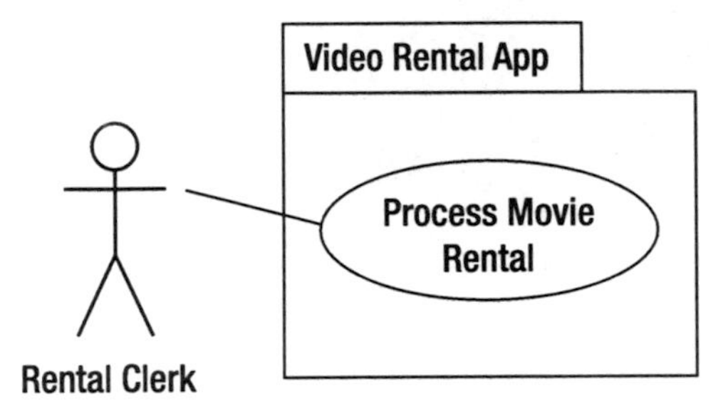

Figure 3-1. *Process Movie Rental use case*

The following scenario describes the internal processing of the Process Movie Rental use case:

- The movie is verified to be in stock.
- The number of available copies in stock is decremented.
- The due date is determined.
- The rental information is recorded. This information includes the movie title, copy number, current date, and due date.
- The customer is informed of the rental information.

This scenario describes the best possible execution of the use case. Because exceptions can occur, a single use case can spawn multiple scenarios. For example, another scenario created for the Process Movie Rental use case could describe what happens when a movie is not in stock.

After you map out the various scenarios for a use case, you can create interaction diagrams to determine which classes of objects will be involved in carrying out the functionality of the scenarios. The interaction diagram also reveals what operations will be required of these classes of objects. Interaction diagrams come in two flavors: sequence diagrams and collaboration diagrams.

Introducing Sequence Diagrams

A sequence diagram models how the classes of objects interact with each other over time as the system runs. The sequence diagram is a visual, two-dimensional model of the interaction taking place and is based on a scenario. Figure 3-2 shows a generic sequence diagram.

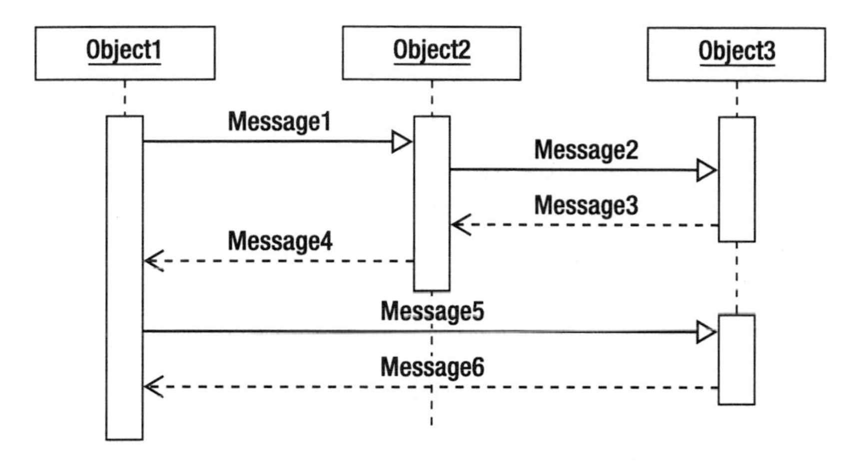

Figure 3-2. *Generic sequence diagram*

As Figure 3-2 demonstrates, the flow of messages from object to object is represented horizontally. The time flow of the interactions taking place is depicted vertically, starting from the top and progressing downward. Objects are next to each other, and a dashed line extends from each of them downward. This dashed line represents the lifeline of the object. Rectangles on the lifeline represent activations of the object. The height of the rectangle represents the duration of the object's activation.

In OOP, objects interact by passing messages to each other. An arrow starting at the initiating object and ending at the receiving object depicts the interaction. A dashed arrow drawn back to the initiating object represents a return message. The messages depicted in the sequence diagram will form the basis of the methods of the classes of the system. Figure 3-3 shows a sample sequence diagram for the Process Movie Rental scenario presented in the previous section.

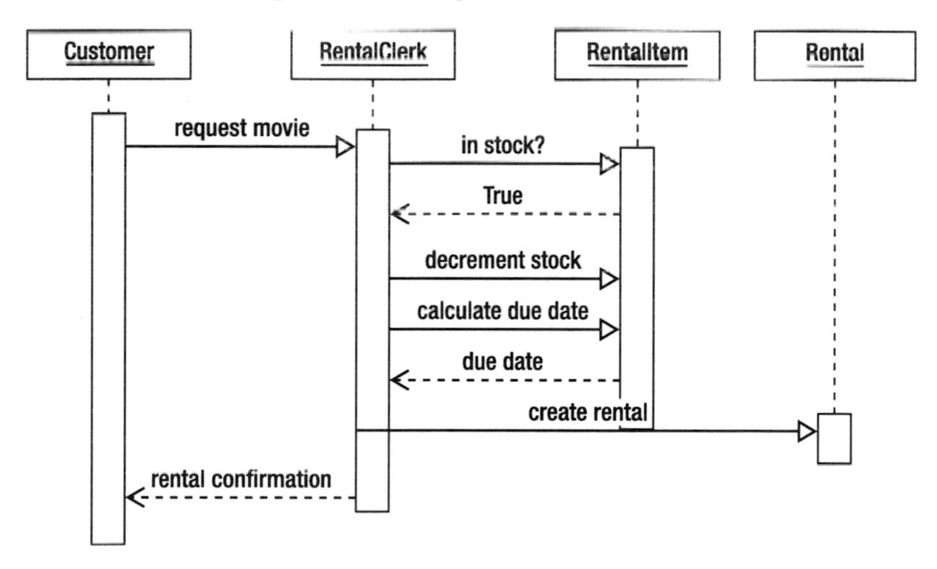

Figure 3-3. *Process Movie Rental sequence diagram*

As you analyze the sequence diagram, you gain an understanding of the classes of objects that will be involved in carrying out the program processing and what methods you will need to create and attach to those classes. You should also model the classes and methods depicted in the sequence diagram in the class diagram. These design documents must be continually cross-referenced and revised as necessary.

The sequence diagram in Figure 3-3 reveals that there will be four objects involved in carrying out the Process Movie Rental scenario.

- The Customer object is an instance of the Customer class and is responsible for encapsulating and maintaining the information pertaining to a customer.
- The RentalClerk object is an instance of the RentalClerk class and is responsible for managing the processing involved in renting a movie.
- The RentalItem object is an instance of the RentalItem class and is responsible for encapsulating and maintaining the information pertaining to a video available for rent.
- The Rental object is an instance of the Rental class and is responsible for encapsulating and maintaining the information pertaining to a video currently being rented.

Message Types

By analyzing the sequence diagram, you can determine what messages must be passed between the objects involved in the processing. In OOP, messages are passed synchronously or asynchronously.

When messages are passed synchronously, the sending object suspends processing and waits for a response before continuing. A line drawn with a closed arrowhead in the sequence diagram represents synchronous messaging.

When an object sends an asynchronous message, the object continues processing and is not expecting an immediate response from the receiving object. A line drawn with an open arrowhead in the sequence diagram represents asynchronous messaging. A dashed arrow usually depicts a response message. These lines are shown in Figure 3-4.

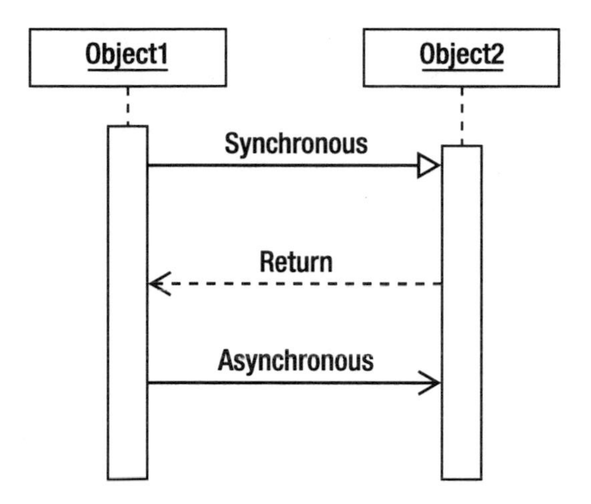

Figure 3-4. *Different types of messages*

By studying the sequence diagram for the Process Movie Rental scenario shown in Figure 3-3, you can see the types of messages that must be passed. For example, the RentalClerk object initiates a synchronous message with the RentalItem object, requesting information about whether a copy of the movie is in stock. The RentalItem object then sends a response back to the RentalClerk object, indicating a copy is in stock.

Recursive Messages

In OOP, it is not uncommon for an object to have an operation that invokes another object instance of itself. This is referred to as recursion. A message arrow that loops back toward the calling object represents recursion in the sequence diagram. The end of the arrow points to a smaller activation rectangle, representing a second object activation drawn on top of the original activation rectangle (see Figure 3-5). For example, an Account object calculates compound interest for overdue payments. To calculate the interest over several compound periods, it needs to invoke itself several times.

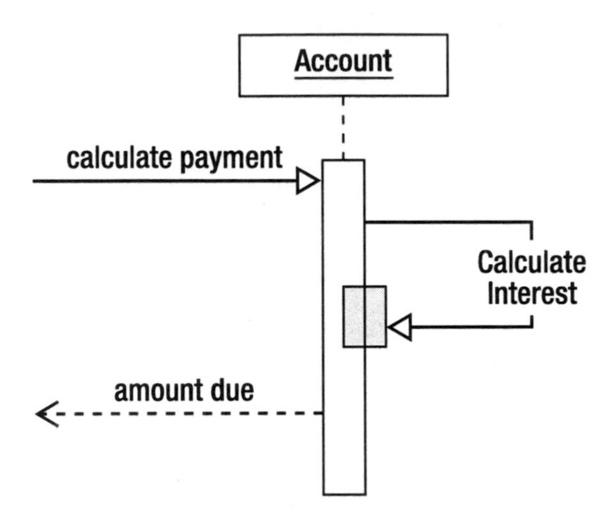

Figure 3-5. *Diagramming a recursive message*

Message Iteration

Sometimes, a message call is repeated until a condition is met. For example, when totaling rental charges, an Add method is called repeatedly until all rentals charged to the customer have been added to the total. In programming terminology, this is iteration. A rectangle drawn around the iterating messages represents an iteration in a sequence diagram. The binding condition of the iteration is depicted in the upper-left corner of the rectangle. Figure 3-6 shows an example of an iteration depicted in a sequence diagram.

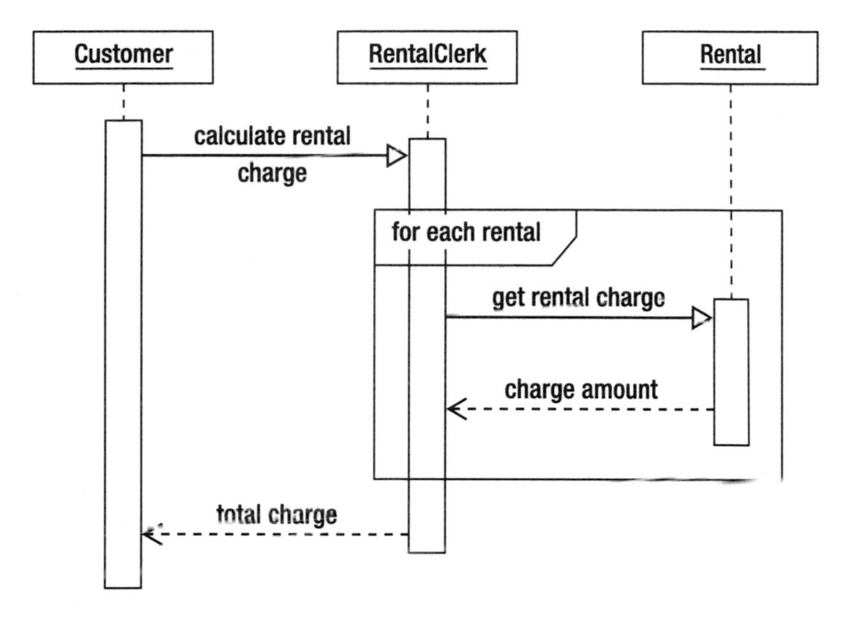

Figure 3-6. *Depicting an iterative message*

Message Constraints

Message calls between objects may have a conditional constraint attached to them. For example, customers must be in good standing in order to be allowed to rent a movie. You place the condition of the constraint within brackets ([]) in the sequence. The message will be sent only if the condition evaluates to true (see Figure 3-7).

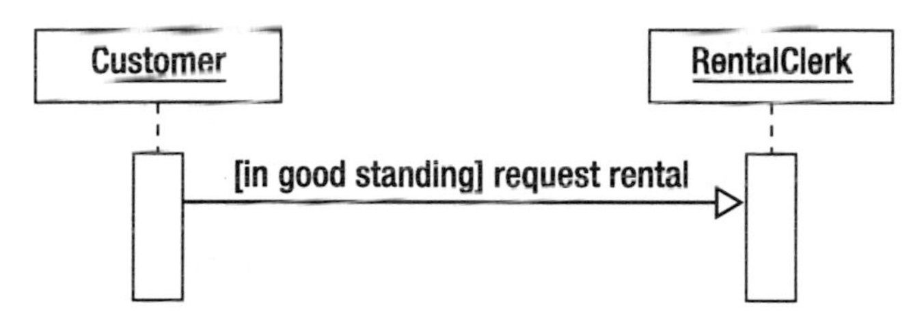

Figure 3-7. *Identifying conditional constraints*

Message Branching

When conditional constraints are tied to message calling, you often run into a branching situation where, depending on the condition, different messages may be invoked. Figure 3-8 represents a conditional constraint when requesting a movie rental. If the status of the rental item is in stock, a message is sent to the Rental object to create a rental. If the status of the rental item is out of stock, a message is sent to the Reservation object to create a reservation. A rectangle drawn around the messages shows the alternate paths that can occur depending on the condition.

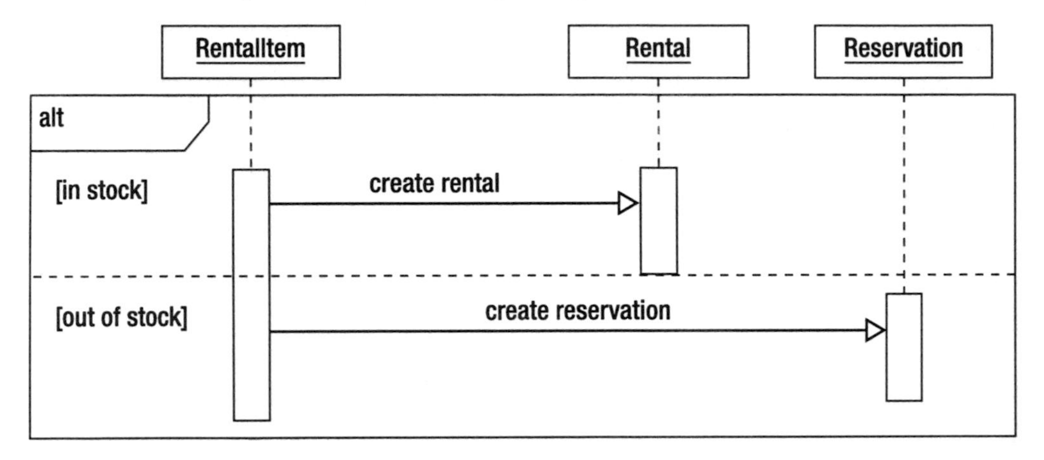

Figure 3-8. *Branching messages in a sequence diagram*

ACTIVITY 3-1. CREATING A SEQUENCE DIAGRAM

After completing this activity, you should be familiar with the following:

- Producing a sequence diagram to model object interaction.
- Using a UML modeling tool to create a sequence diagram.
- Adding methods to the class diagram.

Examining the Scenario

The following scenario was created for a use case in the user group library application introduced in Activity 2-1. It describes the processing involved when a member borrows an item from the library.

When a member makes a request to borrow an item, the librarian checks the member's records to make sure no outstanding fines exist. Once the member passes these checks, the item is checked to see if it is available. Once the item availability has been confirmed, a loan is created recording the item number, member number, checkout date, and return date.

1. By examining the noun phrases in the scenario, you can identify which objects will be involved in carrying out the processing. The objects identified should also have a corresponding class depicted in the class diagram that has been previously

created. From the scenario depicted, identify five objects that will carry out the processing.

2. After the objects have been identified and cross-referenced with the class diagram, the next step is to identify the messaging that must occur between these objects to carry out the task. You can look at the verb phrases in the scenario to help identify these messages. For example, the "request to borrow item" phase indicates a message interaction between the Member object and the Librarian object. What are the other interactions depicted in the scenario?

See the end of the chapter for Activity 3-1 answers.

Creating a Sequence Diagram

Follow these steps to create a sequence diagram using UMLet:

1. Start UMLet. Locate the drop-down list at the top of the template window. Change the template type to Sequence (see Figure 3-9).

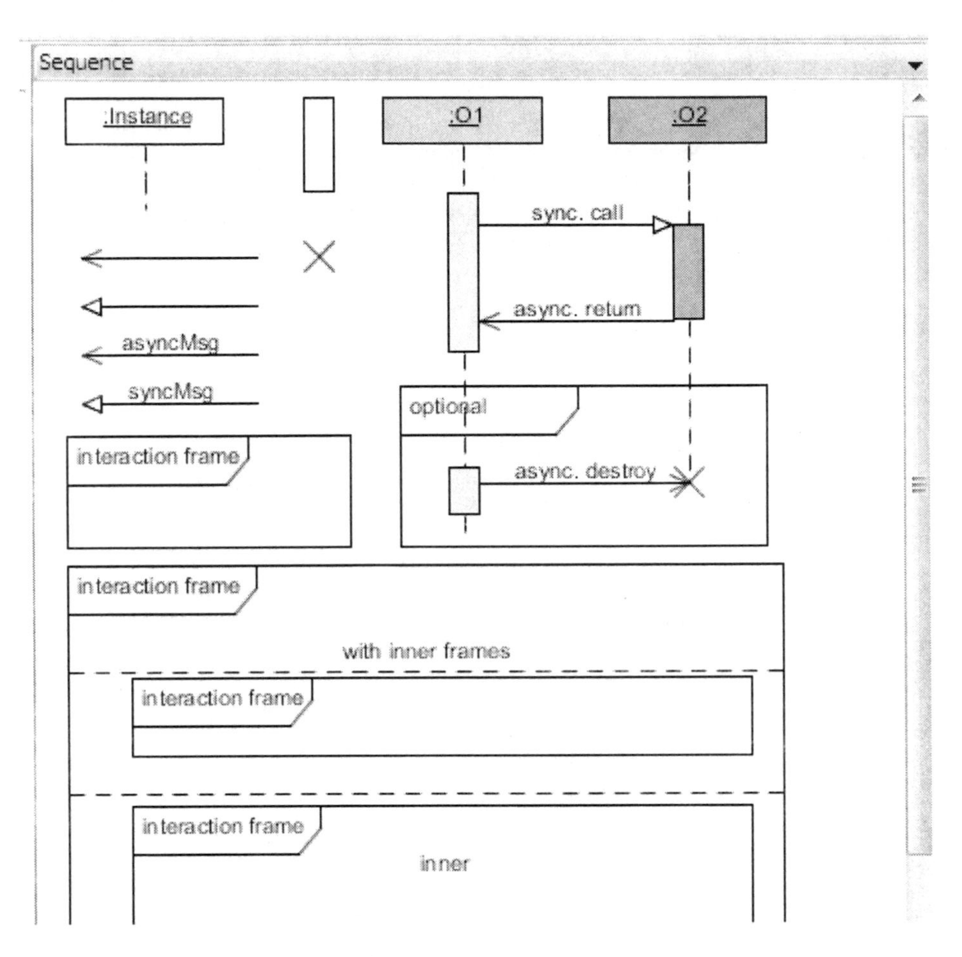

Figure 3-9. *Changing template shape types*

2. Double-click the Instance shape in the template window. An Instance shape will appear in the upper left corner of the design surface. In the properties window, change the name of the shape to Member.

3. From the shapes window, locate the lifeline and activation shapes and add them to the Member instance, as shown in Figure 3-10.

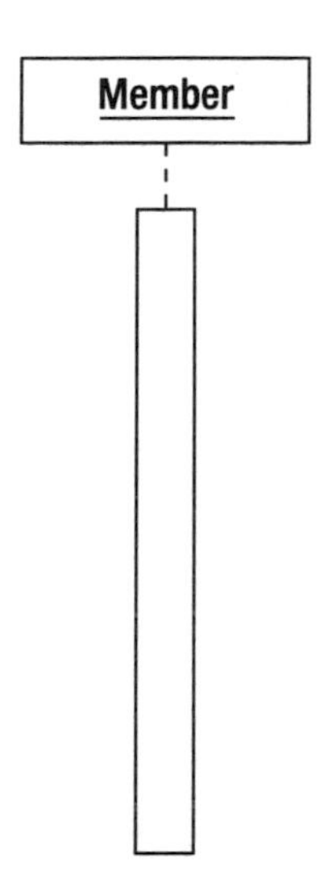

Figure 3-10. *Adding shapes to the sequence diagram*

4. Repeat steps 2 and 3 to add a Librarian, LoanHistory, Item, and Loan object to the diagram. Lay them out from left to right as shown in Figure 3-11.

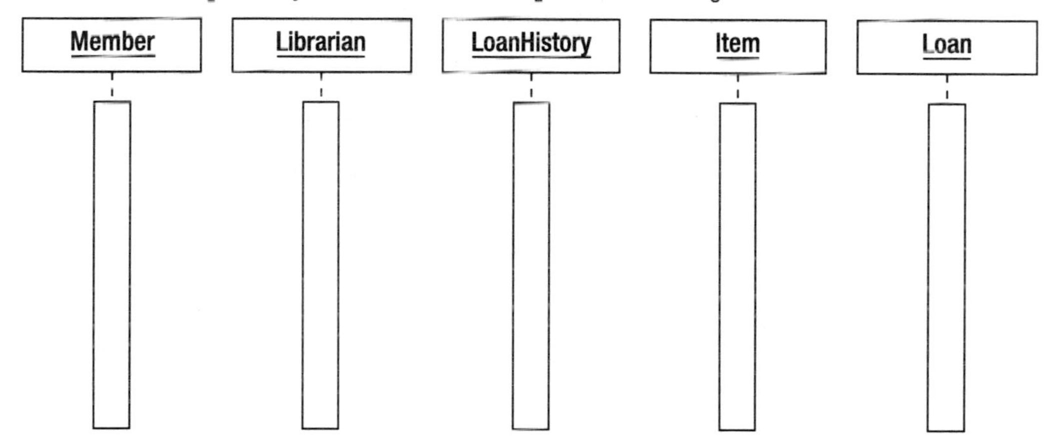

Figure 3-11. *Object layout in the sequence diagram*

5. From the shapes template window, double-click the Sequence Message arrow shape. Attach the tail end of the arrow to the Member object's lifeline and the head of the arrow to the Librarian object's lifeline. In the properties window, change the name of the message to "request item."
6. To create a return arrow, double-click on the solid arrow with the open arrow head in the shapes template window. In the properties window, change the first line to

It=.< This should change the arrow from solid to dash. Attach the tail end to the Librarian object and the head end to the Member object. Change the name to "return loan info." Your diagram should look similar to Figure 3-12.

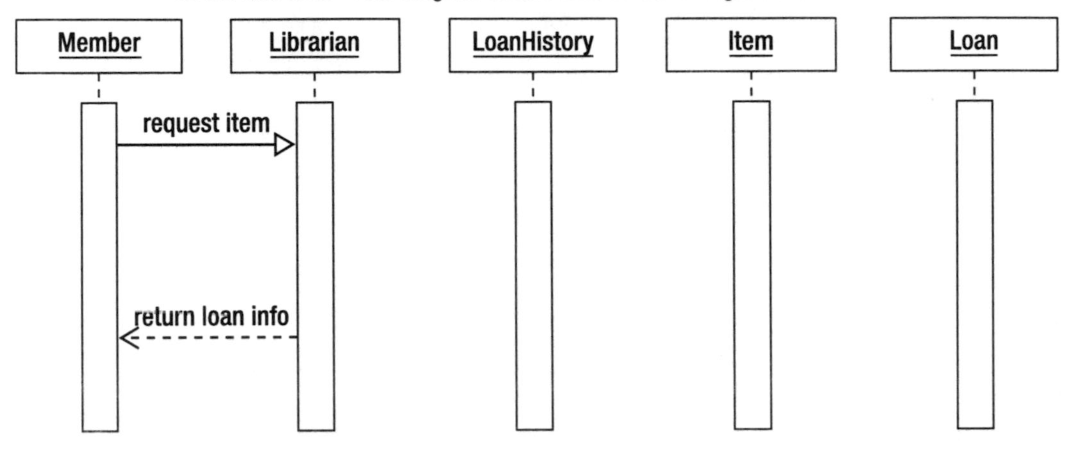

Figure 3-12. *Message layout in the sequence diagram*

7. Repeat steps 5 and 6 to create a message from the Librarian object to the LoanHistory object. Name the calling message (the solid line) "check history." Name the return message (the dashed line) "return history info."
8. Create a message from the Librarian object to the Item object. Name the calling message "check availability." Name the return message "return availability info."
9. Create a message from the Librarian object to the Item object. Name the calling message "update status." Name the return message "return update confirmation."
10. Create a message from the Librarian object to the Loan object. Name the calling message "create loan." Name the return message "return loan confirmation."
11. Rearrange the shapes so that your diagram looks similar to Figure 3-13. Save the diagram as UML_Act3_1.

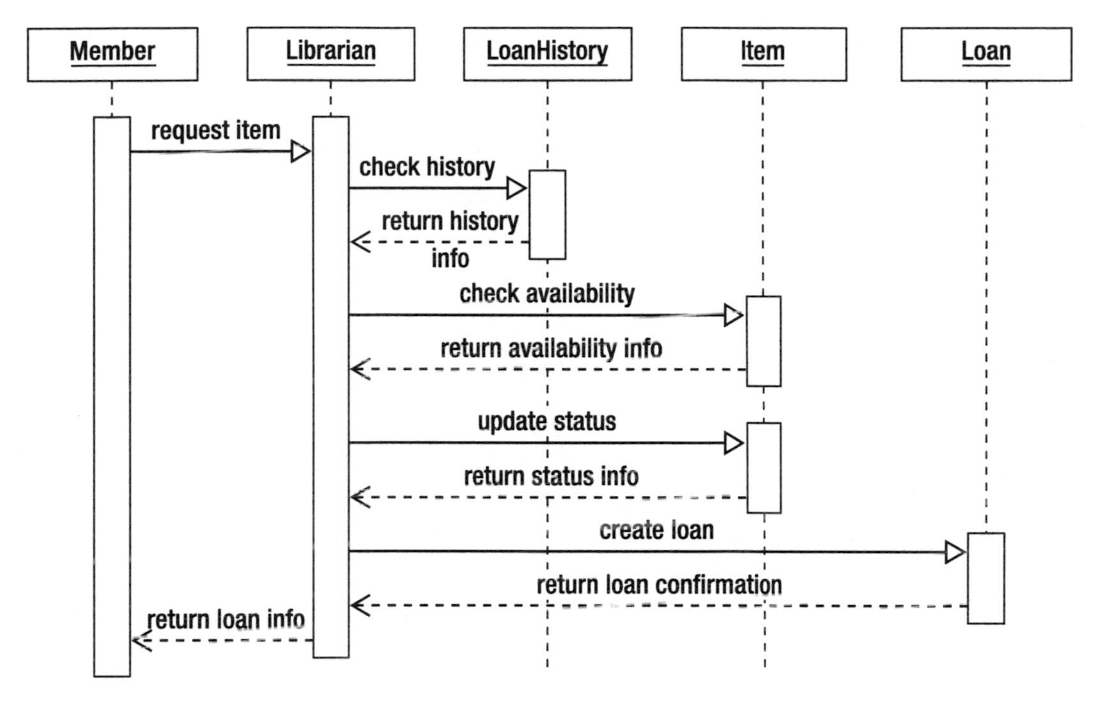

Figure 3-13. *Completed sequence diagram*

Adding Methods to the Class Diagram

After you have developed the sequence diagram, you begin to gain an understanding of the methods that must be included in the various classes of the application. You achieve the message interaction depicted in the sequence diagram by a method call from the initiating object (client) to the receiving object (server). The method being called is defined in the class that the server object is instantiated as. For example, the "check availability" message in the sequence diagram indicates that the Item class needs a method that processes this message call.

Follow these steps to add the methods:

1. In UMLet, chose File ➤ New to create a new diagram. Locate the drop-down list at the top of the template window. Change the template type to Class.
2. Double-click on the Simple Class shape template. Select the shape in the design window.
3. In the properties window, change the name of the class to Item. Underneath the name in the properties window enter two dashes. This will create a new section in the class shape. This section is where you enter the attributes of the class.

4. In the properties window, add the ItemNumber attribute to the class followed by two more dashes. This creates a third section in the class shape that is used to add the methods of the class.
5. Add a checkAvailability and an updateStatus method to the class as shown in Figure 3-14.

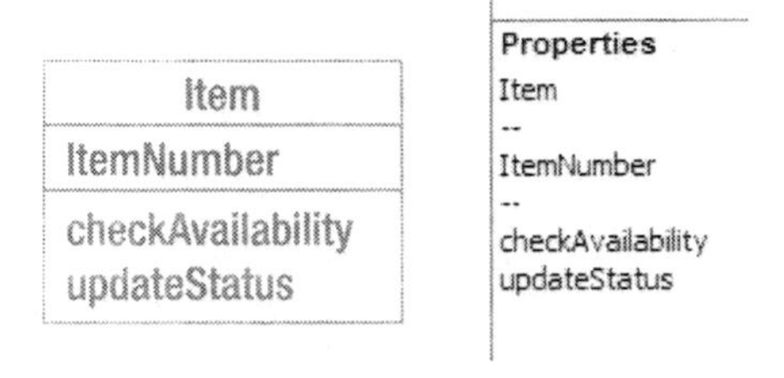

Figure 3-14. *Adding methods to a class*

6. Save the diagram as UML_Act3_1b.

Understanding Activity Diagrams

An activity diagram illustrates the flow of activities that need to occur during an operation or process. You can construct the activity diagram to view the workflow at various levels of focus.

- A high, system-level focus represents each use case as an activity and diagrams the workflow among the different use cases.
- A mid-level focus diagrams the workflow occurring within a particular use case.
- A low-level focus diagrams the workflow that occurs within a particular operation of one of the classes of the system.

The activity diagram consists of the starting point of the process represented by a solid circle and transition arrows representing the flow or transition from one activity to the next. Rounded rectangles represent the activities, and a bull's eye circle represents the ending point of the process. For example, Figure 3-15 shows a generic activity diagram that represents a process that starts with activity A, proceeds to activity B, and concludes.

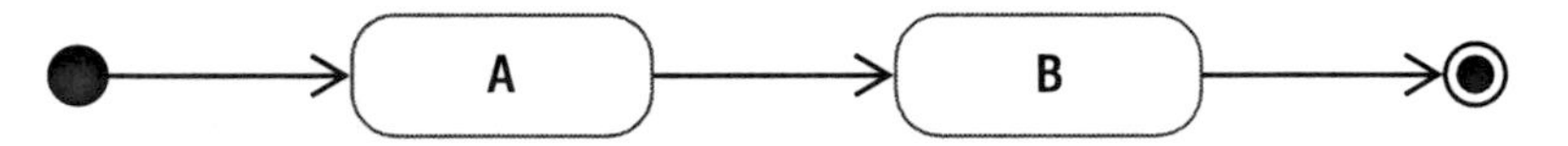

Figure 3-15. *Generic activity diagram*

Decision Points and Guard Conditions

Often, one activity will conditionally follow another. For example, in order to rent a video, a PIN verifies membership. An activity diagram represents conditionality by a decision point (represented by a diamond) with the guard condition (the condition that must be met to proceed) in brackets next to the flow line (see Figure 3-16).

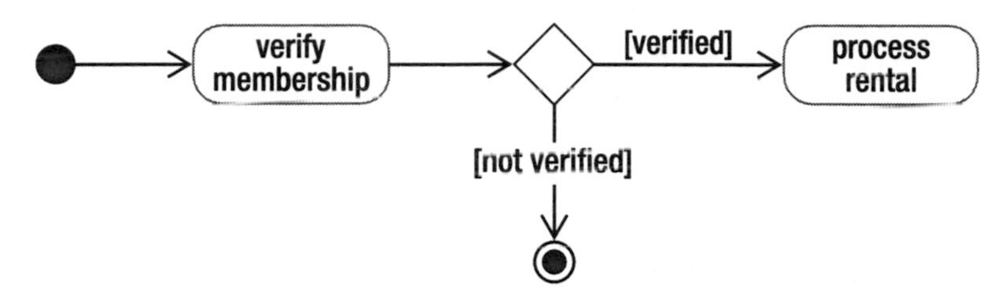

Figure 3-16. *Indicating decision points and guard conditions*

Parallel Processing

In some cases, two or more activities can run in parallel instead of sequentially. A solid, bold line drawn perpendicularly to the transition arrow represents the splitting of the paths. After the split, a second solid, bold line represents the merge. Figure 3-17 shows an activity diagram for the processing of a movie return. The order in which the Increment Inventory and the Remove Rental activities occur does not matter. The parallel paths in the diagram represent this parallel processing.

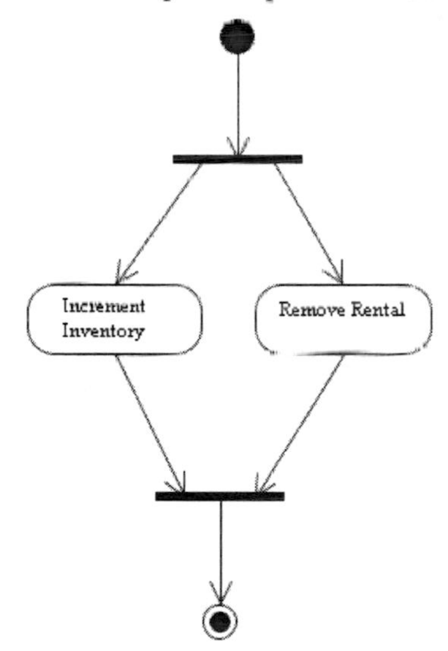

Figure 3-17. *Parallel processing depicted in an activity diagram*

Activity Ownership

The activity diagram's purpose is to model the control flow from activity to activity as the program processes. The diagrams shown thus far do not indicate which objects have responsibility for these activities. To signify object ownership of the activities, you segment the activity diagram into a series of vertical partitions (also called swim lanes). The object role at the top of the partition is responsible for the activities in that partition. Figure 3-18 shows an activity diagram for processing a movie rental, with swim lanes included.

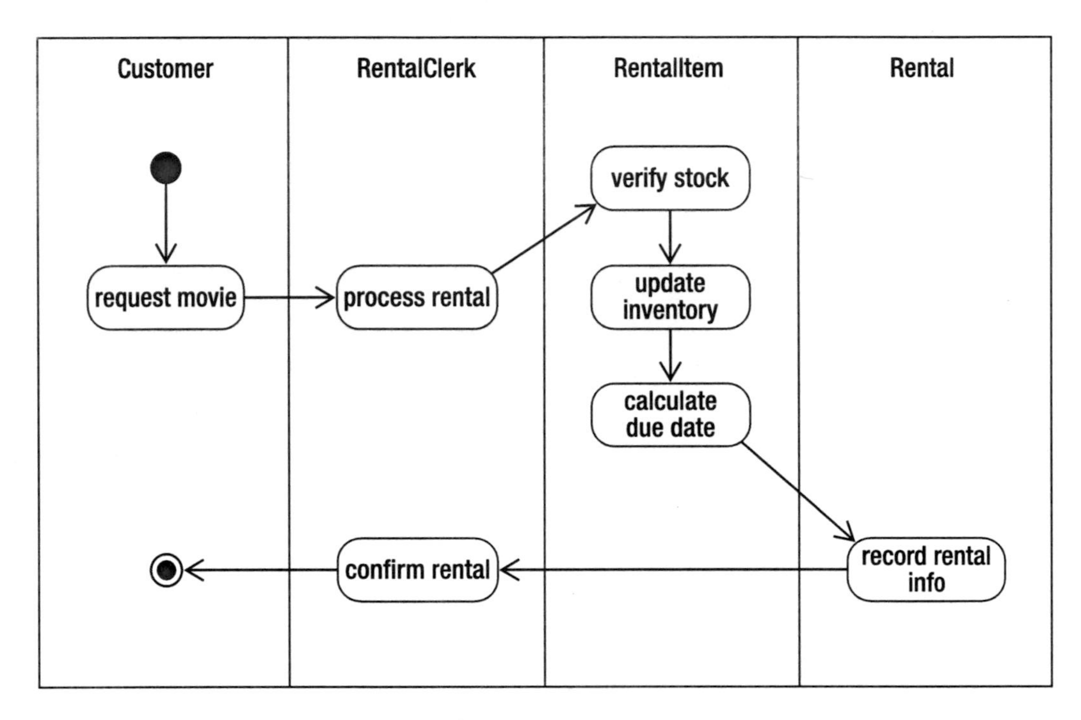

Figure 3-18. *Swim lanes in an activity diagram*

ACTIVITY 3-2. CREATING AN ACTIVITY DIAGRAM

After completing this activity, you should be familiar with the following:

- Using an activity diagram to model control flow as the program completes an activity.
- Using a UML modeling tool to create an activity class diagram.

Identifying Objects and Activities

Examine the following scenario developed for a use case from the user group library application:

After viewing the list of available loan items, a member requests an item to check out on loan. The librarian enters the member number and retrieves information about outstanding loans and any unpaid fines. If the member has fewer than four outstanding loans and does not have any outstanding fines, the loan is processed. The librarian retrieves information on the loan item to determine if it is currently on loan. If the item is available, it is checked out to the member.

By identifying the nouns and noun phrases in the use case scenario, you can get an idea of what objects will perform the tasks in carrying out the activities. Remember that these objects are instances of the classes identified in the class diagram. The following objects will be involved in carrying out the activities: Member, Librarian, LoanHistory, Item, and Loan.

The verb phrases help identify the activities carried out by the objects. These activities should correspond to the methods of the classes in the system. Match the following activities to the appropriate objects:

A. Request Movie

B. Process Rental

C. Check Availability

D. Check Member's Loan Status

E. Update Item Status

F. Calculate Due Date

G. Record Rental Info

H. Confirm Rental

See the end of the chapter for Activity 3-2 answers.

Creating an Activity Diagram

Follow these steps to create a sequence diagram using UMLet:

1. Start UMLet. Locate the drop-down list at the top of the template window. Change the template type to Activity.
2. Double-click the System box shape in the template window. A System box shape will appear in the upper left corner of the design surface. In the properties window, change the name of the shape to Member to represent the Member partition.
3. Repeat step 2 to add a partition for the Librarian, LoanHistory, Item, and Loan objects. Align the partitions from left to right as in Figure 3-19.

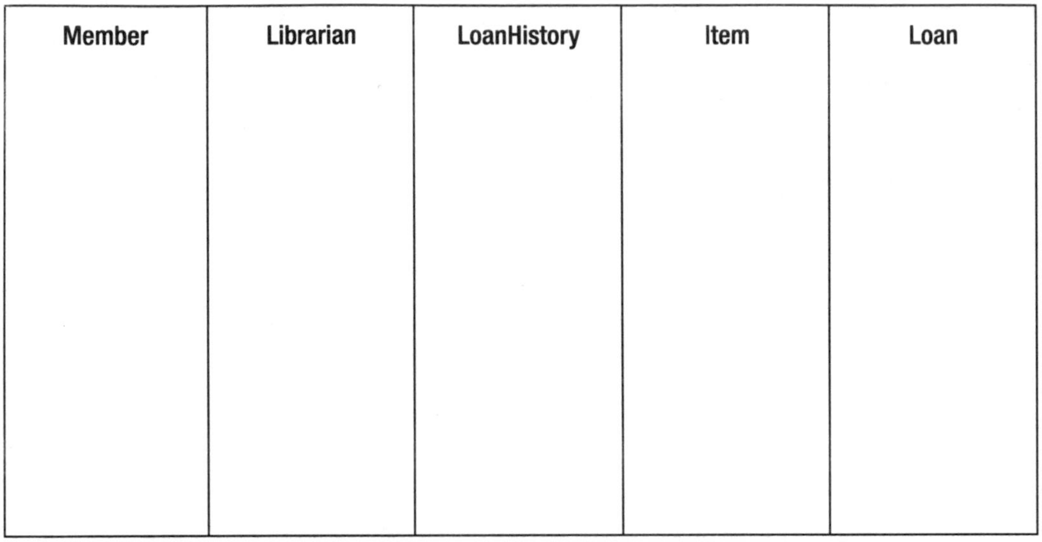

Member	Librarian	LoanHistory	Item	Loan

Figure 3-19. *Creating the activity diagram partitions*

4. From the Shapes window, double-click the Initial State shape and add it to the Member partition. Below the Initial State in the Member partition, add a State shape. Rename the State to "request item." Add a transition shape (arrow) from the Initial State to the Request Item action state.
5. Under the Librarian partition, add a Process Loan state and a Transition shape from the Request Item state to the Process Loan state.
6. Under the LoanHistory partition, add a Check Member Status action state and a Transition shape from the Process Loan action to the Check Member Status action state.
7. From the Shapes window, double-click the Conditional Branch shape (diamond) and add it to the LoanHistory partition below the Check Member Status action state. Add a Transition shape from the Check Member Status state to the Conditional Branch. From the Conditional Branch, add a Transition shape to a Deny Loan state under the Librarian partition. Add a label to the Transition shape with a condition of fail. Also add a Transition shape to a Check Item Status action state under the Item partition with a label condition of pass. Your diagram should be similar to Figure 3-20.

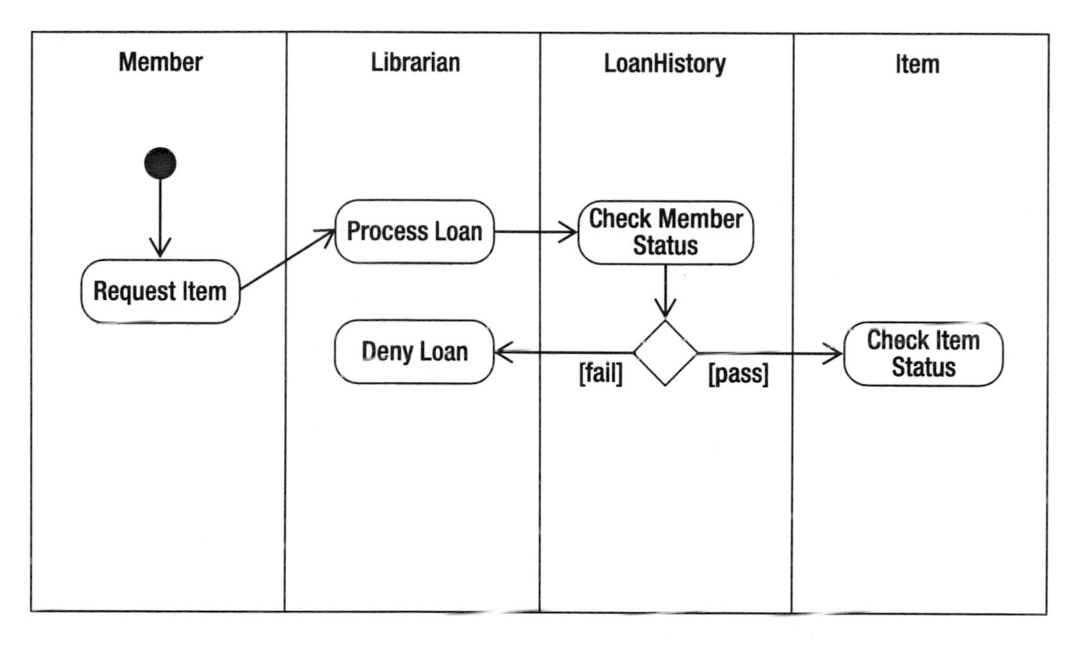

Figure 3-20. *Adding a branching condition*

8. Repeat step 7 to create a Conditional Branch from the Check Item Status state. If the item is in stock, add a Transition shape to an Update Item Status state under the Item partition. If the item is out of stock, add a Transition shape to the Deny Loan state under the Librarian partition.

9. From the Update Item Status state, add a Transition shape to a Record Loan Info state under the Loan partition.

10. From the Record Loan Info state, add a Transition shape to a Confirm Loan state under the Librarian partition.

11. From the Shapes window, click the Final State shape and add it to the bottom of the Member partition. Add a Transition shape from the Deny Loan state to the Final action state. Add another Transition shape from the Confirm Loan state to the Final action state.

Your completed diagram should resemble the one shown in Figure 3-21. Save the diagram as UMLAct3_2 and exit UMLet.

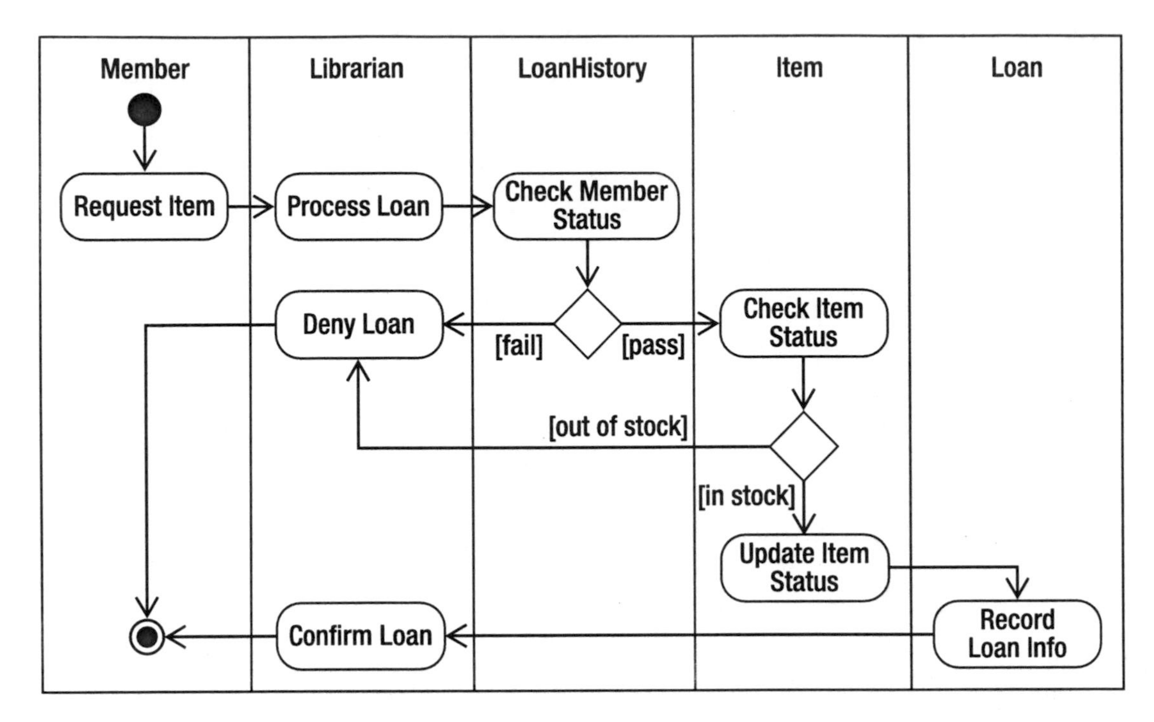

Figure 3-21. *Completed activity diagram*

Exploring GUI Design

Thus far, the discussions of object-oriented analysis and design have focused on modeling the functional design and the internal processing of the application. Successful modern software applications rely on a rich set of graphical user interfaces (GUIs) to expose this functionality to the users of the application.

In modern software systems, one of the most important aspects of an application is how well it interacts with the users. Gone are the days when users would interact with the application by typing cryptic commands at the DOS prompt. Modern operating systems employ GUIs that are, for the most part, intuitive to use. Users have also grown accustomed to the polished interfaces of the commercial office-productivity applications. Users have come to expect the same ease of use and intuitiveness built into applications developed in-house.

The design of the user interface should not be done haphazardly; rather, it should be planned in conjunction with the business logic design. The success of most applications is judged by the response of the users toward the application. If users are not comfortable when interacting with the application and the application does not improve the productivity of the user, it is doomed to failure. To the user, the application is the interface. It does not matter how pristine and clever the business logic code may be; if the user interface is poorly designed and implemented, the application will not be acceptable to the users. It is often hard for developers to remember that it is the user who drives the software development.

Although UML was not specifically designed for GUI design, many software architects and programmers have employed some of the UML diagrams to help model the user interface of an application.

GUI Activity Diagrams

The first step in developing a user interface design is to perform a task analysis to discover how users will interact with the system. The task analysis is based on the use cases and scenarios that have been modeled previously. You can then develop activity diagrams to model how the interaction between the user and the system will take place. Figure 3-22 shows an activity diagram modeling the activities the user goes through to record rental information.

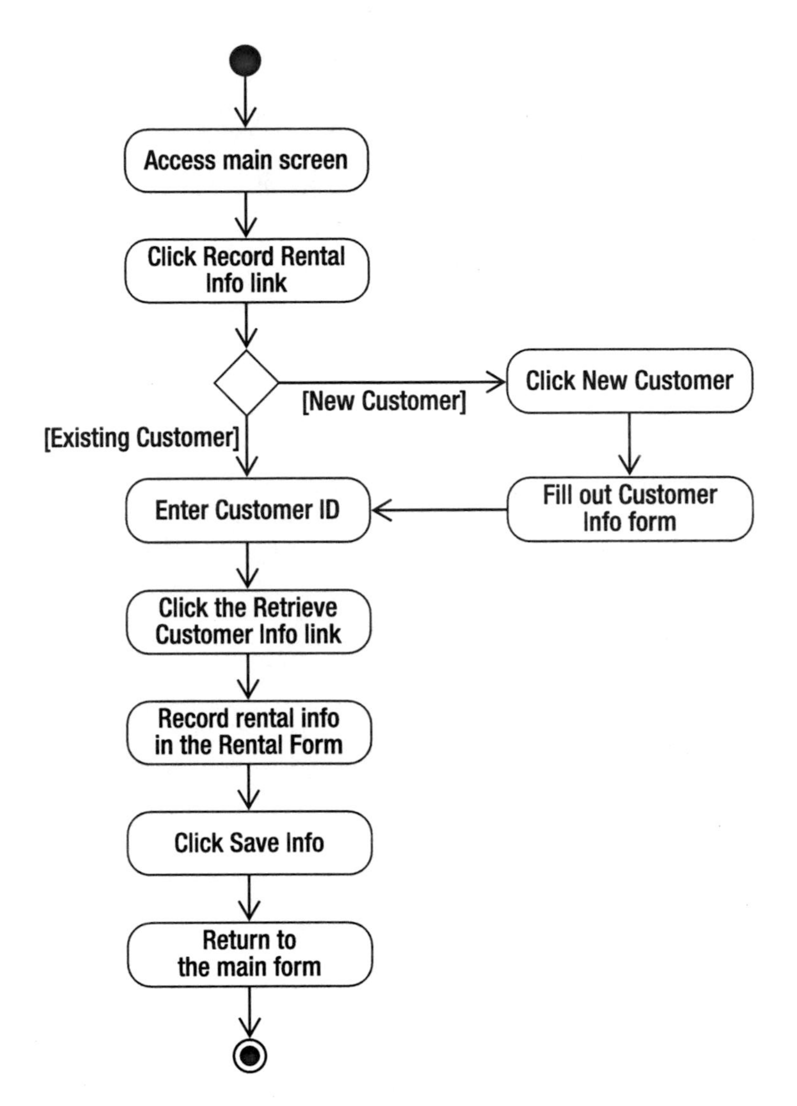

Figure 3-22. *GUI modeling with an activity diagram*

Interface Prototyping

After you have identified and prioritized the necessary tasks, you can develop a prototype sketch of the various screens that will make up the user interface. Figure 3-23 shows a prototype sketch of the Customer Info screen. Although you can use paper and pencil to develop your diagrams, there are some nice GUI prototyping tools available that offer common GUI design templates and the ability to link screens, plus other useful features.

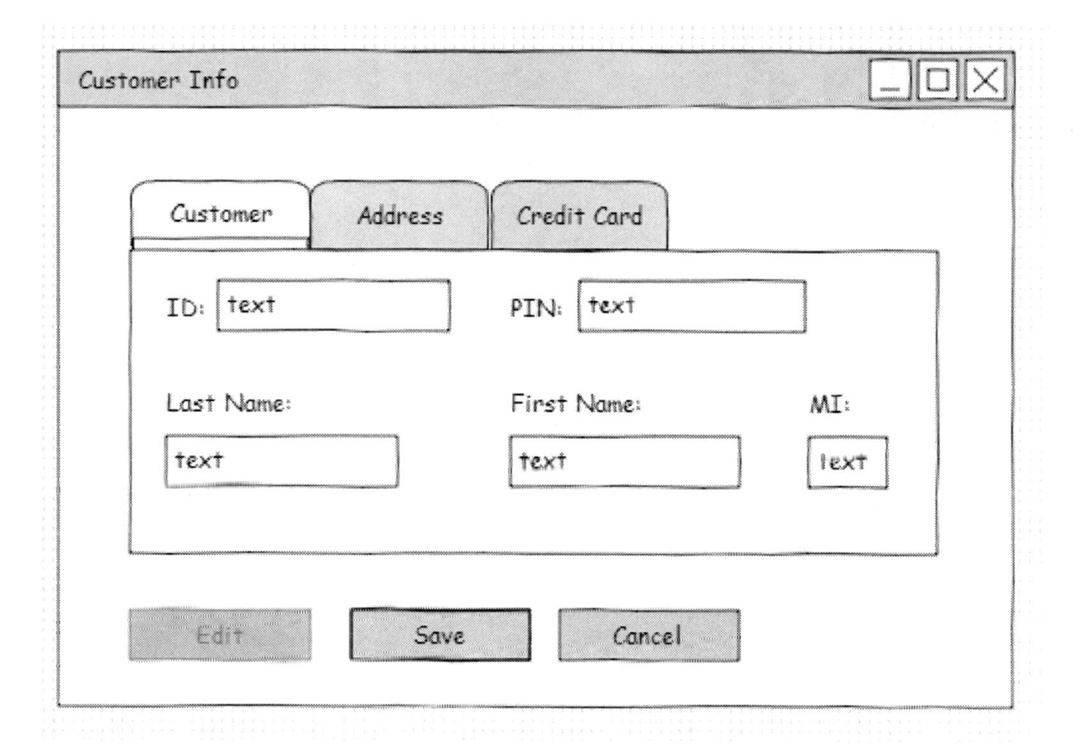

Figure 3-23. *GUI prototype sketch*

Interface Flow Diagrams

Once you have prototyped the various screens, you can use interface flow diagrams to model the relationships and flow patterns among the screens that make up the user interface. Figure 3-24 shows a partial interface flow diagram for the video rental application.

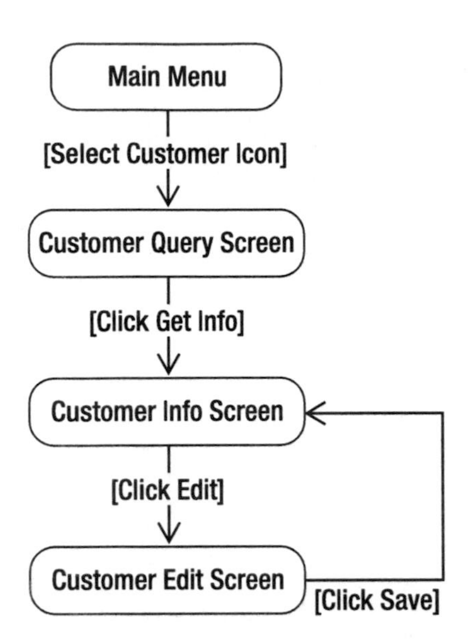

Figure 3-24. *Interface flow diagramming*

Application Prototyping

Once you have roughed out the screen layout and the design of the user interface, you can develop a simple prototype. The prototype should contain skeleton code that simulates the functionality of the system. At this point, you should not put a great effort into integrating the user interface front end with the business functionality of the application. The idea is to let the users interact with a working prototype to generate feedback on the user interface.

The processes of refining and testing the user interface will be iterative and will most likely continue through several cycles. Once the user interface design and the internal functional design of the application have been completed and prototyped, the next step in the application development cycle is to start coding the application.

Summary

This chapter introduced scenarios, sequence diagrams, collaboration diagrams, and activity diagrams. You saw how to use these diagrams for modeling object interaction. Additionally, you learned how some of the UML diagrams might be used to help model the user interface of the application.

The goal of this and the previous chapters has been to introduce you to some of the common modeling diagrams and concepts involved in software design and UML. In Chapter 4, you will take the concepts developed thus far and use them to implement a solution design for a sample case study.

ACTIVITY ANSWERS

Activity 3-1 Answers

Member, Librarian, Item, Loan, Loan History. These five objects are involved in the processing depicted in the scenario.

The other messaging interactions depicted in the scenario are as follows:

1. The Librarian object checks the lending history of the member with the LoanHistory object.
2. The Librarian object checks the availability of the item through the Item object.
3. The Librarian object updates the availability of the item through the Item object.
4. The Librarian creates a Loan object containing loan information.
5. The Librarian returns loan information to the Member object.

Activity 3-2 Answers

A. Member, B. Librarian, C. Item, D. LoanHistory, E. Item, F. Loan, G. Loan, H. Librarian.

The Member object is responsible for the Request Movie activity. The Librarian object is responsible for the Process Rental and Confirm Rental activities. The LoanHistory object is responsible for the Check Member's Loan Status activity. The Item object is responsible for the Check Availability and Update Item Status activities. The Loan object is responsible for the Calculate Due Date and Record Rental Info activities.

CHAPTER 4

Designing OOP Solutions: A Case Study

Designing solutions for an application is not an easy endeavor. Becoming an accomplished designer takes time and a conscious effort, which explains why many developers avoid it like the plague. You can study all the theories and know all the buzzwords, but the only way to truly develop your modeling skills is to roll up your sleeves, get your hands dirty, and start modeling. In this chapter, you will go through the process of modeling an office-supply ordering system. Although this is not a terribly complex application, it will serve to help solidify the modeling concepts covered in the previous chapters. By analyzing the case study, you will also gain a better understanding of how a model is developed and how the pieces fit together.

After reading this chapter, you should be familiar with the following:

- How to model an OOP solution using UML.
- Some common OOP design pitfalls to avoid.

Developing an OOP Solution

In the case-study scenario, your company currently has no standard way for departments to order office supplies. Each department separately implements its own ordering process. As a result, it is next to impossible to track company-wide spending on supplies, which impacts the ability to forecast budgeting and identify abuses. Another problem with the current system is that it does not allow for a single contact person who could negotiate better deals with the various vendors.

As a result, you have been asked to help develop a company-wide office-supply ordering (OSO) application. To model this system you will complete the following steps:

- Create an SRS.
- Develop the use cases.
- Diagram the use cases.
- Model the classes.
- Model the user interface design.

Creating the System Requirement Specification

After interviewing the various clients of the proposed system, you develop the SRS. Remember from Chapter 2 that the SRS scopes the system requirements, defines the system boundaries, and identifies the users of the system.

You have identified the following system users:

- *Purchaser*: Initiates a request for supplies.
- *Department manager*: Tracks and approves supply requests from department purchasers.
- *Supply vendor processing application*: Receives order files generated by the system.
- *Purchase manager*: Updates the supply catalog, tracks supply requests, and checks in delivered items.

You have identified the following system requirements:

- Users must log in to the system by supplying a username and password.
- Purchasers will view a list of supplies that are available to be ordered.
- Purchasers will be able to filter the list of supplies by category.
- Purchasers can request multiple supplies in a single purchase request.
- A department manager can request general supplies for the department.
- Department managers must approve or deny supply requests for their department at the end of each week.
- If department managers deny a request, they must supply a short explanation outlining the reason for the denial.
- Department managers must track spending within their departments and ensure there are sufficient funds for approved supply requests.
- A purchase manager maintains the supply catalog and ensures it is accurate and current.
- A purchase manager checks in the supplies when they are received and organizes the supplies for distribution.
- Supply requests that have been requested but not approved are marked with a status of pending.
- Supply requests that have been approved are marked with a status of approved and an order is generated.
- Once an order is generated, a file containing the order details is placed in an order queue. Once the order has been placed in the queue, it is marked with a status of placed.

- A separate supply vendor processing application will retrieve the order files from the queue, parse the documents, and distribute the line items to the appropriate vendor queues. Periodically, the supply vendor processing application will retrieve the orders from a vendor queue and send them to the vendor.
- When all the items of an order are checked in, the order is marked with a status of fulfilled and the purchaser is informed that the order is ready for pick up.

Developing the Use Cases

After generating the SRS and getting the appropriate system users to sign off on it, the next task is to develop the use cases, which will define how the system will function from the users' perspective. The first step in developing the use cases is to define the actors. Remember from Chapter 2 that the actors represent the external entities (human or other systems) that will interact with the system. From the SRS, you can identify the following actors that will interact with the system:

- Purchaser
- Department manager
- Purchase manager
- Supply vendor processing application

Now that you have identified the actors, the next step is to identify the various use cases with which the actors will be involved. By examining the requirement statements made in the SRS, you can identify the various use cases. For example, the statement "Users must log in to the system by supplying a username and password" indicates the need for a Login use case. Table 4-1 identifies the use cases for the OSO application.

Table 4-1. *Use Cases for the OSO Application*

Name	Actor(s)	Description
Login	Purchaser, Department manager, Purchase manager	Users see a login screen. They then enter their username and password. They either click Log In or Cancel. After login, they see a screen containing product information.
View Supply Catalog	Purchaser, Department manager, Purchase manager	Users see a catalog table that contains a list of supplies. The table contains information such as the supply name, category, description, and cost. Users can filter supplies by category.

(continued)

Table 4-1. *(continued)*

Name	Actor(s)	Description
Purchase Request	Purchaser, Department manager	Purchasers select items in the table and click a button to add them to their cart. A separate table shows the items in their cart, the number of each item requested and the cost, as well as the total cost of the request.
Department Purchase Request	Department manager	Department managers select items in the table and click a button to add them to their cart. A separate table shows the items in their cart, the number of each item requested and the cost, as well as the total cost of the request.
Request Review	Department manager	Department managers see a screen that lists all pending supply requests for members of their department. They review the requests and mark them as approved or denied. If they deny the request, they enter a brief explanation.
Track Spending	Department manager	Department managers see a screen that lists the monthly spending of department members as well as the running total of the department.
Maintain Catalog	Purchase manager	The purchase manager has the ability to update product information, add products, or mark products as discontinued. The administrator can also update category information, add categories, and mark categories as discontinued.
Item Check In	Purchase manager	The purchase manager sees a screen for entering the order number. The purchase manager then sees the line items listed for the order. The items that have been received are marked. When all the items for an order are received, it is marked as fulfilled.
Order Placement	Supply vendor processing application	The supply vendor processing application checks the queue for outgoing order files. Files are retrieved, parsed, and sent to the appropriate vendor queue.

Diagramming the Use Cases

Now that you have identified the various use cases and actors, you are ready to construct a diagram of the use cases. Figure 4-1 shows a preliminary use case model developed with UMLet, which was introduced in Chapter 2.

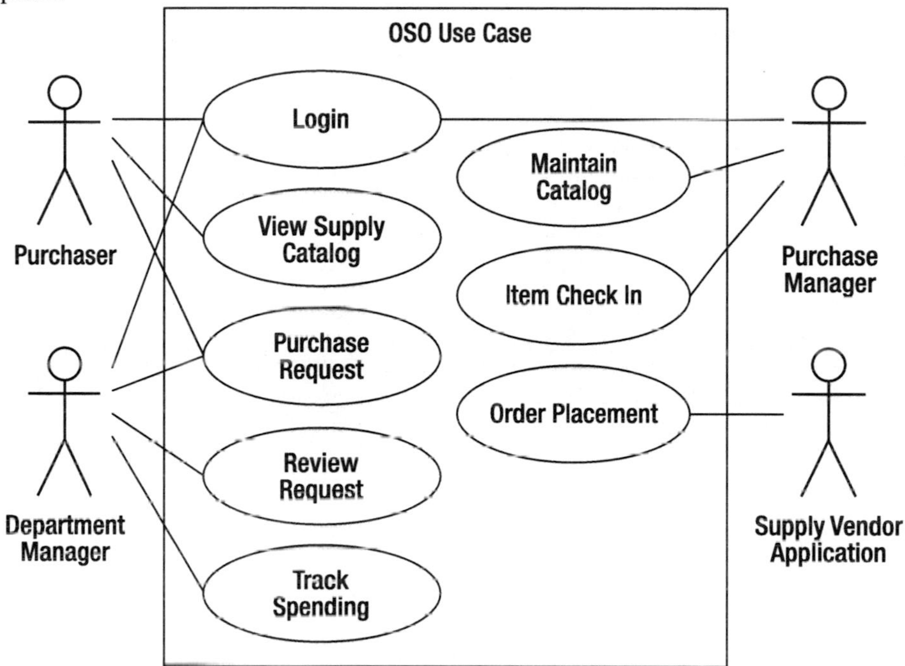

Figure 4-1. *Preliminary OSO use case diagram*

After you have diagrammed the use cases, you now look for any relationships that may exist between the use cases. Two relationships that may exist are the includes relationship and the extends relationship. Remember from the discussions in Chapter 2 that when a use case includes another use case, the use case being included needs to run as a precondition. For example, the Login use case of the OSO application needs to be included in the View Supply Catalog use case. The reason you make Login a separate use case is that the Login use case can be reused by one or more other use cases. In the OSO application, the Login use case will also be included with the Track Spending use case. Figure 4-2 depicts this includes relationship.

■Note In some modeling tools, the includes relationship may be indicated in the use case diagram by the uses keyword.

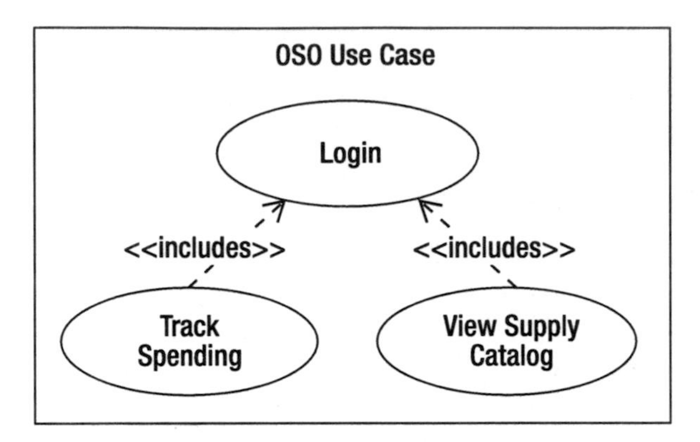

Figure 4-2. *Including the Login use case*

The extends relationship exists between two use cases when, depending on a condition, a use case will extend the behavior of the initial use case. In the OSO application, when a manager is making a purchase request, she can indicate that she will be requesting a purchase for the department. In this case, the Department Purchase Request use case becomes an extension of the Purchase Request use case. Figure 4-3 diagrams this extension.

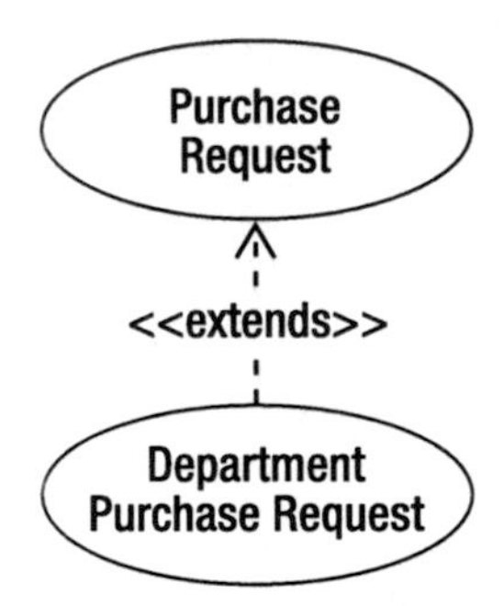

Figure 4-3. *Extending the Purchase Request use case*

After analyzing the system requirements and use cases, you can make the system development more manageable by breaking up the application and developing it in phases. For example, you can develop the Purchase Request portion of the application first. Next, you can develop Request Review portion, and then the Item Check In portion. The rest of this chapter focuses on the Purchase Request portion of the application. Employees and department managers will use this part of the application to make purchase requests. Figure 4-4 shows the use case diagram for this phase.

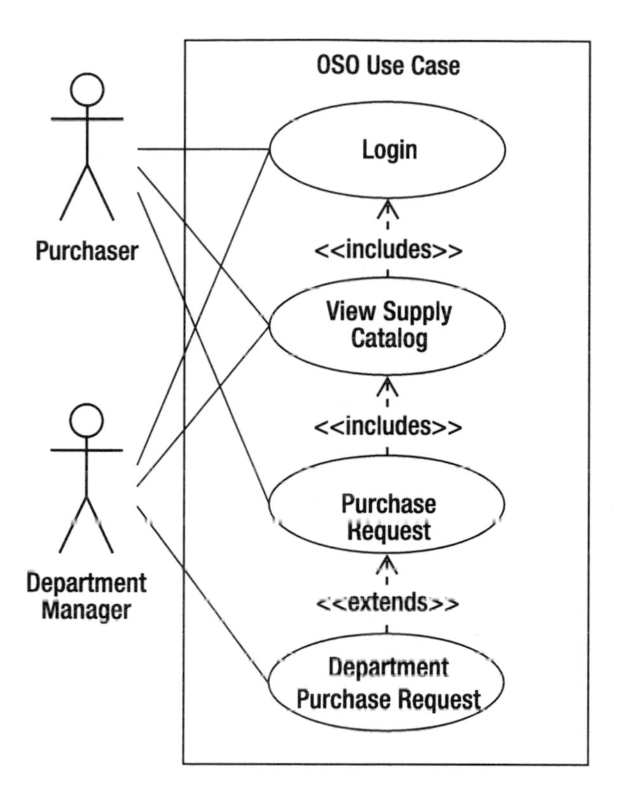

Figure 4-4. *Purchase Request use case diagram*

Developing the Class Model

Developing the class model involves several tasks. You begin by identifying the classes, and then you add attributes, associations, and behaviors.

Identifying the Classes

After you have identified the various use cases, you can start identifying the classes the system needs to include to carry out the functionality described in the use cases. To identify the classes, you drill down into each use case and define a series of steps needed to carry it out. It is also helpful to identify the noun phrases in the use case descriptions. The noun phrases are often good indicators of the classes that will be needed.

For example, the following steps describe the View Supply Catalog use case:

- User has logged in and been assigned a user status level. (This is the precondition.)
- Users are presented with a catalog table that contains a list of supplies. The table contains information such as the supply name, category, description, and cost.
- Users can filter supplies by category.
- Users are given the choice of logging out or making a purchase request. (This is the postcondition.)

From this description, you can identify a class that will be responsible for retrieving product information from the database and filtering the products being displayed. The name of this class will be the ProductCatalog class.

Examining the noun phrases in the use case descriptions dealing with making purchase requests reveals the candidate classes for the OSO application, as listed in Table 4-2.

Table 4-2. *Candidate Classes Used to Make Purchase Requests*

Use Case	Candidate Classes
Login	User, username, password, success, failure
View Supply Catalog	User, catalog table, supplies, information, supply name, category, description, cost
Purchase Request	Purchaser, items, cart, number, item requested, cost, total cost
Department Purchase Request	Department manager, items, cart, number, item requested, cost, total cost, department purchase request

Now that you have identified the candidate classes, you need to eliminate the classes that indicate redundancy. For example, a reference to items and line items would represent the same abstraction. You can also eliminate classes that represent attributes rather than objects. Username, password, and cost are examples of noun phrases that represent attributes. Some classes are vague or generalizations of other classes. User is actually a generalization of purchaser and manager. Classes may also actually refer to the same object abstraction but indicate a different state of the object. For example, the supply request and order represent the same abstraction before and after approval. You should also filter out classes that represent implementation constructs such as list and table. For example, a cart is really a collection of order items for a particular order.

Using these elimination criteria, you can whittle down the class list to the following candidate classes:

- Employee
- DepartmentManager
- Order
- OrderItem
- ProductCatalog
- Product

You can also include classes that represent the actors that will interact with the system. These are special classes called actor classes and are included in the class diagram to model the interface between the system and the actor. For example, you could designate a Purchaser(UI) actor class that represents the GUI that a Purchaser (Employee or DepartmentManager) would interact with to make a purchase request. Because these classes are not actually part of the system, the internal implementations of these classes are encapsulated, and they are treated as black boxes to the system.

You can now start formulating the class diagram for the Purchase Request portion of the OSO application. Figure 4-5 shows the preliminary class diagram for the OSO application.

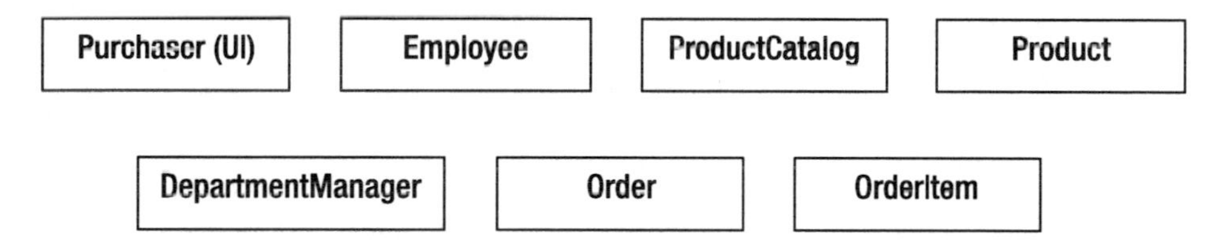

Figure 4-5. Preliminary OSO class diagram

Adding Attributes to the Classes

The next stage in the development of the class model is to identify the level of abstraction the classes must implement. You determine what state information is relevant to the OSO application. This required state information will be implemented through the attributes of the class. Analyzing the system requirements for the Employee class reveals the need for a login name, password, and department. You also need an identifier such as an employee ID to uniquely identify various employees. An interview with managers revealed the need to include the first and last names of the employee so that they can track spending by name. Table 4-3 summarizes the attributes that will be included in the OSO classes.

Table 4-3. *OSO Class Attributes*

Class	Attribute	Type
Employee	EmployeeID	Integer
	LoginName	String
	Password	String
	Department	String
	FirstName	String
	LastName	String
DepartmentManager	EmployeeID	Integer
	LoginName	String
	Password	String
	Department	String
	FirstName	String
	LastName	String
Order	OrderNumber	Long
	OrderDate	Date
	Status	String
OrderItem	ProductNumber	String
	Quantity	Short
	UnitPrice	Decimal
Product	ProductNumber	String
	ProductName	String
	Description	String
	UnitPrice	Decimal
	Category	String
	VendorCode	String
ProductCatalog	None	

Figure 4-6 shows the OSO class diagram with the class attributes. I have left out the attributes for the DepartmentManager class. The DepartmentManager class will probably inherit the attributes listed for the Employee class.

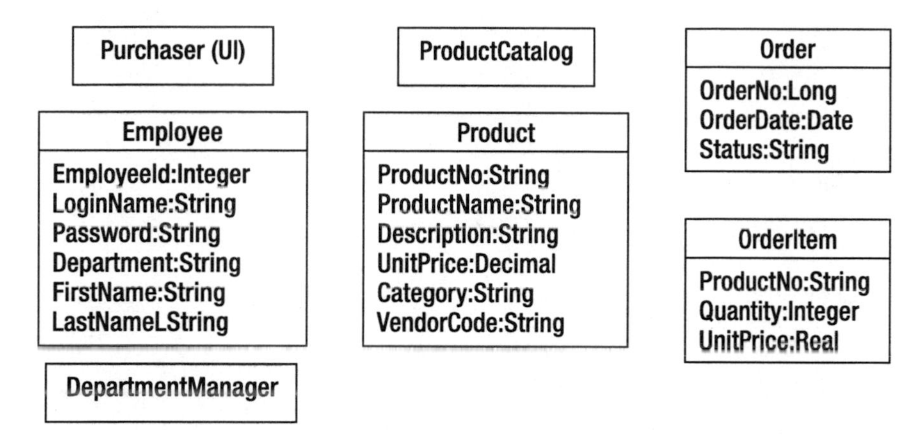

Figure 4-6. *The Purchase Request component class diagram with attributes added*

Identifying Class Associations

The next stage in the development process is to model the class associations that will exist in the OSO application. If you study the use cases and SRS, you can gain an understanding of what types of associations you need to incorporate into the class structural design.

■ **Note** You may find that you need to further refine the SRS to expose the class associations.

For example, an employee will be associated with an order. By examining the multiplicity of the association, you discover that an employee can have multiple orders, but an order can be associated with only one employee. Figure 4-7 models this association.

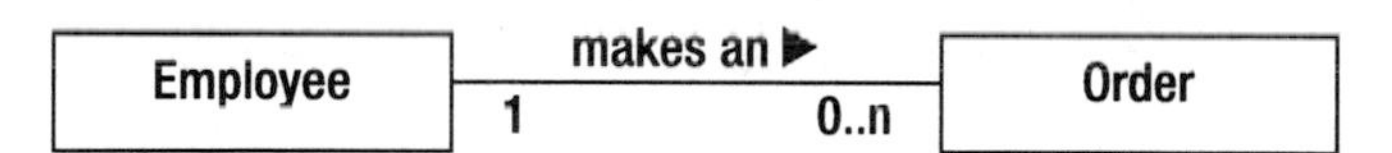

Figure 4-7. *Depicting the association between the Employee class and the Order class*

As you start to identify the class attributes, you will notice that the Employee class and the DepartmentManager class have many of the same attributes. This makes sense, because a manager is also an employee. For the purpose of this application, a manager represents an employee with specialized behavior. This specialization is represented by an inheritance relationship, as shown in Figure 4-8.

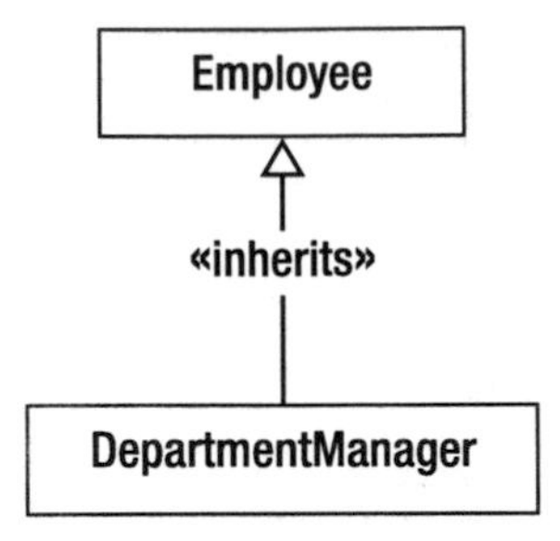

Figure 4-8. *The DepartmentManager class inheriting from the Employee class*

The following statements sum up the associations in the OSO class structure:

- An Order is a collection of OrderItem objects.
- An Employee can have multiple Order objects.
- An Order is associated with one Employee.
- The ProductCatalog is associated with multiple Product objects.
- A Product is associated with the ProductCatalog.
- An OrderItem is associated with one Product.
- A Product may be associated with multiple OrderItem objects.
- A DepartmentManager is an Employee with specialized behavior.

Figure 4-9 shows these various associations (excluding the class attributes for clarity).

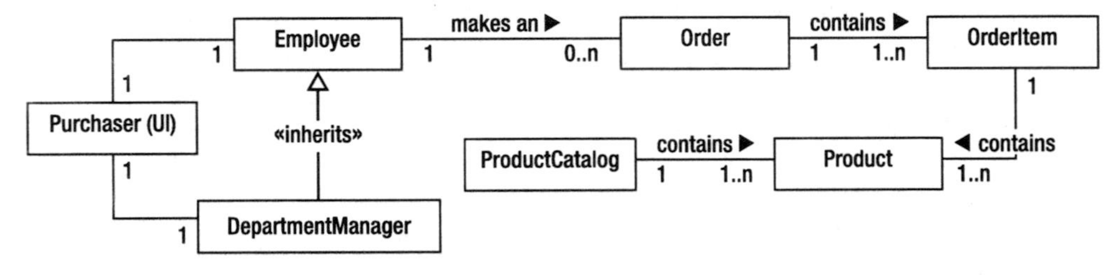

Figure 4-9. *The Purchase Request component class diagram with associations added*

Modeling the Class Behaviors

Now that you have sketched out the preliminary structure of the classes, you are ready to model how these classes will interact and collaborate. The first step in this process is to drill down into the use case descriptions and create a more detailed scenario of how the use case will be carried out. The following scenario describes one possible sequence for carrying out the Login use case.

1. The user is presented with a login dialog box.
2. The user enters a login name and a password.

3. The user submits the information.
4. The name and password are checked and verified.
5. The user is presented with a supply request screen.

Although this scenario depicts the most common processing involved with the Login use case, you may need other scenarios to describe anticipated alternate outcomes. The following scenario describes an alternate processing of the Login use case:

1. The user is presented with a login dialog box.
2. The user enters a login name and a password.
3. The user submits the information.
4. The name and password are checked but cannot be verified.
5. The user is informed of the incorrect login information.
6. The user is presented with a login dialog box again.
7. The user either tries again or cancels the login request.

At this point, it may help to create a visual representation of the scenarios outlined for the use case. Remember from Chapter 3 that activity diagrams are often used to visualize use case processing. Figure 4-10 shows an activity diagram constructed for the Login use case scenarios.

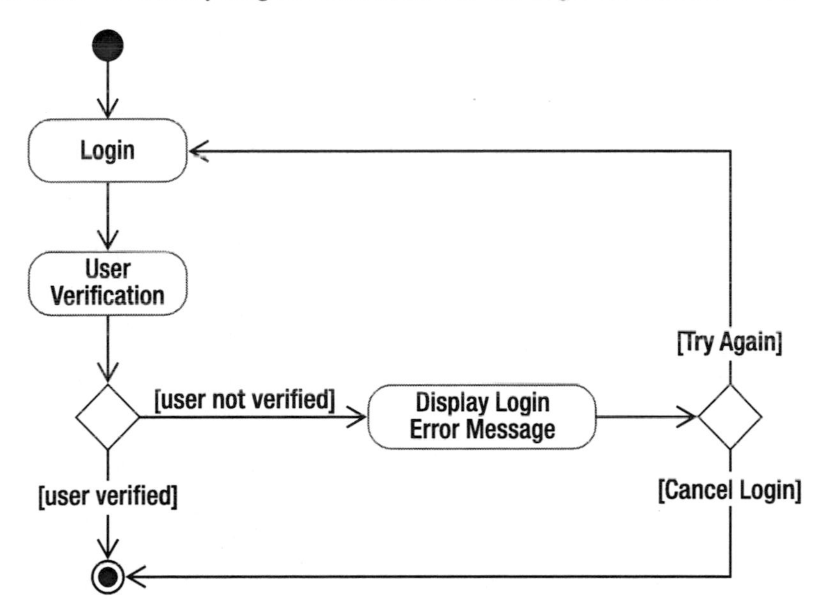

Figure 4-10. *An activity diagram depicting the Login use case scenarios*

After analyzing the process involved in the use case scenarios, you can now turn your attention to assigning the necessary behaviors to the classes of the system. To help identify the class behaviors and interactions that need to occur, you construct a sequence diagram, as discussed in Chapter 3.

Figure 4-11 shows a sequence diagram for the Login use case scenarios. The Purchaser (UI) class calls the Login method that has been assigned to the Employee class. The message returns information that will indicate whether the login has been verified.

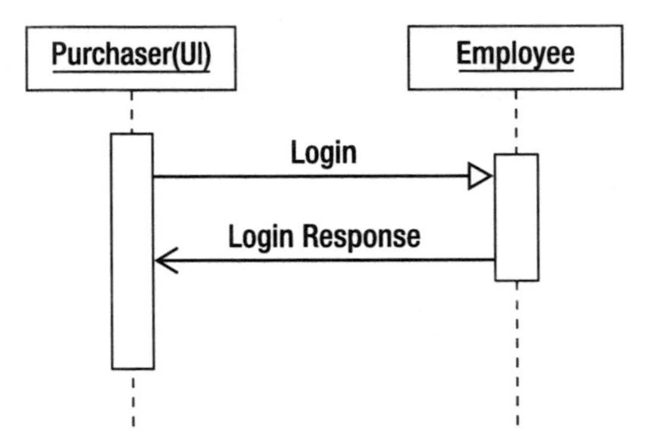

Figure 4-11. *A sequence diagram depicting the Login use case scenarios*

Next, let's analyze the View Supply Catalog use case. The following scenario describes the use case:

1. User logged in and has been verified.
2. User views a catalog table that contains product information, including the supply name, category, description, and price.
3. User chooses to filter the table by category, selects a category, and refreshes the table.

From this scenario, you can see that you need a method of the ProductCatalog class that will return a listing of product categories. The Purchaser class will invoke this method. Another method the ProductCatalog class needs is one that will return a product list filtered by category. The sequence diagram in Figure 4-12 shows the interaction that occurs between the Purchaser (UI) class and the ProductCatalog class.

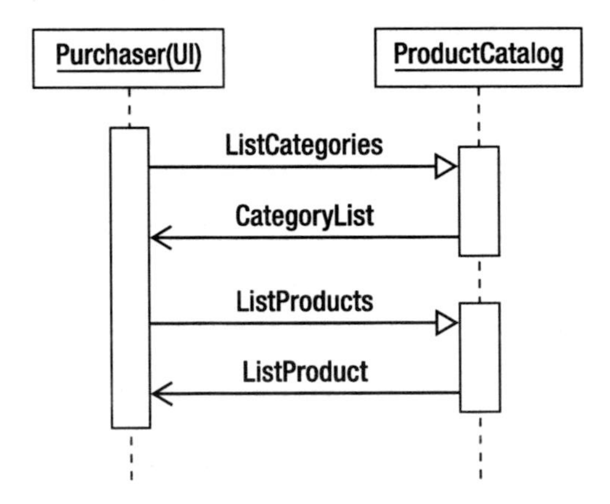

Figure 4-12. *A sequence diagram depicting the View Supply Catalog scenario*

The following scenario was developed for the Purchase Request use case:

1. A purchaser has logged in and has been verified as an employee.
2. The purchaser selects items from the product catalog and adds them to the order request (shopping cart), indicating the number of each item requested.
3. After completing the item selections for the order, the purchaser submits the order.
4. Order request information is updated, and an order ID is generated and returned to the purchaser.

From the scenario, you can identify an AddItem method of the Order class that needs to be created. This method will accept a product ID and a quantity, and then return the subtotal of the order. The Order class will need to call a method of the OrderItem class, which will create an instance of an order item. You also need a SubmitOrder method of the Order class that will submit the request and the return order ID of the generated order. Figure 4-13 shows the associated sequence diagram for this scenario.

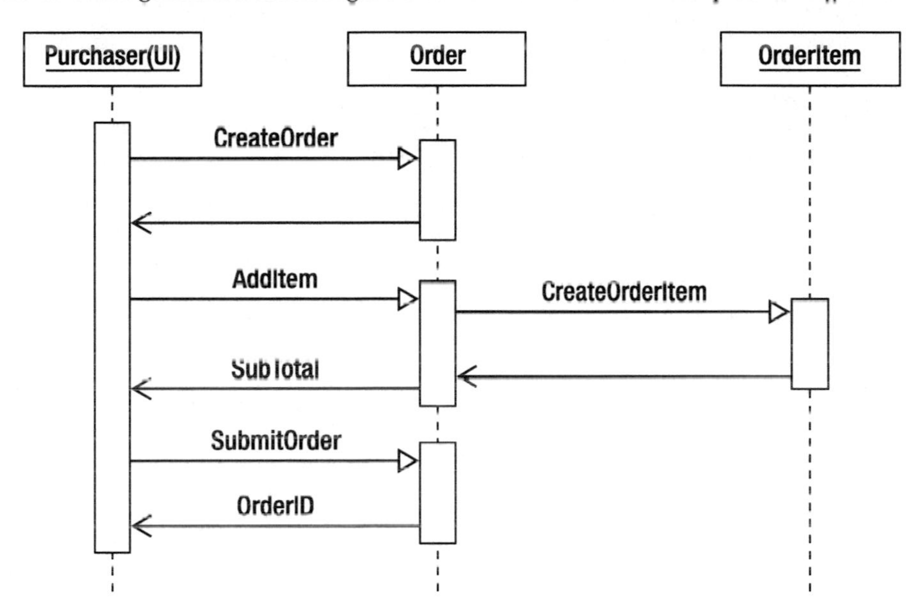

Figure 4-13. *A sequence diagram depicting the Purchase Request scenario*

Some other scenarios that need to be included are deleting an item from the shopping cart, changing the quantity of an item in the cart, and canceling the order process. You will also need to include similar scenarios and create similar methods for the Department Purchase Request use case. After analyzing the scenarios and interactions that need to take place, you can develop a class diagram for the Purchase Request portion of the application, as shown in Figure 4-14.

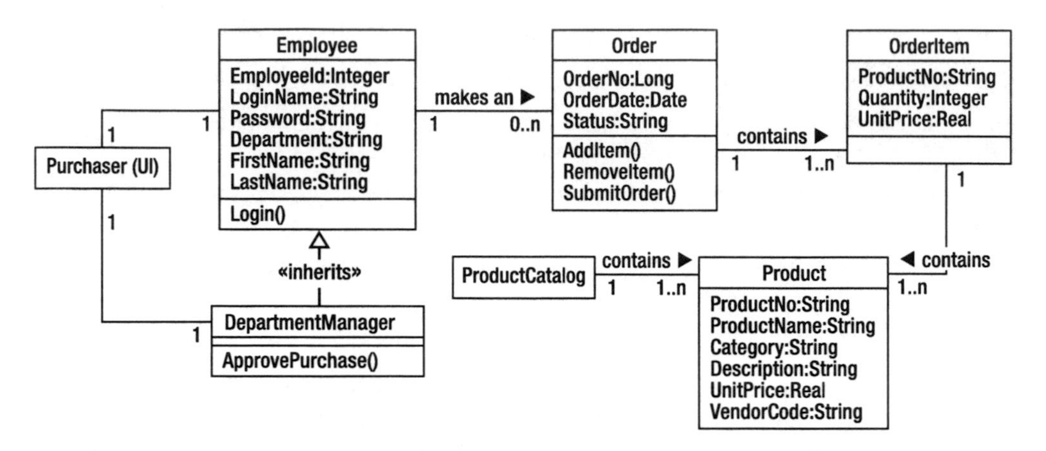

Figure 4-14. *Purchase Request class diagram*

Developing the User Interface Model Design

At this point in the application design process, you don't want to commit to a particular GUI implementation (in other words, a technology-specific one). It is helpful, however, to model some of the common elements and functionality required of a GUI for the application. This will help you create a prototype user interface that you can use to verify the business logic design that has been developed. The users will be able to interact with the prototype and provide feedback and verification of the logical design.

The first prototype screen that you need to implement is the one for logging in. You can construct an activity diagram to help define the activities the user needs to perform when logging in to the system, as shown in Figure 4-15.

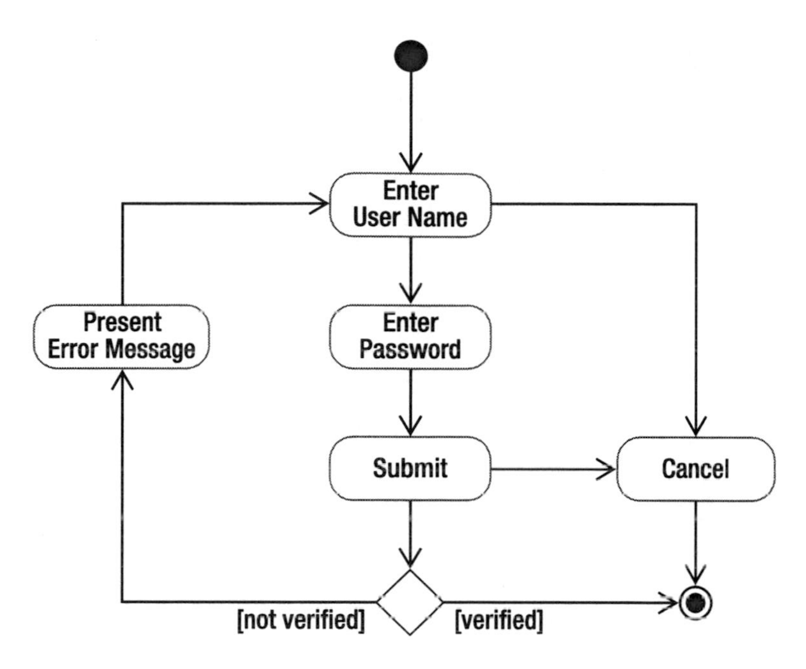

Figure 4-15. *An activity diagram depicting user login activities*

Analyzing the activity diagram reveals that you can implement the login screen as a fairly generic interface. This screen should allow the user to enter a username and password. It should include a way to indicate that the user is logging in as either an employee or a manager. The final requirement is to include a way for the user to abort the login process. Figure 4-16 shows a prototype of the login screen.

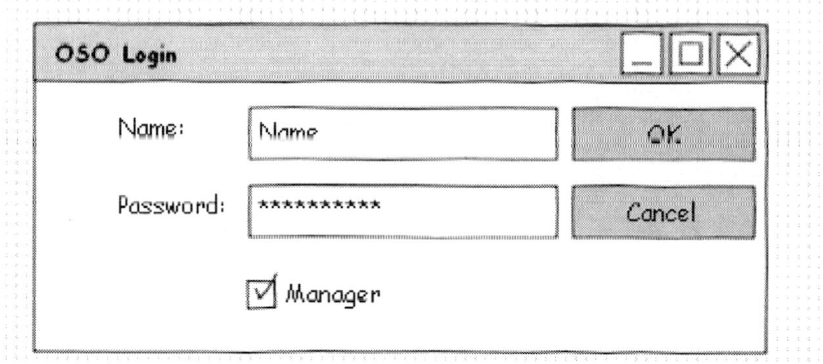

Figure 4-16. *Login screen prototype*

The next screen you need to consider is the product catalog screen. Figure 4-17 depicts the activity diagram for viewing and filtering the products.

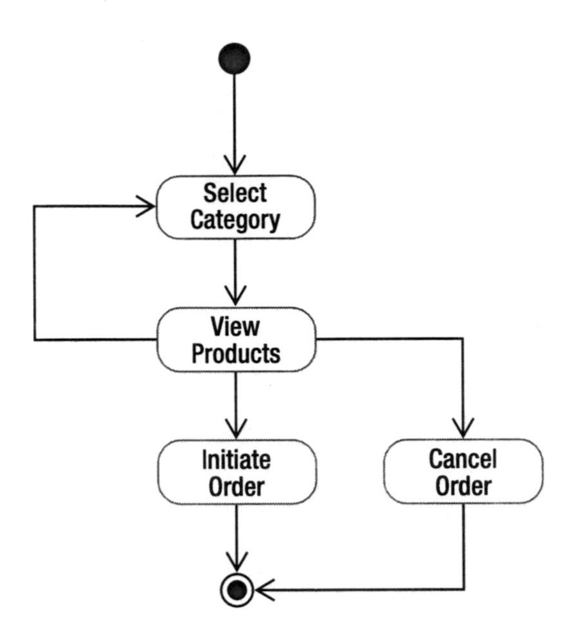

Figure 4-17. *An activity diagram depicting activities for viewing products*

The activity diagram reveals that the screen needs to show a table or list of products and product information. Users must be able to filter the products by category, which can be initiated by selecting a category from a category list. Users also need to be able to initiate an order request or exit the application. Figure 4-18 shows a prototype screen that can be used to view the products.

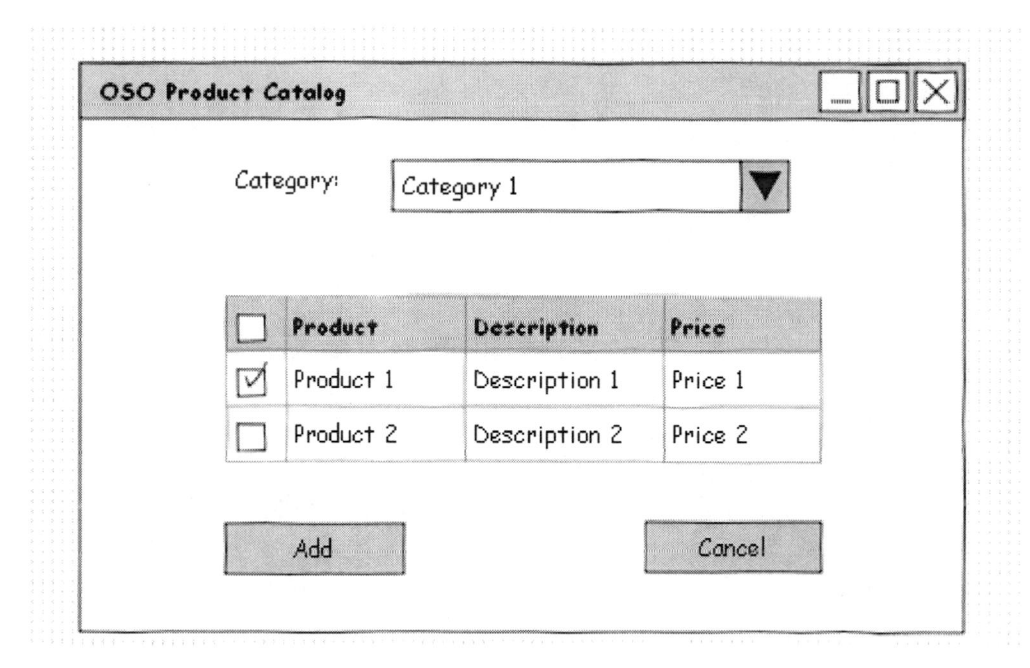

Figure 4-18. *View products screen prototype*

The final screen that needs to be prototyped for this part of the application is the shopping cart interface. This will facilitate the adding and removing items from an order request. It also needs to allow the user to submit the order or abort an order request. Figure 4-19 shows a prototype of the order request screen.

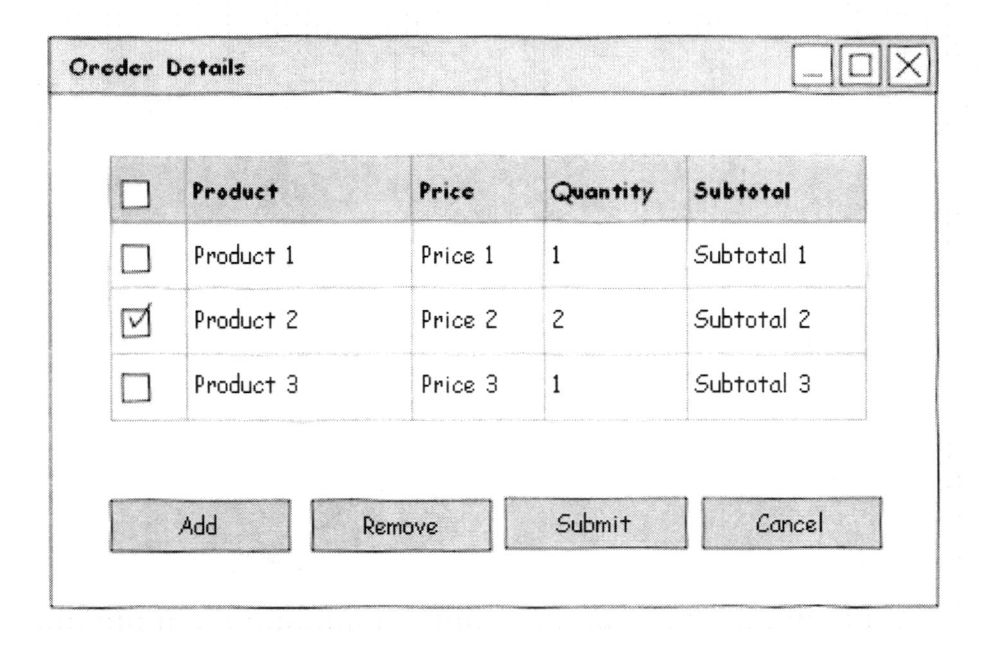

Figure 4-19. *Order request screen prototype*

That completes the preliminary design for this phase of the OSO application. You applied what you learned in Chapters 2 and 3 to model the design. Next, let's review some common mistakes to avoid during this process.

Avoiding Some Common OOP Design Pitfalls

When you start to model your own OOP designs, you want to be sure to follow good practice. The following are some of the common traps that you should avoid:

- *Confusing modeling with documenting*: The main value in modeling is not the diagrams produced, but rather the process you go through to produce the diagrams.
- *Not involving the users in the process*: It is worth emphasizing that users are the consumers of your product. They are the ones who define the business processes and functional requirements of the system.
- *Trying to model the whole solution at one time*: When developing complex systems, break up the system design and development into manageable components. Plan to produce the software in phases. This will provide for faster modeling, developing, testing, and release cycles.

- *Striving to create a perfect model*: No model will be perfect from the start. Successful modelers understand that the modeling process is iterative, and models are continuously updated and revised throughout the application development cycle.
- *Thinking there is only one true modeling methodology*: Just as there are many different equally viable OOP languages, there are many equally valid modeling methodologies for developing software. Choose the one that works best for you and the project at hand.
- *Reinventing the wheel*: Look for patterns and reusability. If you analyze many of the business processes that applications attempt to solve, a consistent set of modeling patterns emerge. Create a repository where you can leverage these existing patterns from project to project and from programmer to programmer.
- *Letting the data model drive the business logic model*: It is generally a bad idea to develop the data model (database structure) first and then build the business logic design on top of it. The solution designer should first ask what business problem needs to be solved, and then build a data model to solve the problem.
- *Confusing the problem domain model with the implementation model*: You should develop two distinct but complementary models when designing applications. A domain model design describes the scope of the project and the processing involved in implementing the business solutions. This includes what objects will be involved, their properties and behaviors, and how they interact and relate to each other. The domain model should be implementation-agnostic. You should be able to use the same domain model as a basis for several different architecturally specific implementations. In other words, you should be able to take the same domain model and implement it using a Visual Basic rich-client, two-tier architecture or a C# (or Java, for that matter) n-tier distributed web application.

Summary

Now that you have analyzed the domain model of an OOP application, you are ready to transform the design into an actual implementation. The next part of this book will introduce you to the C# language. You will look at the .NET Framework and see how C# applications are built on top of the framework. You will be introduced to working in the Visual Studio IDE and become familiar with the syntax of the C# language. The next section will also demonstrate the process of implementing OOP constructs such as class structures, object instantiation, inheritance, and polymorphism in C#. You will revisit the case study introduced in this chapter in Chapter 14, at which time you will look at transforming the application design into actual implementation code.

CHAPTER 5

Introducing the .NET Framework and Visual Studio

Business application programming has evolved from a two-tier, tightly coupled model into a multitiered, loosely coupled model, often involving data transfer over the Internet or a corporate intranet. In an effort to allow programmers to be more productive and deal with the complexities of this type of model, Microsoft developed the .NET Framework. To effectively program in C#, you need to understand this underlying framework upon which it is built.

After reading this chapter, you should be familiar with the following:

- The .NET Framework.
- The features of the Common Language Runtime (CLR).
- How the just-in-time (JIT) compiler works.
- The .NET Framework base class library.
- Namespaces and assemblies
- The features of the Visual Studio integrated development environment.

Introducing the .NET Framework

The .NET Framework is a collection of fundamental classes designed to provide the common services needed to run applications. Let's look at the goals of the .NET Framework and then review its components.

Goals of the .NET Framework

Microsoft designed the .NET Framework with certain goals in mind. The following sections examine these goals and how the .NET Framework achieves them.

Support of Industry Standards

Microsoft wanted the .NET Framework to be based on industry standards and practices. As a result, the framework relies heavily on industry standards such as the Extensible Markup Language (XML) and

Simple Object Access Protocol (SOAP). Microsoft has also submitted a Common Language Infrastructure (CLI) Working Document to the European Computer Manufacturers Association (ECMA), which oversees many of the common standards in the computer industry.

The CLI is a set of specifications needed to create compilers that conform to the .NET Framework. Third-party vendors can use these specifications to create .NET-compliant language compilers; for example, Interactive Software Engineering (ISE) has created a .NET compiler for Eifle. Third-party vendors can also create a CLR that will allow .NET-compliant languages to run on different platforms. One example, Mono is an open source, cross platform implementation of the CLR that gives C# applications the ability to run on the Linux platform.

Extensibility

To create a highly productive environment in which to program, Microsoft realized the .NET Framework had to be extensible. As a result, Microsoft has exposed the framework class hierarchy to developers. Through inheritance and interfaces, you can easily access and extend the functionality of these classes. For example, you could create a button control class that not only inherits its base functionality from the button class exposed by the .NET Framework, but also extends the base functionality in a unique way required by your application.

Microsoft has also made it much easier to work with the underlying operating system. By repackaging and implementing the Windows operating system application programming interface (API) functions in a class-based hierarchy, Microsoft has made it more intuitive and easier for OOP programmers to work with the functionality exposed by the underlying operating system.

Unified Programming Models

Another important goal Microsoft incorporated into the .NET Framework was cross-language independence and integration. To achieve this goal, all languages that support the Common Language Specification (CLS) compile into the same intermediate language, support the same set of basic data types, and expose the same set of code-accessibility methods. As a result, not only can classes developed in the different CLS-compliant languages communicate seamlessly with one another, but you can also implement OOP constructs across languages. For example, you could develop a class written in C# that inherits from a class written using Visual Basic (VB). Microsoft has developed several languages that support the .NET Framework. Along with C#, the languages are VB, managed C++, JScript, and F#. In addition to these languages, many third-party vendors have developed versions of other popular languages designed to run under the .NET Framework, such as Pascal and Python.

Easier Deployment

Microsoft needed a way to simplify application deployment. Before the development of the .NET Framework, when components were deployed, component information had to be recorded in the system registry. Many of these components, especially system components, were used by several different client applications. When a client application made a call to the component, the registry was searched to determine the metadata needed to work with the component. If a newer version of the component was deployed, it replaced the registry information of the old component. Often, the new components were incompatible with the old version and caused existing clients to fail. You have probably experienced this problem after installing a service pack that ended up causing more problems than it fixed!

The .NET Framework combats this problem by storing the metadata for working with the component in a manifest, which is packaged in the assembly containing the component code. An assembly is a package containing the code, resources, and metadata needed to run an application. By default, an assembly is marked as private and placed in the same directory as the client assembly. This ensures that the component assembly is not inadvertently replaced or modified and also allows for a simpler deployment because there is no need to work with the registry. If a component needs to be shared, its assembly is deployed to a special directory referred to as the Global Assembly Cache (GAC). The manifest of the assembly contains versioning information, so newer versions of the component can be deployed side by side with the older versions in the GAC. By default, client assemblies continue to request and use the versions of the components they were intended to use. Older client assemblies will no longer fail when newer versions of the component are installed.

Improved Memory Management

A common problem of programs developed for the Windows platform has been memory management. Often, these programs have caused memory leaks. A memory leak occurs when a program allocates memory from the operating system but fails to release the memory after it is finished working with the memory. This problem is compounded when the program is intended to run for a long time, such as a service that runs in the background. To combat this problem, the .NET Framework uses nondeterministic finalization. Instead of relying on the applications to deallocate the unused memory, the framework uses a garbage collection object. The garbage collector periodically scans for unused memory blocks and returns them to the operating system.

Improved Security Model

Implementing security in today's highly distributed, Internet-based applications is an extremely important issue. In the past, security has focused on the user of the application. Security identities were checked when users logged in to an application, and their identities were passed along as the application made calls to remote servers and databases. This type of security model has proven to be inefficient and complicated to implement for today's enterprise-level, loosely coupled systems. In an effort to make security easier to implement and more robust, the .NET Framework uses the concept of code identity and code access.

When an assembly is created, it is given a unique identity. When a server assembly is created, you can grant access permissions and rights. When a client assembly calls a server assembly, the runtime will check the permissions and rights of the client, and then grant or deny access to the server code accordingly. Because each assembly has an identity, you can also restrict access to the assembly through the operating system. If a user downloads a component from the Web, for example, you can restrict the component's ability to read and write files on the user's system.

Components of the .NET Framework

Now that you have seen some of the major goals of the .NET Framework, let's take a look at the components it comprises.

Common Language Runtime

The fundamental component of the .NET Framework is the CLR. The CLR manages the code being executed and provides for a layer of abstraction between the code and the operating system. Built into the CLR are mechanisms for the following:

- Loading code into memory and preparing it for execution.
- Converting the code from the intermediate language to native code.
- Managing code execution.
- Managing code and user-level security.
- Automating deallocation and release of memory.
- Debugging and tracing code execution.
- Providing structured exception handling.

Framework Base Class Library

Built on top of the CLR is the .NET Framework base class library. Included in this class library are reference types and value types that encapsulate access to the system functionality. *Types* are data structures. A reference type is a complex type—for example, classes and interfaces. A value type is simple type—for example, integer or Boolean. Programmers use these base classes and interfaces as the foundation on which they build applications, components, and controls. The base class library includes types that encapsulate data structures, perform basic input/output operations, invoke security management, manage network communication, and perform many other functions.

Data Classes

Built on top of the base classes are classes that support data management. This set of classes is commonly referred to as ADO.NET. Using the ADO.NET object model, programmers can access and manage data stored in a variety of data storage structures through managed providers. Microsoft has written and tuned the ADO.NET classes and object model to work efficiently in a loosely coupled, disconnected, multitiered environment. ADO.NET not only exposes the data from the database, but also exposes the metadata associated with the data. Data is exposed as a sort of mini-relational database. This means that you can get the data and work with it while disconnected from the data source, and later synchronize the data with the data source.

Microsoft has provided support for several data providers. Data stored in Microsoft SQL Server can be accessed through the native SQL data provider. OLEDB and Open Database Connectivity (ODBC) managed providers are two generic providers for systems currently exposed through the OLEDB or ODBC standard APIs. Because these managed data providers do not interface directly with the database engine but rather talk to the unmanaged provider, which then talks to the database engine, using nonnative data providers is less efficient and robust than using a native provider. Because of the extensibility of the .NET Framework and Microsoft's commitment to open-based standards, many data storage vendors now supply native data providers for their systems.

Built on top of the ADO.NET provider model is the ADO.NET Entity Framework. The Entity Framework bridges the gap between the relation data structure of the database and the object oriented structure of the programming language. It provides an Object/Relational Mapping (ORM) framework that eliminates the need for programmers to write most of the plumbing code for data access. The framework provides services such as change tracking, identity resolution, and query translation. Programmers retrieve data using Language Integrated Query (LINQ) and manipulate data as strongly typed objects. Chapter 10 takes a detailed look at ADO.NET and data access.

Windows Applications

Prior to the .NET Framework, developing Windows GUIs was dramatically different depending on whether you were developing using C++ or Visual Basic. Although developing GUIs in VB was easy and could be accomplished very quickly, VB developers were isolated and not fully exposed to the underlying features of the Windows API. On the other hand, although exposed to the full features of the Windows API, developing GUIs in C++ was very tedious and time consuming. With the .NET Framework Microsoft has incorporated a set of base classes exposing advanced Windows GUI functionality equally among the .NET-compliant languages. This has allowed Windows GUI development to become consistent across the various .NET-enabled programming languages, combining the ease of development with the full features of the API.

Along with Windows forms and controls, .NET Framework includes a set of classes collectively referred to as the Windows Presentation Foundation (WPF). WPF integrates a rendering engine that is built to take advantage of modern graphics hardware. It also includes application development features such as controls, data binding, layout, graphics, and animation. With the WPF set of classes, programmers can create applications that provide an extremely rich user experience. You will look more closely at building WPF based applications in Chapter 11.

Web Applications

The .NET Framework exposes a base set of classes that can be used on a web server to create user interfaces and services exposed to web-enabled clients. These classes are collectively referred to as ASP.NET. Using ASP.NET, you can develop one user interface that can dynamically respond to the type of client device making the request. At runtime, the .NET Framework takes care of discovering the type of client making the request (browser type and version) and exposing an appropriate interface. The GUIs for web applications running on a Windows client have become more robust because the .NET Framework exposes much of the API functionality that previously had been exposed only to traditional Windows Forms-based C++ and VB applications. Another improvement in web application development using the .NET Framework is that server-side code can be written in any .NET-compliant language. Prior to .NET, server-side code had to be written in a scripting language such as VBScript or JScript.

In order to provide users with web-based applications that rival the feature-rich Windows-based GUI applications, Microsoft has developed Silverlight. Silverlight includes a subset of the WPF technology, which greatly extends the elements in the browser for creating UI. Silverlight includes support for graphics, animation, media, advanced data integration, and multithreading. Chapter 12 covers developing web applications with Silverlight.

Application Services

Included in the .NET Framework are base class and interface support for exposing services that can be consumed by other applications. Previous to the .NET Framework, applications developed in C++ and VB used COM technology. Because COM was based on binary standards, application-to-application communication through firewalls and across the Internet was not easy to implement. The proprietary nature of the COM also limited the types of clients that could effectively use and interact with applications exposing services through COM.

Microsoft has addressed these limitations by exposing services through Internet standards. Included in the .NET Framework is a set of classes collectively referred to as the Windows Communication Foundation (WCF). Using WCF, you can send data as messages from one application to another. The message transport and content can be easily changed depending on the consumer and environment. For example, if the service is exposed over the Web, a text-based message over HTTP can be used. On the other hand, if the client is on the same corporate network, a binary message over TCP can be used. Chapter 13 covers exposing and consuming application services using WCF.

Working with the .NET Framework

To work with the .NET Framework, you should understand how it is structured and how managed code is compiled and executed. .NET applications are organized and packaged into assemblies. All code executed by the .NET runtime must be contained in an assembly.

Understanding Assemblies and Manifests

The assembly contains the code, resources, and a manifest (metadata about the assembly) needed to run the application. Assemblies can be organized into a single file where all this information is incorporated into a single dynamic link library (DLL) file or executable (EXE) file, or multiple files where the information is incorporated into separate DLL files, graphics files, and a manifest file. One of the main functions of an assembly is to form a boundary for types, references, and security. Another important function of the assembly is to form a unit for deployment.

One of the most crucial portions of an assembly is the manifest; in fact, every assembly must contain a manifest. The purpose of the manifest is to describe the assembly. It contains such things as the identity of the assembly, a description of the classes and other data types the assembly exposes to clients, any other assemblies this assembly needs to reference, and security details needed to run the assembly.

By default, when an assembly is created, it is marked as private. A copy of the assembly must be placed in the same directory or a bin subdirectory of any client assembly that uses it. If the assembly must be shared among multiple client assemblies, it is placed in the GAC, a special Windows folder. To convert a private assembly into a shared assembly, you must run a utility program to create encryption keys, and you must sign the assembly with the keys. After signing the assembly, you must use another utility to add the shared assembly into the GAC. By mandating such stringent requirements for creating and exposing shared assemblies, Microsoft is trying to ensure that naming collisions and malicious tampering of shared assemblies will not occur.

Referencing Assemblies and Namespaces

To make the .NET Framework more manageable, Microsoft has given it a hierarchical structure. This hierarchical structure is organized into what are referred to as namespaces. By organizing the framework into namespaces, the chances of naming collisions are greatly reduced. Organizing related functionality of the framework into namespaces also greatly enhances its usability for developers. For example, if you want to build a window's GUI, it is a pretty good bet the functionality you need exists in the `System.Windows` namespace.

All of the .NET Framework classes reside in the System namespace. The System namespace is further subdivided by functionality. The functionality required to work with a database is contained in the System.Data namespace. Some namespaces run several levels deep; for example, the functionality used to connect to a SQL Server database is contained in the System.Data.SqlClient namespace.

An assembly may be organized into a single namespace or multiple namespaces. Several assemblies may also be organized into the same namespace.

To gain access to the classes in the .NET Framework, you need to reference the assembly that contains the namespace in your code. Then you can access classes in the assembly by providing their fully qualified names. For example, if you want to add a text box to a form, you create an instance of the System.Windows.Controls.TextBox class, like so:

```
private System.Windows.Controls.TextBox newTextBox;
```

Fortunately, in C#, you can use the using statement at the top of the code file so that you do not need to continually reference the fully qualified name in the code:

```
using System.Windows.Controls;
private TextBox newTextBox;
```

Compiling and Executing Managed Code

When .NET code is compiled, it is converted into a .NET portable executable (PE) file. The compiler translates the source code into Microsoft intermediate language (MSIL) format. MSIL is CPU-independent code, which means it needs to be further converted into native code before executing.

Along with the MSIL code, the PE file includes the metadata information contained within the manifest. The incorporation of the metadata in the PE file makes the code self-describing. There is no need for additional type library or Interface Definition Language (IDL) files.

Because the source code for the various .NET-compliant languages is compiled into the same MSIL and metadata format based on a common type system, the .NET platform supports language integration. This is a step beyond Microsoft's COM components, where, for example, client code written in VB could instantiate and use the methods of a component written in C++. With .NET language integration, you could write a .NET class in VB that inherits from a class written in C# and then overrides some of its methods.

Before the MSIL code in the PE file is executed, a .NET Framework just-in-time (JIT) compiler converts it into CPU-specific native code. To improve efficiency, the JIT compiler does not convert all the MSIL code into native code at the same time. MSIL code is converted on an as-needed basis. When a method is executed, the compiler checks to see if the code has already been converted and placed in cache. If it has, the compiled version is used; otherwise, the MSIL code is converted and stored in the cache for future calls.

Because JIT compilers are written to target different CPUs and operating systems, developers are freed from needing to rewrite their applications to target various platforms. It is conceivable that the programs you write for a Windows server platform will also run on a UNIX server. All that is needed is a JIT compiler for the UNIX architecture.

Using the Visual Studio Integrated Development Environment

You can write C# code using a simple text editor and compile it with a command-line compiler. You will find, however, that programming enterprise-level applications using a text editor can be frustrating and inefficient. Most programmers who code for a living find an integrated development environment (IDE) invaluable in terms of ease of use and increased productivity. Microsoft has developed an exceptional

IDE in Visual Studio (VS). Integrated into VS are many features that make programming for the .NET Framework more intuitive, easier, and more productive. Some of Visual Studio's useful features are:

- Editor features such as automatic syntax checking, auto completion, and color highlighting.
- One IDE for all .NET languages.
- Extensive debugging support, including the ability to set breakpoints, step through code, and view and modify variables.
- Integrated help documentation.
- Drag-and-drop GUI development.
- XML and HTML editing.
- Automated deployment tools that integrate with Windows Installer.
- The ability to view and manage servers from within the IDE.
- A fully customizable and extensible interface.

The following activities will introduce you to some of the many features available in the VS IDE. As you work through these steps, don't worry about the coding details. Just concentrate on getting used to working within the VS IDE. You'll learn more about the code in upcoming chapters.

■ Note If you do not have Visual Studio 2010 installed, refer to Appendix C for installation instruction.

ACTIVITY 5-1. TOURING VISUAL STUDIO

In this activity, you will become familiar with the following:

- Customizing the IDE.
- Creating a .NET project and setting project properties.
- Using the various editor windows in the VS IDE.
- Using the auto syntax check and auto completion features of the VS IDE.
- Compiling assemblies with the VS IDE.

Customizing the IDE

To customize the IDE, follow these steps:

1. Launch VS by selecting Start ➤ Programs ➤ Microsoft Visual Studio 2010.

■Note If this is the first time you have launched VS, you will be asked to choose a default development setting. Choose the Visual C# Development Settings.

---

2. You will be presented with the Start Page. The Start Page contains several panes, including one that has links to useful documentation posted on the MSDN (Microsoft Developer Network) web site. Clicking one of these links will launch a browser window hosted inside VS, which will open the documentation on the MSDN site. Take some time to investigate the information and the various links exposed to you on the Start Page.

3. Microsoft has taken considerable effort to make VS a customizable design environment. You can customize just about every aspect of the layout, from the various windows and menus down to the color coding used in the code editor. Select Tools ➤ Options to open the Options dialog box, shown in Figure 5-1, that allows you to customize many aspects of the IDE.

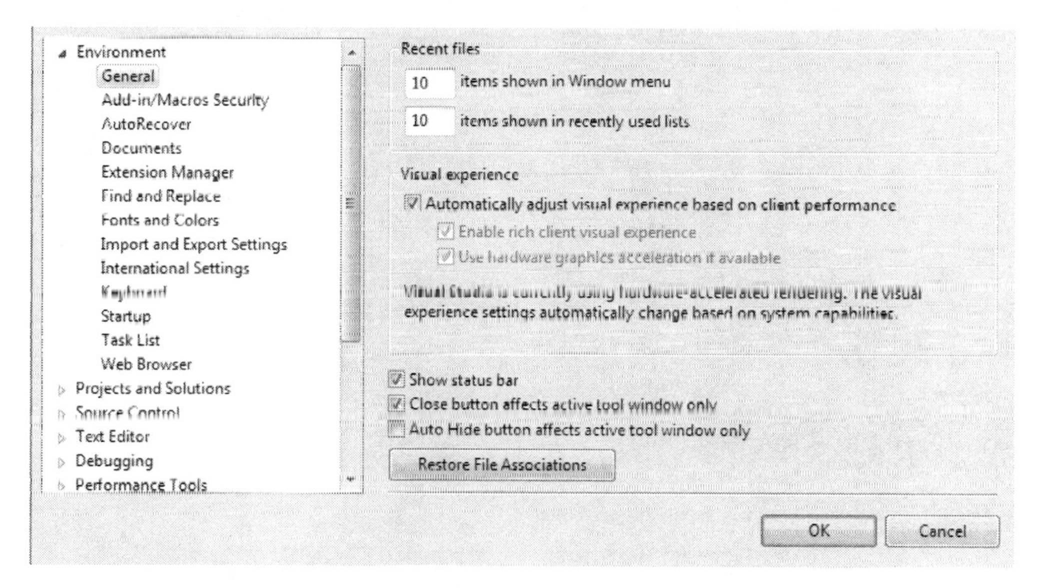

Figure 5-1. *VS Options dialog box*

4. Click Projects and Solutions in the category list on the left side of the dialog box. You are presented with options to change the default location of projects and what happens when you build and run a project. Select the Always Show Solution the Show Output Window When Build Starts option.

5. Investigate some of the other customizable options available. Close the Options dialog box when you are finished by clicking the OK button.

Creating a New Project

To create a new project, follow these steps:

1. On the Start Page, click the Create Project link, which launches the New Project dialog box. (You can also choose File ➤ New ➤ Project to open this dialog box.)
2. The New Project dialog box allows you to create various projects using built-in templates. There are templates for creating Windows projects, Web projects, WCF projects, as well as many others, depending on what options you chose when installing VS.
3. In the Installed Templates pane, expand the Visual C# node and select the Windows node, as shown in Figure 5-2. Observe the various C# project templates. There are templates for creating various types of Windows applications, including Windows Forms-based applications, class libraries, and console applications.

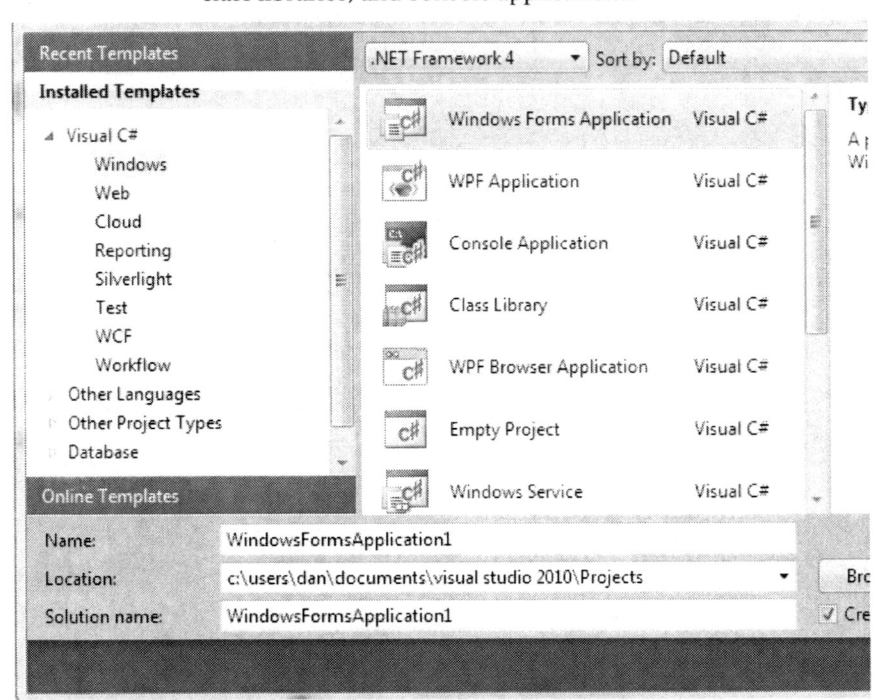

Figure 5-2. *VS New Project dialog box*

4. Click the Windows Application template. Change the name of the application to DemoChapter5 and click the OK button.

When the project opens, you will be presented with a form designer for a default form (named Form1) that has been added to the project. To the right of this window, you should see the Solution Explorer.

Investigating the Solution Explorer and Class View

The Solution Explorer displays the projects and files that are part of the current solution, as shown in Figure 5-3. By default, when you create a project, a solution is created with the same name as the project. The solution contains some global information, project-linking information, and customization settings, such as a task list and debugging information. A solution may contain more than one related project.

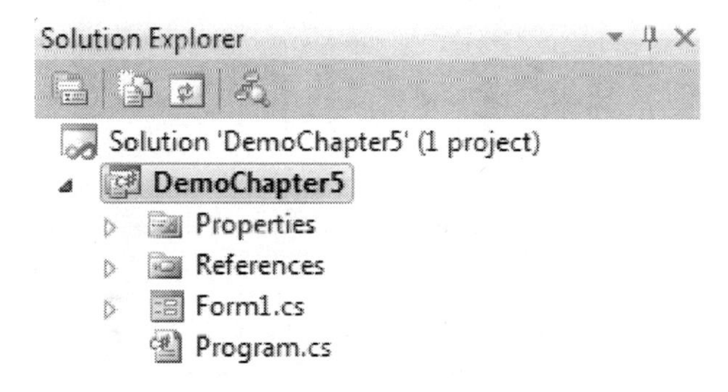

Figure 5-3. *Solution Explorer*

Under the solution node is the project node. The project node organizes the various files and settings related to a project. The project file organizes this information in an XML document, which contains references to the class files that are part of the project, any external references needed by the project, and compilation options that have been set. Under the Project node is a Properties node, References node, a class file for the Form1 class, and a Program class file.

To practice using the Solution Explorer and some VS features and views, follow these steps:

1. In the Solution Explorer window, right-click the Properties node and select Open. This launches the Project Properties window. Along the left side of the window are several tabs you can use to explore and set various application settings.
2. Select the Application tab, as shown in Figure 5-4. Notice that, by default, the assembly name and default namespace are set to the name of the project.

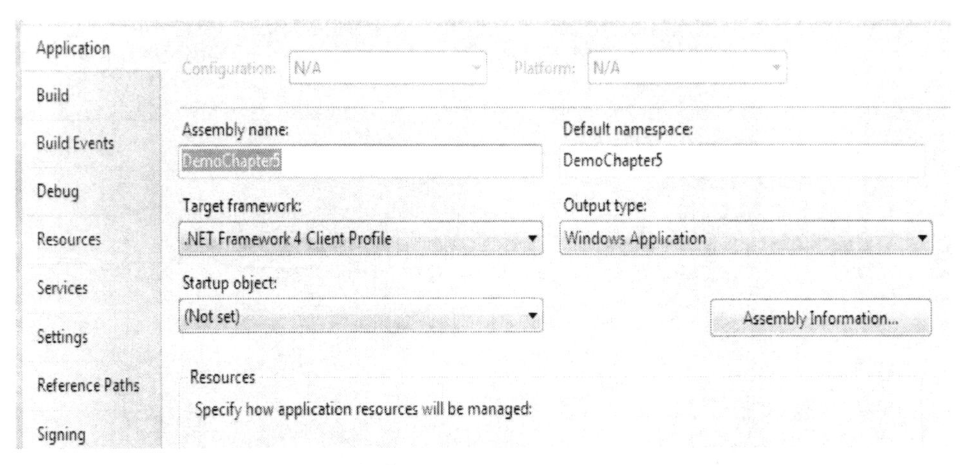

Figure 5-4. *Project Properties Window*

3. Explore some of the other tabs in the Project Properties window. Close the window when you are finished by clicking on the x in the tab of the window.

4. In the Solution Explorer window, expand the References node. Under the node are the external assemblies referenced by the application. Notice that several references have been included by default. The default references depend on the type of project. For example, since this is a Windows Application project, a reference to the System.Windows.Forms namespace is included by default.

5. The Form1 class file under the Solution Explorer's project node has a .cs extension to indicate it is written in C# code. By default, the name of the file has been set to the same name as the form. Double-click the file in the Solution Explorer window. The form is shown in Design View. Click the View Code button in the toolbar at the top of the Solution Explorer, and the code editor for the Form1 class will open.

6. Select View ➤ Other Windows ➤ Class View to launch the Class View window. The top part of the Class View window organizes the project files in terms of the namespace hierarchy. Expanding the DemoChap5 root node reveals three sub nodes: a References node, the DemoChap5 namespace node, and DemoChap5 properties node. A namespace node is designated by the {} symbol to the left of the node name.

7. Listed under the DemoChap5 namespace node are the classes that belong to the namespace. Expanding the Form1 node reveals a Base Types folder. Expanding Base Types shows the classes and interfaces inherited and implemented by the Form1 class, as shown in Figure 5-5. You can further expand the nodes to show the classes and interfaces inherited and implemented by the Form base class.

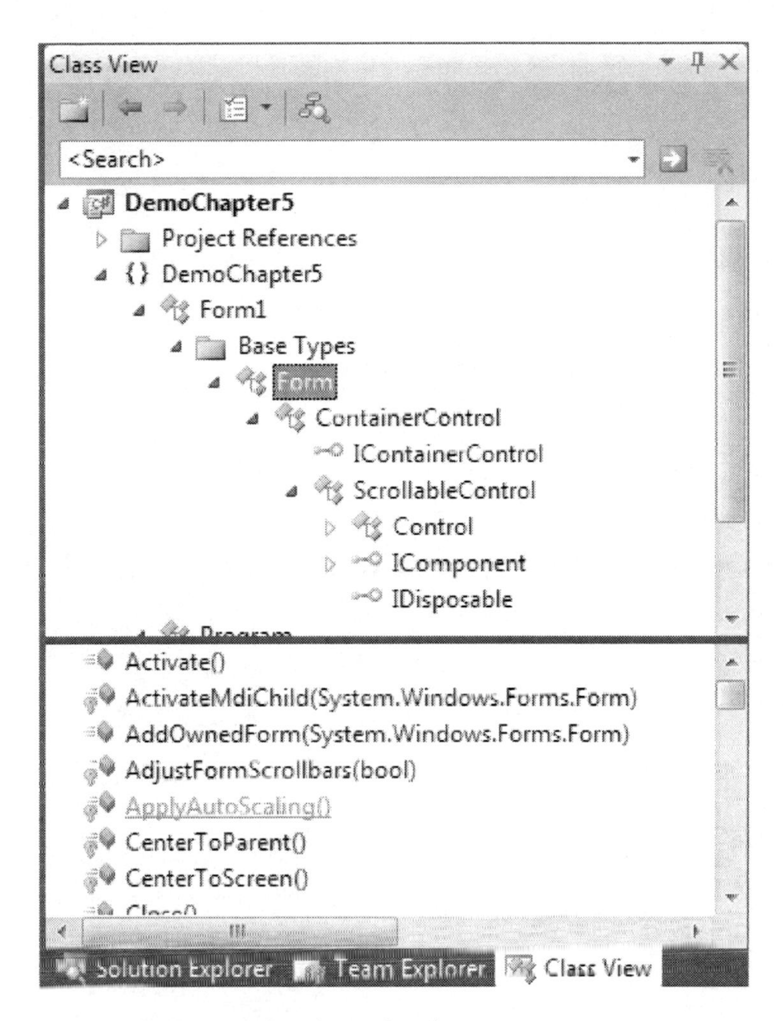

Figure 5-5. *Expanded nodes in the Class View*

8. The bottom section of the Class View window is a listing of the class's methods, properties, and events. Select the Form node in the top section of the Class View window. Notice the considerable number of methods, properties, and events listed in the bottom section of the window.

9. Right-click the DemoChap5 project node and select Add ➤ Class. Name the class DemoClass1 and click the Add button. If the class code is not visible in the code editor, double-click the DemoClass1 node in the Class View window to display it. Wrap the class definition code in a namespace declaration as follows:

```
namespace DemoChapter5
{
    namespace MyDemoNamespace
    {
        class DemoClass1
        {
        }
    }
}
```

10. From the Build menu, chose Build Solution. Notice the updated hierarchy in the Class View. DemoClass1 now belongs to the MyDemoNamespace, which belongs to the DemoChapter5 namespace. The fully qualified name of DemoClass1 is now DemoChapter5.MyDemoNamespace.DemoClass1.

11. Add the following code to the DemoClass1 definition. As you add the code, notice the auto selection drop-down list provided (see Figure 5-6). Pressing the Tab key will select the current item on the list.

```
class DemoClass1: System.Collections.CaseInsensitiveComparer
{
}
```

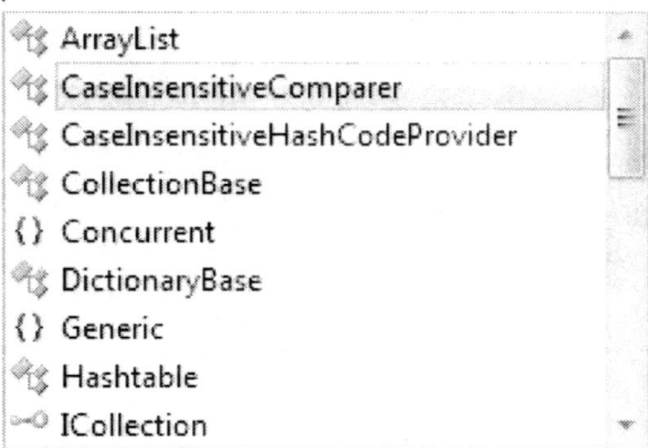

Figure 5-6. *Code selection drop-down list*

12. From the Build menu, chose Build Solution. Notice the updated hierarchy in the Class View. Expand the Base Types node under the DemoClass1 node, and you will see the base CaseInsensitiveComparer class node. Select this node and you will see the methods and properties of the CaseInsensitiveComparer class in the lower section of the Class View window.

13. Right-click the Compare method of the CaseInsensitiveComparer class node and choose Browse Definition. The Object Browser window is opened as a tab in the main window and information about the Compare method is displayed. Notice it takes two object arguments, compares them, and returns an integer value based on the result (see Figure 5-7).

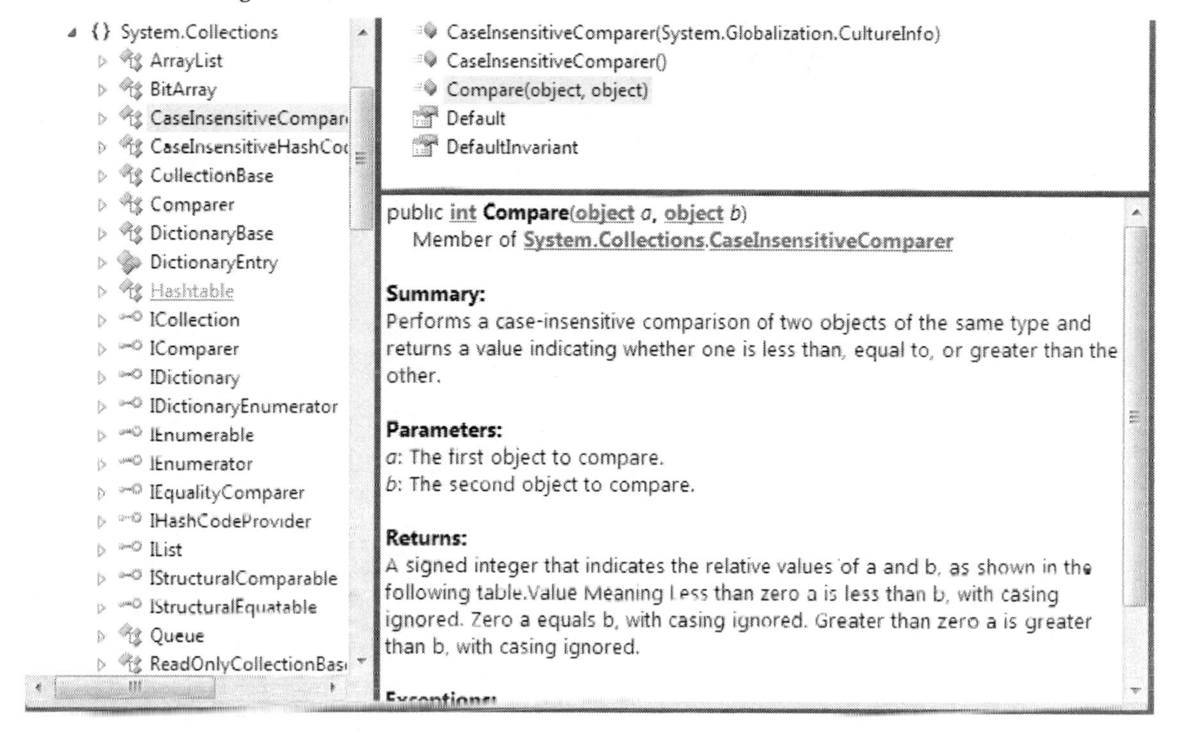

Figure 5-7. *Object Browser*

14. The Object Browser enables you to explore the object hierarchies and to view information about items and methods within the hierarchy. Take some time to explore the Object Browser. When you are finished, close the Object Browser and close the Class View window.

Exploring the Toolbox and Properties Window

To explore the VS Toolbox and Properties window, follow these steps:

1. In the Solution Explorer window, double-click the Form1.cs node. This brings up the Form1 design tab in the main editing window. Locate the Toolbox tab to the left of the main editing window. Hover the cursor over the tab, and the Toolbox window should expand, as shown in Figure 5-8. In the upper-right corner of the Toolbox, you should see the Auto Hide icon, which looks like a thumbtack. Click the icon to turn off the auto hide feature.

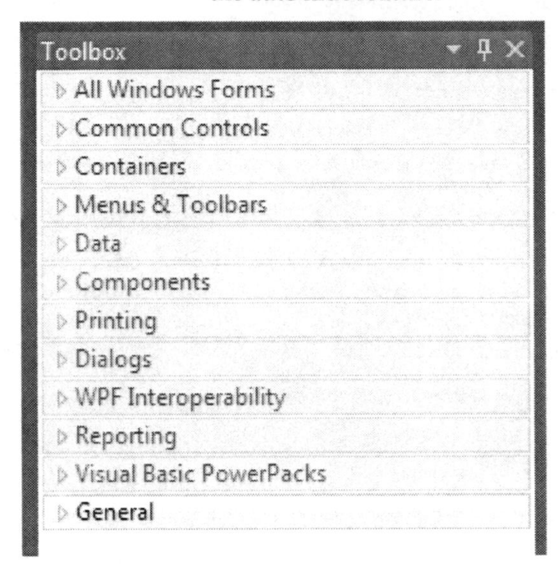

Figure 5-8. *VS Toolbox*

2. Under the All Windows Forms node of the Toolbox are controls that you can drag and drop onto your form to build the GUI. There are also other nodes that contain nongraphical components that help make some common programming tasks easier to create and manage. For example, the Data node contains controls for accessing and managing data stores. Scroll down the Toolbox window and observe the various controls exposed by the designer.

3. Under the All Windows Forms node, select the Label control. Move the cursor over the form; it should change to a crosshairs pointer. Draw a label on the form by clicking, dragging, and then releasing the mouse. In a similar fashion, draw a TextBox control and a Button control on the form. Figure 5-9 shows how the form should look.

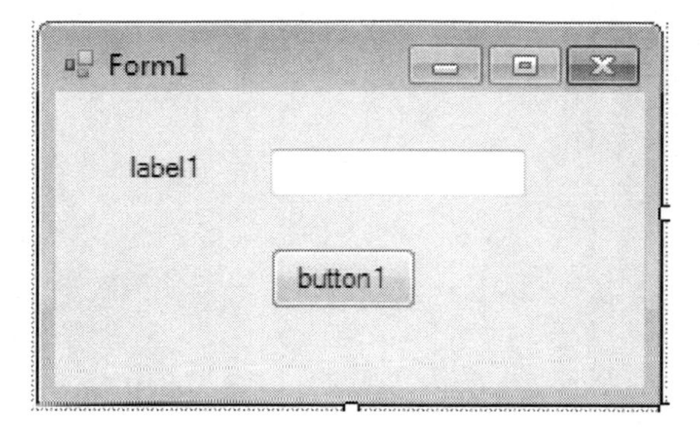

Figure 5-9. *Sample form layout*

4. Turn the auto hide feature of the Toolbox back on by clicking the Auto Hide (thumbtack) icon in the upper-right corner of the Toolbox window.
5. Locate the Properties tab to the right of the main editing window, or select View ➤ Properties Window to open the Properties window. The Properties window displays the properties of the currently selected object in the Design View. You can also edit many of the object's properties through this window.
6. In the Form1 design window, click Label1. The Label1 control should be selected in the drop-down list at the top of the Properties window (see Figure 5-10). Locate the Text property and change it to "Enter your password:" (minus the quotes).

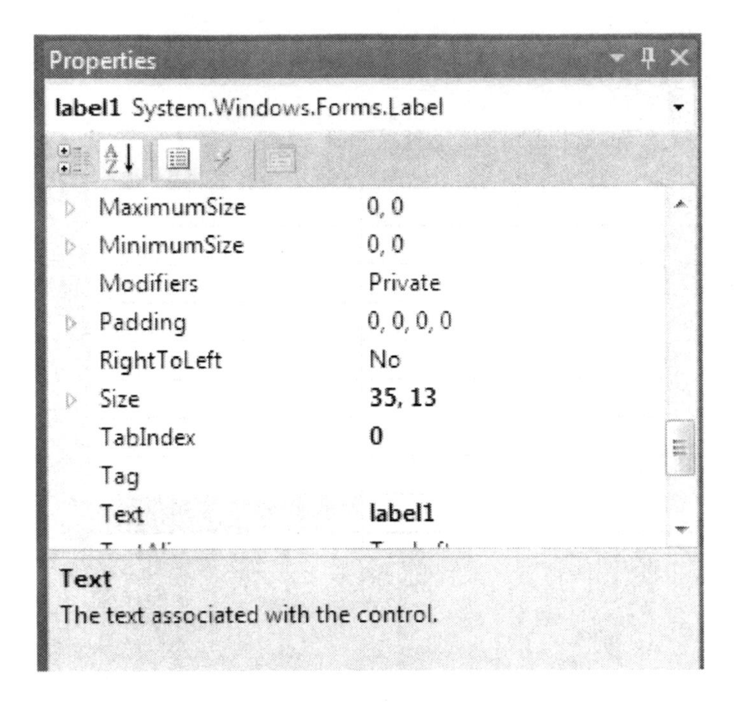

Figure 5-10. *VS Properties window*

■ Note You may need to resize the label on the form to see all the text.

---

7. Set the PasswordChar property of TextBox1 to *. Change the Text property of Button1 to OK. (Click the control on the form or use the drop-down list at the top of the Properties window to see the control's properties.)

8. Save the project by choosing File ➤ Save All.

Building and Executing the Assembly

To build and execute the assembly, follow these steps:

1. In the Solution Explorer, click Form1. At the top of the Solution Explorer, click the View Designer toolbar button.

2. In the form designer double click the Button1 control. The code editor for Form1 will be displayed in the main editing window. A method that handles the button click event is added to the code editor.

3. Add the following code to the method. This code will display the password entered in TextBox1 on the title bar of the form.

```
private void button1_Click(object sender, EventArgs e)
{
        this.Text = "Your password is " + textBox1.Text;
}
```

4. Select Build ➤ Build Solution. The Output window shows the progress of compiling the assembly (see Figure 5-11). Once the assembly has been compiled, it is ready for execution. (If you can't locate the Output window, select View menu ➤ Output.)

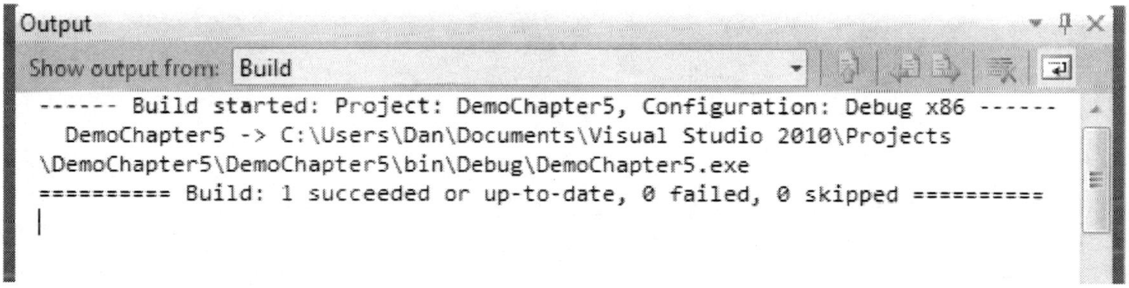

```
Output
Show output from: Build
------ Build started: Project: DemoChapter5, Configuration: Debug x86 ------
  DemoChapter5 -> C:\Users\Dan\Documents\Visual Studio 2010\Projects
\DemoChapter5\DemoChapter5\bin\Debug\DemoChapter5.exe
========== Build: 1 succeeded or up-to-date, 0 failed, 0 skipped ==========
```

Figure 5-11. *Progress of build displayed in the Output window*

5. Select Debug ➤ Start Debugging. This runs the assembly in debug mode. Once the form loads, enter a password and click the OK button. You should see the message containing the password in the form's title bar. Close the form by clicking the x in the upper right corner.

6. Select File ➤ Save All, and then exit VS by selecting File ➤ Exit.

ACTIVITY 5-2. USING THE DEBUGGING FEATURES OF VS

In this activity, you will become familiar with the following:

- Setting breakpoints and stepping through the code.
- Using the various debugging windows in the VS IDE.
- Locating and fixing build errors using the Error List window.

Stepping Through Code

To step through your code, follow these steps:

1. Start VS. Select File ➤ New ➤ Project.

2. Under the C# Windows templates, select the Console Application. Rename the project Activity5_2.

3. You will see a Program class file open in the code editor. The class file has a Main method that gets executed first when the application runs. Add the following code to the program class. This code contains a method that loads a list of numbers and displays the contents of the list in the console window.

```
class Program
    {
        static List<int> numList = new List<int>();
        static void Main(string[] args)
        {
            LoadList(10);
            foreach (int i in numList)
            {
                System.Console.WriteLine(i);
            }
            Console.ReadLine();
        }
        static void LoadList(int iMax)
        {
            for (int i = 1; i <= 10; i++)
            {
                numList.Add(i);
            }
        }
    }
```

4. To set a breakpoint, place the cursor on the declaration line of the Main method, right-click, and choose Breakpoint ➤ Insert Breakpoint. A red dot will appear in the left margin to indicate that a breakpoint has been set (see Figure 5-12).

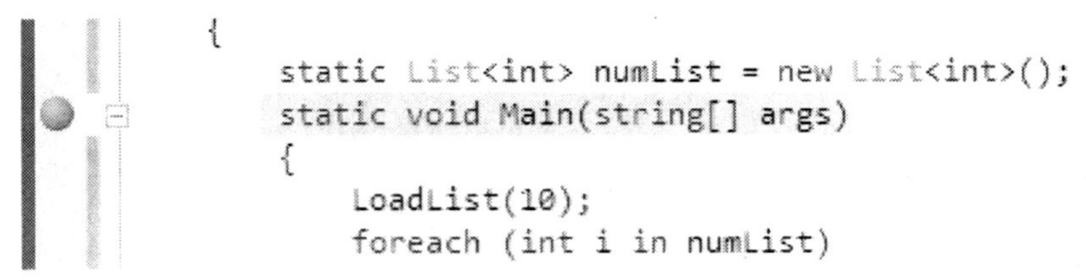

Figure 5-12. *Setting a breakpoint in the code editor*

5. Select Debug ➤ Start Debugging. Program execution will pause at the breakpoint. A yellow arrow indicates the next line of code that will be executed.

6. Select View ➤ Toolbars and click the Debug toolbar. (A check next to the toolbar name indicates it is visible.) To step through the code one line at a time, select the Step Into button on the Debug toolbar (see Figure 5-13). (You can also press the F11 key.) Continue stepping through the code until you get to the LoadList.

Figure 5-13. *Using the Debug toolbar*

7. Step through the code until the `for` loop has looped a couple of times. At this point, you are probably satisfied that this code is working and you want to step out of this method. On the Debug toolbar, click the Step Out button. You should return to the Main method.
8. Continue stepping through the code until the `for-each loop` has looped a couple of times. At this point, you may want to return to runtime mode. To do this, click the Continue button on the Debug toolbar. When the Console window appears, hit the enter key to close the window.
9. Start the application in debug mode again. Step through the code until you get to the method `call LoadList(10);`.
10. On the Debug toolbar, choose the Step Over button. This will execute the method and reenter break mode after execution returns to the calling code. After stepping over the method, continue stepping through the code for several lines, and then choose the Stop button on the Debug toolbar. Click the red dot in the left margin to remove the breakpoint.

Setting Conditional Breakpoints

To set conditional breakpoints, follow these steps:

1. In the Program.cs file locate the `LoadList` method. Set a breakpoint on the following line of code:

```
numList.Add(i);
```

2. Open the Breakpoints window by selecting Debug ➤ Windows ➤ Breakpoints. You should see the breakpoint you just set listed in the Breakpoints window (see Figure 5-14).

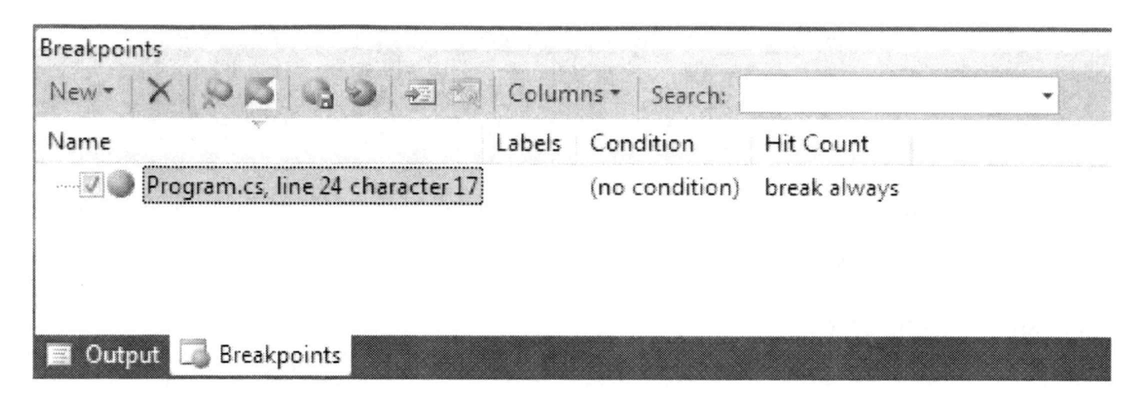

Figure 5-14. *Breakpoints window*

3. Right-click the breakpoint in the Breakpoints window and select Condition. You will see the Breakpoint Condition dialog box. Enter i == 3 as the condition expression and click the OK button (see Figure 5-15).

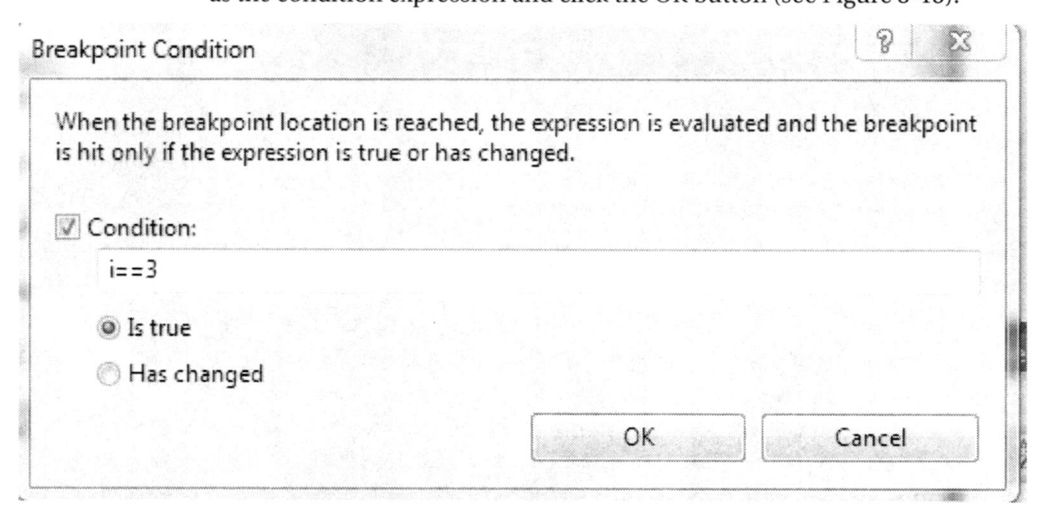

Figure 5-15. *Breakpoint Condition dialog box*

4. Select Debug ➤ Start. When the form appears, click the Load List button. Program execution will pause, and you will see a yellow arrow indicating the next line that will be executed.

5. Select Debug ➤ Windows ➤ Locals. The Locals window is displayed at the bottom of the screen (see Figure 5-16). The value of i is displayed in the Locals window. Verify that it is 3. Step through the code using the Debug toolbar and watch the value of i change in the Locals window. Click the Stop Debugging button in the Debug toolbar.

Locals

Name	Value	Type
iMax	10	int
i	3	int

Figure 5-16. *Locals window*

6. Locate the Output window at the bottom of your screen and click the Breakpoints tab. Right-click the breakpoint in the Breakpoints window and select Condition. Clear the current condition by clearing the Condition check box, and then click the OK button.

7. Right-click the breakpoint in the Breakpoints window and select Hit Count. Set the breakpoint to break when the hit count equals 4, and then click OK.

8. Select Debug ➤ Start. Program execution will pause and the yellow arrow indicates the next line of code that will execute.

9. Right-click the numList statement and select Add Watch. A Watch window will be displayed with numList in it. Notice that numList is a System.Collections.Generics.List type. Click the plus sign next to numList. Verify that the list contains three items (see Figure 5-17). Step through the code and watch the array fill with items. Click the Stop button in the Debug toolbar.

Watch 1

Name	Value	Type
numList	Count = 3	System.Collections.Generic.List<int>
[0]	1	int
[1]	2	int
[2]	3	int
Raw View		

Locals Watch 1

Figure 5-17. *The Watch window*

Locating and Fixing Build Errors

To locate and fix build errors, follow these steps:

1. In the Program class, locate the following line of code and comment it out by placing a two slashes in front of it, as shown here:

```
//static List<int> numList = new List<int>();
```

2. Notice the red squiggly lines under the numList in the code. This indicates a build error that must be fixed before the application can run. Hovering over the line reveals more information about the error.

3. Select Build ➤ Build Solution. The Error List window will appear at the bottom of the screen, indicating a build error (see Figure 5-18).

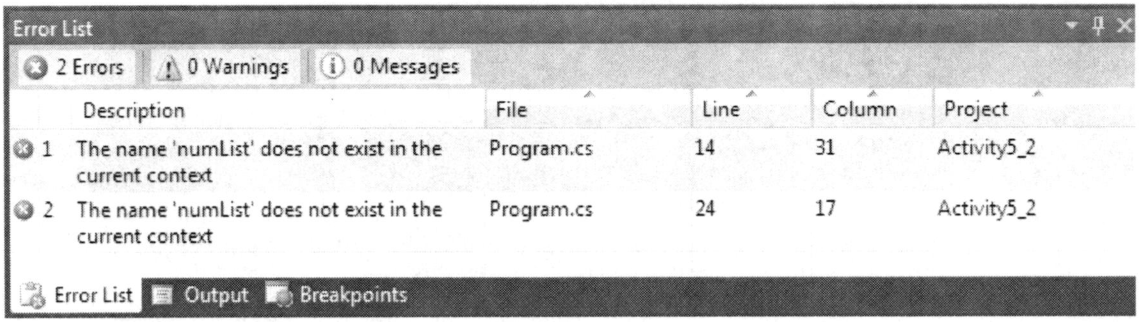

Error List

2 Errors | 0 Warnings | 0 Messages

	Description	File	Line	Column	Project
1	The name 'numList' does not exist in the current context	Program.cs	14	31	Activity5_2
2	The name 'numList' does not exist in the current context	Program.cs	24	17	Activity5_2

Error List | Output | Breakpoints

Figure 5-18. *Locating build errors with the Error List window*

4. Double-click the line containing the build error in the Error List window. The corresponding code will become visible in the code editor.

5. Uncomment the line you commented in step 1 by deleting the slashes. Select Build ➤ Build Solution. This time, the Output window is displayed at the bottom of the screen, indicating that there were no build errors.

6. Save the project and exit VS.

Summary

This chapter introduced you to the fundamentals of the .NET Framework. You reviewed some of the underlying goals of the .NET Framework. You also looked at how the .NET Framework is structured and how code is compiled and executed by the CLR. These concepts are relevant and consistent across all .NET-compliant programming languages. In addition, you explored some of the features of the Visual Studio integrated development environment.

The next chapter is the first in a series that looks at how the OOP concepts—such as class structure, inheritance, and polymorphism—are implemented in C# code.

CHAPTER 6

Creating Classes

In the previous chapter, you looked at how the .NET Framework was developed and how programs execute under the framework. That chapter introduced you to the Visual Studio IDE, and you gained some familiarity with working in it. You are now ready to start coding! This chapter is the first of a series that will introduce you to how classes are created and used in C#. It covers the basics of creating and using classes. You will create classes, add attributes and methods, and instantiate object instances of the classes in client code.

After reading this chapter, you should be familiar with the following:

- How objects used in OOP depend on class definition files.
- The important role encapsulation plays in OOP.
- How to define the properties and methods of a class.
- The purpose of class constructors.
- How to use instances of classes in client code.
- The process of overloading class constructors and methods.
- How to create and test class definition files with Visual Studio.

Introducing Objects and Classes

In OOP, you use objects in your programs to encapsulate the data associated with the entities with which the program is working. For example, a human resources application needs to work with employees. Employees have attributes associated with them that need to be tracked. You may be interested in such things as the employee names, addresses, departments, and so on. Although you track the same attributes for all employees, each employee has unique values for these attributes. In the human resources application, an `Employee` object obtains and modifies the attributes associated with an employee. In OOP, the attributes of an object are referred to as properties.

Along with the properties of the employees, the human resource application also needs an established set of behaviors exposed by the `Employee` object. For example, one employee behavior of interest to the human resources department is the ability to request time off. In OOP, objects expose behaviors through methods. The `Employee` object contains a `RequestTimeOff` method that encapsulates the implementation code.

The properties and methods of the objects used in OOP are defined through classes. A class is a blueprint that defines the attributes and behaviors of the objects that are created as instances of the class. If you have completed the proper analysis and design of the application, you should be able to refer to the UML design documentation to determine which classes need to be constructed and what properties and methods these classes will contain. The UML class diagram contains the initial information you need to construct the classes of the system.

To demonstrate the construction of a class using C#, you will look at the code for a simple `Employee` class. The `Employee` class will have properties and methods that encapsulate and work with employee data as part of a fictitious human resources application.

Defining Classes

Let's walk through the source code needed to create a class definition. The first line of code defines the code block as a class definition using the keyword `Class` followed by the name of the class. The body of the class definition is enclosed by an open and closing curly bracket. The code block is structured like this:

```
class Employee
{
}
```

Creating Class Properties

After defining the starting and ending point of the class code block, the next step is to define the instance variables (often referred to as fields) contained in the class. These variables hold the data that an instance of your class will manipulate. The `Private` keyword ensures that these instance variables can be manipulated only by the code inside the class. Here are the instance variable definitions:

```
    private int _empID;
    private string _loginName;
    private string _password;
    private string _department;
    private string _name;
```

When a user of the class (client code) needs to query or set the value of these instance variables, public properties are exposed to them. Inside the property block of code are a Get block and a Set block. The Get block returns the value of the private instance variable to the user of the class. This code provides a readable property. The Set block provides a write-enabled property; it passes a value sent in by the client code to the corresponding private instance variable. Here is an example of a property block:

```
public string Name
{
    get { return _name; }
    set { _name = value; }
}
```

There may be times when you want to restrict access to a property so that client code can read the property value but not change it. By eliminating the Set block inside the Property block, you create a read-only property. The following code shows how to make the EmployeeID property read-only:

```
public int EmployeeID
{
    get { return _empID; }
}
```

■ **Note** The private and public keywords affect the scope of the code. For more information about scoping, see Appendix A.

Newcomers to OOP often ask why it's necessary to go through so much work to get and set properties. Couldn't you just create public instance variables that the user could read and write to directly? The answer lies in one of the fundamental tenets of OOP: data encapsulation. Data encapsulation means that the client code does not have direct access to the data. When working with the data, the client code must use clearly defined properties and methods accessed through an instance of the class. The following are some of the benefits of encapsulating the data in this way:

- Preventing unauthorized access to the data.
- Ensuring data integrity through error checking.
- Creating read-only or write-only properties.
- Isolating users of the class from changes in the implementation code.

For example, you could check to make sure the password is at least six characters long via the following code:

```
public string Password
{
    get { return _password; }
    set
    {
        if (value.Length >= 6)
        {
            _password = value;
        }
        else
        {
            throw new Exception("Password must be at least 6 characters");
        }
    }
}
```

Creating Class Methods

Class methods define the behaviors of the class. For example, the following defines a method for the Employee class that verifies employee logins:

```
public void Login(string loginName, string password)
{
    if (loginName == "Jones" & password == "mj")
    {
        _empID = 1;
        Department = "HR";
```

```
            Name = "Mary Jones";
        }
        else if (loginName == "Smith" & password == "js")
        {
            _empID = 2;
            Department = "IS";
            Name = "Jerry Smith";
        }
        else
        {
            throw new Exception("Login incorrect.");
        }
    }
```

When client code calls the Login method of the class, the login name and password are passed into the method (these are called input parameters). The parameters are checked. If they match a current employee, the instance of the class is populated with attributes of the employee. If the login name and password do not match a current employee, an exception is passed back to the client code.

■ Note Exception handling is an important part of application processing. For more information about exceptions, see Appendix B.

In the previous method, a value is not returned to the client code. This is indicated by the void keyword. Sometimes the method returns a value back to the client calling code (called an output parameter). The following AddEmployee method is another method of the Employee class. It's called when an employee needs to be added to the database, and it returns the newly assigned employee ID to the client. The method also populates the object instance of the Employee class with the attributes of the newly added employee.

```
public int AddEmployee(string loginName, string password,
            string department, string name)
{
    //Data normally saved to database.
    _empID = 3;
    LoginName = loginName;
    Password = password;
    Department = department;
    Name = name;
    return EmployeeID;
}
```

ACTIVITY 6-1. CREATING THE EMPLOYEE CLASS

In this activity, you will become familiar with the following:

- Creating a C# class definition file using Visual Studio.
- Creating and using an instance of the class from client code.

■ Note If you have not already done so, download the starter files from the source code area of the Apress web site (www.apress.com).

Defining the Employee Class

To create the Employee class, follow these steps:

1. Start Visual Studio. Select File ➤ Open ➤ Project.
2. Navigate to the Activity6_1Starter folder, click the Act6_1.sln file, and click Open. When the project opens, it will contain a login form. You will use this form later to test the Employee class you create.
3. Select Project ➤ Add Class. In the Add New Item dialog box, rename the class file to Employee.cs, and then click Open. Visual Studio adds the Employee.cs file to the project and adds the following class definition code to the file:

```
class Employee
{
}
```

4. Enter the following code between the opening and closing brackets to add the private instance variables to the class body in the definition file:

```
private int _empID;
private string _loginName;
private string _password;
private int _securityLevel;
```

5. Next, add the following public properties to access the private instance variables defined in step 4:

```
public int EmployeeID
{
    get { return _empID; }
}
public string LoginName
{
    get { return _loginName; }
    set { _loginName = value; }
}
public string Password
{
    get { return _password; }
    set { _password = value; }
}
public int SecurityLevel
{
    get { return _securityLevel; }
```

```
}
```

6. After the properties, add the following `Login` method to the class definition:

```
public void Login(string loginName, string password)
{
    LoginName = loginName;
    Password = password;
    //Data nomally retrieved from database.
    //Hard coded for demo only.
    if (loginName == "Smith" & password == "js")
    {
        _empID = 1;
        _securityLevel = 2;

    }
    else if (loginName == "Jones" & password == "mj")
    {
        _empID = 2;
        _securityLevel = 4;
    }
    else
    {
        throw new Exception("Login incorrect.");
    }
}
```

7. Select Build ➤ Build Solution. Make sure there are no build errors in the Error List window. If there are, fix them, and then rebuild.

Testing the Employee Class

To test the Employee class, follow these steps:

1. Open frmLogin in the code editor and locate the btnLogin click event code.

■ Tip Double-clicking the Login button in the form designer will also bring up the event code in the code editor.

---

2. In the body of the btnLogin click event, declare and instantiate a variable of type Employee called oEmployee:

```
Employee oEmployee = new Employee();
```

3. Next, call the Login method of the oEmployee object, passing in the values of the login name and the password from the text boxes on the form:

```
oEmployee.Login(txtName.Text,txtPassword.Text);
```

4. After calling the Login method, show a message box stating the user's security level, which is retrieved by reading the SecurityLevel property of the oEmployee object:

```
MessageBox.Show("Your security level is " + oEmployee.SecurityLevel);
```

5. Select Build ➤ Build Solution. Make sure there are no build errors in the Error List window. If there are, fix them, and then rebuild.

6. Select Debug ➤ Start to run the project. Test the login form by entering a login name of Smith and a password of js. You should get a message indicating a security level of 2. Try entering your name and a password of pass. You should get a message indicating the login failed.

7. After testing the login procedure, close the form; this will stop the debugger.

Using Constructors

In OOP, you use constructors to perform any processing that needs to occur when an object instance of the class becomes instantiated. For example, you could initialize properties of the object instance or establish a database connection. The class constructor method is named the same as the class. When an object instance of a class is instantiated by client code, the constructor method is executed. The following constructor is used in the Employee class to initialize the properties of an object instance of the Employee class. An employee ID is passed in to the constructor to retrieve the values from data storage, like so:

```
public Employee(int empID)
{
    //Retrieval of data hardcoded for demo
    if (empID == 1)
```

```
        {
            _empID = 1;
            LoginName = "Smith";
            Password = "js";
            Department = "IT";
            Name = "Jerry Smith";

        }
        else if (empID == 2)
        {
            _empID = 2;
            LoginName = "Jones";
            Password = "mj";
            Department = "HR";
            Name = "Mary Jones";
        }
        else
        {
            throw new Exception("Invalid EmployeeID");
        }
    }
```

Overloading Methods

The ability to overload methods is a useful feature of OOP languages. You overload methods in a class by defining multiple methods that have the same name but contain different signatures. A method signature is a combination of the name of the method and its parameter type list. If you change the parameter type list, you create a different method signature. For example, the parameter type lists can contain a different number of parameters or different parameter types. The compiler will determine which method to execute by examining the parameter type list passed in by the client.

■ **Note** Changing how a parameter is passed (in other words, from `byVal` to `byRef`) does not change the method signature. Altering the return type of the method also does not create a unique method signature. For a more detailed discussion of method signatures and passing arguments, refer to Appendix A.

Suppose you want to provide two methods of the `Employee` class that will allow you to add an employee to the database. The first method assigns a username and password to the employee when the employee is added. The second method adds the employee information but defers the assignment of username and password until later. You can easily accomplish this by overloading the `AddEmployee` method of the `Employee` class, as the following code demonstrates:

```
public int AddEmployee(string loginName, string password,
            string department, string name)
{
    //Data normally saved to database.
    _empID = 3;
    LoginName = loginName;
    Password = password;
```

```
        Department = department;
        Name = name;
        return EmployeeID;
    }

    public int AddEmployee(string department, string name)
    {
        //Data normally saved to database.
        _empID = 3;
        Department = department;
        Name = name;
        return EmployeeID;
    }
```

Because the parameter type list of the first method (string, string) differs from the parameter type list of the second method (string, string, string, string), the compiler can determine which method to invoke. A common technique in OOP is to overload the constructor of the class. For example, when an instance of the Employee class is created, one constructor could be used for new employees and another could be used for current employees by passing in the employee ID when the class instance is instantiated by the client. The following code shows the overloading of a class constructor:

```
public Employee()
{
    _empID = -1;
}

public Employee(int empID)
{
    //Retrieval of data hard coded for demo
    if (empID == 1)
    {
        _empID = 1;
        LoginName = "Smith";
        Password = "js";
        Department = "IT";
        Name = "Jerry Smith";

    }
    else if (empID == 2)
    {
        _empID = 2;
        LoginName = "Jones";
        Password = "mj";
        Department = "HR";
        Name = "Mary Jones";
    }
    else
    {
        throw new Exception("Invalid EmployeeID");
    }
}
```

ACTIVITY 6-2. CREATING CONSTRUCTORS AND OVERLOADING METHODS

In this activity, you will become familiar with the following:

- Creating and overloading the class constructor method.
- Using overloaded constructors of a class from client code.
- Overloading a method of a class.
- Using overloaded methods of a class from client code.

Creating and Overloading Class Constructors

To create and overload class constructors, follow these steps:

1. Start Visual Studio. Select File ➤ Open ➤ Project.
2. Navigate to the Activity6_2Starter folder, click the `Act6_2.sln` file, and then click Open. When the project opens, it will contain a frmEmployeeInfo form that you will use to test the `Employee` class. The project also includes the `Employee.cs` file, which contains the `Employee` class definition code.
3. Open `Employee.cs` in the code editor and examine the code. The class contains several properties pertaining to employees that need to be maintained.
4. After the property declaration code, add the following private method to the class. This method simulates the generation of a new employee ID.

```
private int GetNextID()
{
    //simulates the retrieval of next
    //available id from database
    return 100;
}
```

5. Create a default class constructor, and add code that calls the `GetNextID` method and assigns the return value to the private instance variable `_empID`:

```
public Employee()
{
    _empID = GetNextID();
}
```

6. Overload the default constructor method by adding a second constructor method that takes an integer parameter of `empID`, like so:

```
public Employee(int empID)
{
    //Constructor for existing employee
}
```

7. Add the following code to the overloaded constructor, which simulates extracting the employee data from a database and assigns the data to the instance properties of the class:

```
//Simulates retrieval from database
if (empID == 1)
{
    _empID = empID;
    LoginName = "smith";
    PassWord = "js";
    SSN = 123456789;
    Department = "IS";
}
else if (empID == 2)
{
    _empID = empID;
    LoginName = "jones";
    PassWord = "mj";
    SSN = 987654321;
    Department = "HR";
}
else
{
    throw new Exception("Invalid Employee ID");
}
```

8. Select Build ➤ Build Solution. Make sure there are no build errors in the Error List window. If there are, fix them, and then rebuild.

Testing the Employee Class Constructors

To test the Employee class constructors, follow these steps:

1. Open the EmployeeInfoForm in the form editor and double click the New Employee button to bring up the click event code in the code editor.

2. In the Click Event method body, declare and instantiate a variable of type Employee called oEmployee:

```
Employee oEmployee = new Employee();
```

3. Next, update the EmployeeID text box with the employee ID, disable the EmployeeID text box, and clear the remaining textboxes:

```
Employee oEmployee = new Employee();
txtEmpID.Text = oEmployee.EmpID.ToString();
txtEmpID.Enabled = false;
txtLoginName.Text = "";
txtPassword.Text = "";
txtSSN.Text = "";
txtDepartment.Text = "";
```

4. Select Build ➤ Build Solution. Make sure there are no build errors in the Error List window. If there are, fix them, and then rebuild.

5. Open the EmployeeInfoForm in the form editor and double click the Existing Employee button to bring up the click event code in the code editor.

6. In the `Click Event` method body, declare and instantiate a variable of type Employee called `oEmployee`. Retrieve the employee ID from the txtEmpID text box and pass it as an argument in the constructor. The `int.Parse` method converts the text to an integer data type:

```
Employee oEmployee = new Employee(int.Parse(txtEmpID.Text));
```

7. Next, disable the Employee ID textbox and fill in the remaining text boxes with the values of the `Employee` object's properties:

```
txtEmpID.Enabled = false;
txtLoginName.Text = oEmployee.LoginName;
txtPassword.Text = oEmployee.PassWord;
txtSSN.Text = oEmployee.SSN.ToString();
txtDepartment.Text = oEmployee.Department;
```

8. Select Build ➤ Build Solution. Make sure there are no build errors in the Error List window. If there are, fix them, and then rebuild.

9. Select Debug ➤ Start to run the project and test the code.

10. When the EmployeeInfo form is displayed, click the New Employee button. You should see that a new employee ID has been generated in the Employee ID textbox.

11. Click the Reset button to clear and enable the Employee ID text box.

12. Enter a value of 1 for the employee ID and click the Get Existing Employee button. The information for the employee is displayed on the form.

13. After testing the constructors, close the form, which will stop the debugger.

Overloading a Class Method

To overload a class method, follow these steps:

1. Open the `Employee.cs` code in the code editor.

2. Add the following `Update` method to the `Employee` class. This method simulates the updating of the employee security information to a database:

```
public string Update(string loginName, string password)
{
    LoginName = loginName;
    PassWord = password;
    return "Security info updated.";
}
```

3. Add a second `Update` method to simulate the updating of the employee human resources data to a database:

```
public string Update(int ssNumber, string department)
{
```

```
        SSN = ssNumber;
        Department = department;
        return "HR info updated.";
    }
```

4. Select Build ➤ Build Solution. Make sure there are no build errors in the Error List window. If there are, fix them, and then rebuild.

Testing the Overloaded Update Method

To test the overloaded Update method, follow these steps:

1. Open the EmployeeInfo Form in the Form editor and double click the Update SI button. You are presented with the click event code in the Code Editor window.
2. In the Click Event method, declare and instantiate a variable of type Employee called oEmployee. Retrieve the employee ID from the txtEmpID text box and pass it as an argument in the constructor:

```
Employee oEmployee = new Employee(int.Parse(txtEmpID.Text));
```

3. Next, call the Update method, passing the values of the login name and password from the text boxes. Show the method return message to the user in a message box:

```
MessageBox.Show(oEmployee.Update(txtLoginName.Text, txtPassword.Text));
```

4. Update the login name and password text boxes with the property values of the Employee object:

```
txtLoginName.Text = oEmployee.LoginName;
txtPassword.Text = oEmployee.PassWord;
```

5. Repeat this process to add similar code to the Update HR button Click Event method to simulate updating the human resources information. Add the following code to the Click Event method:

```
Employee oEmployee = new Employee(int.Parse(txtEmpID.Text));
MessageBox.Show(oEmployee.Update(int.Parse(txtSSN.Text), txtDepartment.Text));
txtSSN.Text = oEmployee.SSN.ToString();
txtDepartment.Text = oEmployee.Department;
```

6. Select Build ➤ Build Solution. Make sure there are no build errors in the Error List window. If there are, fix them, and then rebuild.
7. Select Debug ➤ Start to run the project and test the code.
8. Enter a value of 1 for the employee ID and click the Get Existing Employee button.
9. Change the values for the security information and click the Update button.
10. Change the values for the human resources information and click the Update button.

11. You should see that the correct `Update` method is called in accordance with the parameters passed in to it. After testing the `Update` method, close the form.

Summary

This chapter gave you a firm foundation in creating and using classes in C# code. Now that you are comfortable constructing and using classes, you are ready to look at implementing some of the more advanced features of OOP. In the next chapter, you will concentrate on how inheritance and polymorphism are implemented in C# code. As an object-oriented programmer, it is important for you to become familiar with these concepts and learn how to implement them in your programs.

CHAPTER 7

Creating Class Hierarchies

In the previous chapter, you learned how to create classes, add attributes and methods, and instantiate object instances of the classes in client code. This chapter introduces the concepts of inheritance and polymorphism.

Inheritance is one of the most powerful and fundamental features of any OOP language. Using inheritance, you create base classes that encapsulate common functionality. Other classes can be derived from these base classes. The derived classes inherit the properties and methods of the base classes and extend the functionality as needed.

A second fundamental OOP feature is polymorphism. *Polymorphism* lets a base class define methods that must be implemented by any derived classes. The base class defines the message signature that derived classes must adhere to, but the implementation code of the method is left up to the derived class. The power of polymorphism lies in the fact that clients know they can implement methods of classes of the base type in the same fashion. Even though the internal processing of the method may be different, the client knows the inputs and outputs of the methods will be the same.

After reading this chapter, you will learn the following:

- How to create and use base classes.
- How to create and use derived classes.
- How access modifiers control inheritance.
- How to override base class methods.
- How to implement interfaces.
- How to implement polymorphism through inheritance and through interfaces.

Understanding Inheritance

One of the most powerful features of any OOP language is inheritance. Inheritance is the ability to create a base class with properties and methods that can be used in classes derived from the base class.

Creating Base and Derived Classes

The purpose of inheritance is to create a base class that encapsulates properties and methods that can be used by derived classes of the same type. For example, you could create a base class Account. A GetBalance method is defined in the Account class. You can then create two separate classes: SavingsAccount and CheckingAccount. Because the SavingsAccount class and the CheckingAccount class use the same logic to retrieve balance information, they inherit the GetBalance method from the base class Account. This enables you to create one common code base that is easier to maintain and manage.

Derived classes are not limited to the properties and methods of the base class, however. The derived classes may require additional methods and properties that are unique to their needs. For example, the business rules for withdrawing money from a checking account may require that a minimum balance be maintained. A minimum balance, however, may not be required for withdrawals from a savings account. In this scenario, the derived CheckingAccount and SavingsAccount classes would each need their own unique definition for a Withdraw method.

To create a derived class in C#, you enter the name of the class, followed by a colon (:) and the name of the base class. The following code demonstrates how to create a CheckingAccount class that derives from an Account base class:

```
class Account
{
    long _accountNumber;

    public long AccountNumber
    {
        get { return _accountNumber; }
        set { _accountNumber = value; }
    }
    public double GetBalance()
    {
        //code to retrieve account balance from database
        return (double)10000;
    }
}

class CheckingAccount : Account
{
    double _minBalance;

    public double MinBalance
    {
        get { return _minBalance; }
        set { _minBalance = value; }
    }
    public void Withdraw(double amount)
    {
        //code to withdraw from account
    }
}
```

The following code could be implemented by a client creating an object instance of CheckingAccount. Notice that the client perceives no distinction between the call to the GetBalance method and the call to the Withdraw method. In this case, the client has no knowledge of the Account class; instead, both methods appear to have been defined by CheckingAccount.

```
CheckingAccount oCheckingAccount = new CheckingAccount();
double balance;
oCheckingAccount.AccountNumber = 1000;
balance = oCheckingAccount.GetBalance();
oCheckingAccount.Withdraw(500);
```

Creating a Sealed Class

By default, any C# class can be inherited. When creating classes that can be inherited, you must take care that they are not modified in such a way that derived classes no longer function as intended. If you are not careful, you can create complex inheritance chains that are hard to manage and debug. For example, suppose you create a derived CheckingAccount class based on the Account class. Another programmer can come along and create a derived class based on the CheckingAccount and use it in ways you never intended. (This could easily occur in large programming teams with poor communication and design.)

By using the sealed modifier, you can create classes that you know will not be derived from. This type of class is often referred to as a *sealed* or *final* class. By making a class not inheritable, you avoid the complexity and overhead associated with altering the code of base classes. The following code demonstrates the use of the sealed modifier when constructing a class definition:

```
sealed class CheckingAccount : Account
```

Creating an Abstract Class

At this point in the example, a client can access the GetBalance method through an instance of the derived CheckingAccount class or directly through an instance of the base Account class. Sometimes, you may want to have a base class that can't be instantiated by client code. Access to the methods and properties of the class must be through a derived class. In this case, you construct the base class using the abstract modifier. The following code shows the Account class definition with the abstract modifier:

```
abstract class Account
```

This makes the Account class an abstract class. For clients to gain access to the GetBalance method, they must instantiate an instance of the derived CheckingAccount class.

Using Access Modifiers in Base Classes

When setting up class hierarchies using inheritance, you must manage how the properties and methods of your classes are accessed. Two access modifiers you have looked at so far are public and private. If a method or property of the base class is exposed as public, it is accessible by both the derived class and any client of the derived class. If you expose the property or method of the base class as private, it is not accessible directly by the derived class or the client.

You may want to expose a property or method of the base class to a derived class, but not to a client of the derived class. In this case, you use the protected access modifier. The following code demonstrates the use of the protected access modifier:

```
protected double GetBalance()
{
    //code to retrieve account balance from database
    return (double)10000;
}
```

By defining the GetBalance method as protected, it becomes accessible to the derived class CheckingAccount, but not to the client code accessing an instance of the CheckingAccount class.

ACTIVITY 7-1. IMPLEMENTING INHERITANCE USING BASE AND DERIVED CLASSES

In this activity, you will become familiar with the following:

- Creating a base class and derived classes that inherit its methods.
- Using the protected access modifier to restrict use of base class methods.
- Creating an abstract base class.

Creating a Base Class and Derived Classes

To create the Account class, follow these steps:

1. Start Visual Studio. Select File ➤ Open ➤ Project.
2. Navigate to the Activity7_1Starter folder, click the Activity7_1.sln file, and then click Open. When the project opens, it will contain a teller form. You will use this form later to test the classes you create.
3. In the Solution Explorer window, right click the Project node and select Add ➤ Class.
4. In the Add New Item dialog box, rename the class file as Account.cs and click Open. The Account.cs file is added to the project, and the Account class definition code is added to the file.
5. Add the following code to the class definition file to create the private instance variable (private is the default modifier for instance variables):

```
int _accountNumber;
```

6. Add the following GetBalance method to the class definition:

```
    public double GetBalance(int accountNumber)
{
    _accountNumber = accountNumber;
    //Data normally retrieved from database.
    if (_accountNumber == 1)
    {
        return 1000;
    }
    else if (_accountNumber == 2)
    {
        return 2000;
    }
    else
    {
        throw new Exception("Account number is incorrect");
    }
}
```

7. After the Account class, add the following code to create the CheckingAccount and SavingsAccount derived classes:

```
class CheckingAccount : Account
{
}
class SavingsAccount : Account
{
}
```

8. Select Build ➤ Build Solution. Make sure there are no build errors in the Error List window. If there are, fix them, and then rebuild.

Testing the Classes

To test the classes, follow these steps:

1. Open the Teller form in the code editor and locate the btnGetBalance click event code.

2. Inside the event procedure, prior to the Try block, declare and instantiate a variable of type CheckingAccount called oCheckingAccount, a variable of type SavingsAccount called oSavingsAccount, and a variable of type Account called oAccount:

```
CheckingAccount oCheckingAccount = new CheckingAccount();
SavingsAccount oSavingsAccount = new SavingsAccount();
Account oAccount = new Account();
```

3. Depending on which radio button is selected, call the GetBalance method of the appropriate object and pass the account number value from the Account Number text box. Show the return value in the Balance text box. Place the following code in the Try block prior to the Catch statement:

```
if (rdbChecking.Checked)
{
    txtBalance.Text =
    oCheckingAccount.GetBalance(int.Parse(txtAccountNumber.Text)).ToString();
}
else if (rdbSavings.Checked)
{
    txtBalance.Text =
    oSavingsAccount.GetBalance(int.Parse(txtAccountNumber.Text)).ToString();
 }
 else if (rdbGeneral.Checked)
 {
     txtBalance.Text =
     oAccount.GetBalance(int.Parse(txtAccountNumber.Text)).ToString();
  }
```

4. Select Build ➤ Build Solution. Make sure there are no build errors in the Error List window. If there are, fix them, and then rebuild.

5. Select Debug ➤ Start to run the project. Enter an account number of 1 and click the Get Balance button for the Checking Account type. You should get a balance of 1,000. Test the other account types. You should get the same result, since all classes are using the same GetBalance function defined in the base class.

6. After testing, close the form, which will stop the debugger.

Restricting Use of a Base Class Method to Its Derived Classes

At this point, the GetBalance method of the base class is public, which means that it can be accessed by derived classes and their clients. Let's alter this so that the GetBalance method can be accessed only by the derived classes alone, and not by their clients. To protect the GetBalance method in this way, follow these steps:

1. Locate the GetBalance method of the Account class.
2. Change the access modifier of the GetBalance method from `public` to `protected`.
3. Switch to the frmTeller code editor and locate the btnGetBalance click event code.
4. Hover the cursor over the call to the GetBalance method of the oCheckingAccount object. You will see a warning stating that it is a protected function and is not accessible in this context.
5. Comment out the code between the Try and the Catch statements.
6. Switch to the Account.cs code editor.

7. Add the following code to create the following private instance variable to the SavingsAccount class definition file:

```
double _dblBalance;
```

8. Add the following Withdraw method to the SavingsAccount class. This function calls the protected method of the Account base class:

```
public double Withdraw(int accountNumber, double amount)
{
    _dblBalance = GetBalance(accountNumber);
    if (_dblBalance >= amount)
    {
        _dblBalance -= amount;
        return _dblBalance;
    }
    else
    {
        throw new Exception("Not enough funds.");
    }
}
```

9. Select Build ➤ Build Solution. Make sure there are no build errors in the Error List window. If there are, fix them, and then rebuild.

Testing the Protected Base Class Method

To test the Withdraw method, follow these steps:

1. Open the frmTeller form in the code editor and locate the btnWithdraw click event code.

2. Inside the event procedure, prior to the Try block, declare and instantiate a variable of type SavingsAccount called oSavingsAccount.

```
SavingsAccount oSavingsAccount = new SavingsAccount();
```

3. Call the Withdraw method of the oSavingsAccount. Pass the account number value from the Account Number text box and the withdrawal amount from the Amount text box. Show the return value in the Balance text box. Place the following code in the Try block prior to the Catch statement:

```
txtBalance.Text = oSavingsAccount.Withdraw
(int.Parse(txtAccountNumber.Text),double.Parse(txtAmount.Text)).ToString();
```

4. Select Build ➤ Build Solution. Make sure there are no build errors in the Error List window. If there are, fix them and then rebuild.

5. Select Debug ➤ Start to run the project.

6. Test the Withdraw method of the SavingsAccount class by entering an account number of 1 and a withdrawal amount of 200. Click the Withdraw button. You should get a resulting balance of 800.

7. Enter an account number of 1 and a withdrawal amount of 2000. Click the Withdraw button. You should get an insufficient funds message.
8. After testing the Withdraw method, close the form, which will stop the debugger.

Restricting Use of All Members of a Base Class to its Derived Classes

Because the Account base class is public, it can be instantiated by clients of the derived classes. You can alter this by making the Account base class an abstract class. An abstract class can be accessed only by its derived classes and can't be instantiated and accessed by their clients. To create and test the accessibility of the abstract class, follow these steps:

1. Locate the Account class definition in the Account.cs code.
2. Add the abstract keyword to the class definition code, like so:

```
abstract class Account
```

3. Select Build ➤ Build Solution. You should receive a build error in the Error List window. Find the line of code causing the error.

```
Account oAccount = new Account();
```

4. Comment out the line of code, and select Build ➤ Build Solution again. It should now build without any errors.
5. Save and close the project.

Overriding the Methods of a Base Class

When a derived class inherits a method from a base class, it inherits the implementation of that method . As the designer of the base class, you may want to let a derived class implement the method in its own unique way. This is known as overriding the base class method.

By default, a derived class can't override the implementation code of its base class. To allow a base class method to be overridden, you must include the keyword virtual in the method definition. In the derived class, you define a method with the same method signature and indicate it is overriding a base class method with the override keyword. The following code demonstrates the creation of an overridable Deposit method in the Account base class:

```
public virtual  void Deposit(double amount)
{
    //Base class implementation
}
```

To override the Deposit method in the derived CheckingAccount class, use the following code:

```
public override void Deposit(double amount)
{
    //Derived class implementation
}
```

One scenario to watch for is when a derived class inherits from the base class and a second derived class inherits from the first derived class. When a method overrides a method in the base class, it becomes overridable by default. To limit an overriding method from being overridden further up the inheritance chain, you must include the sealed keyword in front of the override keyword in the method definition of the derived class. The following code in the CheckingAccount class prevents the overriding of the Deposit method if the CheckingAccount class is derived from:

```
public sealed override void Deposit(double amount)
{
    //Derived class implementation
}
```

When you indicate that a base class method is overridable, derived classes have the option of overriding the method or using the implementation provided by the base class. In some cases, you may want to use a base class method as a template for the derived classes. The base class has no implementation code, but is used to define the method signatures used in the derived classes. This type of class is referred to as an *abstract base class*. You define the class and the methods with the abstract keyword. The following code is used to create an abstract Account base class with an abstract Deposit method:

```
public  abstract class Account
{
    public abstract void Deposit(double amount);
}
```

Note that because there is no implementation code defined in the base class for the Deposit method, the body of the method is omitted.

Calling a Derived Class Method from a Base Class

A situation may arise in which you are calling an overridable method in the base class from another method of the base class, and the derived class overrides the method of the base class. When a call is made to the base class method from an instance of the derived class, the base class will call the overridden method of the derived class. The following code shows an example of this situation. A CheckingAccount base class contains an overridable GetMinBalance method. The InterestBearingCheckingAccount class, inheriting from the CheckingAccount class, overrides the GetMinBalance method.

```
class CheckingAccount
{
    private double _balance = 2000;

    public double Balance
    {
        get { return _balance; }
    }
    public virtual double GetMinBalance()
    {
        return 200;
    }
    public virtual void Withdraw(double amount)
```

```
    {
        double minBalance = GetMinBalance();
        if (minBalance < (Balance - amount))
        {
            _balance -= amount;
        }
        else
        {
            throw new Exception("Minimum balance error.");
        }
    }
}
class InterestBearingCheckingAccount : CheckingAccount
{
    public override double GetMinBalance()
    {
        return 1000;
    }
}
```

A client instantiates an object instance of the InterestBearingCheckingAccount class and calls the Withdraw method. In this case, the overridden GetMinimumBalance method of the InterestBearingCheckingAccount class is executed, and a minimum balance of 1,000 is used.

```
InterestBearingCheckingAccount oAccount = new InterestBearingCheckingAccount();
oAccount.Withdraw(500);
```

When the call was made to the Withdraw method, you could have prefaced it with the `this` qualifier:

```
double minBalance = this.GetMinBalance();
```

Because the `this` qualifier is the default qualifier if none is used, the code would execute the same way as previously demonstrated. The most derived class implementation (that has been instantiated) of the method is executed. In other words, if a client instantiates an instance of the InterestBearingCheckingAccount class, as was demonstrated previously, the base class's call to GetMinimumBalance is made to the derived class's implementation. On the other hand, if a client instantiates an instance of the CheckingAccount class, the base class's call to GetMinimumBalance is made to its own implementation.

Calling a Base Class Method from a Derived Class

In some cases, you may want to develop a derived class method that still uses the implementation code in the base class but also augments it with its own implementation code. In this case, you create an overriding method in the derived class and call the code in the base class using the base qualifier. The following code demonstrates the use of the base qualifier:

```
public override void Deposit(double amount)
{
    base.Deposit(amount);
    //Derived class implementation.
}
```

Overloading Methods of a Base Class

Methods inherited by the derived class can be overloaded. The method signature of the overloaded class must use the same name as the overloaded method, but the parameter lists must differ. This is the same as when you overload methods of the same class. The following code demonstrates the overloading of a derived method:

```
class CheckingAccount
{
    public void Withdraw(double amount)
    {
    }
}
class InterestBearingCheckingAccount : CheckingAccount
{
    public void Withdraw(double amount, double minBalance)
    {
    }
}
```

Client code instantiating an instance of the InterestBearingCheckingAccount has access to both Withdraw methods.

```
InterestBearingCheckingAccount oAccount = new InterestBearingCheckingAccount();
oAccount.Withdraw(500);
oAccount.Withdraw(500, 200);
```

Hiding Base Class Methods

If a method in a derived class has the same method signature as that of the base class method but it is not marked with the override key word, it effectively hides the method of the base class. Although this may be the intended behavior, sometimes it can occur inadvertently. Although the code will still compile, the IDE will issue a warning asking if this is the intended behavior. If you intend to hide a base class method, you should explicitly use the new keyword in the definition of the method of the derived class. Using the new keyword will indicate to the IDE this is the intended behavior and dismiss the warning. The following code demonstrates hiding a base class method:

```
class CheckingAccount
{
    public virtual void Withdraw(double amount)
    {
    }
}

class InterestBearingCheckingAccount : CheckingAccount
{
    public new void Withdraw(double amount)
    {
    }
    public void Withdraw(double amount, double minBalance)
    {
```

```
    }
}
```

ACTIVITY 7-2. OVERRIDING BASE CLASS METHODS

In this activity, you will become familiar with the following:

- Overriding methods of a base class.
- Using the base qualifier in a derived classes.

Overriding Base Class Methods

To override the Account class, follow these steps:

1. Start VS. Select File ➤ Open ➤ Project.
2. Navigate to the Activity7_2Starter folder, click the Act7_2.sln file, and then click Open. When the project opens, it will contain a teller form. You will use this form later to test the classes you will create. The project also contains a BankClasses.cs file. This file contains code for the Account base class and the derived classes SavingsAccount and CheckingAccount.
3. Examine the Withdraw method defined in the base class Account. This method checks to see whether there are sufficient funds in the account and, if there are, updates the balance. You will override this method in the CheckingAccount class to ensure that a minimum balance is maintained.
4. Change the Withdraw method definition in the Account class to indicate it is overridable, like so:

```
public virtual double Withdraw(double amount)
```

5. Add the following GetMinimumBalance method to the CheckingAccount class definition:

```
public double GetMinimumBalance()
{
    return 200;
}
```

6. Add the following overriding Withdraw method to the CheckingAccount class definition. This method adds a check to see that the minimum balance is maintained after a withdrawal.

```
public override double Withdraw(double amount)
{
    if (Balance >= amount + GetMinimumBalance())
    {
        _balance -= amount;
```

```
            return Balance;
        }
        else
        {
            throw new ApplicationException("Not enough funds.");
        }
    }
```

7. Select Build ➤ Build Solution. Make sure there are no build errors in the Error List window. If there are, fix them and then rebuild.

Testing the Overwritten Methods

To test the modified Withdraw methods you have created, follow these steps:

1. Open the frmTeller form in the code editor and locate the btnWithdraw click event code.

2. Depending on which radio button is selected, call the Withdraw method of the appropriate object and pass the value of the txtAmount text box. Add the following code in the try block to show the return value in the txtBalance text box:

```
if (rdbChecking.Checked)
{
    oCheckingAccount.AccountNumber = int.Parse(txtAccountNumber.Text);
    txtBalance.Text =
oCheckingAccount.Withdraw(double.Parse(txtAmount.Text)).ToString();
}
else if (rdbSavings.Checked)
{
     oSavingsAccount.AccountNumber = int.Parse(txtAccountNumber.Text);
     txtBalance.Text =
oSavingsAccount.Withdraw(double.Parse(txtAmount.Text)).ToString();
}
```

3. Select Build ➤ Build Solution. Make sure there are no build errors in the Error List window. If there are, fix them, and then rebuild.

4. Select Debug ➤ Start to run the project.

5. Enter an account number of 1, choose the Checking option button, and click the Get Balance button.You should get a balance of 1000.

6. Enter a withdrawal amount of 200 and click the Withdraw button. You should get a resulting balance of 800.

7. Enter a withdrawal amount of 700 and click the Withdraw button. You should get an insufficient funds message because the resulting balance would be less than the minimum balance of 200.

8. Enter an account number of 1, choose the Savings option button, and click the Get Balance button. You should get a balance of 1000.

9. Enter a withdrawal amount of 600 and click the Withdraw button. You should get a resulting balance of 400.
10. Enter a withdrawal amount of 400 and click the Withdraw button. You should get a resulting balance of 0 because there is no minimum balance for the savings account that uses the Account base class's Withdraw method.
11. After testing, close the form, which will stop the debugger.

Using the Base Qualifier to Call a Base Class Method

At this point, the Withdraw method of the CheckingAccount class overrides the Account class's Withdraw method. None of the code in the base class's method is executed. You will now alter the code so that when the CheckingAccount class's code is executed, it also executes the base class's Withdraw method . Follow these steps:

1. Locate the Withdraw method of the Account class.
2. Change the implementation code so that it decrements the balance by the amount passed to it.

```
public virtual double Withdraw(double amount)
{
    _balance -= amount;
    return Balance;
}
```

3. Change the Withdraw method of the CheckingAccount class so that after it checks for sufficient funds, it calls the Withdraw method of the Account base class.

```
public override double Withdraw(double amount)
{
    if (Balance >= amount + GetMinimumBalance())
    {
        return base.Withdraw(amount);
    }
    else
    {
        throw new ApplicationException("Not enough funds.");
    }
}
```

4. Add a Withdraw method to the SavingsAccount class that is similar to the Withdraw method of the CheckingAccount class but does not check for a minimum balance.

```
public override double Withdraw(double amount)
{
    if (Balance >= amount)
    {
        return base.Withdraw(amount);
    }
    else
    {
```

```
            throw new ApplicationException("Not enough funds.");
        }
    }
```

5. Select Build ➤ Build Solution. Make sure there are no build errors in the Error List window. If there are, fix them, and then rebuild.

Testing the Use of the Base Modifier

To test the Withdraw method, follow these steps:

1. Select Debug ➤ Start.
2. Enter an account number of 1, choose the Checking option button, and click the Get Balance button. You should get a balance of 1000.
3. Enter a withdrawal amount of 600 and click the Withdraw button. You should get a resulting balance of 400.
4. Enter a withdrawal amount of 300 and click the Withdraw button. You should get an insufficient funds message because the resulting balance would be less than the 200 minimum.
5. Enter an account number of 1, choose the Savings option button, and click the Get Balance button. You should get a balance of 1000.
6. Enter a withdrawal amount of 600 and click the Withdraw button. You should get a resulting balance of 400.
7. Enter a withdrawal amount of 300 and click the Withdraw button. You should get a resulting balance of 100, because there is no minimum balance for the savings account that uses the Account base class's Withdraw method.
8. After testing, close the form, which will stop the debugger.

Implementing Interfaces

As you saw earlier, you can create an abstract base class that does not contain any implementation code but defines the method signatures that must be used by any class that inherits from the base class. When you use an abstract class, classes that derive from it must implement its inherited methods. You could use another technique to accomplish a similar result. In this case, instead of defining an abstract class, you define an interface that defines the method signatures.

Classes that implement an interface are contractually required to implement the interface signature definition and can't alter it. This technique is useful to ensure that client code using the classes know which methods are available, how they should be called, and the return values to expect. The following code shows how you declare an interface definition:

```
public interface IAccount
{
   string GetAccountInfo(int accountNumber);
}
```

A class implements the interface by using a semicolon followed by the name of the interface after the class name. When a class implements an interface, it must provide implementation code for all methods defined by the interface. The following code demonstrates how a CheckingAccount implements the IAccount interface:

```
public class CheckingAccount : IAccount
{
    public string GetAccountInfo(int accountNumber)
    {
        return "Printing checking account info";
    }
}
```

Because implementing an interface and inheriting from an abstract base class are similar, you might ask why you should bother using an interface. One advantage of using interfaces is that a class can implement multiple interfaces. The .NET Framework does not support inheritance from more than one class. As a workaround to multiple inheritance, the ability to implement multiple interfaces was included. Interfaces are also useful to enforce common functionality across disparate types of classes.

Understanding Polymorphism

Polymorphism is the ability of derived classes inheriting from the same base class to respond to the same method call in their own unique way. This simplifies client code because the client code does not need to worry about which class type it is referencing, as long as the class types implement the same method interfaces.

For example, suppose you want all account classes in a banking application to contain a GetAccountInfo method with the same interface definition but different implementations based on account type. Client code could loop through a collection of account-type classes, and the compiler would determine at runtime which specific account-type implementation needs to be executed. If you later added a new account type that implements the GetAccountInfo method, you would not need to alter existing client code.

You can achieve polymorphism either by using inheritance or by implementing interfaces. The following code demonstrates the use of inheritance. First, you define the base and derived classes.

```
public abstract class Account
{
   public abstract string GetAccountInfo();
}

public class CheckingAccount : Account
{
   public override string GetAccountInfo()
   {
       return "Printing checking account info";
   }
```

```
}
public class SavingsAccount : Account
{
    public override string GetAccountInfo()
    {
        return "Printing savings account info";
    }
}
```

You then create a list of type Account and add a CheckingAccount and a SavingsAccount.

```
List<Account> AccountList = new List<Account>();
CheckingAccount oCheckingAccount = new CheckingAccount();
SavingsAccount oSavingsAccount = new SavingsAccount();
AccountList.Add(oCheckingAccount);
AccountList.Add(oSavingsAccount);
```

You then loop through the List and call the GetAccountInfo method of each Account. Each Account type will implement its own implementation of the GetAccountInfo.

```
foreach (Account a in AccountList)
{
    MessageBox.Show(a.GetAccountInfo());
}
```

You can also achieve a similar result by using interfaces. Instead of inheriting from the base class Account, you define and implement an IAccount interface.

```
public interface IAccount
 {
    string GetAccountInfo();
 }

public class CheckingAccount : IAccount
{
    public string GetAccountInfo()
    {
        return "Printing checking account info";
    }
}
public class SavingsAccount : IAccount
{
    public string GetAccountInfo()
    {
        return "Printing savings account info";
    }
}
```

You then create a list of type IAccount and add a CheckingAccount and a SavingsAccount.

```
List<IAccount> AccountList = new List<IAccount>();
CheckingAccount oCheckingAccount = new CheckingAccount();
SavingsAccount oSavingsAccount = new SavingsAccount();
AccountList.Add(oCheckingAccount);
AccountList.Add(oSavingsAccount);
```

You then loop through the List and call the GetAccountInfo method of each Account. Each Account type will implement its own implementation of the GetAccountInfo.

```
foreach (IAccount a in AccountList)
{
    MessageBox.Show(a.GetAccountInfo());
}
```

ACTIVITY 7-3. IMPLEMENTING POLYMORPHISM

In this activity, you will become familiar with the following:

- Creating polymorphism through inheritance.
- Creating polymorphism through interfaces.

Implementing Polymorphism Using Inheritance

To implement polymorphism using inheritance, follow these steps:

1. Start Visual Studio. Select File ➤ New ➤ Project.
2. Select the Console Application template under the C# templates. Name the project Activity7_3.
3. The project includes a Program.cs file. This file contains a Main method that launches a Windows Console application. Right click the project node in the Solution Explorer Window and select Add ➤ class. Name the file Account.cs.
4. In the Account.cs file alter the code to an abstract base Account class. Include an accountNumber property and an abstract method GetAccountInfo that takes no parameters and returns a string.

```
public abstract class Account
{
    private int _accountNumber;

    public int AccountNumber
    {
        get { return _accountNumber; }
        set { _accountNumber = value; }
    }

    public abstract string GetAccountInfo();
}
```

5. Add the following code to create two derived classes: CheckingAccount and SavingsAccount. These classes will override the GetAccountInfo method of the base class.

```
public class CheckingAccount : Account
{
    public override string GetAccountInfo()
    {
        return "Printing checking account info for account number "
            + AccountNumber.ToString();
    }
}
public class SavingsAccount : Account
{
    public override string GetAccountInfo()
    {
        return "Printing savings account info for account number "
            + AccountNumber.ToString();
    }
}
```

6. Select Build ➤ Build Solution. Make sure there are no build errors in the Error List window. If there are, fix them, and then rebuild.

Testing the Polymorphic Inheritance Method

To test the polymorphic method, follow these steps:

1. Open the Program.cs file in the code editor and locate the Main method.
2. Instantiate an instance of a list of Account types.

```
List<Account> AccountList = new List<Account>();
```

3. Instantiate an instance of the CheckingAccount and SavingsAccount.

```
CheckingAccount oCheckingAccount = new CheckingAccount();
oCheckingAccount.AccountNumber = 100;
SavingsAccount oSavingsAccount = new SavingsAccount();
oSavingsAccount.AccountNumber = 200;
```

4. Add the oCheckingAccount and oSavingsAccount to the list using the Add method of the list.

```
AccountList.Add(oCheckingAccount);
AccountList.Add(oSavingsAccount);
```

5. Loop through the list and call the GetAccountInfo method of each Account type in the list and show the results in a console window.

```
foreach (Account a in AccountList)
{
    Console.WriteLine(a.GetAccountInfo());
}
Console.ReadLine();
```

6. Select Build ➤ Build Solution. Make sure there are no build errors in the Error List window. If there are, fix them, and then rebuild.

7. Select Debug ➤ Start to run the project. You should see a console window with the return string for the GetAccountInfo method of each object in the list.
8. After testing the polymorphism, hit the enter key to close the console window, which will stop the debugger.

Implementing Polymorphism Using an Interface

To implement polymorphism using an interface, follow these steps:

1. View the code for the Account.cs file in the code editor.
2. Comment out the code for the Account, CheckingAccount, and SavingsAccount classes.
3. Define an interface IAccount that contains the GetAccountInfo method.

```
public interface IAccount
 {
    string GetAccountInfo();
 }
```

4. Add the following code to create two classes: CheckingAccount and SavingsAccount. These classes will implement the IAccount interface.

```
public class CheckingAccount : IAccount
{
    private int _accountNumber;

    public int AccountNumber
    {
        get { return _accountNumber; }
        set { _accountNumber = value; }
    }
    public string GetAccountInfo()
    {
        return "Printing checking account info for account number "
            + AccountNumber.ToString();
    }
}
public class SavingsAccount : IAccount
{
    private int _accountNumber;

    public int AccountNumber
    {
        get { return _accountNumber; }
        set { _accountNumber = value; }
    }
    public string GetAccountInfo()
    {
        return "Printing savings account info for account number "
            + AccountNumber.ToString();
```

```
    }
}
```

5. Select Build ➤ Build Solution. Make sure there are no build errors in the Error List window. If there are, fix them, and then rebuild.

Testing the Polymorphic Interface Method

To test the polymorphic method, follow these steps:

1. Open the Program.cs file in the code editor and locate the Main method.
2. Change the code to instantiate an instance of a list of IAccount types.

```
List<IAccount> AccountList = new List<IAccount>();
```

3. Change the for each loop to loop through the list and call the GetAccountInfo() method of each IAccount type in the list.

```
foreach (IAccount a in AccountList)
{
    Console.WriteLine(a.GetAccountInfo());
}
Console.ReadLine();
```

4. Select Build ➤ Build Solution. Make sure there are no build errors in the Error List window. If there are, fix them, and then rebuild.
5. Select Debug ➤ Start to run the project. You should see a console window with the return string for the GetAccountInfo method of each object in the list.
6. After testing the polymorphism, hit the enter key to close the console window, which will stop the debugger.

Summary

This chapter introduced you to two of OOP's most powerful features: inheritance and polymorphism. Knowing how to implement these features is fundamental to becoming a successful object-oriented programmer, regardless of the language you use.

In the next chapter, you will take a closer look at how the objects in your applications collaborate. The topics covered include how objects pass messages to one another, how events drive your programs, how data is shared among instances of a class, and how exceptions are handled.

CHAPTER 8

Implementing Object Collaboration

In the previous chapter, you learned how to create and use class hierarchies in C#. That chapter also introduced the concepts of inheritance, polymorphism, and interfaces. In this chapter, you'll learn how to get the objects of an application to work together to perform tasks. You will see how objects communicate through messaging and how events initiate application processing. You'll also learn how the objects respond and communicate exceptions that may occur as they carry out their assigned tasks.

After reading this chapter, you should be familiar with the following:

- The process of object communication through messaging.
- The different types of messaging that can occur.
- How to use delegation in C# applications.
- How objects can respond to events and publish their own events.
- The process of issuing and responding to exceptions.
- How to create shared data and procedures among several instances of the same class.
- How to issue message calls asynchronously.

Communicating Through Messaging

One of the advantages of OOP is that OOP applications function in much the same way that people do in the real world. You can think of your application as a large company. In large companies, the employees perform specialized functions. For example, one person is in charge of accounts payable processing, and another is responsible for the accounts receivable operations. When an employee needs to request a service—paid time off (PTO), for example—the employee (the client) sends a message to her manager (the server). This client/server request can involve just two objects, or it can be a complex chain of client/server requests. For example, the employee requests the PTO from her manager, who, in turn, checks with the human resources (HR) department to see if the employee has enough accumulated time. In this case, the manager is both a server to the employee and a client to the HR department.

Defining Method Signatures

When a message passes between a client and server, the client may or may not expect a response. For example, when an employee requests PTO, she expects a response indicating approval or denial.

However, when the accounting department issues paychecks, the staff members do not expect everyone in the company to issue a response e-mail thanking them!

A common requirement when a message is issued is to include the information necessary to carry out the request. When an employee requests PTO, her manager expects her to provide him with the dates she is requesting off. In OOP terminology, you refer to the name of the method (requested service) and the input parameters (client-supplied information) as the method signature.

The following code demonstrates how methods are defined in C#. The access modifier is first followed by the return type (void is used if no return value is returned) and then the name of the method. Parameter types and names are listed in parenthesis separated by commas. The body of the method is contained in opening and closing curly brackets.

```
public int AddEmployee(string firstName,string lastName)
{
    //Code to save data to database
}
public void LogMessage(string message)
{
    //Code to write to log file.
}
```

Passing Parameters

When you define a method in the class, you also must indicate how the parameters are passed. Parameters may be passed by value or by reference.

If you choose to pass the parameters by value, a copy of the parameter data is passed from the client to the server. The server works with the copy and, if changes are made to the data, the server must pass the copy back to the client so that the client can choose to discard the changes or replicate them. Returning to the company analogy, think about the process of updating your employee file. The HR department does not give you direct access to the file; instead, it sends you a copy of the values in the file. You make changes to the copy, and then you send it back to the HR department. The HR department then decides whether to replicate these changes to the actual employee file. In C#, passing parameters by value is the default, so no keyword is used. In the following method, the parameter is passed by value:

```
public int AddEmployee(string firstName)
        {
            //Code to save data to database
        }
```

Another way you can pass parameters is by reference. In this case, the client does not pass in a copy of the data but instead passes a reference to where the data is located. Using the previous example, instead of sending you a copy of the data in your employee file when you want to make updates, the HR department informs you where the file is located, and tells you to go to it to make the changes. In this case, clearly it would be better to pass the parameters by reference. In C# code, when passing parameters by reference the ref keyword is used. The following code shows how you define the method to pass values by reference:

```
public int AddEmployee(ref string firstName)
{
    //Code to save data to database
}
```

In highly distributed applications, it is advantageous to pass parameters by value instead of by reference. Passing parameters by reference can cause increased overhead, because when the server object must work with parameter information, it needs to make calls across processing boundaries and the network. Passing values by reference is also less secure when maintaining data integrity. The client is opening a channel for the data to be manipulated without the client's knowledge or control.

On the other hand, passing values by reference may be the better choice when the client and server are in the same process space (they occupy the same cubicle, so to speak) and have a clearly established trust relationship. In this situation, allowing direct access to the memory storage location and passing the parameters by reference may offer a performance advantage over passing the parameters by value.

The other situation where passing parameters by reference may be advantageous is if the object is a complex data type, such as another object. In this case, the overhead of copying the data structure and passing it across process and network boundaries outweighs the overhead of making repeated calls across the network.

■ **Note** The .NET Framework addresses the problem of complex data types by allowing you to efficiently copy and pass those types by serializing and deserializing them in an XML structure.

Understanding Event-Driven Programming

So far, you have been looking at messaging between the objects in which the client initiates the message interaction. If you think about how you interact with objects in real life, you often receive messages in response to an event that has occurred. For example, when the sandwich vendor comes into the building, a message is issued over the intercom informing employees that the lunch has arrived. This type of messaging is referred to as broadcast messaging. The server issues the message, and the clients decide to ignore or respond to the message.

Another way this event message could be issued is by the receptionist sending an e-mail to a list of interested employees when the sandwich vendor shows up. In this case, the interested employees would subscribe to receive the event message with the receptionist. This type of messaging is often referred to as subscription-based messaging.

Applications built with the .NET Framework are object-oriented, event-driven programs. If you trace the client/server processing chains that occur in your applications, you can identify the event that kicked off the processing. In the case of Windows applications, the user interacting with a GUI usually initiates the event. For example, a user might initiate the process of saving data to a database by clicking a button. Classes in applications can also initiate events. A security class could broadcast an event message when an invalid login is detected. You can also subscribe to external events. You could create a web service that would issue an event notification when a change occurs in a stock you are tracking in the stock market. You could write an application that subscribes to the service and responds to the event notification.

Understanding Delegation

In order to implement event-based programming in C#, you must first understand delegation. Delegation is when you request a service from a server by making a method call. The server then reroutes this service request to another method, which services the request. The delegate class can examine the service request and dynamically determines at runtime where to route the request. Returning to the company analogy, when a manager receives a service request, she often delegates it to a member of her department. (In fact, many would argue that a common trait among successful managers is the ability to know when and how to delegate responsibilities.)

When you create a delegated method, you first define the delegated method's signature. Because the delegate method does not actually service the request, it does not contain any implementation code. The following code shows a delegated method used to compare integer values:

```
public delegate Boolean CompareInt(int I1, int I2);
```

Once the delegated method's signature is defined, you can then create the methods that will be delegated to. These methods must have the same parameters and return types as the delegated method. The following code shows two methods that the delegated method will delegate to:

```
private Boolean AscendOrder(int I1, int I2)
{
    if (I1 < I2)
    { return true;}
    else
    { return false; }
}
private Boolean DescendOrder(int I1, int I2)
{
    if (I1 > I2)
    { return true; }
    else
    { return false; }
}
```

Once the delegate and its delegating methods have been defined, you are ready to use the delegate. The following code shows a portion of a sorting routine that determines which delegated method to call depending on a SortType passed in as a parameter:

```
public void SortIntegers(SortType sortDirection, int[] intArray)
{
    CompareInt CheckOrder;
    if (sortDirection == SortType.Ascending)
        { CheckOrder = new CompareInt(AscendOrder); }
    else
        { CheckOrder = new CompareInt(DescendOrder); }
    // Code continues ...
}
```

Implementing Events

In C#, when you want to issue event messages, first you declare a delegate type for the event. The delegate type defines the set of arguments that will be passed to the method that handles the event.

```
public delegate void DataUpdateEventHandler(string msg);
```

Once the delegate is declared an event of the delegate type is declared.

```
public event DataUpdateEventHandler DataUpdate;
```

When you want to raise the event, you call the event passing in the appropriate arguments.

```
public void SaveInfo()
{
    try
    {
        DataUpdate("Data has been updated");
    }
    catch
    {
        DataUpdate("Data could not be updated");
    }
}
```

Responding To Events

To consume an event in client code, an event handling method is declared that executes program logic in response to the event. This event handler must have the same method signature as the event delegate declared in the class issuing the event.

```
void odata_DataUpdate(string msg)
{
    MessageBox.Show(msg);
}
```

This event handler is registered with the event source using the += operator. This process is referred to as event wiring. The following code wires up the event handler for the DataUpdate event declared previously:

```
Data odata = new Data();
odata.DataUpdate += new DataUpdateEventHandler(odata_DataUpdate);
odata.SaveInfo();
```

Windows Control Event Handling

Windows Forms also implement event handlers by using the += operator to wire up the event handler to the event. The following code wires up a button to a click event and a textbox to a mouse down event:

```
this.button1.Click += new System.EventHandler(this.button1_Click);
this.textBox1.MouseDown += new
System.Windows.Forms.MouseEventHandler(this.textBox1_MouseDown);
```

The event handler methods for control events take two parameters: the first parameter, sender, provides a reference to the object that raised the event. The second parameter passes an object containing information specific to the event that is being handled. The following code shows an event handler method for a button click event and an event handler for the textbox mouse down event. Notice how e is used to determine if the left button was clicked.

```
private void button1_Click(object sender, EventArgs e)
{
```

```
}
private void textBox1_MouseDown(object sender, MouseEventArgs e)
{
    if (e.Button == System.Windows.Forms.MouseButtons.Left)
    {
        //code goes here.
    }
}
```

ACTIVITY 8-1. ISSUING AND RESPONDING TO EVENT MESSAGES

In this activity, you will learn to do the following:

- Create and raise events from a server class.
- Handle events from client classes.
- Handle GUI events.

Adding and Raising Event Messaging in the Class Definition

To add and raise event messaging in a class definition file, follow these steps:

1. Start Visual Studio. Select File ➤ New ➤ Project.
2. Choose a Windows Application project. Name the project `Act8_1`.
3. A default form is included in the project. Add controls to the form and change the property values, as listed in Table 8-1. Your completed form should look similar to Figure 8-1.

Table 8-1. *Login Form and Control Properties*

Object	Property	Value
Form1	Name	frmLogin
	Text	Login
Label1	Name	lblName
	Text	Name:
Label2	Name	lblPassword
	Text	Password:

(continued)

Table 8-1. *(continued)*

Object	Property	Value
Textbox1	Name	txtName
	Text	(empty)
Textbox2	Name	txtPassword
	Text	(empty)
	PasswordChar	*
Button1	Name	btnLogin
	Text	Login
Button2	Name	btnClose
	Text	Close

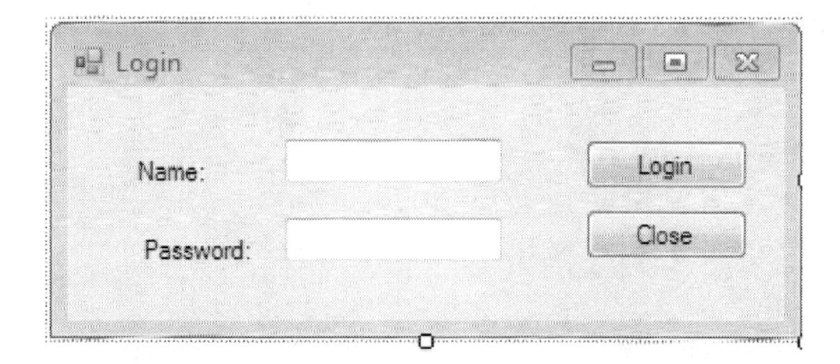

Figure 8-1. *The completed login form*

4. Select Project ➤ Add Class. Name the class Employee. Open the Employee class code in the code editor.
5. Above the class declaration, add the following line of code to define the Login event handler delegate. You will use this event to track employee logins to your application.

```
public delegate void LoginEventHandler(string loginName, Boolean status);
```

6. Inside the class declaration, add the following line of code to define the LoginEvent as the delegate type:

```
public event LoginEventHandler LoginEvent;
```

7. Add the following Login method to the class, which will raise the LoginEvent:

```
public void Login(string loginName, string password)
{
    //Data normally retrieved from database.
    if (loginName == "Smith" && password == "js")
    {
        LoginEvent(loginName, true);
    }
    else
    {
        LoginEvent(loginName, false);
    }
}
```

8. Select Build ➤ Build Solution. Make sure there are no build errors in the Error List window. If there are, fix them, and then rebuild.

Receiving Events in the Client Class

To receive events in the client class, follow these steps:

1. Open the frmLogin in the design window.
2. Double-click the Login button to view the Login button click event handler.
3. Add the following code to wire up the Employee class's LoginEvent with an event handler in the form class:

```
private void btnLogin_Click(object sender, EventArgs e)
{
    Employee oEmployee = new Employee();
    oEmployee.LoginEvent += new LoginEventHandler(oEmployee_LoginEvent);
    oEmployee.Login(txtName.Text, txtPassword.Text);
}
```

4. Add the following event handler method to the form that gets called when the Employee class issues a LoginEvent:

```
void oEmployee_LoginEvent(string loginName, bool status)
{
    MessageBox.Show("Login status :" + status);
}
```

5. Select Build ➤ Build Solution. Make sure there are no build errors in the Error List window. If there are, fix them, and then rebuild.
6. Select Debug ➤ Start to run the project.
7. To test to make sure the Login event is raised, enter a login name of Smith and a password of js. This should trigger a login status of true.

8. After testing the Login event, close the form, which will stop the debugger.

Handling Multiple Events with One Method

To handle multiple events with one method, follow these steps:

1. Open frmLogin in the form designer by right-clicking the frmLogin node in the Solution Explorer and choosing View Designer.
2. From the Toolbox, add a MenuStrip control to the form. Click where it says "Type Here" and enter File for the top-level menu and Exit for its submenu, as shown in Figure 8-2.

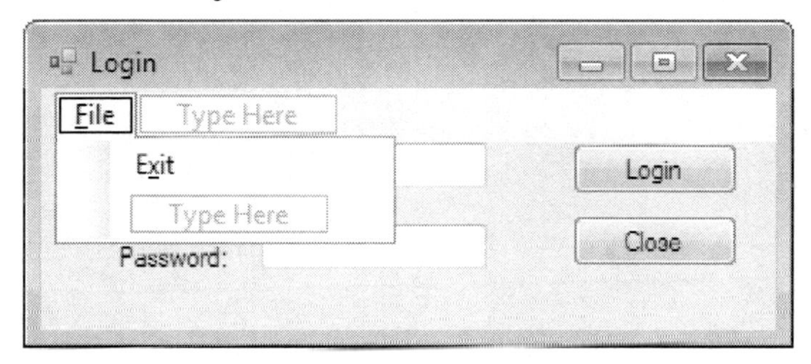

Figure 8-2. *Adding the MenuStrip control*

3. Add the following method to handle the click event of the menu and the Close button:

```
private void FormClose(object sender, EventArgs e)
{
    this.Close();
}
```

4. Open the frmLogin in the designer window. In the properties window, select the exitToolStripMenuItem. Select the event button at the top of the properties window to show the events of the control. In the click event drop-down, select the FormClose method (see Figure 8-3).

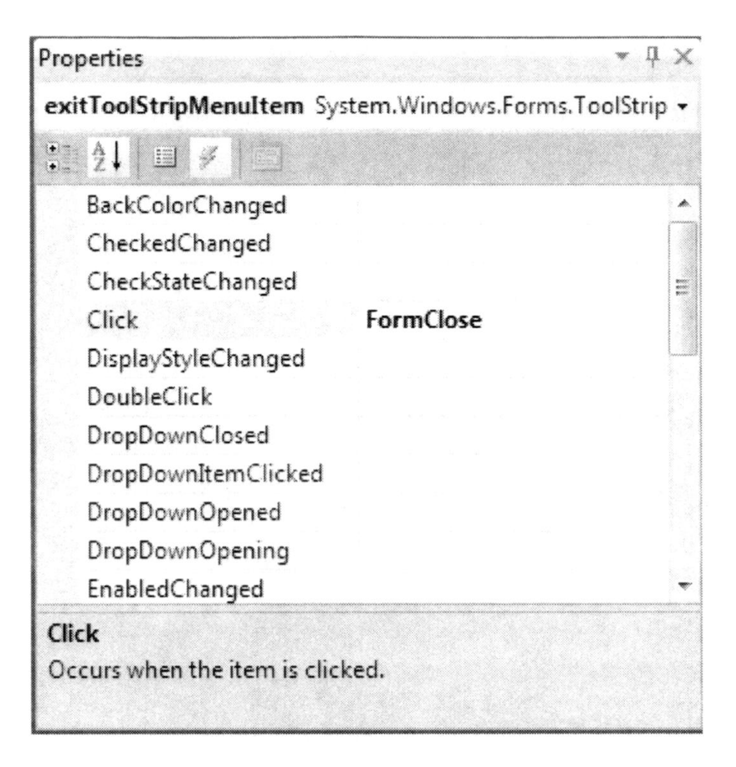

Figure 8-3. *Wiring up an event handler*

5. Repeat step 4 to wire up the btnClose button click event to the FormClose method.
6. Expand the frmLogin node in the Solution window. Right click on the frmLogin.Designer.cs node and select View Code.
7. In the code editor, expand the Windows Form Designer generated code region. Search for the following code:

```
this.btnClose.Click += new System.EventHandler(this.FormClose);
this.exitToolStripMenuItem.Click += new System.EventHandler(this.FormClose);
```

8. This code was generated by the form designer to wire up the events to the FormClose method.
9. Select Build ➤ Build Solution. Make sure there are no build errors in the Error List window. If there are, fix them, and then rebuild.
10. Select Debug ➤ Start to run the project. Test the Exit menu and the Close button.
11. After testing, save the project, and then exit Visual Studio.

Handling Exceptions in the .NET Framework

When objects collaborate, things can go wrong. Exceptions are things that you do not expect to occur during normal processing. For example, you may be trying to save data to a database over the network when the connection fails, or you may be trying to save to a drive without a disk in the drive. Your applications should be able to gracefully handle any exceptions that occur during application processing.

The .NET Framework uses a structured exception handling mechanism. The following are some of the benefits of this structured exception handling:

- Common support and structure across all .NET languages.
- Support for the creation of protected blocks of code.
- The ability to filter exceptions to create efficient robust error handling.
- Support of termination handlers to guarantee that cleanup tasks are completed, regardless of any exceptions that may be encountered.

The .NET Framework also provides an extensive number of exception classes used to handle common exceptions that might occur. For example, the FileNotFoundException class encapsulates information such as the file name, error message, and the source for an exception that is thrown when there is an attempt to access a file that does not exist. In addition, the .NET Framework allows the creation of application-specific exception classes you can write to handle common exceptions that are unique to your application.

Using the Try-Catch Block

When creating code that could end up causing an exception, you should place it in a Try block. Code placed inside the Try block is considered protected. If an exception occurs while the protected code is executing, code processing is transferred to the Catch block, where it is handled. The following code shows a method of a class that tries to read from a file that does not exist. When the exception is thrown, it is caught in the Catch block.

```
public string ReadText(string filePath)
{
    StreamReader sr;
    try
    {
        sr = File.OpenText(filePath);
        string fileText = sr.ReadToEnd();
        sr.Close();
        return fileText;
    }
    catch(Exception ex)
    {
        return ex.Message;
    }
}
```

All Try blocks require at least one nested Catch block. You can use the Catch block to catch all exceptions that may occur in the Try block, or you can use it to filter exceptions based on the type of exception. This enables you to dynamically respond to different exceptions based on the exception type. The following code demonstrates filtering exceptions based on the different exceptions that could occur when trying to read a text file from disk:

```
public string ReadText(string filePath)
{
    StreamReader sr;
    try
    {
        sr = File.OpenText(filePath);
        string fileText = sr.ReadToEnd();
        sr.Close();
        return fileText;
    }
    catch (DirectoryNotFoundException ex)
    {
        return ex.Message;
    }
    catch (FileNotFoundException ex)
    {
        return ex.Message;
    }
    catch(Exception ex)
    {
        return ex.Message;
    }
}
```

Adding a Finally Block

Additionally, you can nest a Finally block at the end of the Try block. Unlike the Catch block, the use of the Finally block is optional. The Finally block is for any cleanup code that needs to occur, even if an exception is encountered. For example, you may need to close a database connection or release a file. When the code of the Try block is executed and an exception occurs, processing will jump to the appropriate Catch block. After the Catch block executes, the Finally block will execute. If the Try block executes and no exception is encountered, the Catch blocks don't execute, but the Finally block will still get processed. The following code shows a Finally block being used to close and dispose a StreamReader:

```
public string ReadText(string filePath)
{
    StreamReader sr = null;
    try
    {
        sr = File.OpenText(filePath);
        string fileText = sr.ReadToEnd();
        return fileText;
    }
    catch (DirectoryNotFoundException ex)
    {
```

```
            return ex.Message;
        }
        catch (FileNotFoundException ex)
        {
            return ex.Message;
        }
        catch (Exception ex)
        {
            return ex.Message;
        }
        finally
        {
            if (sr != null)
            {
                sr.Close();
                sr.Dispose();
            }
        }
    }
```

Throwing Exceptions

During code execution, when an exception occurs that does not fit into one of the predefined system exception classes, you can throw your own exception. You normally throw your own exception when the error will not cause problems with execution but rather with the processing of your business rules. For example, you could look for an order date that is in the future and throw an ApplicationException. The ApplicationException class inherits from the System.Exception class. The following code shows an example of throwing an ApplicationException:

```
    public void LogOrder(long orderNumber, DateTime orderDate)
    {
        try
        {
            if (orderDate > DateTime.Now)
            {
                throw new ApplicationException("Order date can not be in the future.");
            }
            //Processing code...
        }
        catch(Exception ex)
        {
            //Exception handler code...
        }
    }
}
```

Nesting Exception Handling

In some cases, you may be able to correct an exception that occurred and continue processing the rest of the code in the Try block. For example, a division-by-zero error may occur, and it would be acceptable to assign the result a value of zero and continue processing. In this case, a Try-Catch block could be nested around the line of code that would cause the exception. After the exception is handled, processing would return to the line of code in the outer Try-Catch block immediately after the nested Try block. The following code demonstrates nesting one Try block within another:

```
try
{
    try
    {
        Y = X1 / X2;
    }
    catch (DivideByZeroException ex)
    {
        Y = 0;
    }
    //Rest of processing code.
}
catch (Exception ex)
{
    //Outer exception processing
}
```

Note For more information about handling exceptions and the .NET Framework exception classes, refer to Appendix B.

Static Properties and Methods

When you declare an object instance of a class, the object instantiates its own instances of the properties and methods of the class it implements. For example, if you were to write a counting routine that increments a counter, then instantiated two object instances of the class, the counters of each object would be independent of each other; when you incremented one counter, the other would not be affected. Normally, this object independence is the behavior you want. However, sometimes you may want different object instances of a class to access the same, shared variables. For example, you might want to build in a counter that logs how many of the object instances have been instantiated. In this case, you would create a static property value in the class definition. The following code demonstrates how you create a static TaxRate property in a class definition:

```
public class AccountingUtilities
{
    private static double _taxRate = 0.06;

    public static double TaxRate
    {
        get { return _taxRate; }
    }
}
```

To access the static property, you don't create an object instance of the class; instead, you refer to the class directly. The following code shows a client accessing the static TaxRate property defined previously:

```
public class Purchase
{
    public double CalculateTax(double purchasePrice)
    {
        return purchasePrice * AccountingUtilities.TaxRate;
    }
}
```

Static methods are useful if you have utility functions that clients need to access, but you don't want the overhead of creating an object instance of a class to gain access to the method. Note that static methods can access only static properties. The following code shows a static method used to count the number of users currently logged in to an application:

```
public class UserLog
{
    private static int _userCount;
    public static void IncrementUserCount()
    {
        _userCount += 1;
    }
    public static void DecrementUserCount()
    {
        _userCount -= 1;
    }
}
```

When client code accesses a static method, it does so by referencing the class directly. The following code demonstrates accessing the static method defined previously:

```
public class User
{
    //other code ...
    public void Login(string userName, string password)
    {
        //code to check credentials
        //if successful
        UserLog.IncrementUserCount();
    }
}
```

Although you may not use static properties and methods often when creating the classes in your applications, they are useful when creating base class libraries and are used throughout the .NET Framework system classes. The following code demonstrates the use of the Compare method of the System.String class. This is a static method that compares two strings alphabetically. It returns a positive value if the first string is greater, a negative value if the second string is greater, or zero if the strings are equal.

```
public Boolean CheckStringOrder(string string1, string string2)
{
    if (string.Compare(string1, string2) >= 0)
```

```
            {
                return true;
            }
            else
            {
                return false;
            }
        }
```

ACTIVITY 8-2. IMPLEMENTING EXCEPTION HANDLING AND STATIC METHODS

In this activity, you will learn how to do the following:

- Create and call static methods of a class.
- Use structured exception handling.

Creating Static Methods

To create the static methods, follow these steps:

1. Start Visual Studio. Select File ➤ New ➤ Project.
2. Choose a Windows Application project. Name the project Act8_2.
3. Visual Studio creates a default form for the project which you'll use to create a login form named Logger. Add controls to the form and change the property values, as listed in Table 8-2. Your completed form should look similar to Figure 8-4.

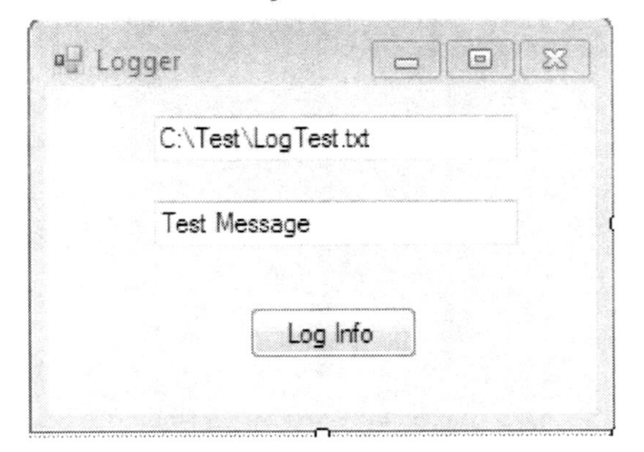

Figure 8-4. *The completed logger form*

Table 8-2. *Logger Form and Control Properties*

Object	Property	Value
Form1	Name	frmLogger
	Text	Logger
Textbox1	Name	txtLogPath
	Text	c:\Test\LogTest.txt
Textbox2	Name	txtLogInfo
	Text	Test Message
Button1	Name	btnLogInfo
	Text	Log Info

4. Select Project ➤ Add Class. Name the class Logger.
5. Because you will be using the System.IO class within the Logger class, add a using statement to the top of the file:

```
using System.IO;
```

6. Add as static LogWrite method to the class. This method will write information to a log file. To open the file, create a FileStream object. Then create a StreamWriter object to write the information to the file.

```
public static string LogWrite(string logPath, string logInfo)
{
    FileStream oFileStream = new FileStream(logPath, FileMode.Open, FileAccess.Write);
    StreamWriter oStreamWriter = new StreamWriter(oFileStream);
    oFileStream.Seek(0, SeekOrigin.End);
    oStreamWriter.WriteLine(DateTime.Now);
    oStreamWriter.WriteLine(logInfo);
    oStreamWriter.WriteLine();
    oStreamWriter.Close();
    return "Info Logged";
}
```

7. Open frmLogger in the visual design editor. Double click the btnLogInfo button to bring up the btnLogInfo_Click event method in the code editor. Add the following code, which runs the LogWrite method of the Logger class and displays the results in the form's text property. Note that because you designated the LogWrite method as static (in step 6), the client does not need to create an object instance of the Logger class. Static methods are accessed directly through a class reference.

```
private void btnLogInfo_Click(object sender, EventArgs e)
{
    this.Text = Logger.LogWrite(txtLogPath.Text, txtLogInfo.Text);
}
```

8. Select Build ➤ Build Solution. Make sure there are no build errors in the Error List window. If there are, fix them, and then rebuild.

9. Select Debug ➤ Run. When the form launches, click the Log Info button. You should get an unhandled exception message of type System.IO.FileNotFoundException. Stop the debugger.

Creating the Structured Exception Handler

To create the structured exception handler, follow these steps:

1. Open the Logger class code in the code editor.
2. Locate the LogWrite method and add a Try-Catch block around the current code. In the Catch block, return a string stating the logging failed.

```
try
{
    FileStream oFileStream =
        new FileStream(logPath, FileMode.Open, FileAccess.Write);
    StreamWriter oStreamWriter = new StreamWriter(oFileStream);
    oFileStream.Seek(0, SeekOrigin.End);
    oStreamWriter.WriteLine(DateTime.Now);
    oStreamWriter.WriteLine(logInfo);
    oStreamWriter.WriteLine();
    oStreamWriter.Close();
    return "Info Logged";
}
catch
{
    return "Logging Failed";
}
```

3. Select Build ➤ Build Solution. Make sure there are no build errors in the Error List window. If there are, fix them, and then rebuild.
4. Select Debug ➤ Run. When the form launches, click the Log Info button. This time, you should not get the exception message because it was handled by the LogWrite method. You should see the message "Logging Failed" in the form's caption. Close the form.

Filtering Exceptions

To filter exceptions, follow these steps:

1. Alter the Catch block to return different messages depending on which exception is thrown.

```
catch (FileNotFoundException ex)
{
    return ex.Message;
}
catch (IOException ex)
{
    return ex.Message;
}
catch
{
    return "Logging Failed";
}
```

2. Select Build ➤ Build Solution. Make sure there are no build errors in the Error List window. If there are, fix them, and then rebuild.
3. Select Debug ➤ Start to run the project. Test the FileNotFoundException catch by clicking the Log Info button. Test the IOException by changing the file path to the A drive and clicking the Log Info button. These errors should be caught and the appropriate message presented in the form's caption.
4. After testing, close the form.
5. Using Notepad, create the LogTest.txt file in a Test folder on the C drive and close the file. Make sure the file and folder are not marked as read only.
6. Select Debug ➤ Start to run the project. Test the WriteLog method by clicking the Log Info button. This time, the form's caption should indicate that the log write was successful.
7. Stop the debugger.
8. Open the LogTest.txt file using Notepad and verify that the information was logged.
9. Save the project, and then exit Visual Studio.

Using Asynchronous Messaging

When objects interact by passing messages back and forth, they can pass the message synchronously or asynchronously.

When a client object makes a synchronous message call to a server object, the client suspends processing and waits for a response back from the server before continuing. Synchronous messaging is the easiest to implement and is the default type of messaging implemented in the .NET Framework. However, sometimes this is an inefficient way of passing messages. For example, the synchronous messaging model is not well suited for long-running file reading and writing, making service calls across slow networks, or message queuing in disconnected client scenarios. To more effectively handle these types of situations, the .NET Framework provides the plumbing needed to pass messages between objects asynchronously.

When a client object passes a message asynchronously, the client can continue processing. After the server completes the message request, the response information will be sent back to the client.

If you think about it, you interact with objects in the real world both synchronously and asynchronously. A good example of synchronous messaging is when you are in the checkout line at the grocery store. When the clerk can't determine the price of one of the items, he calls the manager for a price check and suspends the checkout process until a result is returned. An example of an asynchronous message call is when the clerk notices that he is running low on change. He alerts the manager that he will need change soon, but he can continue to process his customer's items until the change arrives.

In the .NET Framework, when you want to call a method of the server object asynchronously, you first need to create a delegate. Instead of making the call directly to the server, the call is passed to the delegate. When a delegate is created, the compiler also creates two methods you can use to interact with a server class asynchronously. These methods are called BeginInvoke and EndInvoke.

The BeginInvoke method takes the parameters defined by the delegate plus an AsyncCallback delegate. The delegate is used to pass a callback method that the server will call to return information to the client when the asynchronous method completes. Another parameter that can be sent in the BeginInvoke method is a context object that the client can use to keep track of the context of the asynchronous call. When the client calls the BeginInvoke method, it returns a reference to an object that implements the IAsynchResult interface. The BeginInvoke method also starts the execution of the asynchronous method call on a different thread from the main thread used by the client when initiating the call.

The EndInvoke method takes the parameters and the IAsyncResult object returned by the BeginInvoke method and blocks the thread used by the BeginInvoke method until a result is returned. When the results are returned by the asynchronous method, the EndInvoke method intercepts the results and passes them back to the client thread that initiated the call.

■ **Note** The method of the server class is not altered to enable a client to call its methods asynchronously. It is up to the client to decide whether to call the server asynchronously and implement the functionality required to make the call.

The following code demonstrates the process to make a call to a server method asynchronously. In this example, the client code is making a call to a server method over a slow connection to read log information. The first step is to define a delegate type that will be used to make the call.

```
private delegate string AsyncReadLog(string filePath);
```

The next step is to declare a variable of the delegate type and instantiate it, passing in the method you are calling asynchronously.

```
private AsyncReadLog LogReader = new AsyncReadLog(Logger.LogRead);
```

■ **Note** Because the LogRead method of the Logger class is a static method, you call it directly.

You then declare a variable of type AsyncCallback and instantiate it, passing in the method that you have set up to process the results of the asynchronous call.

```
AsyncCallback aCallBack = new AsyncCallback(LogReadCallBack);
```

You are now ready to call the server method asynchronously by implementing the BeginInvoke method of the delegate type. You need to declare a variable of type IAsyncResult to capture the return value and pass the parameters required by the server method and a reference to the AsyncCallback object declared previously.

```
IAsyncResult aResult = LogReader.BeginInvoke(txtLogPath.Text, aCallBack,null);
```

You can now implement the callback method in the client, which needs to accept an input parameter of type IAsyncCallback that will be passed to it. Inside this method, you will make a call to the delegate's EndInvoke method. This method takes the IAsyncCallback object type returned by the BeginInvoke method. The following code displays the results of the call in a message box:

```
public void LogReadCallBack(IAsyncResult asyncResult)
{
    MessageBox.Show(LogReader.EndInvoke(asyncResult));
}
```

■ **Note** You can also use the BackgroundWorker component to call methods using a thread separate from the UI thread. For more information about using the BackgroundWorker thread, consult the Visual Studio help files.

ACTIVITY 8-3. CALLING METHODS ASYNCHRONOUSLY

In this activity, you will learn how to do the following:

- Call methods synchronously.
- Call methods asynchronously.

Creating a Method and Calling It Synchronously

To create the method and call it synchronously, follow these steps:

1. Start Visual Studio. Select File ➤ Open ➤ Project.
2. Open the solution file you completed in Act8_2.
3. Add the buttons shown in Table 8-3 to the frmLogger form. Figure 8-5 shows the completed form.

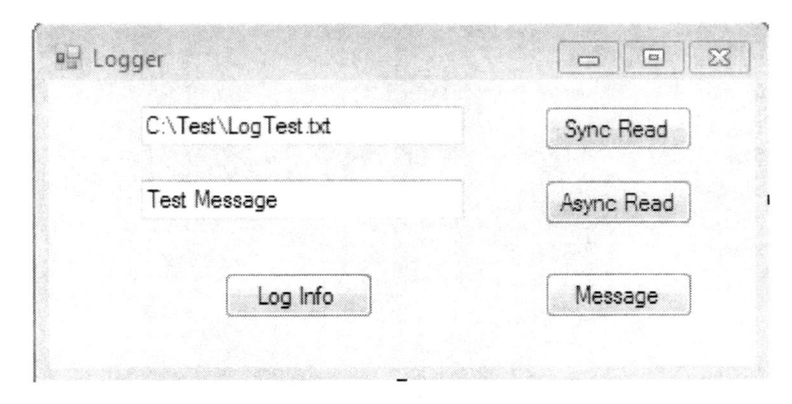

Figure 8-5. *The completed logger form for synchronous and asynchronous reading*

Table 8-3. *Additional Buttons for the Logger Form*

Object	Property	Value
Button1	Name	btnSyncRead
	Text	Sync Read
Button2	Name	btnAsyncRead
	Text	Async Read
Button3	Name	btnMessage
	Text	Message

4. Open the Logger class in the code editor.
5. Recall that because you are using the System.IO namespace within the Logger class, you added a using statement to the top of the file. You are also going to use System.Threading namespace, so add a using statement to include this namespace.

```
using System.Threading;
```

6. Add a static LogRead function to the class. This function will read information from a log file. To open the file, create a FileStream object. Then create StreamReader object to read the information from the file. You are also using the Thread class to suspend processing for five seconds to simulate a long call across a slow network.

```
public static string LogRead(string filePath)
{
    StreamReader oStreamReader;
    string fileText;
```

```
        try
        {
            oStreamReader = File.OpenText(filePath);
            fileText = oStreamReader.ReadToEnd();
            oStreamReader.Close();
            Thread.Sleep(5000);
            return fileText;
        }
        catch (FileNotFoundException ex)
        {
            return ex.Message;
        }
        catch (IOException ex)
        {
            return ex.Message;
        }
        catch
        {
            return "Logging Failed";
        }
    }
```

7. Open frmLogger in the visual design editor. Double click the btnMessage button to bring up the btnMessage_Click event method in the code editor. Add code to display a message box.

```
private void btnMessage_Click(object sender, EventArgs e)
{
    MessageBox.Show("Hello");
}
```

8. Open frmLogger in the visual design editor. Double-click the btnSyncRead button to bring up the btnSyncRead_Click event method in the code editor. Add code that calls the LogRead method of the Logger class and displays the results in a message box.

```
private void btnSyncRead_Click(object sender, EventArgs e)
{
   MessageBox.Show(Logger.LogRead(txtLogPath.Text));
}
```

9. Select Build ➤ Build Solution. Make sure there are no build errors in the Error List window. If there are, fix them, and then rebuild.

10. Select Debug ➤ Run. When the form launches, click the Sync Read button. After clicking the Sync Read button, try clicking the Message button. You should not get a response when clicking the Message button because you called the ReadLog method synchronously. After the ReadLog method returns a result, the Message button will respond when clicked.

11. When you have finished testing, close the form.

Calling a Method Asynchronously

To call a method asynchronously, follow these steps:

1. Open the frmLogger class code in the code editor.
2. After the class definition statement at the beginning of the class file, add code to create a delegate definition that will be used to make the asynchronous call. On the next line, declare a LogReader variable of the delegate type and instantiate it, passing the LogRead method of the Logger class.

```
public partial class frmLogger : Form
{
    private delegate string AsyncReadLog(string filePath);
    private AsyncReadLog LogReader = new AsyncReadLog(Logger.LogRead);
```

3. Create a callback method that will be used to retrieve the results of the asynchronous message call. This method needs to accept a parameter of type IAsyncResult.

```
public void LogReadCallBack(IAsyncResult asyncResult)
{
}
```

4. Open frmLogger in the visual design editor. Double-click the btnAsyncRead button to bring up the btnAsyncRead_Click event method in the code editor. Add code that declares a variable of type AsyncCallback and instantiate it, passing in the LogReadCallBack method you created. On the next line of code, call the BeginInvoke method of the LogReader delegate, passing in the file path and the AsyncCallback variable. Capture the return value in a variable of type IAsyncResult.

```
private void btnAsyncRead_Click(object sender, EventArgs e)
{
    AsyncCallback aCallBack = new AsyncCallback(LogReadCallBack);
    IAsyncResult aResult = LogReader.BeginInvoke(txtLogPath.Text,
aCallBack,null);
}
```

5. Add code to the LogReadCallBack method that calls the EndInvoke method of the LogReader delegate, passing in the file path and the IAsyncResult parameter. Display the results in a message box.

```
public void LogReadCallBack(IAsyncResult asyncResult)
{
    MessageBox.Show(LogReader.EndInvoke(asyncResult));
}
```

6. Select Build ➤ Build Solution. Make sure there are no build errors in the Error List window. If there are, fix them, and then rebuild.
7. Select Debug ➤ Run. When the form launches, click the Async Read button. After clicking the Async Read button, click the Message button. This time, you should get

a response because you called the ReadLog method asynchronously. After five seconds you should see a message box containing the results of the Logger.LogRead method.

8. When you have finished testing, close the form.
9. Save the project, and then exit Visual Studio.

Summary

This chapter described how the objects in your applications collaborate. You saw how objects pass messages to one another, how events drive your programs, how instances of a class share data, and how to handle exceptions.

In the next chapter, you will look at collections and arrays. Collections and arrays organize similar objects into a group. Working with collections is one of the most common programming constructs you will need to apply in your applications. You will examine some of the basic types of collections available in the NET Framework and learn how to employ collections in your code.

CHAPTER 9

Working with Collections

In the previous chapter, you looked at how objects collaborate and communicate in object-oriented programs. That chapter introduced the concepts of messaging, events, delegation, exception handling, and asynchronous programming. In this chapter, you will look at how collections of objects are organized and processed. The .NET Framework contains an extensive set of classes and interfaces for creating and managing collections of objects. You will look at the various types of collection structures .NET provides and learn what they are designed for and when to use each. You will also look at how to use generics to create highly reusable, efficient collections.

In this chapter, you will learn the following:

- The various types of collections exposed by the .NET Framework.
- How to work with arrays and array lists.
- How to create generic collections.
- How to implement queues and stacks.

Introducing the .NET Framework Collection Types

Programmers frequently need to work with collections of types. For example, if you are working with employee time records in a payroll system, you need to group the records by employee, loop through the records, and add up the hours for each.

All collections need a basic set of functionality, such as adding objects, removing objects, and iterating through their objects. In addition to the basic set, some collections need additional specialized functionality. For example, a collection of help desk e-mail requests needs to implement a first-in, first-out functionality when adding and removing items from the collection.

The .NET Framework provides a variety of basic and specialized collection classes for you to use. The System.Collections namespace contains interfaces and classes that define various types of collections, such as lists, queues, hash tables, and dictionaries. Table 9-1 lists and describes some of the commonly used collection classes. If you do not find a collection class with the functionality you need, you can extend a .NET Framework class to create your own.

Table 9-1. *Commonly Used Collection Classes*

Class	Description
Array	Provides the base class for language implementations that support strongly typed arrays.
ArrayList	Represents a weakly typed list of objects using an array whose size is dynamically increased as required.
SortedList	Represents a collection of key/value pairs that are sorted by the keys and are accessible by key and by index.
Queue	Represents a first-in, first-out (FIFO) collection of objects.
Stack	Represents a simple last-in, first-out (LIFO), nongeneric collection of objects.
Hashtable	Represents a collection of key/value pairs that are organized based on the hash code of the key.
CollectionBase	Provides the abstract base class for a strongly typed collection.
DictionaryBase	Provides the abstract base class for a strongly typed collection of key/value pairs.

Table 9-2 describes some of the interfaces implemented by these collection classes.

Table 9-2. *Collection Class Interfaces*

Interface	Description
ICollection	Defines size, enumerators, and synchronization methods for all nongeneric collections.
IComparer	Exposes a method that compares two objects.
IDictionary	Represents a nongeneric collection of key/value pairs.
IDictionaryEnumerator	Enumerates the elements of a nongeneric dictionary.
IEnumerable	Exposes the enumerator, which supports a simple iteration over a nongeneric collection.
IEnumerator	Supports a simple iteration over a nongeneric collection.
IList	Represents a nongeneric collection of objects that can be individually accessed by index.

In this chapter, you will work with some of the commonly used collection classes, beginning with the Array and ArrayList classes.

Working with Arrays and Array Lists

An array is one of the most common data structures in computer programming. An array holds data elements of the same data type. For example, you can create an array of integers, strings, or dates. Arrays are often used to pass values to methods as parameters. For example, when you use a Console application, it's common to provide command line switches. The following DOS command is used to copy a file on your computer:

```
copy win.ini c:\windows /y
```

The source file, destination path, and overwrite indicator are passed into the copy program as an array of strings.

You access the elements of an array through its index. The index is an integer representing the position of the element in the array. For example, an array of strings representing the days of the week has the following index values:

Index	Value
0	Sunday
1	Monday
2	Tuesday
3	Wednesday
4	Thursday
5	Friday
6	Saturday

This days-of-the-week example is a one-dimensional array, which means the index is represented by a single integer. Arrays can also be multidimensional. The index of an element of a multidimensional array is a set of integers equal to the number of dimensions. Figure 9-1 shows a seating chart that represents a two-dimensional array where the student's name (value) is referenced by the ordered pair of row number, seat number (index).

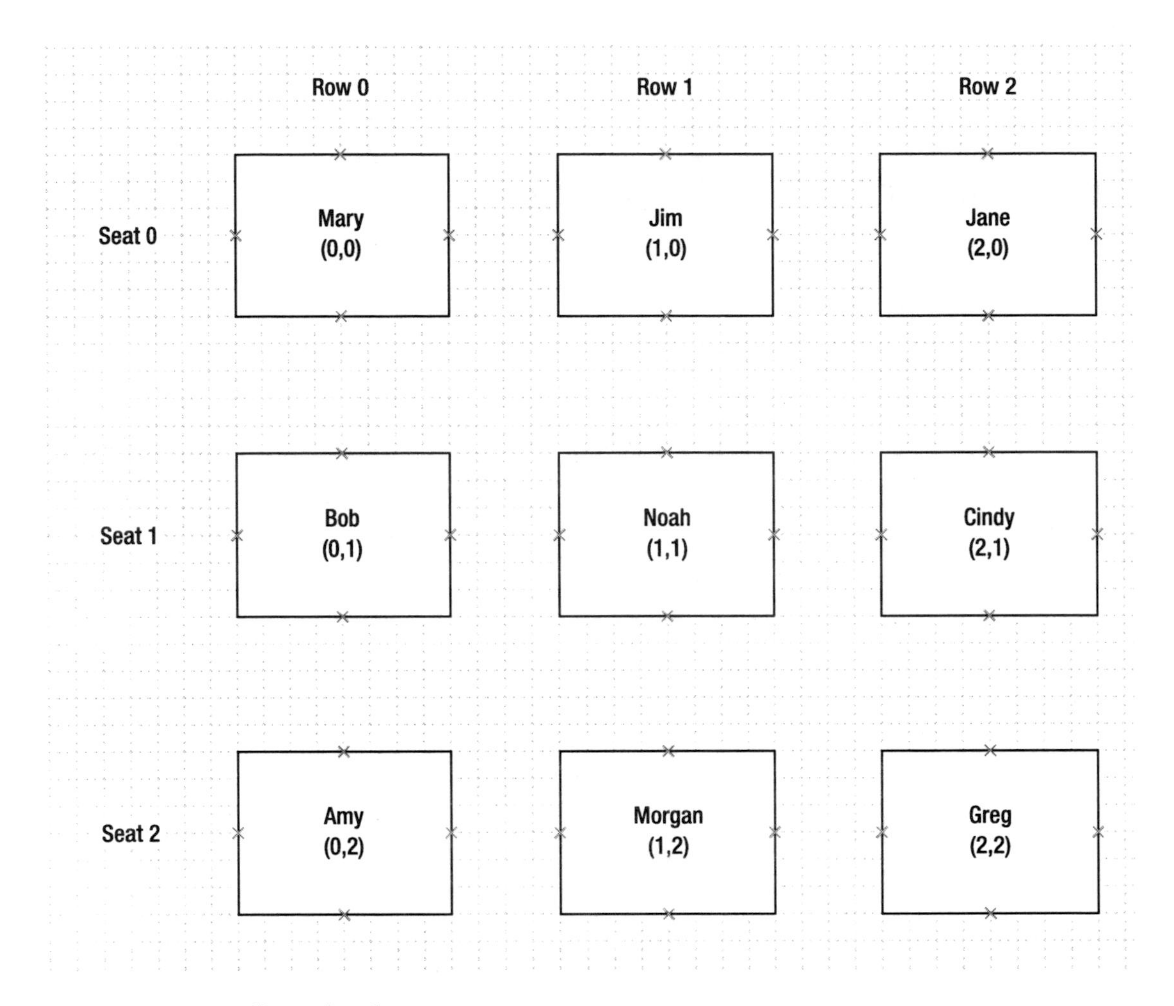

Figure 9-1. *A two-dimensional array*

You implement array functionality when you declare its type. The common types implemented as arrays are numeric types such as integers or double types, as well as the character and string types. When declaring a type as an array, you use square brackets ([ ]) after the type, followed by the name of the array. The elements of the array are designated by a comma separated list enclosed by curly brackets ({}). For example, the following code declares an array of type Integer and fills it with five values:

```
int[] intArray = { 1, 2, 3, 4, 5 };
```

Once a type is declared as an array, the properties and methods of the Array class are exposed. Some of the functionality includes querying for the upper and lower bounds of the array, updating the elements of the array, and copying the elements of the array. The Array class contains many static methods used to work with arrays, such as methods for clearing, reversing, and sorting its elements.

The following code demonstrates declaring and working with an array of integers. It also uses several static methods exposed by the Array class. Notice the foreach loop used to list the values of the array. The foreach loop provides a way to iterate through the elements of the array. Figure 9-2 shows the output of this code in the Console window.

```
int[] intArray = { 1, 2, 3, 4, 5 };
Console.WriteLine("Upper Bound");
Console.WriteLine(intArray.GetUpperBound(0));
Console.WriteLine("Array elements");
foreach (int item in intArray)
{
    Console.WriteLine(item);
}
Array.Reverse(intArray);
Console.WriteLine("Array reversed");
foreach (int item in intArray)
{
    Console.WriteLine(item);
}
Array.Clear(intArray, 2, 2);
Console.WriteLine("Elements 2 and 3 cleared");
foreach (int item in intArray)
{
    Console.WriteLine(item);
}
intArray[4] = 9;
Console.WriteLine("Element 4 reset");
foreach (int item in intArray)
{
    Console.WriteLine(item);
}
Console.ReadLine();
```

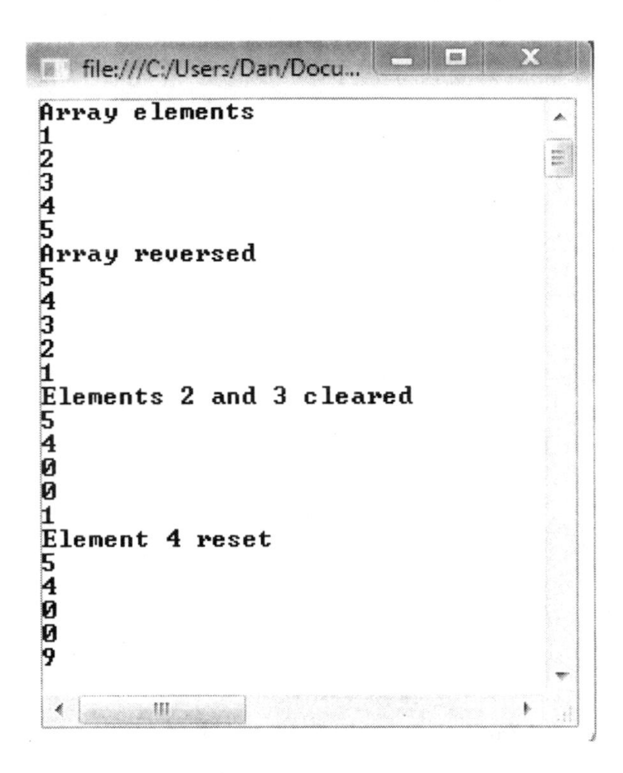

Figure 9-2. *One-dimensional array output*

Although one-dimensional arrays are the most common type you will run into, you should understand how to work with the occasional multidimensional array. Two-dimensional arrays are used to store (in active memory) and process data that fits in the rows and columns of a table. For example, you may need to process a series of measurements (temperature or radiation level) taken at hourly intervals over several days. To create a multidimensional array, you place one or more commas inside the square brackets to indicate the number of dimensions. One comma indicates two dimensions; two commas indicate three dimensions, and so forth. When filling a multidemensional array, curly brackets within curly brackets define the elements. The following code declares and fills a two-dimensional array:

```
int[,] twoDArray = { { 1, 2 }, { 3, 4 }, { 5, 6 } };
//Print the index and value of the elements
for (int i = 0; i <= twoDArray.GetUpperBound(0); i++)
{
     for (int x = 0; x <= twoDArray.GetUpperBound(1); x++)
     {
          Console.WriteLine("Index = [{0},{1}]  Value = {2}", i, x, twoDArray[i, x]);
     }
}
```

Figure 9-3 shows the output of this code in the Console window.

```
file:///C:/Users/Dan/Documents/...
Index = [0,0]  Value = 1
Index = [0,1]  Value = 2
Index = [1,0]  Value = 3
Index = [1,1]  Value = 4
Index = [2,0]  Value = 5
Index = [2,1]  Value = 6
```

Figure 9-3. *Two-dimensional array output*

When you work with collections, you often do not know the number of items it contains until runtime. This is where the ArrayList class fits in. The capacity of an array list automatically expands as required, with the memory reallocation and copying of elements performed automatically. The ArrayList class also provides methods and properties for working with the array elements that the Array class does not provide. The following code demonstrates some of these properties and methods. Notice that the capacity of the list expands dynamically as more names are added.

```
ArrayList nameList = new ArrayList();
nameList.Add("Bob");
nameList.Add("Dan");
nameList.Add("Wendy");
Console.WriteLine("Original Capacity");
Console.WriteLine(nameList.Capacity);
Console.WriteLine("Original Values");
foreach (object name in nameList)
{
    Console.WriteLine(name);
}

nameList.Insert(nameList.IndexOf("Dan"), "Cindy");
nameList.Insert(nameList.IndexOf("Wendy"), "Jim");
Console.WriteLine("New Capacity");
Console.WriteLine(nameList.Capacity);
Console.WriteLine("New Values");
foreach (object name in nameList)
{
    Console.WriteLine(name);
}
```

Figure 9-4 shows the output in the Console window.

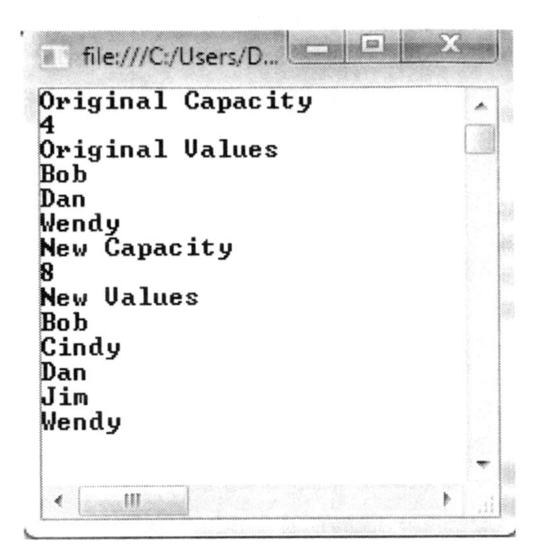

Figure 9-4. *The ArrayList output*

Although it's often easier to work with an ArrayList than with an Array, an ArrayList can have only one dimension. Also, an Array of a specific type offers better performance than an ArrayList, because the elements of ArrayList are of type Object. When types are added to the ArrayList, they are cast to a generic Object type. When the items are retrieved from the list, they must be cast once again to the specific type.

ACTIVITY 9-1. WORKING WITH ARRAYS AND ARRAYLISTS

In this activity, you will become familiar with the following:

- Creating and using arrays.
- Working with multidimensional arrays.
- Working with array lists.

Creating and Using Arrays

To create and populate an array, follow these steps:

1. Start Visual Studio. Select File ➤ New ➤ Project.
2. Choose a Console application project. Name the project Act9_1. The Console application contains a class called Program with a Main method. The Main method is the first method that is accessed when the application is launched.
3. Notice that the Main method accepts an input parameter of a string array called args. The args array contains any command line args passed in when the Console

application is launched. The members of the args array are separated by a space when passed in.

```
static void Main(string[] args)
{
}
```

4. Add the following code to the Main method to display the command line arguments passed in:

```
Console.WriteLine("parameter count = {0}", args.Length);

for (int i = 0; i < args.Length; i++)
{
    Console.WriteLine("Arg[{0}] = [{1}]", i, args[i]);
}
Console.ReadLine();
```

5. In Solution Explorer, right-click the project node and choose Project. In the project properties window, select the Debug tab. In the command line arguments field, enter "C# coding is fun" (see Figure 9-5).

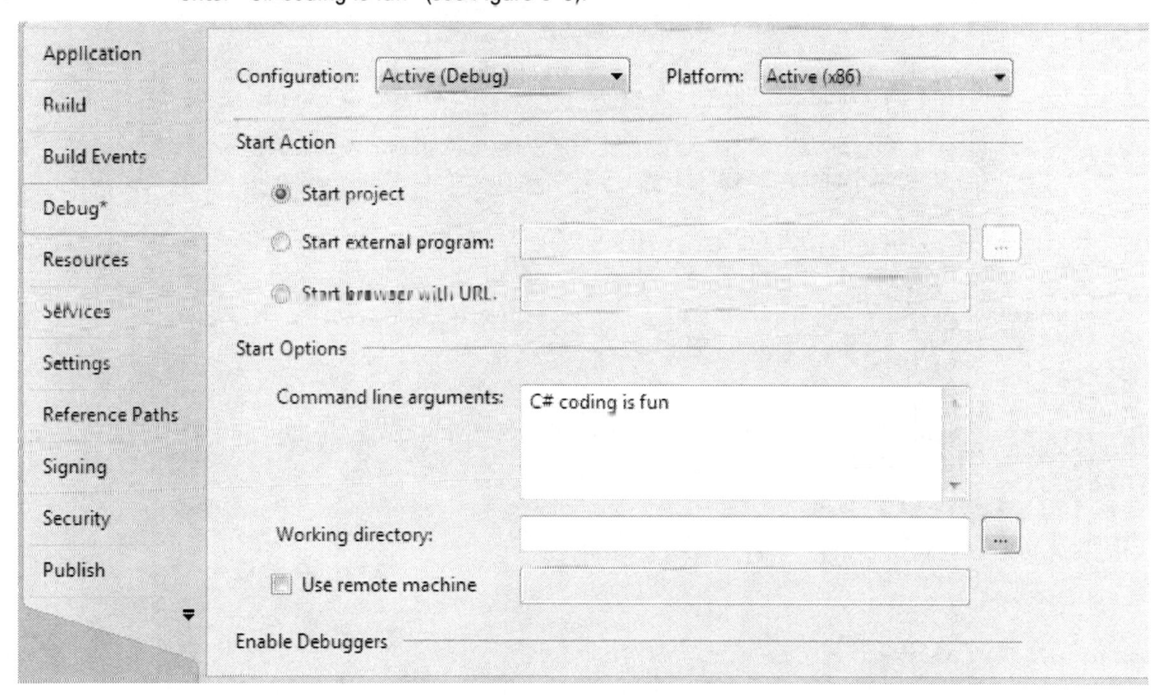

Figure 9-5. *Adding comand line arguments*

6. Select Debug ➤ Start to run the project. The Console window should launch with the output shown in Figure 9-6. After viewing the output, stop the debugger.

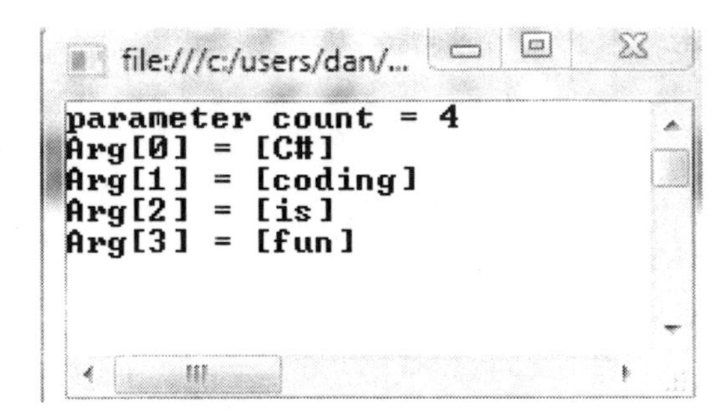

Figure 9-6. *The Console output for the array*

7. Add the following code before the Console.ReadLine() method in the Main method. This code clears the value of the array at index 1 and sets the value at index 3 to "great".

```
Array.Clear(args, 1, 1);
args[3] = "great";
for (int i = 0; i < args.Length; i++)
{
    Console.WriteLine("Arg[{0}] = [{1}]", i, args[i]);
}
```

8. Select Debug ➤ Start to run the project. The Console window should launch with the additional output shown in Figure 9-7. After viewing the output, stop the debugger.

Figure 9-7. *The Console output for the updated array*

Working with Multidimensional Arrays

To create and populate a multidimensional array, follow these steps:

1. Comment out the code in the Main method.
2. Add the following code to the Main method to create and populate a two-dimensional array:

```
string[,] seatingChart = new string[2,2];
seatingChart[0, 0] = "Mary";
seatingChart[0, 1] = "Jim";
seatingChart[1, 0] = "Bob";
seatingChart[1, 1] = "Jane";
```

3. Add the following code to loop through the array and print the names to the Console window:

```
for (int row = 0; row < 2; row++)
{
    for (int seat = 0; seat < 2; seat++)
    {
        Console.WriteLine("Row: {0} Seat: {1} Student: {2}",
            (row + 1),(seat + 1),seatingChart[row, seat]);
    }
}
Console.ReadLine();
```

4. Select Debug ➤ Start to run the project. The Console window should launch with the output that shows the seating chart of the students (see Figure 9-8).

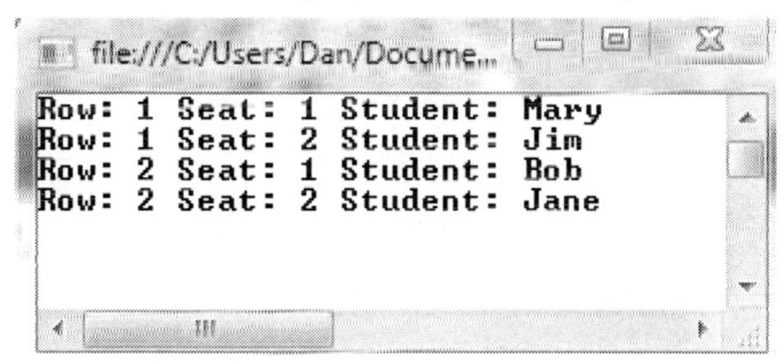

Figure 9-8. *The Console output for the two-dimensional array*

5. After viewing the output, stop the debugger.

Working with ArrayLists

Although the two dimensional array you just created works, it may be more intuitive to store the information about each student's seating assignment in a seating assignment class and then to organize these objects into an ArrayList structure. To create and populate an array list of seating assignments, follow these steps:

1. Add a class file to the project named SeatingAssignment.cs.
2. Add the following code to create the SeatingAssignment class. This class contains a Row, Seat, and Student property. It also contains an overloaded constructor to set these properties.

```
public class SeatingAssignment
{
    int _row;
    int _seat;
    string _student;
    public int Row
    {
        get { return _row; }
        set { _row = value; }
    }
    public int Seat
    {
        get { return _seat; }
        set { _seat = value; }
    }
    public string Student
    {
        get { return _student; }
        set { _student = value; }
    }
   public SeatingAssignment(int row, int seat, string student)
    {
        this.Row = row;
        this.Seat = seat;
        this.Student = student;
    }
}
```

3. In the Main method of the Program class, comment out the previous code.
4. Add the following code to create an ArrayList of SeatingAssignments:

```
ArrayList seatingChart = new ArrayList();
seatingChart.Add(new SeatingAssignment(0, 0, "Mary"));
seatingChart.Add(new SeatingAssignment(0, 1, "Jim"));
seatingChart.Add(new SeatingAssignment(1, 0, "Bob"));
seatingChart.Add(new SeatingAssignment(1, 1, "Jane"));
After the ArrayList is populated, add the following code to write the SeatingAssignment
information to the console window.
foreach (SeatingAssignment sa in seatingChart)
{
    Console.WriteLine("Row: {0} Seat: {1} Student: {2}",
        (sa.Row + 1), (sa.Seat + 1), sa.Student);
}
Console.ReadLine();
```

5. Select Debug ➤ Start to run the project. The Console window should launch with the same output as shown in Figure 9-8 (the seating chart of the students).
6. One of the advantages of the ArrayList class is the ability to add and remove items dynamically. Add the following code after the code in step 4 to add two more students to the seating chart:

```
seatingChart.Add(new SeatingAssignment(2, 0, "Bill"));
seatingChart.Add(new SeatingAssignment(2, 1, "Judy"));
```

7. Select Debug ➤ Start to run the project. The Console window should launch with the output showing the new students.
8. When finished, stop the debugger, and close Visual Studio.

Using Generic Collections

Working with collections is a common requirement of application programming. Most of the data we work with needs to be organized in a collection. For example, you may need to retrieve customers from a database and load them into a drop-down list in the UI (User Interface). The customer information is represented by a customer class, and the customers are organized into a customer collection. The collection can then be sorted, filtered, and looped through for processing.

With the exception of a few of the specialized collections strongly typed to hold strings, the collections provided by the .NET Framework are weakly typed. The items held by the collections are of type Object, and so they can be of any type, since all types derive from the Object type.

Weakly typed collections can cause performance and maintenance problems for your application. One problem is there are no inherent safeguards for limiting the types of objects stored in the collection. The same collection can hold any type of item, including dates, integers, or a custom type such as an employee object. If you build and expose a collection of integers, and that collection inadvertently gets passed a date, the chances are high that the code will fail at some point.

Fortunately, C# supports generics, and the .NET Framework provides generic-based collections in the System.Collections.Generic namespace. Generics let you define a class without specifying its type. The type is specified when the class is instantiated. Using a generic collection provides the advantages of type safety and the performance of a strongly typed collection while also providing the code reuse associated with weakly typed collections.

The following code shows how to create a strongly typed collection of Customers using the Generic.List class. The list type (in this case, Customer) is placed between the angle brackets (<>). Customer objects are added to the collection, and then the Customers in the collection are retrieved, and the Customer information is written out to the Console. (You will look at binding collections to UI controls in Chapter 11.)

```
List<Customer> customerList = new List<Customer>();
customerList.Add(new Customer
    ("WHITC", "White Clover Markets", "Karl Jablonski"));
customerList.Add(new Customer("RANCH", "Rancho grande", "Sergio Gutiérrez"));
customerList.Add(new Customer("ALFKI","Alfreds Futterkiste","Maria Anders"));
customerList.Add
    (new Customer("FRANR", "France restauration", "Carine Schmitt"));
```

```
foreach (Customer c in customerList)
{
    Console.WriteLine("Id: {0} Company: {1} Contact: {2}",
                    c.CompanyId, c.CompanyName, c.ContactName);
}
```

There may be times when you need to extend the functionality of the collection provided by the .NET Framework. For example, you may need the ability to sort the collection of Customers by either the CompanyId or the CompanyName. To implement sorting, you need to define a sorting class that implements the IComparer interface. The IComparer interface ensures the sorting class implements a Compare method with the appropriate signature. (Interfaces were covered in Chapter 7.) The CustomerSorter class shown next sorts a list of `Customer` by `CompanyName`. Note that since the CompanyName property is a string, you can use the String Comparer to sort them.

```
public class CustomerSorter : IComparer<Customer>
{
    public int Compare(Customer customer1, Customer customer2)
    {
        return customer1.CompanyName.CompareTo(customer2.CompanyName);
    }
}
```

Now you can sort the Customers by CompanyName and then display them.

```
customerList.Sort(new CustomerSorter());
```

The output is shown in Figure 9-9.

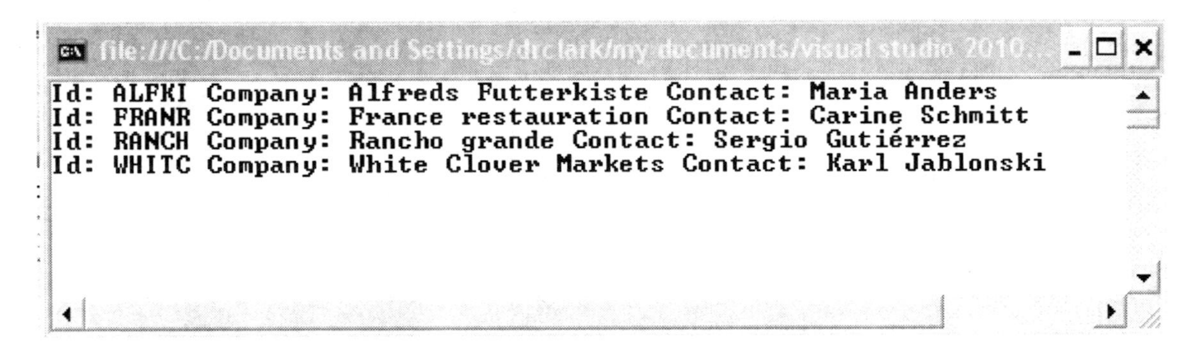

Figure 9-9. *The Console output for the sorted list of* `Customer`

ACTIVITY 9-2. IMPLEMENTING AND EXTENDING GENERIC COLLECTIONS

In this activity, you will become familiar with the following:

- Implementing a generic collection.
- Extending a generic collection to implement sorting.

To create and populate a generic list, follow these steps:

1. Start Visual Studio. Select File ➤ New ➤ Project.
2. Choose a Console Application project. Name the project Act9_2.
3. Select Project ➤ Add Class. Name the class Request.
4. Add the following properties to the Request class:

```
public class Request
 {
     string _requestor;
     int _priority;
     DateTime _date;
     public string Requestor
     {
         get { return _requestor; }
         set { _requestor = value; }
     }
     public int Priority
     {
         get { return _priority; }
         set { _priority = value; }
     }
     public DateTime Date
     {
         get { return _date; }
         set { _date = value; }
     }
```

5. Overload the constructor of the Request class to set the properties in the constructor.

```
public Request(string requestor, int priority, DateTime date)
{
    this.Requestor = requestor;
    this.Priority = priority;
    this.Date = date;
}
```

6. Add a method to override the ToString() method of the base Object class. This will return the request information as a string when the method is called.

```
public override string  ToString()
```

```
{
    return String.Format("{0}, {1}, {2}",this.Requestor,
       this.Priority.ToString(), this.Date);
}
```

7. Open the Program class in the code editor and add the following code to the Main method. This code populates a generic list of type Request and displays the values in the Console window.

```
static void Main(string[] args)
{
    List<Request> reqList = new List<Request>();
    reqList.Add(new Request("Dan",2 ,new DateTime(2011,4,2)));
    reqList.Add(new Request("Alice", 5, new DateTime(2011, 2, 5)));
    reqList.Add(new Request("Bill", 3, new DateTime(2011, 6, 19)));
    foreach (Request req in reqList)
    {
        Console.WriteLine(req.ToString());
    }
    Console.ReadLine();
}
```

8. Select Debug ➤ Start to run the project. The Console window should launch with the request items listed in the order they were added to the reqList.

9. Select Project ➤ Add Class. Name the class DateSorter.

10. Add the following code to the DateSorter class. This class implements the IComparer interface and is used to enable sorting Requests by date.

```
public class DateSorter:IComparer<Request>
 {
    public int Compare(Request R1, Request R2)
    {
        return R1.Date.CompareTo(R2.Date);
    }
 }
```

11. Add the following code in the Main method of the Program class prior to the. Console.WriteLine method. This code sorts the reqList by date and displays the values in the Console window.

```
Console.WriteLine("Sorted by date.");
reqList.Sort(new DateSorter());
foreach (Request req in reqList)
{
    Console.WriteLine(req.ToString());
}
Console.ReadLine();
```

12. Select Debug ➤ Start to run the project. The Console window should launch with the output shown in Figure 9-10. After viewing the output, stop the debugger and exit Visual Studio.

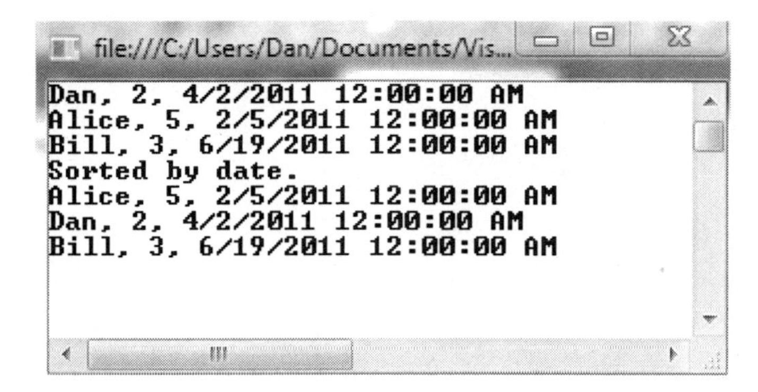

Figure 9-10. *Generic collection unsorted and sorted by date*

Programming with Stacks and Queues

Two special types of collections often used in programming are the stack and the queue. A stack is a last-in, first-out collection of objects. A queue represents a first-in, first-out collection of objects.

A stack is a good way to maintain a list of moves made in a chess game. When a user wants to undo his moves , he begins with his most recent move, which is the last one added to the list and also the first one retrieved . Another example of using a stack occurs when a program executes a series of method calls. A stack maintains the addresses of the methods, and execution returns to the methods in the reverse order in which they were called. When placing items in a stack, you use the push method. The pop method removes items from the stack. The peek method returns the object at the top of the stack without removing it. The following code demonstrates adding and removing items from a stack. In this case, you're using generics to implement a stack of ChessMove objects. The RecordMove method adds the most recent move to the stack. The GetLastMove method returns the most recent move on the stack.

```
Stack<ChessMove> moveStack = new Stack<ChessMove>();
void RecordMove(ChessMove move)
{
    moveStack.Push(move);
}
ChessMove GetLastMove()
{
    return moveStack.Pop();
}
```

An application that services help desk requests is a good example of when to use a queue. A collection maintains a list of help desk requests sent to the application. When requests are retrieved from the collection for processing, the first ones in should be the first ones retrieved. The Queue class uses the enqueue and dequeue methods to add and remove items. It also implements the peek method to return the item at the beginning of the queue without removing the item. The following code demonstrates adding and removing items from a PaymentRequest queue. The AddRequest method adds a request to the queue and the GetNextRequest method removes a request from the queue.

```
Queue<PaymentRequest> payRequest = new Queue<PaymentRequest>();
void AddRequest(PaymentRequest request)
{
    payRequest.Enqueue(request);
}
PaymentRequest GetNextRequest()
{
    return payRequest.Dequeue();
}
```

Summary

In this chapter, you examined the various types of collections exposed by the .NET Framework. You learned how to work with arrays, array lists, queues, stacks, and generic collections.

This chapter is the final one in a series that introduced you to the various OOP constructs such as classes, inheritance, and polymorphism. You should have a firm understanding of how class structures, object collaboration, and collections are implemented in C#. You have been introduced to the Visual Studio IDE and you've practiced using it. You are now ready to put the pieces together and develop a working application.

The next chapter is the first in a series in which you will develop .NET applications. In the process, you will investigate data access using ADO.NET, create a Windows-based GUI using the Widows Presentation Framework, create a web-based GUI using Silverlight, and create web services using the Windows Communication Framework.

CHAPTER 10

Implementing the Data Access Layer

In the past several chapters, you have looked at the various object-oriented programming constructs such as classes, inheritance, and polymorphism as they are implemented in C# code. You have been introduced to and practiced using the Visual Studio integrated development environment. You should also have a firm understanding of how class structures and object collaboration are implemented.

You are now ready to put the pieces together and develop a working application. Because most business applications involve working with and updating data in a back-end relational database, you will look at how the .NET Framework provides the functionality to work with relational data.

After reading this chapter, you will understand the following:

- How to establish a connection to a database using the Connection object.
- How to use a Command object to execute SQL queries.
- How to use a Command object to execute stored procedures.
- How to retrieve records with the DataReader object.
- How to populate DataTables and DataSets.
- How to establish relationships between tables in a DataSet.
- How to edit and update data in a DataSet.
- How to create an Entity Data Model.
- How to use LINQ to EF to query data.
- How to use the Entity Framework to update data.

Introducing ADO.NET

A majority of applications developed for businesses need to interact with a data storage device. Data storage can occur in many different forms: for example, in a flat file system, as is the case with many traditional mainframe systems, or in a relational database management system, such as SQL Server, Oracle, or Sybase. You can also maintain data in a hierarchical textual file structure, as is the case with XML. To access and work with data in a consistent way across these various data stores, the .NET

Framework provides a set of classes organized into the System.Data namespace. This collection of classes is known as ADO.NET.

Looking at the history of Microsoft's data access technologies reveals an evolution from a connected model to a disconnected one. When developing the traditional two-tier client-server applications prevalent in the 1980s and early 1990s, it was often more efficient to open a connection with the database, work with the data implementing server-side cursors, and close the connection when finished working with the data. The problem with this approach became apparent in the late 1990s as companies tried to evolve their data-driven applications from traditional two-tier client-server applications to multitier web-based models: opening and holding a connection open until processing was complete is not scalable. Scalability is the ability of an application to handle an increasing number of simultaneous clients without a noticeable degradation of performance. Microsoft has designed ADO.NET to be highly scalable. To achieve scalability, Microsoft has designed ADO.NET around a disconnected model. A connection is made to the database, the data and metadata are retrieved and cached locally, and the connection is closed.

Another problem with the traditional data access technologies developed during this time was the lack of interoperability. Systems with a high degree of interoperability can easily exchange data back and forth between each other regardless of the implementation technologies of the various systems. Traditional data access technologies rely on proprietary methods of data exchange. Using these techniques, it is hard for a system built using Microsoft technologies such as ADO (pre-.NET) and DCOM to exchange data with a system built using Java technologies such as JDBC and CORBA. The industry as a whole realized it was in the best interest of all parties to develop open standards for exchanging data between disparate systems. Microsoft has embraced these standards and has incorporated support of the standards into the .NET Framework.

Working with Data Providers

To establish a connection to a data source, such as a SQL Server database, and work with its data, you must use the appropriate .NET provider classes. The SQL Server provider classes are located in the System.Data.SQLClient namespace. Other data providers exist, such as the OLEDB data provider for Oracle classes located in the System.Data.OLEDB namespace. Each of these providers implements a similar class structure, which you can use to interact with its intended data source. Table 10-1 summarizes the main classes of the System.Data.SQLClient provider namespace.

Table 10-1. *Classes in the System.Data.SqlClient Namespace*

Class	Responsibility
SqlConnection	Establishes a connection and a unique session with a database.
SqlCommand	Represents a Transact-SQL statement or stored procedure to execute at the database.
SqlDataReader	Provides a means of reading a forward-only stream of rows from the database.
SqlDataAdapter	Fills a DataSet and updates changes back to the database.
SqlParameter	Represents a parameter used to pass information to and from stored procedures.

Class	Responsibility
SqlTransaction	Represents a Transact-SQL transaction to be made in the database.
SqlError	Collects information relevant to a warning or error returned by the database server.
SqlException	Defines the exception that is thrown when a warning or error is returned by the database server.

A similar set of classes exists in the System.Data.OLEDB provider namespace. For example, instead of the SqlConnection class, you have an OleDbConnection class.

Establishing a Connection

The first step to retrieving data from a database is to establish a connection, which is done using a Connection object based on the type of provider being used. To establish a connection to SQL Server, you instantiate a Connection object of type SqlConnection. You also need to provide the Connection object with a ConnectionString. The ConnectionString consists of a series of semicolon-delineated name-value pairs that provide information needed to connect to the database server. Some of the information commonly passed by the ConnectionString is the name of the target server, the name of the database, and security information. The following code demonstrates a ConnectionString used to connect to a SQL Server database:

```
"Data Source=TestServer;Initial Catalog=Pubs;User ID=Dan;Password=training"
```

The attributes you need to provide through the ConnectionString are dependent on the data provider you are using. The following code demonstrates a ConnectionString used to connect to an Access database using the OLEDB provider for Access:

```
"Provider=Microsoft.Jet.OleDb.4.0;Data Source=D:\Data\Northwind.mdb"
```

The next step is to invoke the Open method of the Connection object. This will result in the Connection object loading the appropriate driver and opening a connection to the data source. Once the connection is open, you can work with the data. After you are done interacting with the database, it is important you invoke the Close method of the Connection object, because when a Connection object falls out of scope or is garbage collected, the connection is not implicitly released. The following code demonstrates the process of opening a connection to the Pubs database in SQL Server, working with the data, and closing the connection:

```
SqlConnection pubConnection = new SqlConnection();
string connString;
try
{
    connString = "Data Source=drcsrv01;Initial Catalog=pubs;Integrated Security=True";
    pubConnection.ConnectionString = connString;
    pubConnection.Open();
    //work with data
}
catch (SqlException ex)
```

```
{
    throw ex;
}
finally
{
    if (pubConnection != null)
    {
        pubConnection.Close();
    }
}
```

Executing a Command

Once your application has established and opened a connection to a database, you can execute SQL statements against it. A Command object stores and executes command statements against the database. You can use the Command object to execute any valid SQL statement understood by the data store. In the case of SQL Server, these can be Data Manipulation Language statements (Select, Insert, Update, and Delete), Data Definition Language statements (Create, Alter, and Drop), or Data Control Language statements (Grant, Deny, and Revoke). The CommandText property of the Command object holds the SQL statement that will be submitted. The Command object contains three methods for submitting the CommandText to the database depending on what is returned. If records are returned, as is the case when a Select statement is executed, then you can use the ExecuteReader. If a single value is returned—for example, the results of a Select Count aggregate function—you should use the ExecuteScalar method. When no records are returned from a query—for example, from an Insert statement—you should use the ExecuteNonQuery method. The following code demonstrates using a Command object to execute a SQL statement against the Pubs database that returns the number of employees:

```
SqlConnection pubConnection = new SqlConnection();
string connString;
SqlCommand pubCommand;
try
{
    connString = "Data Source=drcsrv01;Initial Catalog=pubs;Integrated Security=True";
    pubConnection.ConnectionString = connString;
    pubConnection.Open();
    pubCommand = new SqlCommand();
    pubCommand.Connection = pubConnection;
    pubCommand.CommandText = "Select Count(emp_id) from employee";
    return (int)pubCommand.ExecuteScalar();
}
catch (SqlException ex)
{
    throw ex;
}
finally
{
    if (pubConnection != null)
    {
        pubConnection.Close();
```

```
    }
}
```

Using Stored Procedures

In many application designs, instead of executing a SQL statement directly, clients must execute stored procedures. Stored procedures are an excellent way to encapsulate the database logic, increase scalability, and enhance the security of multitiered applications. To execute a stored procedure, you use a Command object, setting its CommandType property to StoredProcedure and its CommandText property to the name of the stored procedure. The following code executes a stored procedure that returns the number of employees in the Pubs database:

```
SqlConnection pubConnection = new SqlConnection();
string connString;
SqlCommand pubCommand;
try
{
    connString = "Data Source=drcsrv01;Initial Catalog=pubs;Integrated Security=True";
    pubConnection.ConnectionString = connString;
    pubConnection.Open();
    pubCommand = new SqlCommand();
    pubCommand.Connection = pubConnection;
    pubCommand.CommandText = "GetEmployeeCount";
    pubCommand.CommandType = CommandType.StoredProcedure;
    return (int)pubCommand.ExecuteScalar();
}
catch (SqlException ex)
{
    throw ex;
}
finally
{
    if (pubConnection != null)
    {
        pubConnection.Close();
    }
}
```

When executing a stored procedure, you often must supply input parameters. You may also need to retrieve the results of the stored procedure through output parameters. To work with parameters, you need to instantiate a parameter object of type SqlParameter, and then add it to the Parameters collection of the Command object. When constructing the parameter, you supply the name of the parameter and the SQL Server data type. For some data types, you also supply the size. If the parameter is an output, input-output, or return parameter, then you must indicate the parameter direction. The following example calls a stored procedure that accepts an input parameter of a letter. The procedure passes back a count of the employees whose last name starts with the letter. The count is returned in the form of an output parameter.

```
SqlConnection pubConnection = new SqlConnection();
string connString;
SqlCommand pubCommand;
```

```
try
{
    connString = "Data Source=drcsrv01;Initial Catalog=pubs;Integrated Security=True";
    pubConnection.ConnectionString = connString;
    pubConnection.Open();
    pubCommand = new SqlCommand();
    pubCommand.Connection = pubConnection;
    pubCommand.CommandText = "GetEmployeeCountByLastInitial";
    SqlParameter inputParameter = pubCommand.Parameters.Add
        ("@LastInitial", SqlDbType.NChar, 1);
    inputParameter.Value = lastInitial.ToCharArray()[0];
    SqlParameter outputParameter = pubCommand.Parameters.Add
        ("@EmployeeCount", SqlDbType.Int);
    outputParameter.Direction = ParameterDirection.Output;
    pubCommand.CommandType = CommandType.StoredProcedure;
    pubCommand.ExecuteNonQuery();
    return (int)outputParameter.Value;
}
catch (SqlException ex)
{
    throw ex;
}
finally
{
    if (pubConnection != null)
    {
        pubConnection.Close();
    }
}
```

Using the DataReader Object to Retrieve Data

A DataReader object accesses data through a forward-only, read-only stream. Oftentimes you will want to loop through a set of records and process the results sequentially without the overhead of maintaining the data in a cache. A good example of this would be loading a list or array with the values returned from the database. After declaring an object of type SqlDataReader, you instantiate it by invoking the ExecuteReader method of a Command object. The Read method of the DataReader object accesses the records returned. The Close method of the DataReader object is called after the records have been processed. The following code demonstrates the use of a DataReader object to retrieve a list of names from a SQL Server database and return it to the client:

```
public ArrayList ListNames()
{
    SqlConnection pubConnection = new SqlConnection();
    string connString;
    SqlCommand pubCommand;
    ArrayList nameArray;
    SqlDataReader employeeDataReader;
    try
    {
```

```
        connString = "Data Source=drcsrv01;" +
            "Initial Catalog=pubs;Integrated Security=True";
        pubConnection.ConnectionString = connString;
        pubConnection.Open();
        pubCommand = new SqlCommand();
        pubCommand.Connection = pubConnection;
        pubCommand.CommandText =
            "Select lname from employee";
        employeeDataReader = pubCommand.ExecuteReader();
        nameArray = new ArrayList();
        while (employeeDataReader.Read())
        {
            nameArray.Add(employeeDataReader["lname"]);
        }
        return nameArray;
    }
    catch (SqlException ex)
    {
        throw ex;
    }
    finally
    {
        if (pubConnection != null)
        {
            pubConnection.Close();
        }
    }
}
```

Using the DataAdapter to Retrieve Data

In many cases, you need to retrieve a set of data from the database, work with the data, and return any updates to the data back to the database. In that case, you use a DataAdapter as a bridge between the data source and the in-memory cache of the data. This in-memory cache of data is contained in a DataSet, which is a major component of the ADO.NET architecture.

Note The DataSet object is discussed in greater detail in the "Working with DataTables and DataSets" section.

To retrieve a set of data from a database, you instantiate a DataAdapter object. You set the SelectCommand property of the DataAdapter to an existing Command object. You then execute the Fill method, passing the name of a DataSet object to fill. Here you see how to use a DataAdapter to fill a DataSet and pass the DataSet back to the client:

```
SqlConnection pubConnection = new SqlConnection();
string connString;
SqlCommand pubCommand;
SqlDataAdapter employeeAdapter;
```

```
DataSet employeeDataSet;
try
{
    connString = "Data Source=drcsrv01;Initial Catalog=pubs;Integrated Security=True";
    pubConnection.ConnectionString = connString;
    pubConnection.Open();
    pubCommand = new SqlCommand();
    pubCommand.Connection = pubConnection;
    pubCommand.CommandText = "Select emp_id, lname, Hire_Date from employee";
    employeeAdapter = new SqlDataAdapter();
    employeeAdapter.SelectCommand = pubCommand;
    employeeDataSet = new DataSet();
    employeeAdapter.Fill(employeeDataSet);
    return employeeDataSet;
}
catch (SqlException ex)
{
    throw ex;
}
finally
{
    if (pubConnection != null)
    {
        pubConnection.Close();
    }
}
```

You may find that you need to retrieve a set of data by executing a stored procedure as opposed to passing in a SQL statement. The following code demonstrates executing a stored procedure that accepts an input parameter and returns a set of records. The records are loaded into a DataSet object and returned to the client.

```
SqlConnection pubConnection = new SqlConnection();
string connString;
SqlCommand pubCommand;
SqlDataAdapter employeeAdapter;
DataSet employeeDataSet;
try
{
    connString = "Data Source=drcsrv01;Initial Catalog=pubs;Integrated Security=True";
    pubConnection.ConnectionString = connString;
    pubConnection.Open();
    pubCommand = new SqlCommand();
    pubCommand.Connection = pubConnection;
    pubCommand.CommandText = "GetEmployeeCountByLastInitial";
    SqlParameter inputParameter = pubCommand.Parameters.Add
        ("@LastInitial", SqlDbType.NChar, 1);
    inputParameter.Value = lastInitial.ToCharArray()[0];
    pubCommand.CommandType = CommandType.StoredProcedure;
    employeeAdapter = new SqlDataAdapter();
    employeeAdapter.SelectCommand = pubCommand;
    employeeDataSet = new DataSet();
```

```
        employeeAdapter.Fill(employeeDataSet);
        return employeeDataSet;
    }
    catch (SqlException ex)
    {
        throw ex;
    }
    finally
    {
        if (pubConnection != null)
        {
            pubConnection.Close();
        }
    }
```

ACTIVITY 10-1. RETRIEVING DATA FROM A SQL SERVER DATABASE

In this activity, you will become familiar with the following:

- Establishing a connection to a SQL Server database.
- Executing queries through a Command object.
- Retrieving data with a DataReader object.
- Executing a stored procedure using a Command object.

■ Note For the activities in this chapter to work, you must have access to a SQL Server 2005 or higher database server with the sample Microsoft Pubs and Northwind databases installed. You must be logged on under a Windows account that has been given the appropriate rights to these databases. You may have to alter the ConnectionString depending on your settings. For more information, refer to the "Software Requirements" section in the Introduction and Appendix C.

Creating a Connection and Executing SQL Queries

To create a connection and execute SQL queries, follow these steps:

1. Start Visual Studio. Select File ➤ New ➤ Project.
2. Choose a Console Application project. Name the project Act10_1.
3. After the project opens, add a new class to the project named Author.
4. Open the Author class code in the code editor. Add the following using statements at the top of the file:

```
using System.Data;
using System.Data.SqlClient;
```

5. Add this code to declare a private class-level variable of type SQLConnection:

```
public class Author
{
    SqlConnection _pubConnection;
    string _connString;
```

6. Create a class constructor that instantiates the Pubs Connection object and sets up the ConnectionString property.

```
public Author()
{
    _connString =
        "Data Source=localhost;Initial Catalog=pubs;Integrated Security=True";
    _pubConnection = new SqlConnection();
    _pubConnection.ConnectionString = _connString;
}
```

7. Add a method to the class that will use a Command object to execute a query to count the number of authors in the Authors table. Because you are only returning a single value, you will use the ExecuteScalar method of the Command object.

```
public int CountAuthors()
{
   try
   {
       SqlCommand pubCommand = new SqlCommand();
       pubCommand.Connection = _pubConnection;
       pubCommand.CommandText = "Select Count(au_id) from authors";
       _pubConnection.Open();
       return (int)pubCommand.ExecuteScalar();
    }
    catch (SqlException ex)
    {
        throw ex;
    }
    finally
    {
        if (_pubConnection != null)
        {
             _pubConnection.Close();
        }
    }
}
```

8. Add the following code to the Main Method of the Program class, which will execute the GetAuthorCount method defined in the Author class:

```
static void Main(string[] args)
{
    try
```

```
    {
         Author author = new Author();
         Console.WriteLine(author.CountAuthors());
         Console.ReadLine();
    }
    catch (Exception ex)
    {
        Console.WriteLine(ex.Message);
        Console.ReadLine();
    }
}
```

9. Select Debug ➤ Start to run the project. The Console window should launch with the number of authors displayed. After viewing the output, stop the debugger.

Using the DataReader Object to Retrieve Records

To use the DataReader object to retrieve records, follow these steps:

1. Open the Author class code in the code editor.
2. Add a public method to the class definition called GetAuthorList that returns an generic List of strings:

```
public List<string> GetAuthorList()
{
}
```

3. Add the following code, which executes a SQL Select statement to retrieve the authors' last names. A DataReader object then loops through the records and creates a list of names that gets returned to the client.

```
SqlCommand authorsCommand = new SqlCommand();
SqlDataReader authorDataReader;
List<string> nameList = new List<string>();
try
{
    authorsCommand.Connection = _pubConnection;
    authorsCommand.CommandText = "Select au_lname from authors";
    _pubConnection.Open();
    authorDataReader = authorsCommand.ExecuteReader();
    while (authorDataReader.Read() == true)
    {
        nameList.Add(authorDataReader.GetString(0));
    }
    return nameList;
}
catch (SqlException ex)
{
    throw ex;
}
finally
```

```
{
    if (_pubConnection != null)
    {
        _pubConnection.Close();
    }
}
```

4. Change the code in the Main Method of the Program class to show the list of names in the console window.

```
static void Main(string[] args)
{
    try
    {
        Author author = new Author();
        foreach (string name in author.GetAuthorList())
        {
            Console.WriteLine(name);
        }
        Console.ReadLine();
    }
    catch (Exception ex)
    {
        Console.WriteLine(ex.Message);
        Console.ReadLine();
    }
}
```

5. Select Debug ➤ Start to run the project. The Console window should launch with the names of the authors displayed. After viewing the output, stop the debugger.

Executing a Stored Procedure Using a Command Object

To execute a stored procedure using a Command object, follow these steps:

1. Open the Author class code in the code editor.
2. Add a public method that overloads the GetAuthorList method by accepting an integer parameter named Royalty. This function will call the stored procedure by royalty in the Pubs database. The procedure takes an integer input of royalty percentage and returns a list of author IDs with the percentage.

```
public List<string> GetAuthorList(int royalty)
{
    SqlCommand authorsCommand = new SqlCommand();
    SqlDataReader authorDataReader;
    List<string> nameList = new List<string>();
    SqlParameter inputParameter = new SqlParameter();
    try
    {
        authorsCommand.Connection = _pubConnection;
        authorsCommand.CommandType = CommandType.StoredProcedure;
        authorsCommand.CommandText = "byroyalty";
```

```
            inputParameter.ParameterName = "@percentage";
            inputParameter.Direction = ParameterDirection.Input;
            inputParameter.SqlDbType = SqlDbType.Int;
            inputParameter.Value = royalty;
            authorsCommand.Parameters.Add(inputParameter);
            _pubConnection.Open();
            authorDataReader = authorsCommand.ExecuteReader();
            while (authorDataReader.Read() == true)
            {
                nameList.Add(authorDataReader.GetString(0));
            }
            return nameList;
        }
        catch (SqlException ex)
        {
            throw ex;
        }
        finally
        {
            if (_pubConnection != null)
            {
                _pubConnection.Close();
            }
        }

}
```

3. In the Main method of the Program class, supply an input parameter of 25 to the GetAuthorList method.

```
foreach (string name in author.GetAuthorList(25))
```

4. Select Debug ➤ Start to run the project. The Console window should launch with the IDs of the authors displayed. After viewing the output, stop the debugger.

5. When finished testing, exit Visual Studio.

Working with DataTables and DataSets

DataSets and DataTables are in-memory caches of data that provide a consistent relational programming model for working with data regardless of the data source. A DataTable represents one table of relational data and consists of columns, rows, and constraints. You can think of a DataSet as a minirelational database, which includes the data tables and the relational integrity constraints between them. If you are retrieving data from a single table, you can populate and use the DataTable directly without the overhead of creating a DataSet first. There are several ways to create a DataTable or DataSet. The most obvious method is to populate a DataTable or DataSet from an existing relational database management system (RDBMS) such as a SQL Server database. As mentioned previously, a DataAdapter object provides the bridge between the RDBMS and the DataTable or DataSet. By using a DataAdapter object, the DataTable or DataSet is totally independent from the data source. Although you need to use a specific set of provider classes to load either type of object, you use the same set of .NET Framework classes to work with a DataTable or DataSet, regardless of how it was created and populated. The System.Data namespace contains the framework classes for working with DataTable or DataSet objects. Table 10-2 lists some of the main classes contained in the System.Data namespace.

Table 10-2. *The Main Members of the System.Data Namespace*

Class	Description
DataSet	Represents a collection of DataTable and DataRelation objects. Organizes an in-memory cache of relational data.
DataTable	Represents a collection of DataColumn, DataRow, and Constraint objects. Organizes records and fields related to a data entity.
DataColumn	Represents the schema of a column in a DataTable.
DataRow	Represents a row of data in a DataTable.
Constraint	Represents a constraint that can be enforced on DataColumn objects.
ForeignKeyConstraint	Enforces referential integrity of a parent/child relationship between two DataTable objects.
UniqueConstraint	Enforces uniqueness of a DataColumn or set of DataColumns. This is required to enforce referential integrity in a parent/child relationship.
DataRelation	Represents a parent/child relation between two DataTable objects.

Populating a DataTable from a SQL Server Database

To retrieve data from a database, you set up a connection with the database using a Connection object. After a connection is established, you create a Command object to retrieve the data from the database. As stated earlier, if you are retrieving data from a single table or result set, you can populate and work with a DataTable directly without creating a DataSet object. The Load method of the DataTable fills the table with the contents of a DataReader object. The following code fills a DataTable with data from the publishers table of the Pubs database:

```
SqlConnection pubConnection = new SqlConnection();
string connString;
SqlCommand pubCommand;
SqlDataReader pubDataReader;
DataTable pubTable;
try
{
    connString = "Data Source=drcsrv01;" +
        "Initial Catalog=pubs;Integrated Security=True";
    pubConnection.ConnectionString = connString;
```

```
    pubCommand = new SqlCommand();
    pubCommand.Connection = pubConnection;
    pubCommand.CommandText =
        "Select pub_id, pub_name, city from publishers";
    pubConnection.Open();
    pubDataReader = pubCommand.ExecuteReader();
    pubTable = new DataTable();
    pubTable.Load(pubDataReader);
    return pubTable;
}
catch (SqlException ex)
{
    throw ex;
}
finally
{
    if (pubConnection != null)
    {
        pubConnection.Close();
    }
}
```

Populating a DataSet from a SQL Server Database

When you need to load data into multiple tables and maintain the referential integrity between the tables, you need to use the DataSet object as a container for the DataTables. To retrieve data from a database and fill the DataSet, you set up a connection with the database using a Connection object. After a connection is established, you create a Command object to retrieve the data from the database, and then create a DataAdapter to fill the DataSet, setting the previously created Command object to the SelectCommand property of the DataAdapter. Create a separate DataAdapter for each DataTable. The final step is to fill the DataSet with the data by executing the Fill method of the DataAdapter. The following code demonstrates filling a DataSet with data from the publishers table and the titles table of the Pubs database:

```
SqlConnection pubConnection = new SqlConnection();
string connString;
SqlCommand pubCommand;
SqlCommand titleCommand;
SqlDataAdapter pubDataAdapter;
SqlDataAdapter titleDataAdapter;
DataSet bookInfoDataSet;
try
{
    connString = "Data Source=drcsrv01;" +
        "Initial Catalog=pubs;Integrated Security=True";
    pubConnection.ConnectionString = connString;
    //Create pub table command
    pubCommand = new SqlCommand();
    pubCommand.Connection = pubConnection;
    pubCommand.CommandText =
```

```
            "Select pub_id, pub_name, city from publishers";
        pubDataAdapter = new SqlDataAdapter();
        pubDataAdapter.SelectCommand = pubCommand;
        //Create title table command
        titleCommand = new SqlCommand();
        titleCommand.Connection = pubConnection;
        titleCommand.CommandText =
            "Select pub_id, title, city, ytd_sales from titles";
        titleDataAdapter = new SqlDataAdapter();
        titleDataAdapter.SelectCommand = titleCommand;
        //Create and fill dataset
        bookInfoDataSet = new DataSet();
        pubDataAdapter.Fill(bookInfoDataSet, "Publishers");
        titleDataAdapter.Fill(bookInfoDataSet, "Titles");
        return bookInfoDataSet;
    }
    catch (SqlException ex)
    {
        throw ex;
    }
    finally
    {
        if (pubConnection != null)
        {
            pubConnection.Close();
        }
    }
```

Establishing Relationships between Tables in a DataSet

In an RDBMS system, referential integrity between tables is enforced through a primary key and foreign key relationship. Using a DataRelation object, you can enforce data referential integrity between the tables in the DataSet. This object contains an array of DataColumn objects that define the common field(s) between the parent table and the child table used to establish the relation. Essentially, the field identified in the parent table is the primary key, and the field identified in the child table is the foreign key. When establishing a relationship, create two DataColumn objects for the common column in each table. Next, create a DataRelation object, pass a name for the DataRelation, and pass the DataColumn objects to the constructor of the DataRelation object. The final step is to add the DataRelation to the Relations collection of the DataSet object. The following code establishes a relationship between the publishers and the titles tables of the bookInfoDataSet created in the previous section:

```
//Create relationahip between tables
DataRelation Pub_TitleRelation;
DataColumn Pub_PubIdColumn;
DataColumn Title_PubIdColumn;
Pub_PubIdColumn = bookInfoDataSet.Tables["Publishers"].Columns["pub_id"];
Title_PubIdColumn = bookInfoDataSet.Tables["Titles"].Columns["pub_id"];
Pub_TitleRelation = new DataRelation("PubsToTitles", Pub_PubIdColumn, Title_PubIdColumn);
bookInfoDataSet.Relations.Add(Pub_TitleRelation);
return bookInfoDataSet;
```

Editing Data in the DataSet

Clients often need to be able to update a DataSet. They may need to add records, delete records, or update an existing record. Because DataSet objects are disconnected by design, the changes made to the DataSet are not automatically propagated back to the database. They are held locally until the client is ready to replicate the changes back to the database. To replicate the changes, you invoke the Update method of the DataAdapter, which determines what changes have been made to the records and implements the appropriate SQL command (Update, Insert, or Delete) that has been defined to replicate the changes back to the database.

To demonstrate the process of updating a DataSet, the following code constructs an Author class that will pass a DataSet containing author information to a client when the GetData method is invoked. The Author class will accept a DataSet containing changes made to the author information and replicate the changes back to the Pubs database when its UpdateData method is invoked. The first step is to define the class and include a using statement for the referenced namespaces, like so:

```
using System.Data;
using System.Data.SqlClient;
```

Define class-level variables for SQLConnection, SQLDataAdapter, and DataSet objects:

```
public class Author
{
    private SqlConnection _pubConnection;
    private SqlDataAdapter _authorsDataAdapter;
    private DataSet _pubsDataSet;
```

In the class constructor, initialize a Connection object, like so:

```
public Author()
{
    SqlCommand selectCommand;
    SqlCommand updateCommand;
    string connectionString = "Integrated Security=True;Data Source=LocalHost;" +
                    "Initial Catalog=Pubs";
    _pubConnection = new SqlConnection(connectionString);
```

Then create a Select Command object, like so:

```
string selectSQL = "Select au_id, au_lname, au_fname from authors";
selectCommand = new SqlCommand(selectSQL,_pubConnection);
selectCommand.CommandType = CommandType.Text;
```

Next you create an Update Command. The command text references parameters in the command's Parameters collection that will be created next.

```
string updateSQL = "Update authors set au_lname = @au_lname," +
          " au_fname = @au_fname where au_id = @au_id";
updateCommand = new SqlCommand(updateSQL, _pubConnection);
updateCommand.CommandType = CommandType.Text;
```

A Parameter object is added to the Command object's Parameter collection for each Parameter in the Update statement. The Add method of the Parameters collection is passed information on the name of the Parameter, the SQL data type, size, and the source column of the DataSet, like so:

```
updateCommand.Parameters.Add("@au_id", SqlDbType.VarChar, 11, "au_id");
updateCommand.Parameters.Add("@au_lname", SqlDbType.VarChar, 40, "au_lname");
updateCommand.Parameters.Add("@au_fname", SqlDbType.VarChar, 40, "au_fname");
```

The final step is to create and set up the DataAdapter object. Set the SelectCommand and UpdateCommand properties to the appropriate SQLCommand objects, like so:

```
    _authorsDataAdapter = new SqlDataAdapter();
    _authorsDataAdapter.SelectCommand = selectCommand;
    _authorsDataAdapter.UpdateCommand = updateCommand;
}
```

Now that the SQLDataAdapter has been set up and created in the class constructor, the GetData and UpdateData methods will use the DataAdapter to get and update the data from the database, like so:

```
public DataSet GetData()
{
     _pubsDataSet = new DataSet();
     _authorsDataAdapter.Fill(_pubsDataSet, "Authors");
     return _pubsDataSet;
}
public void SaveData(DataSet authorChanges)
{
    _authorsDataAdapter.Update(authorChanges, "Authors");
}
```

In a similar fashion, you could implement the InsertCommand and the DeleteCommand properties of the DataAdapter to allow clients to insert new records or delete records in the database.

Note For simple updates to a single table in the data source, the .NET Framework provides a CommandBuilder class to automate the creation of the InsertCommand, UpdateCommand, and DeleteCommand properties of the DataAdapter.

ACTIVITY 10-2. WORKING WITH DATASET OBJECTS

In this activity, you will become familiar with the following:

- Populating a DataSet from a SQL Server database.
- Editing data in a DataSet.
- Updating changes from the DataSet to the database.
- Establishing relationships between tables in a DataSet.

Populating a DataSet from a SQL Server Database

To populate a DataSet from a SQL Server database, follow these steps:

1. Start Visual Studio. Select File ➤ New ➤ Project.
2. Choose Windows Application. Rename the project to Act10_2 and click the OK button.
3. After the project opens, add a new class to the project named Author.
4. Open the Author class code in the code editor. Add the following using statements at the top of the file:

```
using System.Data;
using System.Data.SqlClient;
```

5. Add the following code to declare private class level variables of type SQLConnection, SqlDataAdapter, and DataSet:

```
public class Author
{
    SqlConnection _pubConnection;
    string _connString;
    SqlDataAdapter _pubDataAdapter;
    DataSet authorDataSet;
```

6. Create a class constructor that instantiates the Pubs Connection object, sets up the ConnectionString property and creates a select command.

```
public Author()
{
     _connString =
         "Data Source=localhost;Initial Catalog=pubs;Integrated Security=True";
     _pubConnection = new SqlConnection();
     _pubConnection.ConnectionString = _connString;
     SqlCommand selectCommand =
         new SqlCommand("Select au id, au lname,au_fname from authors",
         _pubConnection);
     _pubDataAdapter = new SqlDataAdapter();
     _pubDataAdapter.SelectCommand = selectCommand;
}
```

7. Create a method of the Author class called GetData that will use the DataAdapter object to fill the DataSet and return it to the client.

```
public DataSet GetData()
{
    try
    {
        authorDataSet = new DataSet();
        _pubDataAdapter.Fill(authorDataSet, "Author");
        return authorDataSet;
    }
```

```
        catch (Exception ex)
        {
            throw ex;
        }
    }
```

8. Build the project and fix any errors.

9. Add the controls listed in Table 10-3 to Form1 and set the properties as shown.

Table 10-3. *Form1 Controls*

Control	Property	Value
DataGridView	Name	dgvAuthors
	AllowUserToAddRows	False
	AllowUserToDeleteRows	False
	ReadOnly	False
Button	Name	btnGetData
	Text	Get Data
Button	Name	btnUpdate
	Text	Update

10. Open the Form1 class code file in the code editor. Declare a class-level DataSet object after the class declaration.

```
public partial class Form1 : Form
{
    private DataSet _pubDataSet;
```

11. Open Form1 in the Form Designer. Double-click on the Get Data button to open the button click event method in the code editor.

12. Add the following code to the btnGetData click event procedure, which will execute the GetData method defined in the Author class. This dataset is then loaded into the grid using the DataSource property.

```
private void btnGetData_Click(object sender, EventArgs e)
{
    Author author = new Author();
    _pubDataSet = author.GetData();
    dgvAuthors.DataSource = _pubDataSet.Tables["Authors"];
}
```

13. Build the project and fix any errors. Once the project builds, run the project in debug mode and test the GetData method. You should see the grid filled with author information. After testing, stop the debugger.

Editing and Updating Data in a DataSet

To edit and update data in a DataSet, follow these steps:

1. Open the Author class code in the code editor.

2. At the end of the class constructor, add code to set up a SqlCommand object that will execute an Update query. Create the update parameters in the Parameters collection and set the DataAdapter object's Update Command property to the SqlCommand object.

```
SqlCommand updateCommand = new SqlCommand
    ("Update authors set au_lname = @au_lname," +
     "au_fname = @au_fname where au_id = @au_id",
     _pubConnection);
updateCommand.Parameters.Add("@au_id", SqlDbType.VarChar, 11, "au_id");
updateCommand.Parameters.Add("@au_lname", SqlDbType.VarChar, 40, "au_lname");
updateCommand.Parameters.Add("@au_fname", SqlDbType.VarChar, 40, "au_fname");
_pubDataAdapter.UpdateCommand = updateCommand;
```

3. Create a method of the Author class called UpdateData that will use the Update method of the DataAdapter object to pass updates made to the DataSet to the Pubs database.

```
public void UpdateData(DataSet changedData)
{
    try
    {
        _pubDataAdapter.Update(changedData, "Authors");
    }
    catch (Exception ex)
    {
        throw ex;
    }
}
```

4. Build the project and fix any errors.

5. Open Form1 in the Form Designer. Double-click on the Update Data button to open the button click event method in the code editor.

6. Add the following code to the btnUpdate click event procedure, which will execute the UpdateData method defined in the Author class. By using the GetChanges method of the DataSet object, only data that has changed is passed for updating.

```
private void btnUpdate_Click(object sender, EventArgs e)
{
    Author author = new Author();
```

```
    author.UpdateData(_pubDataSet.GetChanges());
}
```

7. Build the project and fix any errors. Once the project builds, run the project in debug mode and test the Update method. First, click the Get Data button. Change the last name of several authors and click the Update button. Click the Get Data button again to retrieve the changed values back from the database. After testing, stop the debugger.

Establishing Relationships between Tables in a DataSet

To establish relationships between tables in a DataSet, follow these steps:

1. Add a new class named StoreSales to the project.

2. Open the StoreSales class code in the code editor. Add the following using statements at the top of the file:

```
using System.Data;
using System.Data.SqlClient;
```

3. Add the following code to declare private class level variables of type SQLConnection, SqlDataAdapter, and DataSet:

```
class StoreSales
{
    SqlConnection _pubConnection;
    string _connString;
    SqlDataAdapter _storeDataAdapter = new SqlDataAdapter();
    SqlDataAdapter _salesDataAdapter = new SqlDataAdapter();
    DataSet storeSalesDataSet;
```

4. Create a class constructor that instantiates the Pubs Connection object and sets up the ConnectionString property.

```
public StoreSales()
{
     _connString =
         "Data Source=localhost;Initial Catalog=pubs;Integrated Security=True";
     _pubConnection = new SqlConnection();
     _pubConnection.ConnectionString = _connString;
}
```

5. Create a method of the StoreSales class called GetData that will use the select store information and sales information and establish a relationship between them. This information is used to fill a DataSet and return it to the client.

```
public DataSet GetData()
{
    try
    {
        //Get Store Info
        string selectStoresSQL = "SELECT [stor_id] ,[stor_name]," +
```

```
                "[city],[state] FROM [stores]";
            SqlCommand selectStoresCommand =
                new SqlCommand(selectStoresSQL, _pubConnection);
            selectStoresCommand.CommandType = CommandType.Text;
            _storeDataAdapter.SelectCommand = selectStoresCommand;
            //Get Sales Info
            string selectSalesSQL = "SELECT [stor_id],[ord_num]," +
                "[ord_date],[qty] FROM [sales]";
            SqlCommand selectSalesCommand =
                new SqlCommand(selectSalesSQL, _pubConnection);
            selectSalesCommand.CommandType = CommandType.Text;
            _salesDataAdapter.SelectCommand = selectSalesCommand;
            //Get data and fill DataSet
            storeSalesDataSet = new DataSet();
            _storeDataAdapter.Fill(storeSalesDataSet, "Stores");
            _salesDataAdapter.Fill(storeSalesDataSet, "Sales");
            //Create relationahip between tables
            DataColumn Store_StoreIdColumn =
                storeSalesDataSet.Tables["Stores"].Columns["stor_id"];
            DataColumn Sales_StoreIdColumn =
                storeSalesDataSet.Tables["Sales"].Columns["stor_id"];
            DataRelation StoreSalesRelation =
                new DataRelation("StoresToSales", Store_StoreIdColumn, Sales_StoreIdColumn);
            storeSalesDataSet.Relations.Add(StoreSalesRelation);

            return storeSalesDataSet;
        }
        catch (Exception ex)
        {
            throw ex;
        }
    }
```

6. Build the project and fix any errors.

7. Add a second form to the project. Add the controls listed in Table 10-4 to Form2 and set the properties as shown.

Table 10-4. *Form2 Controls*

Control	Property	Value
DataGridView	Name	dgvStores
DataGridView	Name	dgvSales
Button	Name	btnGetData
	Text	Get Data

8. Open the Form2 class code file in the code editor. Declare a class-level DataSet object after the class declaration.

```
public partial class Form2 : Form
{
    DataSet StoreSalesDataSet;
```

9. Open Form2 in the Form Designer. Double-click on the Get Data button to open the button click event method in the code editor.

10. Add the following code to the btnGetData click event procedure, which will execute the GetData method defined in the StoreSales class. This Stores table is then loaded into the Stores grid using the DataSource property. Setting the DataMember property of the Sales grid loads it with the sales data of the store selected in the Stores grid.

```
private void btnGetData_Click(object sender, EventArgs e)
{
    StoreSales storeSales = new StoreSales();
    StoreSalesDataSet = storeSales.GetData();
    dgvStores.DataSource = StoreSalesDataSet.Tables["Stores"];
    dgvSales.DataSource =StoreSalesDataSet.Tables["Stores"];
    dgvSales.DataMember = "StoreSales";
}
```

11. Open the Program class in the code editor. Change the code to launch Form2 when the form loads.

```
Application.Run(new Form2());
```

12. When the form loads, click the Get Data button to load the grids. Selecting a new row in the Stores grid should update the Sales grid to show the store's sales. When you are finished testing stop the debugger and exit Visual Studio.

Working with the Entity Framework

The Entity Framework (EF) is an Object-Relational Mapping (ORM) technology built into ADO.NET. EF tries to eliminate the mismatch between the objected-oriented programming constructs of the .NET language and the relational data constructs of the database system. For example, to load and work with a customer object, a developer has to send a SQL string to the database engine. The developer must be familiar with the relational schema of the data and this information is hardcoded into the application. A big disadvantage of this approach is the application is not shielded from changes in the underlying schema. Another disadvantage is that since the application sends the SQL statements as a string to the database engine for processing, Visual Studio can't implement syntax checking and issue warnings and build errors to the help the programmer.

The Entity Framework provides the mapping schema that allows programmers to work at a higher level of abstraction. They can write code using object-oriented constructs to query and load the entities (objects defined by classes). The mapping schema translates the queries against the entities into the required database specific language needed to perform CRUD (create, read, update, and delete) operations against the data.

In order to use the Entity Framework in your application, you must first add an ADO.NET Entity Data Model to your application. This step launches the Entity Data Model Wizard, which allows you to develop your model from scratch or generate it from an existing database. Choosing to generate it from an existing database allows you to create a connection to the database and select the tables views and stored procedures you want to include in the model. The .edmx file generated by the wizard is an XML-based file that has three sections. The first consists of store schema definition language (SSDL); this describes the tables and relationships where the data is stored. The following code shows a portion of the SSDL for a data model generated from the Pubs database:

```
<EntityContainer Name="pubsModelStoreContainer">
          <EntitySet Name="sales" EntityType="pubsModel.Store.sales"
                     store:Type="Tables" Schema="dbo" />
          <EntitySet Name="stores" EntityType="pubsModel.Store.stores"
                     store:Type="Tables" Schema="dbo" />
          <AssociationSet Name="FK__sales__stor_id__1273C1CD"
                          Association="pubsModel.Store.FK__sales__stor_id__1273C1CD">
            <End Role="stores" EntitySet="stores" />
            <End Role="sales" EntitySet="sales" />
          </AssociationSet>
        </EntityContainer>
        <EntityType Name="sales">
          <Key>
            <PropertyRef Name="stor_id" />
            <PropertyRef Name="ord_num" />
            <PropertyRef Name="title_id" />
          </Key>
          <Property Name="stor_id" Type="char" Nullable="false" MaxLength="4" />
          <Property Name="ord_num" Type="varchar" Nullable="false" MaxLength="20" />
          <Property Name="ord_date" Type="datetime" Nullable="false" />
          <Property Name="qty" Type="smallint" Nullable="false" />
          <Property Name="payterms" Type="varchar" Nullable="false" MaxLength="12" />
          <Property Name="title_id" Type="varchar" Nullable="false" MaxLength="6" />
        </EntityType>
```

The second section consists of conceptual schema definition language (CSDL); it specifies the entities and relationships between them. These entities are used by the application to work with data in the application. The following code comes from the CDSL section of a data model generated from the Pubs database:

```
        <EntityContainer Name="pubsEntities" annotation:LazyLoadingEnabled="true">
          <EntitySet Name="sales" EntityType="pubsModel.sale" />
          <EntitySet Name="stores" EntityType="pubsModel.store" />
          <AssociationSet Name="FK__sales__stor_id__1273C1CD"
                          Association="pubsModel.FK__sales__stor_id__1273C1CD">
            <End Role="stores" EntitySet="stores" />
            <End Role="sales" EntitySet="sales" />
          </AssociationSet>
        </EntityContainer>
        <EntityType Name="sale">
          <Key>
```

```
      <PropertyRef Name="stor_id" />
      <PropertyRef Name="ord_num" />
      <PropertyRef Name="title_id" />
    </Key>
    <Property Name="stor_id" Type="String" Nullable="false"
              MaxLength="4" Unicode="false" FixedLength="true" />
    <Property Name="ord_num" Type="String" Nullable="false"
              MaxLength="20" Unicode="false" FixedLength="false" />
    <Property Name="ord_date" Type="DateTime" Nullable="false" />
    <Property Name="qty" Type="Int16" Nullable="false" />
    <Property Name="payterms" Type="String" Nullable="false"
              MaxLength="12" Unicode="false" FixedLength="false" />
    <Property Name="title_id" Type="String" Nullable="false"
              MaxLength="6" Unicode="false" FixedLength="false" />
    <NavigationProperty Name="store"
              Relationship="pubsModel.FK__sales__stor_id__1273C1CD"
          FromRole="sales" ToRole="stores" />
  </EntityType>
```

The final section of the .edmx file consists of code written in the mapping specification language (MSL). The MSL maps the conceptual model to the storage model. The following code shows a portion of the MSL section of a data model generated from the Pubs database:

```
<EntityContainerMapping StorageEntityContainer="pubsModelStoreContainer"
                                CdmEntityContainer="pubsEntities">
          <EntitySetMapping Name="sales"><EntityTypeMapping TypeName="pubsModel.sale">
            <MappingFragment StoreEntitySet="sales">
            <ScalarProperty Name="stor_id" ColumnName="stor_id" />
            <ScalarProperty Name="ord_num" ColumnName="ord_num" />
            <ScalarProperty Name="ord_date" ColumnName="ord_date" />
            <ScalarProperty Name="qty" ColumnName="qty" />
            <ScalarProperty Name="payterms" ColumnName="payterms" />
            <ScalarProperty Name="title_id" ColumnName="title_id" />
            </MappingFragment></EntityTypeMapping></EntitySetMapping>
```

Querying Entities with LINQ to EF

When creating the ADO.NET entity data model using the Entity Data Model Wizard, an ObjectContext class is created that represents the entity container defined in the model. The ObjectContext class supports CRUD-based queries against the entity model. Queries written against the ObjectContext class are written using LINQ to EF. LINQ stands for Language-Integrated Query. LINQ allows developers to write queries in C# syntax, which, when executed, are converted to the query syntax of the data provider. Once the query is executed and data is returned, the Entity Framework converts the results back to the entity object model.

The following code uses the Select method to return all the rows from the Stores table and return the results as a list of Store entities. The Store names are then written to the console window.

```
var context = new pubsEntities();
var query = from s in context.stores
            select s;
var stores = query.ToList();
```

```
foreach (store s in stores)
{
    Console.WriteLine(s.stor_name);
}
    Console.ReadLine();
```

LINQ to EF provides a rich set of query operations including filtering, ordering, and grouping operations. The following code demonstrates filtering stores by state:

```
var context = new pubsEntities();
var query = from s in context.stores
            where  s.state == "WA"
            select s;
var stores = query.ToList();
```

The following code selects sales entities that have ordered more than 25 objects and then orders them by descending date:

```
var context = new pubsEntities();
var query = from s in context.sales
            where s.qty > 25
            orderby s.ord_date descending
            select s;
var sales = query.ToList();
```

Since the Entity Framework includes navigation properties between entities, you can easily build complex queries based on related entities. The following query selects stores with more than five sales orders:

```
var context = new pubsEntities();
var query = from s in context.stores
            where s.sales.Count > 5
            select s;
var stores = query.ToList();
```

■Note For more information on the LINQ query language, refer to the MSDN library at http://msdn.microsoft.com.

Updating Entities with the Entity Framework

The Entity Framework tracks changes made to the entity types represented in the Context object. You can add, update or delete entity objects. When you are ready to persist the changes back to the database, you call the SaveChanges method of the context object. The EF creates and executes the insert, update, or delete statements against the database. You can also explicitly map stored procedures to implement the database commands. The following code selects a store using the store ID, updates the store name, and sends it back to the database:

```
var context = new pubsEntities();
var store = (from s in context.stores
             where s.stor_id == storeId
             select s).First();
store.stor_name = "DRC Books";
context.SaveChanges();
```

ACTIVITY 10-3. RETRIEVING DATA WITH THE ENTITY FRAMEWORK

In this activity, you will become familiar with the following:

- Creating an Entity Data Model.
- Executing queries using LINQ to EF.

Creating an Entity Data Model

To create an entity data model, follow these steps:

1. Start Visual Studio. Select File ➤ New ➤ Project.
2. Choose Console Application. Rename the project to Act10_3 and click the OK button.
3. Right click on the project node in solution explorer and select Add ➤ New Item.
4. Under the Data node in the Add New Item window, select an ADO.NET Entity Data Model. Name the model Pubs.emdx and click Add.
5. In the Choose Model Contents screen, select the Generate from database and click Next.
6. In the "Choose Your Data Connection" screen, create a connection to the Pubs database and choose Next. (See Figure 10-1)

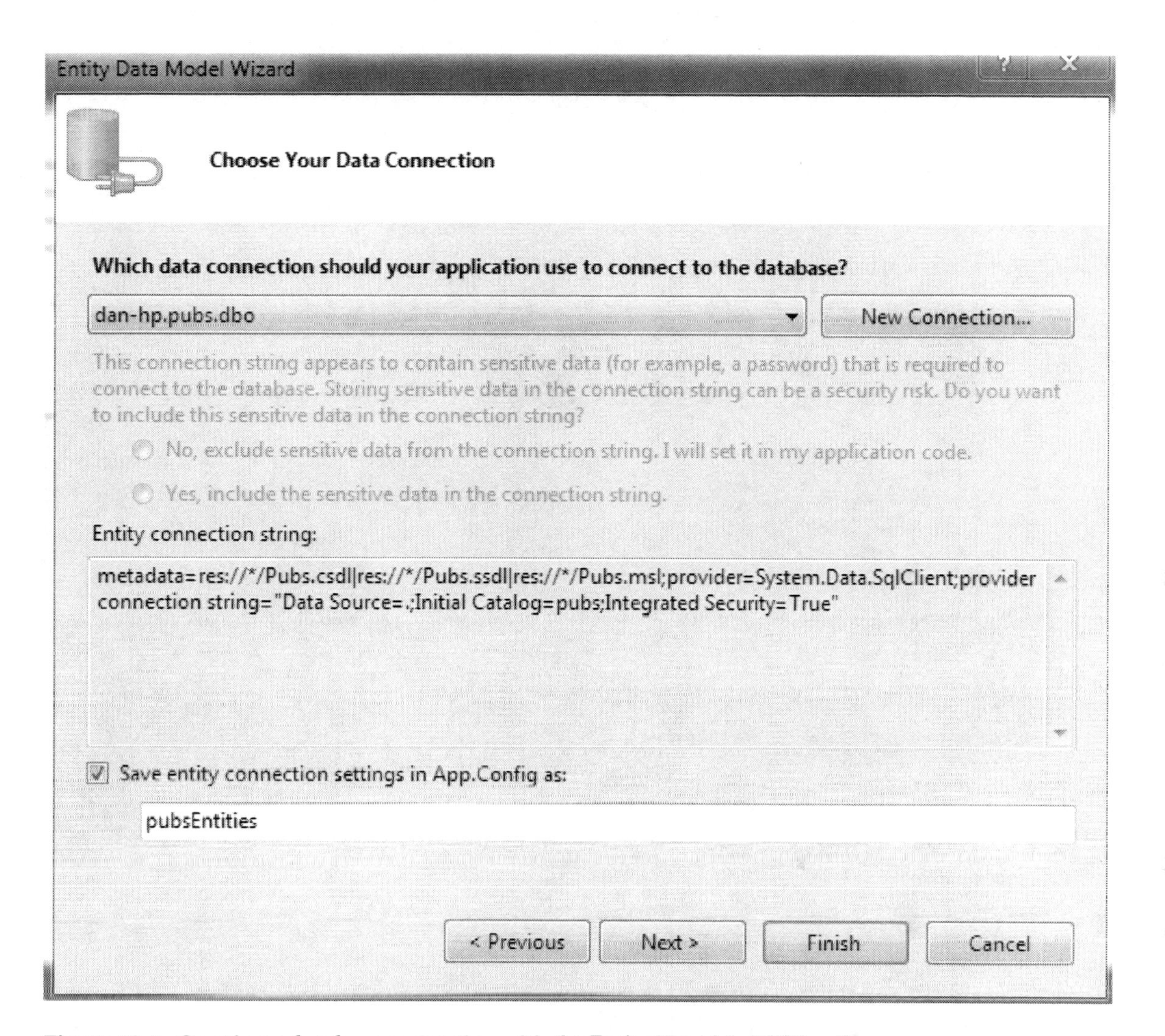

Figure 10-1. *Creating a database connection with the Entity Data Model Wizard*

7. In the "Choose Your Database Objects" screen, expand the Tables node and select the Sales, Stores, and Titles tables, as shown in Figure 10-2. Click Finish.

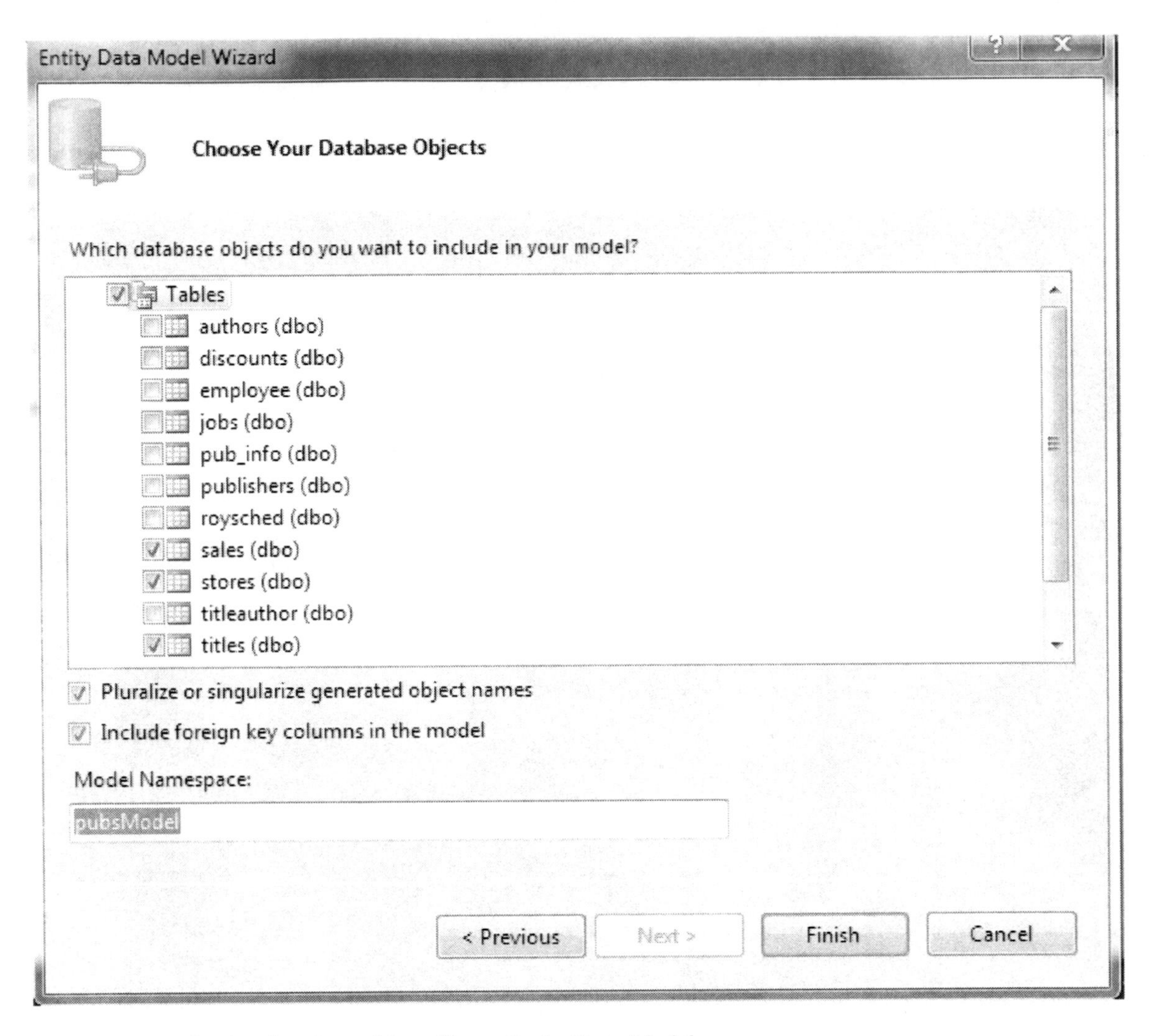

Figure 10-2. *Selecting database objects for an Entity Data Model*

8. You are presented with the Entity Model Designer containing the sales, store, and title entities, as shown in Figure 10-3.

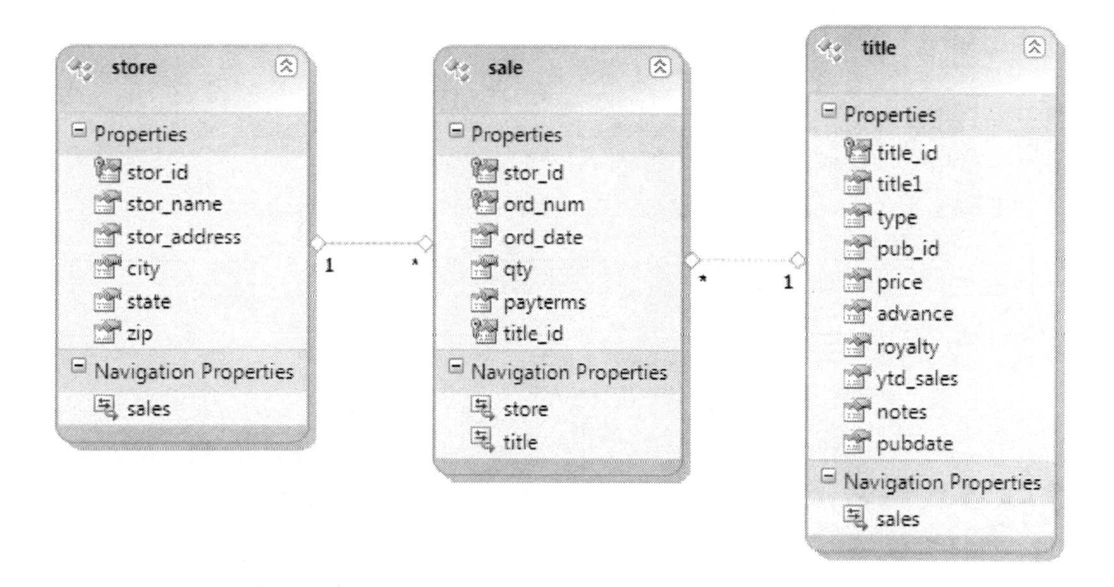

Figure 10-3. *Entity Model Designer*

9. In the Entity Model Designer right click on the title entity and select rename. Rename it to book. In the book entity, rename the title1 property to title.

Querying an Entity Data Model

To query this entity data model using LINQ, follow these steps:

1. Open the Program.cs file in the Code Editor Window.
2. Add the following method to select the book entities and write their titles to the Console window:

```
private static void GetTitles()
{
    var context = new pubsEntities();
    var query = from b in context.books select b;
    var books = query.ToList();
    foreach (book b in books)
    {
        Console.WriteLine(b.title);
    }
    Console.ReadLine();
}
```

3. Call the GetTitles method from the Main method.

```
static void Main(string[] args)
{
    GetTitles();
}
```

4. Run the program in debug mode. You should see the titles listed in the Console window. When you are done testing, stop the debugger.

5. Add the following method that gets books in the 10 to 20 dollar range and orders them by price:

```
private static void GetTitlesByPrice()
{
    var context = new pubsEntities();
    var query = from b in context.books
                where b.price >= (decimal)10.00
                        && b.price <= (decimal)20.00
                orderby b.price
                select b;
    var books = query.ToList();
    foreach (book b in books)
    {
        Console.WriteLine(b.price + " -- " + b.title);
    }
    Console.ReadLine();
}
```

6. Call the GetTitlesByPrice method from the Main method.

```
static void Main(string[] args)
{
    //GetTitles();
    GetTitlesByPrice();
}
```

7. Run the program in debug mode. You should see the titles and prices listed in the Console window. When you are done testing, stop the debugger.

8. Add the following method to list the book titles and the sum of their sales amount. Notice that this query gets the sales amount by adding up the book's related sales entities.

```
private static void GetBooksSold()
{
    var context = new pubsEntities();
    var query = from b in context.books
                select new
                {
                    BookID = b.title_id,
                    TotalSold = b.sales.Sum(s =>(int?) s.qty)
                 };
    foreach (var item in query)
    {
        Console.WriteLine(item.BookID + " -- " + item.TotalSold);
```

```
    }
    Console.ReadLine();
}
```

9. Call the GetBooksSold method from the Main method.

```
static void Main(string[] args)
{
    //GetTitles();
    //GetTitlesByPrice();
    GetBooksSold();
}
```

10. Run the program in debug mode. You should see the book IDs and amount sold listed in the Console window. When you are done testing, stop the debugger and exit Visual Studio.

Summary

This chapter is the first in a series that will show you how to build the various tiers of an OOP application. To implement an application's data access layer, you learned about ADO.NET and the classes used to work with relational data sources. You looked at the various classes that make up the System.Data.SqlClient namespace; these classes retrieve and update data stored in a SQL Server database. You also examined the System.Data namespace classes that work with disconnected data. In addition, you were exposed to the Entity Framework and LINQ and saw how they allow you to query the data using OOP constructs. You wrote queries in terms of entities and the framework translated the queries into the query syntax of the datasource, retrieved the data, and loaded the entities.

In the next chapter, you will look at implementing the user interface (UI) tier of a Windows application. Along the way, you will take a closer look at the classes and namespaces of the .NET Framework used to create rich Windows-based user interfaces.

CHAPTER 11

■ ■ ■

Developing Windows Applications

In the previous chapter, you learned how to build the data access layer of an application. To implement its logic, you used the classes of the System.Data namespace. These classes retrieve and work with relational data, which is a common requirement of many business applications. You are now ready to look at how users will interact with your application. Users interact with an application through the user interface layer. This layer, in turn, interacts with the business logic layer, which, in turn, interacts with the data access layer. In this chapter, you will learn how to build a user interface layer with the .NET Windows Presentation Foundation (WPF). WPF takes advantage of modern graphics hardware and uses a vector-based rendering engine to display its output. It consists of a comprehensive set of application-development features that include Extensible Application Markup Language (XAML), controls, data binding, and layout.

After reading this chapter, you will be comfortable performing the following tasks:

- Using XAML markup to design a user interface.
- Working with layout controls.
- Working with display controls.
- Responding to control events.
- Using data binding controls.
- Creating and using control templates.

Windows Fundamentals

Windows are objects with a visual interface that are painted on the screen to provide users a way to interact with programs. Like most objects you work with in object-oriented languages, .NET windows expose properties, methods, and events. A window's properties define its appearance. Its Background property, for example, determines its color. The methods of a window define its behaviors. For example, calling its Hide method hides it from the user. A window's events define interactions with the user (or other objects). You can use the MouseDown event, for example, to initiate an action when the user clicks the right mouse button on the window.

Controls are components with visual interfaces that give users a way to interact with the program. A window is a special type of control, called a container control, that hosts other controls. You can place many different types of controls on windows. Some common controls used on windows are TextBoxes, Labels, OptionButtons, ListBoxes, and CheckBoxes. In addition to the controls provided by the .NET Framework, you can also create your own custom controls or purchase controls from third-party vendors.

Introducing XAML

WPF user interfaces are built using a declarative markup language called XAML. XAML declares the controls that will make up the interface. An opening angle bracket (<) followed by the name of the control type and a closing bracket defines the control. For example, the following markup defines a button control inside a Grid.

```
<Grid>
      <Button/>
</Grid>
```

Notice the Grid needs a formal closing tag because it contains the Button control. Since the Button control does not contain any other controls, you can use a forward slash (/) in front of the end bracket to close it.

The next step is to define the properties of the controls. For example, you may want to set the background color of the button to red and write some text on it. The properties of the control are set by using attribute syntax, which consists of the property name followed by an equal sign and the attribute value in quotation marks. The following markup shows the Button control with some attributes added:

```
<Grid>
      <Button Content="Click Me" Background="Red"/>
</Grid>
```

For some properties of an object element, attribute syntax is not possible. For these cases, a different syntax known as property element syntax can be used. The syntax for the property element start tag is <typeName.propertyName>. For example, you can create rows and columns in the layout grid to control placement of controls in the grid, as shown:

```
<Grid.ColumnDefinitions>
        <ColumnDefinition Width="100" />
        <ColumnDefinition Width="*" />
</Grid.ColumnDefinitions>
<Grid.RowDefinitions>
        <RowDefinition Height="25" />
        <RowDefinition Height="25" />
        <RowDefinition Height="25" />
</Grid.RowDefinitions>
```

Controls are positioned in the grid by including a Grid.Row and Grid.Column attribute, as shown:

```
<Label Grid.Column="0" Grid.Row="0" Content="Name:" />
<Label Grid.Column="0" Grid.Row="1" Content="Password:" />
<Button Grid.Column="1" Grid.Row="3"
        Content="Click Me" HorizontalAlignment="Right"
        MinWidth="80" Background="Red"/>
```

Figure 11-1 shows the window with two textboxes created by the previous XAML code.

Figure 11-1. *A window created with XAML*

Using Layout Controls

Although you can use fixed positioning to place controls on a WPF window, it's not recommended. Using fixed positioning usually works well for a fixed resolution size but it doesn't scale well to different resolutions and devices. To overcome the limitations of fixed positioning, WPF offers several layout controls. A layout control allows you to position other controls within it using a relative positioning format. One of the main layout controls for positioning other controls is the Grid. As seen previously, a Grid control contains columns and rows to control the placement of its child controls. The height and width of the columns and rows can be set to a fixed value, auto, or *. The auto setting takes up as much space as needed by the contained control. The * setting takes up as much space as is available. The Grid control is often used to lay out data entry forms. The following code lays out a simple data entry form used to collect user information. The resulting form is shown in Figure 11-2.

```
<Grid>
    <Grid.RowDefinitions>
        <RowDefinition Height="Auto" />
        <RowDefinition Height="Auto" />
        <RowDefinition Height="Auto" />
        <RowDefinition Height="Auto" />
        <RowDefinition Height="28" />
        <RowDefinition Height="*" />
    </Grid.RowDefinitions>
    <Grid.ColumnDefinitions>
        <ColumnDefinition Width="Auto" />
        <ColumnDefinition Width="200" />
        <ColumnDefinition Width="*" />
    </Grid.ColumnDefinitions>
    <Label Grid.Row="0" Grid.Column="0" Content="Name:"/>
    <Label Grid.Row="1" Grid.Column="0" Content="Old Password:"/>
    <Label Grid.Row="2" Grid.Column="0" Content="New Password:"/>
    <Label Grid.Row="3" Grid.Column="0" Content="Confirm Password:"/>
    <TextBox Grid.Column="1" Grid.Row="0" Margin="3" />
    <TextBox Grid.Column="1" Grid.Row="1" Margin="3" />
    <TextBox Grid.Column="1" Grid.Row="2" Margin="3" />
    <TextBox Grid.Column="1" Grid.Row="3" Margin="3" />
    <Button Grid.Column="1" Grid.Row="4" HorizontalAlignment="Right"
        MinWidth="80" Margin="0,0,0,8" Content="Submit"  />
</Grid>
```

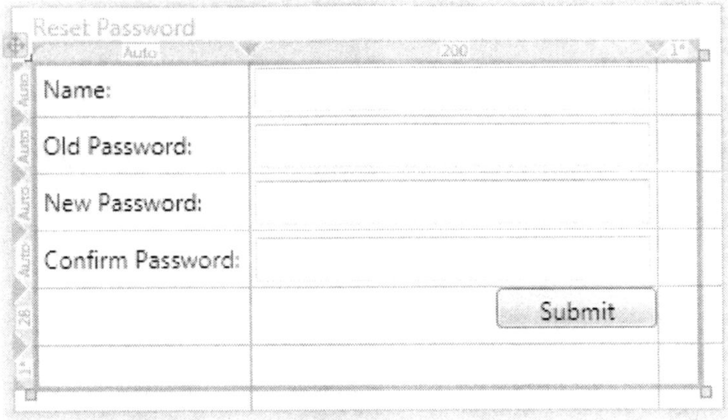

Figure 11-2. *Input form window*

Another useful layout control is the StackPanel. It lays out child controls either vertically or horizontally depending on the orientation setting. The following code shows two buttons in a StackPanel control:

```
<StackPanel Grid.Column="1" Grid.Row="4" Orientation="Horizontal" >
    <Button  MinWidth="80" Margin="0,0,0,8" Content="Submit" />
    <Button  MinWidth="80" Margin="0,0,0,8" Content="Cancel"  />
</StackPanel>
```

Some other layout controls available are the DockPanel, WrapPanel, and Canvas. The DockPanel is used to provide docking of elements to the left, right, top, bottom, or center of the panel. The WrapPanel acts like a StackPanel but will wrap child controls to a new line if no room is left. The Canvas control is used to lay out its child elements with absolute positioning relative to one of its sides. It is typically used for graphics elements and not to lay out user interface controls.

Adding Display Controls

The goal of most business applications is to present data to their users, allow them to update the data and save it back to a database. Some common controls used to facilitate this process are the Textbox, ListBox, ComboBox, Checkbox, DatePicker, and DataGrid. You have already seen the TextBox used on a window; the following code shows how to add a ListBox and ComboBox to a window. Figure 11-3 shows how the window is rendered.

```
<Grid>
    <Grid.ColumnDefinitions>
        <ColumnDefinition Width="*" />
        <ColumnDefinition Width="*" />
    </Grid.ColumnDefinitions>
    <ListBox Margin="20" Grid.Column="0">
        <ListBoxItem>Red</ListBoxItem>
        <ListBoxItem>Blue</ListBoxItem>
```

```
        <ListBoxItem>Green</ListBoxItem>
        <ListBoxItem>Yellow</ListBoxItem>
    </ListBox>
    <ComboBox Grid.Column="1" VerticalAlignment="Top">
        <ComboBoxItem>Small</ComboBoxItem>
        <ComboBoxItem>Medium</ComboBoxItem>
        <ComboBoxItem>Large</ComboBoxItem>
        <ComboBoxItem>X-Large</ComboBoxItem>
    </ComboBox>
</Grid>
```

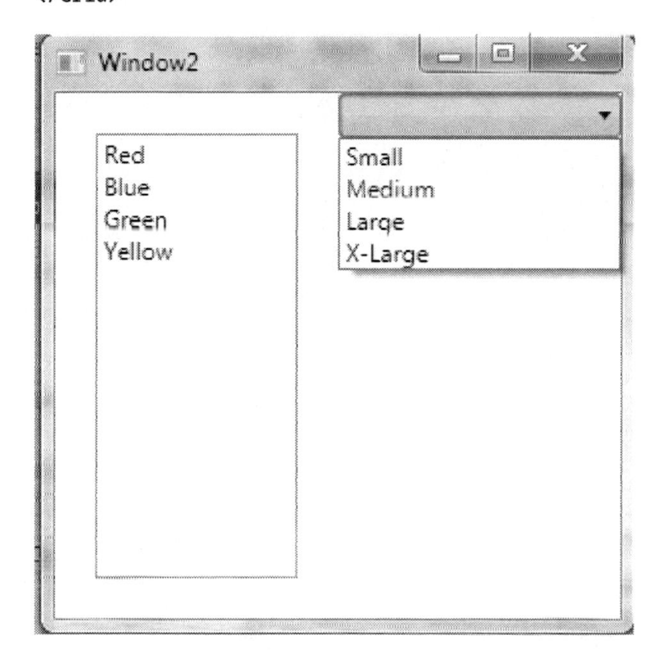

Figure 11-3. *Window containing a ListBox and ComboBox*

Although you can code the items displayed in these controls directly in the XAML markup, it is more likely you will use data binding to display their values. You'll look at data binding shortly.

Using the Visual Studio Designer

Even though it's quite possible to create your window entirely through code using a text editor, you will probably find this process quite tedious and not a very productive use of your time. Thankfully, the Visual Studio IDE includes an excellent designer for creating your WPF windows. Using the designer, you can drag and drop controls from the Toolbox to the Visual Studio designer, set its properties using the Visual Studio Properties window, and get the benefits of auto completion and syntax checking as you enter code using the XAML editor. Figure 11-4 shows a window in the Visual Studio designer.

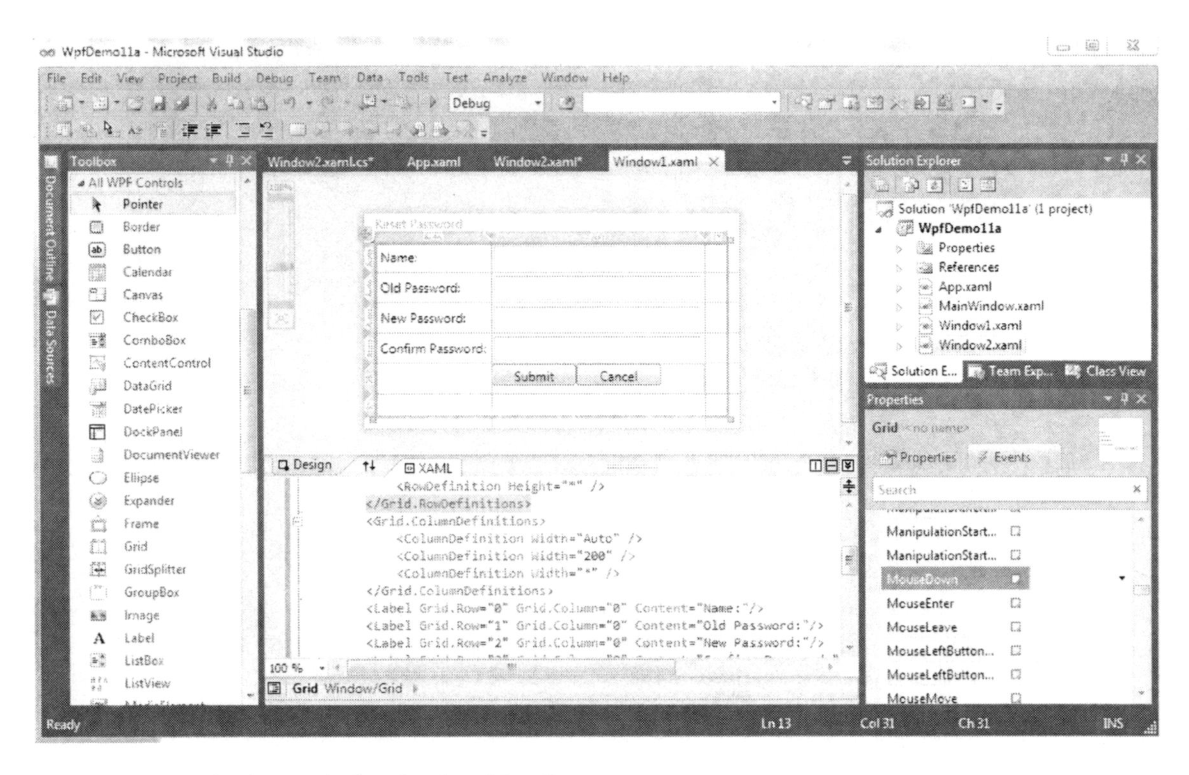

Figure 11-4. *Designing a window in Visual Studio*

Handling Control Events

Windows graphical user interface (GUI) programs are event-driven. Events are actions initiated by either a user or the system, whenever a user clicks a button, for example, or a SqlConnection object issues a StateChange event. Event-driven applications respond to the various events that occur by executing code that you specify. To respond to an event, you define the event handler to execute when a particular event occurs. As you saw in Chapter 8, the .NET Framework uses delegation to bind an event, with the event handler procedures written to respond to the event. A delegation object maintains an invocation list of methods that have subscribed to receive notification when the event occurs. When an event occurs—for example, a button is clicked—the control will raise the event by invoking the delegate for the event, which in turn will call the event handler methods that have subscribed to receive the event notification. Although this sounds complicated, the framework classes do most of the work for you.

In Visual Studio, you can add an event to a WPF control either by writing XAML code or by selecting it in the control's Properties window. Figure 11-5 shows wiring up an event handler in the XAML Editor window; Figure 11-6 shows wiring up an event handler using the Events tab of the Properties window. Note that when working with controls in code, you need to give them a unique name using the Name attribute.

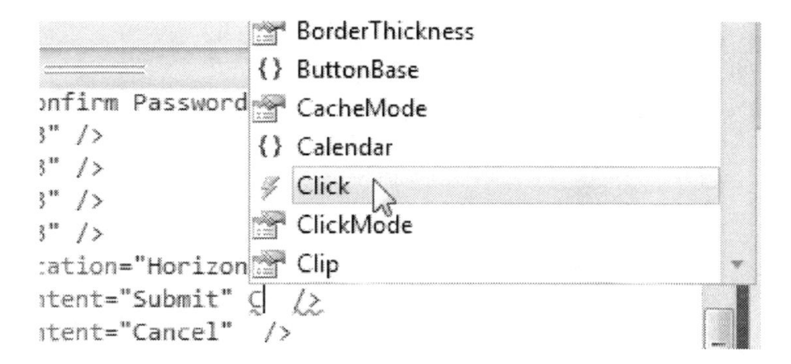

Figure 11-5. *Wiring up an event handler in the XAML editor*

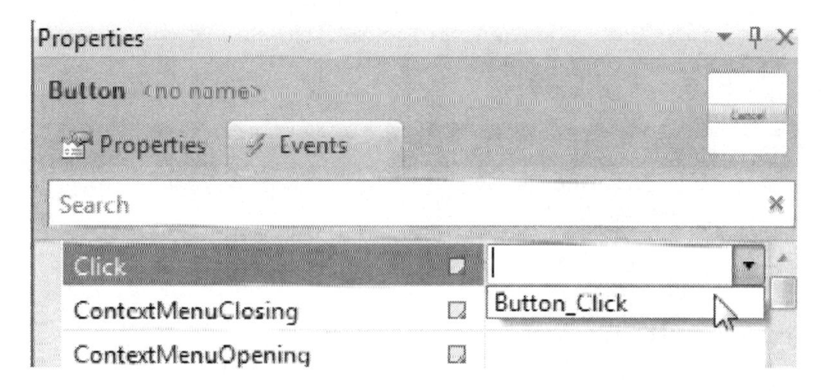

Figure 11-6. *Wiring up an event handler in the Properties window*

Regardless of how you wire up an event handler, the Visual Studio code editor inserts an empty event handler method in the codebehind file. The following code shows the event handler method inserted for the button click event:

```
private void btnCancel_Click(object sender, RoutedEventArgs e)
{
}
```

By convention, the name of the event handler method begins with the name of the object issuing the event followed by an underscore (_) and the name of the event. The actual name of the event handler, however, is unimportant. The Click attribute in the XAML code adds this method to the invocation list of the event's delegation object.

All event handlers must provide two parameters, which are passed to the method when the event is fired. The first parameter is the sender, which represents the object that initiated the event. The second parameter, of type System.Windows.RoutedEventArgs, is an object used to pass any information specific to the particular event.

Because the .NET Framework uses delegates for event notification, you can use the same method to handle more than one event, provided the events have the same signature. For example, you could handle a button click event and a menu click event with the same event handler, but not a button KeyPress event, because it has a different signature. The following code demonstrates how to handle the button click event of two buttons that use the same handler method. The sender parameter is cast as a Button type and interrogated to determine which button fired the event.

```
private void Button_Click(object sender, RoutedEventArgs e)
{
    Button btn = (Button)sender;
    if (btn.Name == "btnCancel")
    {
        //Cancel code goes here
    }
    else if (btn.Name == "btnSubmit")
    {
        //Submit code goes here
    }
}
```

In the following activity, you will work with forms and controls to construct a simple memo viewer application that will allow users to load and view memo documents.

ACTIVITY 11-1. WORKING WITH WINDOWS AND CONTROLS

In this activity, you will become familiar with the following:

- Creating a Windows Form-based GUI application.
- Working with Menu, StatusStrip, and Dialog controls.
- Working with Control events.

Creating the Memo Viewer Interface

To create the memo viewer interface, follow these steps:

1. Start Visual Studio. Select File ➤ New ➤ Project.
2. Choose a WPF Application under the C# Projects folder. Rename the project to Act11_1 and click the OK button.
3. The project contains a MainWindow.xaml file. This file is where you design the user interface. The project also contains a MainWindow.xaml.cs file. This is the codebehind file and it is where you will add the code to respond to the events.
4. In the Window tag in the XAML Editor Window, add a Name attribute with a value of "MemoViewer". Change the Title attribute to "Memo Viewer".

```
<Window x:Class="Act11_1.MainWindow"
    xmlns="http://schemas.microsoft.com/winfx/2006/xaml/presentation"
    xmlns:x="http://schemas.microsoft.com/winfx/2006/xaml"
    Name="MemoViewer" Title="Memo Viewer" Height="350" Width="525">
```

5. Add a DockPanel control in the Grid control.

```
<Grid>
    <DockPanel LastChildFill="True">
    </DockPanel>
</Grid>
```

6. Add a Menu control inside the DockPanel and dock it to the top using the following XAML:

```
<DockPanel LastChildFill="True">
    <Menu DockPanel.Dock="Top">
        <MenuItem Header="_File">
            <MenuItem Name="mnuNew" Header="_New..." />
            <Separator />
            <MenuItem Name="mnuOpen"  Header="_Open..." />
            <Separator />
            <MenuItem Name="mnuSave" Header="_Save" />
            <MenuItem Name="mnuSaveAs" Header="_Save As..." />
            <Separator />
            <MenuItem  Name="mnuExit" Header="_Exit" />
        </MenuItem>
        <MenuItem Header="_Edit">
            <MenuItem Header="_Cut..." />
            <MenuItem Header="_Copy..." />
            <MenuItem Header="_Paste" />
        </MenuItem>
    </Menu>
</DockPanel>
```

7. Add a StatusBar control by inserting the following code between the ending Menu tag and the ending DockPanel tag. Note that you are using a Grid control inside the StatusBar control to layout the items in the StatusBar.

```
<StatusBar DockPanel.Dock="Bottom">
     <Grid>
         <Grid.RowDefinitions>
             <RowDefinition Height="*"/>
         </Grid.RowDefinitions>
         <Grid.ColumnDefinitions>
             <ColumnDefinition Width="4*"/>
             <ColumnDefinition Width="*"/>
         </Grid.ColumnDefinitions>
     </Grid>
     <StatusBarItem Grid.Column="0" HorizontalAlignment="Left">
         <TextBlock Name="sbTextbox1">File Name</TextBlock>
     </StatusBarItem>
     <StatusBarItem Grid.Column="1" HorizontalAlignment="Right">
         <TextBlock Name="sbTextbox2">Date</TextBlock>
     </StatusBarItem>
 </StatusBar>
```

8. Add a RichTextBox control after the StatusBar end tag and before the DockPanel end tag.

```
    </StatusBar>
    <RichTextBox Name="rtbMemo" />
</DockPanel>
```

9. Note that as you add the XAML, the Visual Designer updates the appearance of the window. The MemoEditor window should look similar to the one shown Figure 11-7.

Figure 11-7. *The completed MemoEditor window*

10. Build the solution. If there are any errors, fix them and rebuild.

Coding the Control Events

To code the control events, follow these steps:

1. In the XAML Editor window, add the Loaded event attribute to the Window, as shown:

```
<Window x:Class="Act11_1.MainWindow"
        xmlns="http://schemas.microsoft.com/winfx/2006/xaml/presentation"
```

```
xmlns:x="http://schemas.microsoft.com/winfx/2006/xaml"
Name="MemoViewer" Title="Memo Viewer" Height="350" Width="525"
Loaded="MemoViewer_Loaded">
```

2. Open the codebehind file by right-clicking the XAML code editor and selecting View Code. Add the following code to the MemoViewer_Loaded event handler. When the window loads, it should show the message on the left side of the StatusPanel and the date on the right.

```
private void MemoViewer_Loaded(object sender, RoutedEventArgs e)
{
    sbTextbox1.Text = "Ready to load file";
    sbTextbox2.Text = DateTime.Today.ToShortDateString();
 }
```

3. In the XAML editor, add the Click event to the mnuOpen control.

```
<MenuItem Name="mnuOpen"  Header="_Open..."
        Click="mnuOpen_Click"/>
```

4. In the Code Editor window of the codebehind file, add the following code to the menu click event. This code configures and launches an Open File Dialog box, which returns the file path. The file path is then passed to a FileStream object, which loads the file into the RichTextBox. The file path is also loaded into the StatusBar TextBox.

```
private void mnuOpen_Click(object sender, RoutedEventArgs e)
{
    // Configure open file dialog box
    Microsoft.Win32.OpenFileDialog dlg = new Microsoft.Win32.OpenFileDialog();
    dlg.FileName = "Document"; // Default file name
    dlg.DefaultExt = ".txt"; // Default file extension
    dlg.Filter = "Text documents (.txt)|*.txt"; // Filter files by extension
    // Show open file dialog box
    Nullable<bool> result = dlg.ShowDialog();
    // Process open file dialog box results
    if (result == true)
    {
        // Open document and load RichTextBox
        string fileName = dlg.FileName;
        TextRange range;
        System.IO.FileStream fStream;
        if (System.IO.File.Exists(fileName))
        {
            range = new TextRange(rtbMemo.Document.ContentStart,
            rtbMemo.Document.ContentEnd);
            fStream = new System.IO.FileStream(fileName,
                      System.IO.FileMode.OpenOrCreate);
            range.Load(fStream, System.Windows.DataFormats.Text );
            fStream.Close();
        }
      sbTextbox1.Text = fileName;
   }
```

5. Add a click event for the mnuExit control with the following code to close the window:

```
private void mnuExit_Click(object sender, RoutedEventArgs e)
{
    this.Close();
}
```

6. Build the solution and fix any errors.
7. Create a Memos folder on the C drive. Using Notepad, create a text file containing a test message. Save the file as Test.txt.
8. Select Debug ➤ Start. Test the application by loading the Test.txt file. After viewing the file, close the window by clicking the Exit menu.
9. After testing the application, exit Visual Studio.

Creating and Using Dialog Boxes

Dialog boxes are special windows often used in Windows-based GUI applications to display or retrieve information from users. The difference between a normal window and a dialog box is that a dialog box is displayed modally. A modal window prevents the user from performing other tasks within the application until the dialog box has been dismissed. When you start a new project in Visual Studio, you are presented with a New Project dialog box, as shown in Figure 11-8. You can also use dialog boxes to present the user with critical information and query them for a response. For example, if you try to run an application in debug mode and a build error is encountered, the Visual Studio IDE presents you with a dialog box asking whether you want to continue (see Figure 11-9).

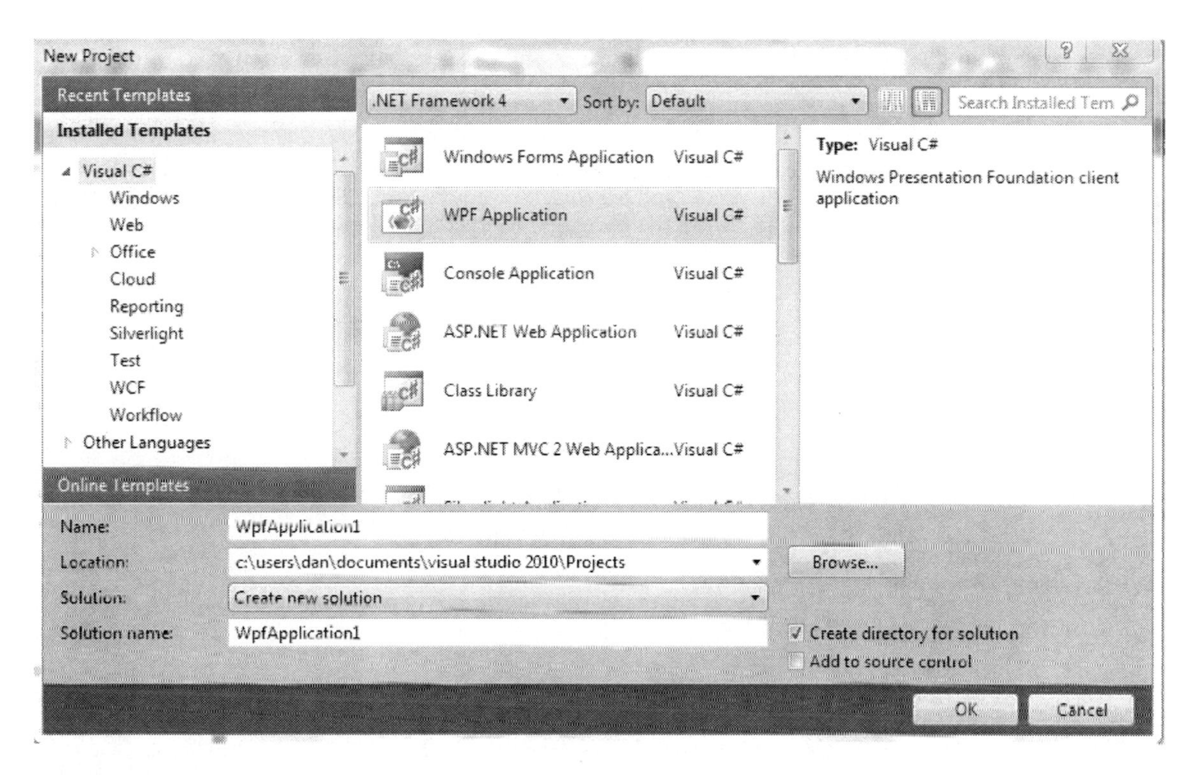

Figure 11-8. *The New Project dialog box*

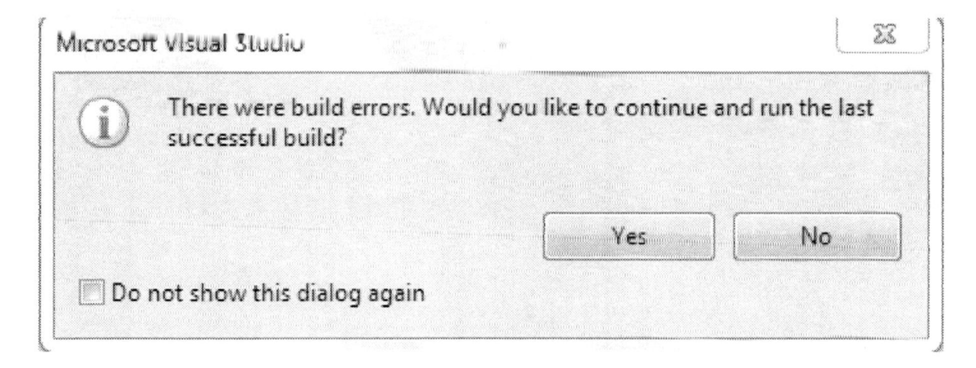

Figure 11-9. *Displaying critical information using a dialog box*

Presenting a MessageBox to the User

The dialog box shown in Figure 11-9 is a special predefined type called a MessageBox. The MessageBox class is part of the System.Windows namespace. The MessageBox class can display a standard Windows message dialog box. To display a MessageBox to the user, you call the static Show method of the MessageBox, like so:

```
MessageBox.Show("File Saved");
```

The Show method is overloaded so that you can optionally show a MessageBox icon, show a title, change the buttons displayed, and set the default button. The only required setting is the text message to be displayed on the form. Figure 11-10 shows the MessageBox displayed by the previous code.

Figure 11-10. *A basic MessageBox*

The following code calls the Show method using some of the other parameters. Figure 11-11 shows the resulting MessageBox that gets displayed. For more information on the various parameters and settings available, look up the MessageBox class in the Visual Studio help file.

```
MessageBox.Show("Are you sure you want to quit?",
          "Closing Application",MessageBoxButton.OKCancel,
          MessageBoxImage.Question);
```

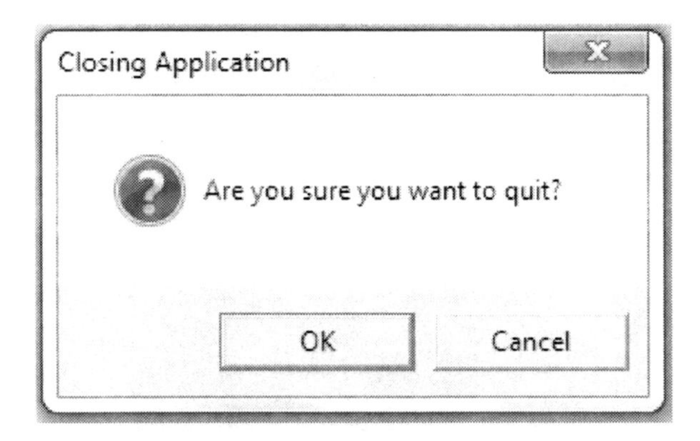

Figure 11-11. *A more complex Messagebox*

You will often use a MessageBox to query for a user response to a question. The user responds by clicking a button. The result is passed back as the return value of the MessageBox.Show method in the form of a MessageBoxResult enumeration. The following code captures the dialog box result entered by a user and closes the window (or not) depending on the result:

```
MessageBoxResult result =  MessageBox.Show("Are you sure you want to quit?",
                    "Closing Application",MessageBoxButton.OKCancel,
                    MessageBoxImage.Question);
if (result == MessageBoxResult.OK)
{
    this.Close();
}
```

Creating a Custom Dialog Box

One of the most exciting features about the .NET Framework is its extensibility. Although there are many types of dialog boxes, you can use "right-out-of-the-box" ones for such tasks as printing, saving files, and loading files. You can also build your own custom dialog boxes. The first step in creating a custom dialog box is to add a new window to the application. Next, add any controls needed to interact with the user. Figure 11-12 shows a dialog box you might use to verify a user's identity

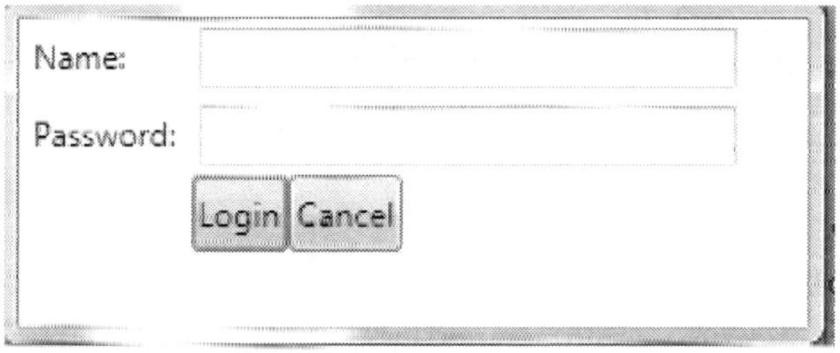

Name:

Password:

Login Cancel

Figure 11-12. *A custom dialog box*

Setting the IsCancel property of the Cancel button to true associates it to the keyboard shortcut of the ESC key. Setting the isDefault property of the Login button to true associates it with the keyboard Enter key. This is shown in the following XAML code:

```
<StackPanel Grid.Column="1"  Grid.Row="3" Orientation="Horizontal">
    <Button Name="loginButton" IsDefault="True">Login</Button>
    <Button Name="cancelButton" IsCancel="True">Cancel</Button>
</StackPanel>
```

When the Login button is clicked, the click event of the button is responsible for validating the user input and setting the DialogResult property to either true or false. This value is returned to the window that called the Show method of the DialogWindow for further processing. The following code shows the LoginDialog window called and the DialogResult property being interrogated. Notice that the calling window has access to the objects defined on the DialogWindow. In this case, it is interrogating the UserName textbox's Text property.

```
LoginDialog dlg = new LoginDialog();
dlg.Owner = this;
dlg.ShowDialog();
```

```
if (dlg.DialogResult == false)
{
    string user = dlg.UserName.Text;
    MessageBox.Show("Invalid login for " + user, "Warning",
                MessageBoxButton.OK, MessageBoxImage.Exclamation);
                this.Close();
}
```

Data Binding in Windows-Based GUIs

Once you have retrieved the data from the business logic tier, you must present it to the user. The user may need to read through the data, edit the data, add records, or delete records. Many of the controls you'll want to add to a window can display data. The choice of what control to use often depends on the type of data you want to display, the ways you want to manipulate it, and the design you have in mind for your interface. Among the controls .NET developers commonly use to present data are the TextBox, DataGrid, Label, ListBox, CheckBox, and Calendar. When different fields of a data source are presented to the user in separate controls (for example, a first name TextBox and last name TextBox), it is important that the controls remain synchronized to show the same record.

The .NET Framework encapsulates much of the complexity of synchronizing controls to a data source through a process called data binding. When you create a binding between a control and some data, you are binding a binding target to a binding source. A binding object handles the interaction between the binding source and the binding target. OneWay binding causes changes to the source property to automatically update the target property, but changes to the target property are not propagated back to the source property. This is useful for read-only scenarios. TwoWay binding causes changes to either the source property or the target property to automatically update the other. This is useful for full data updating scenarios.

Binding Controls Using a DataContext

To bind a control to data, you need a data source object. The DataContext of a container control allows child controls to inherit information from their parent controls about the data source that is used for binding. The following code sets the DataContext property of the top level Window control. It uses a DataSet and a TableAdapter to fill a Table object and set it to the DataContext of the Window.

```
private void Window_Loaded(object sender, RoutedEventArgs e)
{
    pubsDataSet dsPubs = new pubsDataSet();
    pubsDataSetTableAdapters.storesTableAdapter taStores =
        new pubsDataSetTableAdapters.storesTableAdapter();
    taStores.Fill(dsPubs.stores);
    this.DataContext = dsPubs.stores.DefaultView;
}
```

The following XAML code binds the DataGrid columns to the Store table columns using the Path attribute. Using Binding for the source means "look up the container hierarchy until a DataContext is found." In this case, it's the DataContext of the Window container.

```
<DataGrid  AutoGenerateColumns="False"  ItemsSource="{Binding}">
    <DataGrid.Columns>
        <DataGridTextColumn x:Name="stor_idColumn"
             Binding="{Binding Path=stor_id}" Header="Id"  />
        <DataGridTextColumn x:Name="stor_nameColumn"
             Binding="{Binding Path=stor_name}" Header="Name" />
                        <DataGridTextColumn x:Name="stateColumn"Binding="{Binding Path=state}"
        Header="State" />
        <DataGridTextColumn x:Name="zipColumn"
                Binding="{Binding Path=zip}" Header="Zip" />
    </DataGrid.Columns>
</DataGrid>
```

The resulting DataGrid loaded with store data is shown in Figure 11-13.

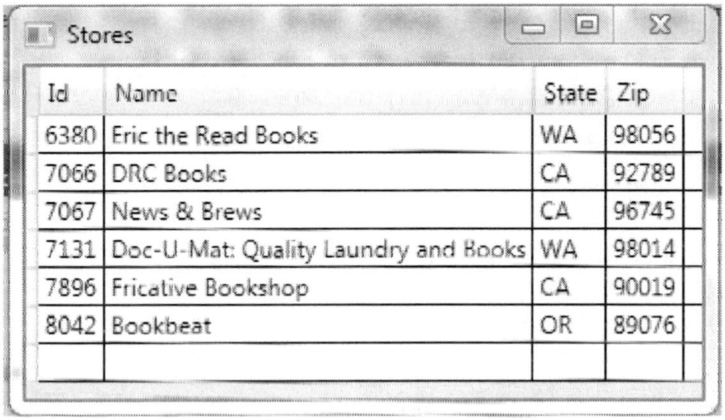

Stores

Id	Name	State	Zip
6380	Eric the Read Books	WA	98056
7066	DRC Books	CA	92789
7067	News & Brews	CA	96745
7131	Doc-U-Mat: Quality Laundry and Books	WA	98014
7896	Fricative Bookshop	CA	90019
8042	Bookbeat	OR	89076

Figure 11-13. *Displaying stored data with a DataGrid*

In the following activity, you will bind a DataGrid control to a DataTable containing data from Pubs database. You will also use a DataAdapter to update data changes made in the DataGrid control back to the Pubs database.

ACTIVITY 10-2. WORKING WITH DATA BOUND CONTROLS

In this activity, you will become familiar with the following:

- Binding a DataGrid to a DataTable.
- Updating data using the DataAdapter.

Binding a DataGrid to a DataTable

To bind a DataGrid to a DataTable object, follow these steps:

Create a DataSet

1. Start Visual Studio. Select File ➤ New ➤ Project.
2. Choose WPF Application. Rename the project to Act11_2 and click the OK button.
3. After the project loads, locate the Data Sources window. Click on the Add New Data Source link.
4. In the Data Source Configuration wizard, choose a data source type of Database.
5. In the Choose a Database Model window, select the Dataset.
6. In the Choose your Data Connection window, select or create a connection to the Pubs database.
7. On the next screen, save the connection to the application configuration file.
8. In the Choose Your Database Objects window, expand the tables' node and select the authors table. Click the Finish button.
9. Note in the Solutions Explorer window a pubsDataSet.xsd file has been added to the file. This file represents a strongly typed dataset object based on the pubs database. Double-click the file node in Solution Explorer to launch the dataset visual editor.
10. The visual editor contains an authors table. Select the authorsTableAdapter, as shown in Figure 11-14. In the Properties window, notice that the select, insert, update, and delete commands have been generated for you (see Figure 11-15).

Figure 11-14. *Selecting authorsTableAdapter*

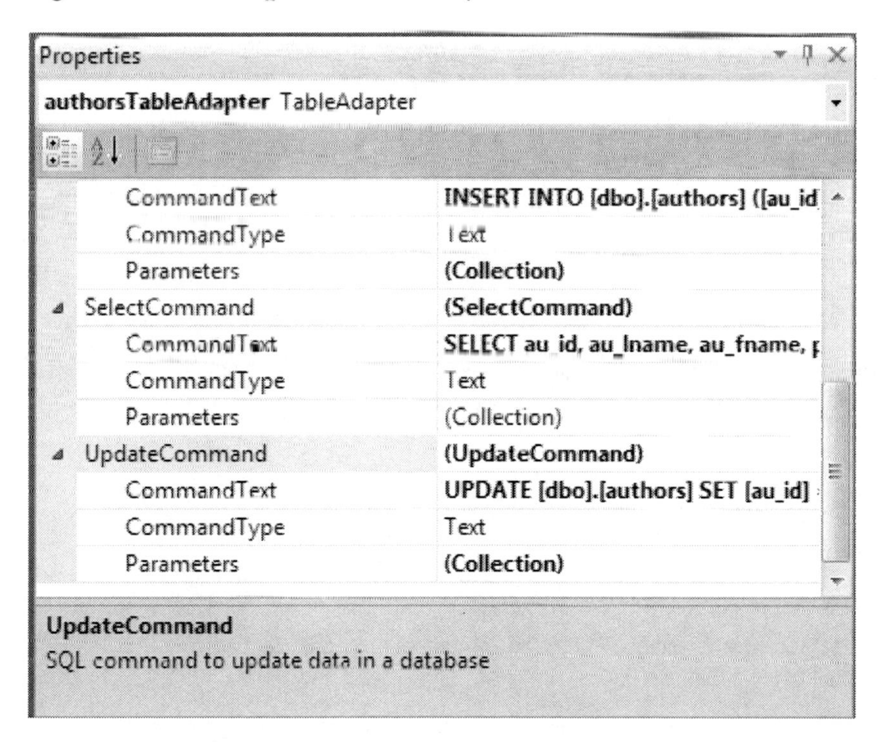

Figure 11-15. *Viewing the generated command text*

Create the Window Layout

1. Open the MainWindow in the XAML Editor window. Change the title of the Window to "Phone List".
2. Inside the Grid tags, add a DockPanel control. Inside the DockPanel, add a StackPanel.

```
<Grid>
    <DockPanel>
        <StackPanel DockPanel.Dock="Top" Orientation="Horizontal">

        </StackPanel>
    </DockPanel>
</Grid>
```

3. Inside the StackPanel, add two buttons—one for getting data and one for updating data. Add a Click event handler for each button.

```
<StackPanel DockPanel.Dock="Top" Orientation="Horizontal">
    <Button Name="btnGetData" Content="Get Data"
            Click="btnGetData_Click" />
    <Button Name="btnSaveData" Content="Save Data"
            Click="btnSaveData_Click" />
</StackPanel>
```

4. Outside the StackPanel but inside the DockPanel, add a DataGrid.

```
        <DataGrid Name="dgAuthors" AutoGenerateColumns="True"
                  DockPanel.Dock="Bottom" />
    </DockPanel>
</Grid>
```

5. Build the solution and make sure there are no build errors.

Load the DataGrid

1. Open the MainWindow.xaml.cs file in the Code Editor window.
2. Add three class level variables of type pubsDataset, authorsTableAdapter, and authorsDataTable.

```
public partial class MainWindow : Window
{
    pubsDataSet _dsPubs;
    pubsDataSetTableAdapters.authorsTableAdapter _taAuthors;
    pubsDataSet.authorsDataTable _dtAuthors;
```

3. In the btnGetData_Click event, add code to fill the _taAuthors table and set it equal to the DataContext of the gdAuthors grid.

```
private void btnGetData_Click(object sender, RoutedEventArgs e)
{
     _dsPubs = new pubsDataSet();
```

```
        _taAuthors = new pubsDataSetTableAdapters.authorsTableAdapter();
        _dtAuthors = new pubsDataSet.authorsDataTable();
        _taAuthors.Fill(_dtAuthors);
        this.dgAuthors.DataContext = _dtAuthors;
}
```

4. Add the ItemSource binding to the DataGrids XAML code. This will bind it to the DataContext.

```
<DataGrid Name="dgAuthors" AutoGenerateColumns="True"
                        DockPanel.Dock="Bottom" ItemsSource="{Binding}" />
```

5. Select Debug ➤ Start. Test the application by loading Get Data button. The DataGrid will load with the Authors' data (see Figure 11-16). Notice that since the AutoGenerateColumns property of the DataGrid is set to true, the grid loads with all the columns in the table. The headers of the grid columns are also the same name as the author's table columns.

6. After viewing the window, stop the debugger.

Phone List

Get Data Save Data

au_id	au_lname	au_fname	phone	address	city
172-32-1176	White	Johnson	408 496-7223	10932 Bigge Rd.	Menlo Pa
213-46-8915	Green	Marjorie	415 986-7020	309 63rd St. #411	Oakland
238-95-7766	Carson	Cheryl	415 548-7723	589 Darwin Ln.	Berkeley
267-41-2394	O'Leary	Michael	408 286-2428	22 Cleveland Av. #14	San Jose
274-80-9391	Straight	Dean	415 834-2919	5420 College Av.	Oakland
341-22-1782	Smith	Meander	913 843-0462	10 Mississippi Dr.	Lawrence
409-56-7008	Bennet	Al	415 658-9932	6223 Bateman St.	Berkeley
427-17-2319	Dull	Ann	415 836-7128	3410 Blonde St.	Palo Alto
472-27-2349	Gringlesby	Burt	707 938-6445	PO Box 792	Covelo
486-29-1786	Locksley	Charlene	415 585-4620	18 Broadway Av.	San Franc
527-72-3246	Greene	Morningstar	615 297-2723	22 Graybar House Rd.	Nashville
648-92-1872	Blotchet-Halls	Reggy	503 745-6402	55 Hillsdale Bl.	Corvallis
672-71-3249	Yokomoto	Akiko	415 935-4228	3 Silver Ct.	Walnut Cr

Figure 11-16. *The author's DataGrid*

Updating Data

1. Open the MainWindow.xaml.cs file in the Code Editor window. Add the following code to update the data in the btnSaveData_Click event handler. This code uses the table adapter's update command to send the changes back to the database.

```
private void btnSaveData_Click(object sender, RoutedEventArgs e)
{
    try
    {
        _taAuthors.Update(_dtAuthors);
        MessageBox.Show("Data Saved.",
               "Information", MessageBoxButton.OK,
                MessageBoxImage.Information);
    }
    catch (Exception ex)
    {
        MessageBox.Show("Could not save data!",
                "Warning",MessageBoxButton.OK,
                 MessageBoxImage.Warning);
    }
}
```

2. Update the Grid's XAML code to only show the first name, last name, and phone columns.

```
<DataGrid Name="dgAuthors" AutoGenerateColumns="False"
          DockPanel.Dock="Bottom" ItemsSource="{Binding}">
    <DataGrid.Columns>
        <DataGridTextColumn Header="Last Name" Binding="{Binding Path='au_lname'}
            " />
        <DataGridTextColumn Header="First Name" Binding="{Binding Path='au_fname'}
            " />
        <DataGridTextColumn Header="Phone" Binding="{Binding Path='phone'}" />
    </DataGrid.Columns>
</DataGrid>
```

3. Select Debug ➤ Start. Test the application by loading the Get Data button. Update some of the Names. Click the Save Data button and then click the Get Data button to verify the names were saved to the database.

4. After testing, stop the debugger and exit Visual Studio.

Creating and Using Control and Data Templates

In WPF, every control has a template that manages its visual appearance. If you don't explicitly set its Style property, then it uses a default template. Creating a custom template and assigning it to the Style property is an excellent way to alter the look and feel of your applications. Figure 11-17 shows a standard button as well as a rounded button created by using a control template.

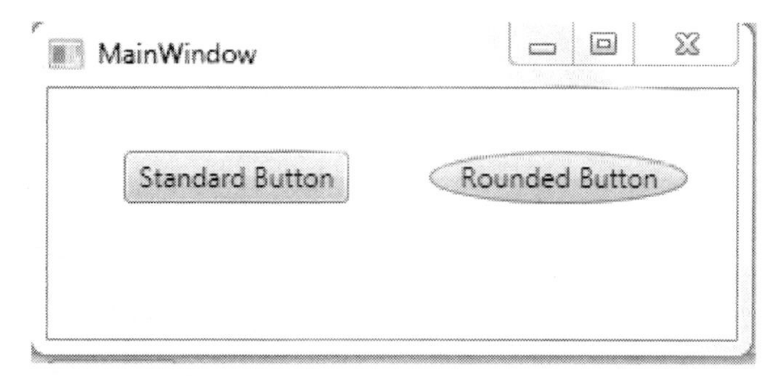

Figure 11-17. *Creating a rounded button with a custom template*

The following XAML is the markup that defines the custom template used to create the rounded button in Figure 11-17.

```
<Window.Resources>
      <Style x:Key="RoundedButtonStyle" TargetType="Button">
          <Setter Property="Template">
              <Setter.Value>
                  <ControlTemplate TargetType="{x:Type Button}">
                      <Grid>
                          <Ellipse Fill="{TemplateBinding Background}"
                           Stroke="{TemplateBinding BorderBrush}"/>
                          <ContentPresenter HorizontalAlignment="Center"
                                        VerticalAlignment="Center"/>
                      </Grid>
                  </ControlTemplate>
              </Setter.Value>
          </Setter>
      </Style>
  </Window.Resources>
```

The following XAML code is used to bind the custom style to a button using the button's Style property:

```
<Button Content="Rounded Button" Style="{StaticResource RoundedButtonStyle}"
```

Along with control style templates, you can also create data templates. Data templates let you customize how your business objects will look when you bind them in your UI. A good example of when you need to use a custom data template is the list box. By default, it renders data as a single line of text. When you try to bind it to a list of employee objects, it calls the ToString() method and writes it out to the display. As you can see in Figure 11-18, this is clearly not what you want.

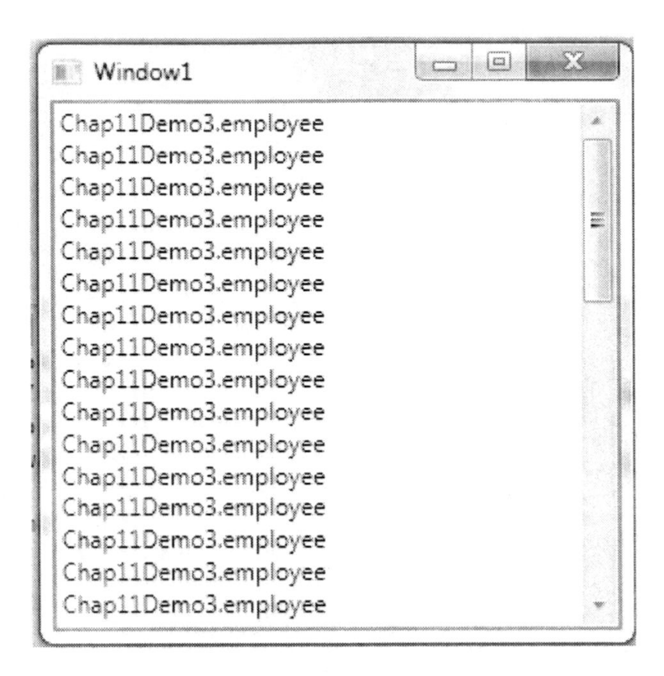

Figure 11-18. *ListBox using the default DataTemplate*

By adding a DataTemplate to the ListBox control, you can not only get the employee data to display, but you can also control how it gets displayed. The following XAML adds a DataTemplate to the ListBox, and Figure 11-19 shows the result:

```
<ListBox ItemsSource="{Binding}" >
    <ListBox.ItemTemplate>
        <DataTemplate>
            <StackPanel Orientation="Horizontal">
                <TextBlock FontWeight="Bold" Text="{Binding Path='lname'}" />
                <TextBlock Text=", " />
                <TextBlock Text="{Binding Path='fname'}" />
                <TextBlock Text=" " />
                <TextBlock Text="{Binding Path = 'minit'}" />
             </StackPanel>
         </DataTemplate>
    </ListBox.ItemTemplate>
</ListBox>
```

Figure 11-19. *ListBox using a custom DataTemplate*

In the following activity, you will bind a ListBox control to an entity created from the Pubs database using an entity data model. You will also create a master detail view by synchronizing a ListBox control and a DataGrid control.

ACTIVITY 10-3. WORKING WITH DATA TEMPLATES

In this activity, you will become familiar with the following:

- Binding a ListBox to an Entity.
- Creating a DataTemplate.
- Creating a Master Detail View.

Binding a ListBox to an Entity

To bind a Listbox to an entity object, follow these steps:

1. Start Visual Studio. Select File ➤ New ➤ Project.
2. Choose WPF Application. Rename the project to Act11_3 and click the OK button.
3. After the project loads locate the Data Sources window. Click on the Add New Data Source link.

4. In the Data Source Configuration wizard, choose a data source type of Database.
5. In the Choose a Database Model window, select the Entity Data Model.
6. In the Choose Model Contents window, select the Generate from database option.
7. In the Choose your Data Connection window, select or create a connection to the Pubs database.
8. On the next screen, save the connection to the application configuration file.
9. In the Choose Your Database Objects window, expand the tables' node and select the stores and sales tables. Click the Finish button.
10. Notice in the Solutions Explorer window a Model1.edmx file has been added to the file. This file contains the relational mapping between the entities and the tables in the pubs database.

Creating the Data Template

1. Add a DockPanel and a ListBox control in the XAML Editor window.

```
<Grid Name="StoresGrid">
    <DockPanel>
        <ListBox Name="StoresList" DockPanel.Dock="Left" ItemsSource="{Binding}">

        </ListBox>
    </DockPanel>
</Grid>
```

2. Add a Window_Loaded event handler in the code file that sets the DataContext of the ListBox to the stores entities.

```
private void Window_Loaded(object sender, RoutedEventArgs e)
{
    pubsEntities db = new pubsEntities();
    this.StoresGrid.DataContext = db.stores;
}
```

3. Add a DataTemplate to display the store name in a TextBox control.

```
<ListBox Name="StoresList" DockPanel.Dock="Left"
         ItemsSource="{Binding}">
    <ListBox.ItemTemplate>
        <DataTemplate>
            <TextBlock FontWeight="Bold" Text="{Binding Path='stor_name'}" />
        </DataTemplate>
    </ListBox.ItemTemplate>
</ListBox>
```

4. Select Debug ➤ Start. Make sure the ListBox shows the store names. When you're done viewing the ListBox, stop the debugger.

5. To implement a master/detail data view, add a DataGrid control to the DockPanel control after the ListBox control. The Binding of the grid is set to the same as the list box, which is the store entity, but the binding path is set to the sales entity. This will cause the data grid to show the sales items of the store selected in the list box.

```
<DataGrid Name="SalesGrid" DockPanel.Dock="Right"
          ItemsSource="{Binding Path='sales'}" AutoGenerateColumns="False">
    <DataGrid.Columns>
        <DataGridTextColumn Header="Order Number"  Binding="{Binding➥
Path='ord_num'}"/>
        <DataGridTextColumn Header="Order Date" Binding="{Binding➥
Path='ord_date'}"/>
    </DataGrid.Columns>
</DataGrid>
```

6. Add the following property to the ListBox control in the XAML code. This will ensure that the ListBox control and DataGrid control will remain in sync.

```
IsSynchronizedWithCurrentItem="True"
```

7. Launch the application in the debugger. Your window should look similar to Figure 11-20. Click on different stores in the list box. You should see the data grid update with the store's sales data. After testing, stop the debugger and close Visual Studio.

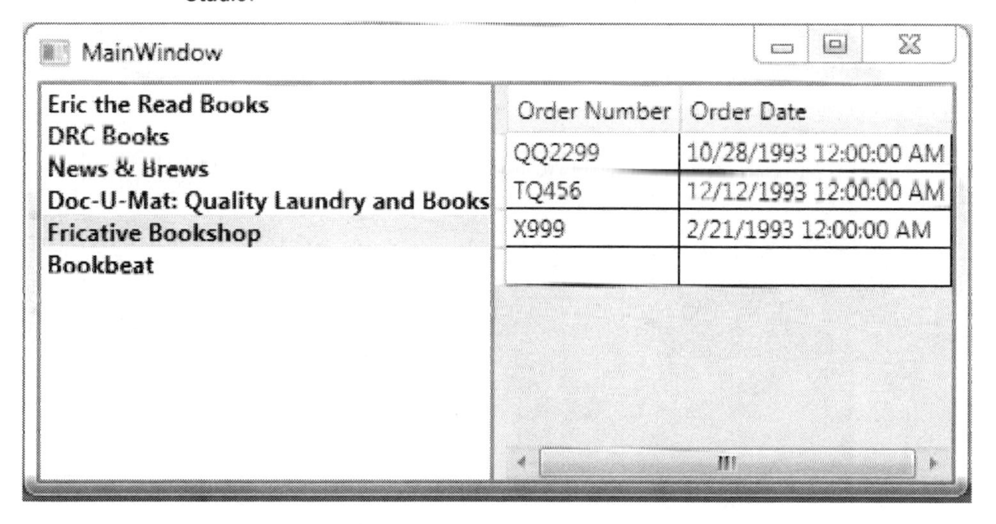

Figure 11-20. *Viewing master/detail data*

Summary

In this chapter, you looked at implementing the interface tier of an application. You implemented the user interface through a WPF-based application front end. Along the way, you took a closer look at the classes and namespaces of the .NET Framework used to implement rich Windows-based user interfaces. You saw how to use XAML syntax to define the controls and layout of the interface. You also saw how easy it is to bind the controls to the data and present it to the users.

In the next chapter, you will revisit the UI tier of a .NET application, but instead of implementing the GUI using WPF, you will implement the GUI as a web-based application using Silverlight. Along the way, you will take a closer look at the namespaces available for creating web-based GUI applications and the techniques involved in implementing the classes contained in these namespaces.

CHAPTER 12

Developing Web Applications

In the previous chapter, you learned how to build a simple Windows-based graphical user interface (GUI) using C# and WPF. Although WPF gives programmers the ability to easily build extremely rich user interfaces, it is not always practical to assume users will access your programs through a traditional Windows-based PC. With the proliferation of intranets, web applications, and mobile devices, applications now need to allow users the ability to access the interface through a variety of browsers and devices. This chapter shows you how to build a web-based user interface using Silverlight. If you experience a sense of déjà vu while reading this chapter, it is by design. Silverlight interface design and programming uses an object model that is remarkably similar to the one used to design and program a WPF interface. As a matter of fact, prior to the release of Silverlight 1.0, it was referred to as Windows Presentation FoundationEverywhere (WPFE).

In this chapter, you will be performing the following tasks with Silverlight:

- Using XAML markup to design the user interface.
- Working with layout controls.
- Working with display controls.
- Responding to control events.
- Working with data binding controls.
- How to perform data validation and conversion.

What Is Silverlight?

Although you can build extremely rich and sophisticated UI for your applications using WPF, it is limited to running on a computer that is running a Windows operating system. More and more users are demanding Rich Internet-based Applications (RIA) that run on a variety of devices and a variety of browsers. This demand is not limited to traditional web-based applications;business users no longer want to be tied to client applications running on their desktop PCs in the office. They want to access the applications on laptops via wireless hotspots or through their Internet-capable cell phones. In response to these demands, Microsoft developed Silverlight.

Silverlight is what is known as a cross-browser, cross-platform technology. It runs in all popular web browsers, including Microsoft Internet Explorer, Mozilla Firefox, Apple Safari, Google Chrome, and on Microsoft Windows and Apple Mac OS X. Running Silverlight requires a free plug-in that automatically installs (with permission) if users don't have it. The download is small and installs quickly. Application code is compiled and runs on the client;it only n eeds to contact the server for resources such as data and media.

Silverlight is based on a subset of the Windows Presentation Foundation (WPF) technology and the .NET Framework. As a result, Silverlight greatly extends the elements and classes available for creating rich UI running in the browser. Silverlight applications are created using any .NET Framework-supported language (including Visual Basic, C#, and JavaScript). Like WPF windows, pages in a Silverlight application are created using XAML. XAML is similar to HTML in that it uses a declarative syntax;however, XAML provides sign ificantly more powerful elements.

Creating a Silverlight Application

You can develop a Silverlight application in Visual Studio much as you would a WPF application. As a matter of fact, if you look at Figure 12-1, you can see that the layout of the designer is almost identical. There is a Visual Design window, XAML Code Editor window, Toolbox, Properties window, and Solution Explorer.

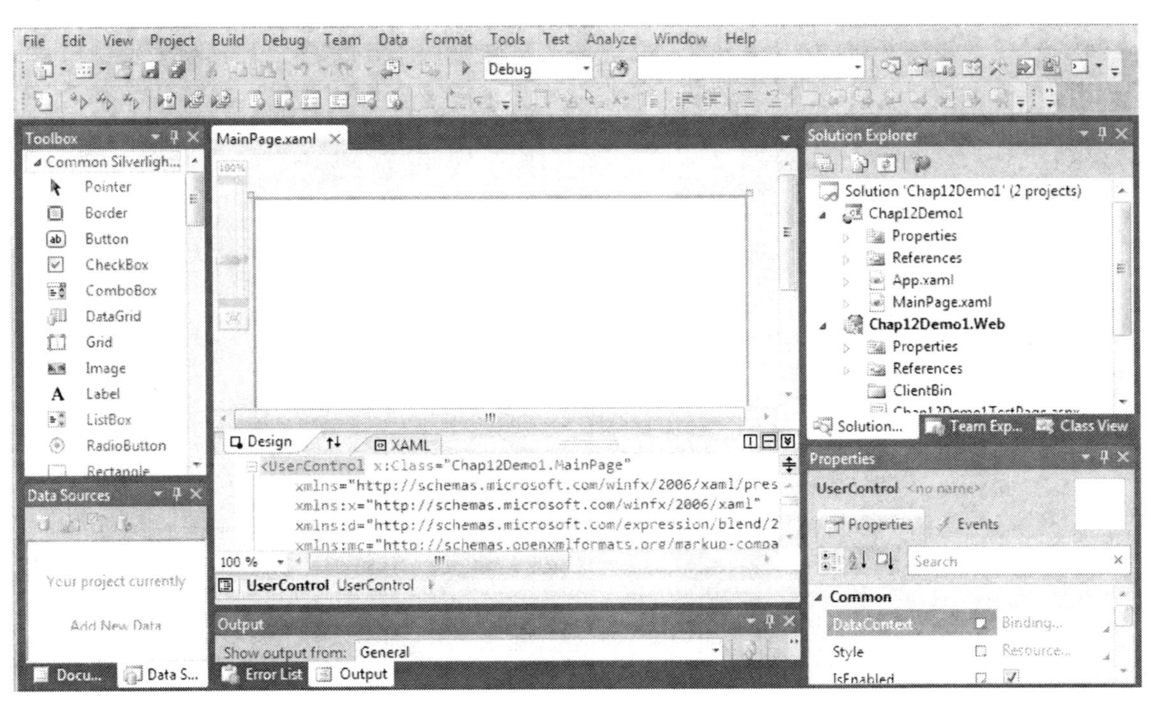

Figure 12-1. *Visual Studio Silverlight designer*

One of the major differences between a WPF application and a Silverlight application is that the Silverlight solution requires two projects. One project is the Silverlight application and the other is a web site to host it. When you build a Silverlight application, the code is compiled and compressed into a XAP file. A link to the XAP file is then hosted in a web page control. When a user loads the web page, the XAP file is downloaded and the code is decompressed and hosted in the browser using the Silverlight plug-in. If the plug-in is not installed, its absence is detected and the user is shown a link where a copy can be found for download. The following markup shows the link to the XAP in an HTML web page:

```
<object data="data:application/x-silverlight-2,"
        type="application/x-silverlight-2" width="100%" height="100%">
    <param name="source" value="ClientBin/Chap12Demo1.xap"/>
    <param name="onError" value="onSilverlightError" />
    <param name="background" value="white" />
    <param name="minRuntimeVersion" value="4.0.50826.0" />
    <param name="autoUpgrade" value="true" />
    <a href="http://go.microsoft.com/fwlink/?LinkID=149156&v=4.0.50826.0"
          style="text-decoration:none">
        <img src="http://go.microsoft.com/fwlink/?LinkId=161376"
              alt="Get Microsoft Silverlight" style="border-style:none"/>
    </a>
</object>
```

Using Layout Controls

The main container for a Silverlight control is the Page element. Inside the Page element, a main layout control must be declared. This can be a Grid, Canvas, or StackPanel. By default, the Visual Studio designer uses the Grid control. The following XAML is the default XAML inserted when you add a new page. Notice that the page element is actually a UserControl hosted by a web page.

```
<UserControl x:Class="Chap12Demo1.MainPage"
    xmlns="http://schemas.microsoft.com/winfx/2006/xaml/presentation"
    xmlns:x="http://schemas.microsoft.com/winfx/2006/xaml"
    xmlns:d="http://schemas.microsoft.com/expression/blend/2008"
    xmlns:mc="http://schemas.openxmlformats.org/markup-compatibility/2006"
    mc:Ignorable="d"
    d:DesignHeight="300" d:DesignWidth="400">
    <Grid x:Name="LayoutRoot" Background="White">

    </Grid>
</UserControl>
```

Just as in WPF, fixed positioning to place controls on a page it is not recommended. Fixed positioning does not scale well to different resolutions and devices. The following code lays out a Silverlight login page used to capture a user's name and password. The resulting form is shown in Figure 12-2.

```
<Grid x:Name="LayoutRoot" Background="White" Margin="10" >
        <Grid.RowDefinitions>
            <RowDefinition Height="Auto" />
            <RowDefinition Height="Auto" />
            <RowDefinition Height="Auto" />
        </Grid.RowDefinitions>
        <Grid.ColumnDefinitions>
            <ColumnDefinition Width="Auto" />
            <ColumnDefinition Width="Auto" />
        </Grid.ColumnDefinitions>
        <sdk:Label Grid.Row="0" Grid.Column="0" Content="Name:"/>
        <sdk:Label Grid.Row="1" Grid.Column="0" Content="Password:"/>
        <TextBox Grid.Column="1" Grid.Row="0" Margin="3" MinWidth="150"/>
```

```
        <TextBox Grid.Column="1" Grid.Row="1" Margin="3" MinWidth="150"/>
        <Button Grid.Column="1" Grid.Row="4" HorizontalAlignment="Right"
            MinWidth="80" Margin="0,0,0,8" Content="Submit"  />
    </Grid>
```

Figure 12-2. *Input page*

You often use layout controls inside other controls. To add a Cancel button to the form and lay it out horizontally alongside the Submit button, you would use a StackPanel inside the Grid control, as shown in the following markup:

```
<StackPanel Grid.Column="1" Grid.Row="4" Orientation="Horizontal" >
    <Button  MinWidth="80" Margin="0,0,0,8" Content="Submit" />
    <Button  MinWidth="80" Margin="0,0,0,8" Content="Cancel"  />
</StackPanel>
```

Adding Display Controls

Silverlight pages can host many of the same controls as a WPF window. Most business applications are designed to present and capture data from the users. Some common controls used to facilitate this process are the Textbox, ListBox, ComboBox, Checkbox, DatePicker, and DataGrid. The following code shows how to add a DatePicker and CheckBoxes to a Silverlight page. The sdk designation in front of the DataPicker control signifies that it's part of the libraries in the Silverlight Software Development K (SDKand is available when you install the SDKFigu re 12-3 shows how the page is displayed to the user.

```
<Grid>
    <Grid.ColumnDefinitions>
        <ColumnDefinition Width="Auto" />
        <ColumnDefinition Width="Auto" />
    </Grid.ColumnDefinitions>
    <sdk:DatePicker Grid.Column="0" VerticalAlignment="Top" MinWidth="175" />
    <StackPanel Grid.Column="1" >
        <CheckBox Content="Morning" />
        <CheckBox Content="Afternoon" />
        <CheckBox Content="Evening" />
    </StackPanel>
</Grid>
```

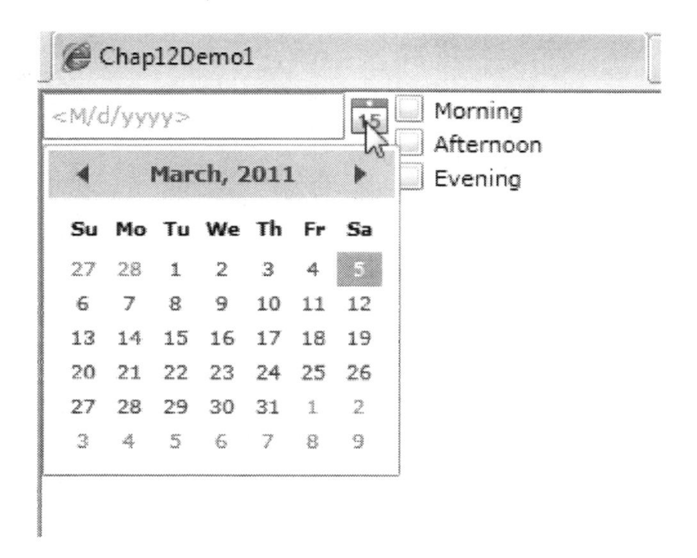

Figure 12-3. *Page containing a DatePicker and CheckBoxes*

Handling Control Events

Silverlight follows an event-driven programming model similar to WPF. Events are messages sent by an object to signal the occurrence of an action. This can be an action initiated by a user, such as a ButtonClick, or an action initiated by the program, such as a LayoutUpdated event.

To add events, you typically wire up an event handler to a control using XAML code. When working with controls in code, you need to give them each a unique name using the Name attribute. The following markup shows how to add a click event to a button:

```
<Button Name="btnSave" Click="btnSave_Click" Grid.Column="2" MinWidth="80"
                    Height="20" Content="Save" VerticalAlignment="Top"/>
```

When an event handler is assigned to an event in the XAML, the code editor inserts an event handler method in the codebehind file. All event handlers include two parameters: the sender parameter contains a reference to the object that initiated the event and the event args passes data specific for a certain kind of event. For example, mouse events may pass information pertaining to the position of the cursor when the event occurred. The following code shows the event handler method inserted for the button click event:

```
private void btnSave_Click(object sender, RoutedEventArgs e)
{
}
```

Remember that by convention, the name of the event handler method is the name of the object issuing the event followed by an underscore character (_) and the name of the event. The actual name of the event handler, however, is unimportant. The Click attribute in the XAML code adds this method to the invocation list of the event's delegation object.

In the following activity, you'll build a Silverlight page, add some common controls, and respond to control events.

ACTIVITY 12-1. WORKING WITH SILVERLIGHT CONTROLS

In this activity, you will become familiar with the following:

- Creating a Silverlight application.
- Adding and working with various controls on a page.
- Implementing control events.

■ **Note** In order to complete the activities in this chapter, you need to install the Silverlight Tools for Visual Studio 2010. Refer to Appendix C for instructions.

Creating a Silverlight Application and Adding Controls

To create the Silverlight application, follow these steps:

1. Start Visual Studio. Select File ➤ New ➤ Project.
2. Choose a Silverlight Application under the C# Projects folder. Rename the project to Act12_1 and click the OK button.
3. The next screen asks if you want to host the Silverlight application in a new web site. It also asks you what version of Silverlight you want to use. Accept the defaults shown in Figure 12-4 and click OK.

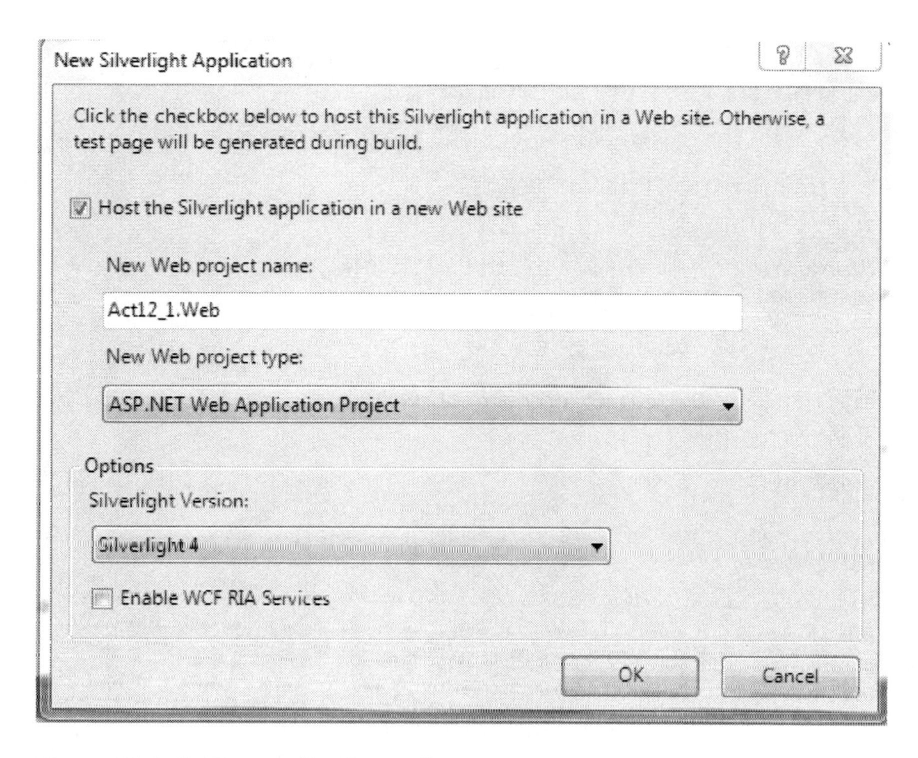

Figure 12-4. *Setting application options*

4. The project contains a MainPage.xaml file. This file is where you design the user interface. The project also contains a MainPage.xaml.cs file. This is the codebehind file and it's where you will add the code to respond to the events.

5. Add a StackPanel inside the main Layout Grid control. Inside the StackPanel, add a TextBox and ComboBox, as shown:

```
<Grid x:Name="LayoutRoot" Background="White" >
    <StackPanel  Orientation="Vertical" HorizontalAlignment="Center">
        <TextBox Name="txtColor"  Text="Color Me!" FontSize="18"/>
        <ComboBox Name="cboColors">
            <ComboBoxItem Name="Item1" Content="Red"/>
            <ComboBoxItem Name="Item2" Content="Blue"/>
            <ComboBoxItem Name="Item3" Content="Green"/>
        </ComboBox>
    </StackPanel>
</Grid>
```

6. Add a SelectionChanged event handler to the ComboBox.

```
<ComboBox Name="cboColors" SelectionChanged="cboColors_SelectionChanged">
```

7. In the codebehind file, add the following code to interrogate the ComboBoxItem's Content and change the font color of the TextBox depending on what was

selected. The SelectionChangedEventArgs parameter (e) passes in a list of selected items. In this case, there is only one item in the list.

```
private void cboColors_SelectionChanged(object sender, SelectionChangedEventArgs e)
{
    ComboBoxItem l = (ComboBoxItem) e.AddedItems[0];
    if (l.Content.ToString() == "Red")
    {
        SolidColorBrush brush = new SolidColorBrush(Colors.Red);
        txtColor.Foreground = brush;
    }
    if (l.Content.ToString() == "Blue")
    {
       SolidColorBrush brush = new SolidColorBrush(Colors.Blue);
       txtColor.Foreground = brush;
    }
    if (l.Content.ToString() == "Green")
    {
        SolidColorBrush brush = new SolidColorBrush(Colors.Green);
        txtColor.Foreground = brush;
    }
}
```

8. Run the application in the debugger. You should see a page with the TextBox and a ComboBox. Test the application by selecting different colors in the ComboBox and verify the text color of the Textbox changes. After testing, stop the debugger.

Adding Event Handling to Silverlight Controls

1. In the XAML Editor below the ComboBox, add a `Canvas` and a `Textbox` control. Note that an event handler for the `Canvas's` MouseEnter and MouseLeave events has been added.

```
<Canvas Width="150" Height="150" Background="Aqua"
        MouseEnter="Canvas_MouseEnter" MouseLeave="Canvas_MouseLeave">
    <TextBox Name="txtMessage" FontSize="18" Visibility="Collapsed"
             Canvas.Left="35" Canvas.Top="46" Background="Aqua" />
</Canvas>
```

2. Open the codebehind file by right-clicking the XAML Editor and selecting View Code. Add the following code to the Canvas_MouseEnter event handler:

```
private void Canvas_MouseEnter(object sender, MouseEventArgs e)
{
    txtMessage.Visibility = Visibility.Visible;
    txtMessage.Text = "Hello";
}
```

3. Add the following code to the Canvas_MouseLeave event handler:

```
private void Canvas_MouseLeave(object sender, MouseEventArgs e)
{
```

```
    txtMessage.Text = "Goodbye";
}
```

4. Run the application in the debugger. You should see the Canvas control on the page. Test the application by moving the mouse cursor in and out of the Canvas control. Verify that the Textbox shows the Hello and Goodbye messages. After testing, stop the debugger.

5. In the XAML Editor, after the Canvas control, add a ProgressBar and a Button control. Note that an event handler for the Button's Click event has been added.

```
<ProgressBar Name="pbProgress" Foreground="Aqua" Background="Gray"
        Value="10" Maximum="100" Width="200" Height="20" Margin="20"/>
<Button Name="btnAdvance" Height="20" Width="60" Content="Advance"
        Click="btnAdvance_Click"/>
```

6. Add the following code to the btnAdvance_Click event handler:

```
private void btnAdvance_Click(object sender, RoutedEventArgs e)
{
    if (pbProgress.Value < pbProgress.Maximum)
    {
        pbProgress.Value+=20;
    }
}
```

7. Run the application in the debugger. You should see the progress bar and button on the page. Click on the Advance button. You should see the progress bar advancing. After testing, stop the debugger and exit Visual Studio.

Data Binding in Silverlight

Binding a Silverlight control to data is done in a way that is very similar to the way it's handled in WPF. When you do the binding with XAML, you use the Binding attribute available with each control. When you bind a control in code, you set its source with the DataContext property. When you set the DataContext for a parent element, such as a Grid control, the child elements will use the same DataContext unless their DataContext is explicitly set.

The .NET Framework encapsulates much of the complexity of synchronizing controls to a data source through the data binding process. The Mode property determines how the data binding flows and reacts to data changes. OneWay binding causes changes to the source property to automatically update the target property, but changes to the target property are not propagated back to the source property. This is useful for read-only scenarios and is the default binding. TwoWay binding causes changes to either the source property or the target property to automatically update the other. This is useful for full data updating scenarios.

The following code shows the DataContext of a Grid control set to a CollectionViewSource that contains a list of authors. The CollectionViewSource allows you to move through the list of authors.

```
CollectionViewSource cvs = new CollectionViewSource();
cvs.Source = authorList;
this.AuthorList.DataContext = cvs;
cvs.View.MoveCurrentToFirst();
```

The following XAML code binds TextBox controls and a CheckBox control to the properties of the Authors class using the Path attribute. Using Binding to designate the source means "look up the container hierarchy until a DataContext is found." In this case, the DataContext will be the one specified for the Grid container.

```
<Grid Name="AuthorList" DataContext="{Binding}">
    <Grid.ColumnDefinitions>
        <ColumnDefinition Width="Auto" />
        <ColumnDefinition Width="Auto" />
    </Grid.ColumnDefinitions>
    <Grid.RowDefinitions>
        <RowDefinition Height="Auto" />
        <RowDefinition Height="Auto" />
        <RowDefinition Height="Auto" />
        <RowDefinition Height="Auto" />
    </Grid.RowDefinitions>
    <sdk:Label Content="First Name:" Grid.Column="0" Grid.Row="0"
               HorizontalAlignment="Left" Margin="3" VerticalAlignment="Center" />
    <TextBox Grid.Column="1" Grid.Row="0" Height="23" HorizontalAlignment="Left"
             Margin="3" Name="txtFirstName" Text="{Binding Path=FirstName}"
             VerticalAlignment="Center" Width="120" />
    <sdk:Label Content="Last Name:" Grid.Column="0" Grid.Row="1"
               HorizontalAlignment="Left" Margin="3" VerticalAlignment="Center" />
    <TextBox Grid.Column="1" Grid.Row="1" Height="23" HorizontalAlignment="Left"
             Margin="3" Name="txtLastName" Text="{Binding Path=LastName}"
             VerticalAlignment="Center" Width="120" />
    <CheckBox Name="chkContract" Content="Under Contract"
              IsChecked="{Binding Path=UnderContract}"
              Grid.Row="2" Grid.ColumnSpan="2" FlowDirection="RightToLeft" />
    <StackPanel Grid.Column="1" Grid.Row="3" Grid.ColumnSpan="2" Orientation="Horizontal">
        <Button Name="btnPrev" Content="Prev" MinWidth="50"/>
        <Button Name="btnNext" Content="Next" MinWidth="50"/>
    </StackPanel>
</Grid>
```

The resulting page loaded with author data is shown in Figure 12-5.

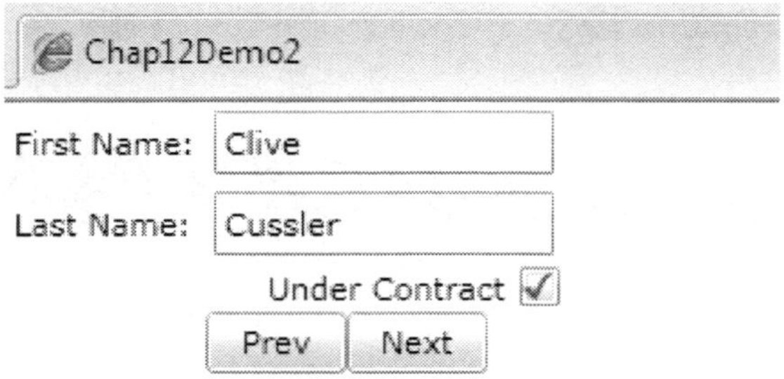

Figure 12-5. *Page displaying author data*

While some controls can only bind to one record at a time, other controls, such as the DataGrid control, bind to and display the entire collection. The following code sets the ItemSource of a DataGrid to the list of authors. In this case, it's not necessary to use a CollectionViewSource.

```
this.AuthorDataGrid.ItemsSource = authorList;
```

The following XAML creates the DataGrid and binds the columns of the grid. The resulting page is shown in Figure 12-6.

```
<sdk:DataGrid Name="AuthorDataGrid" AutoGenerateColumns="False">
    <sdk:DataGrid.Columns>
        <sdk:DataGridTextColumn Header="First Name"
             Width="SizeToHeader" Binding="{Binding FirstName}" />
        <sdk:DataGridTextColumn Header="Last Name"
             Width="SizeToHeader" Binding="{Binding LastName}" />
        <sdk:DataGridCheckBoxColumn Header="Under Contract"
             Width="SizeToHeader" Binding="{Binding UnderContract}" />
    </sdk:DataGrid.Columns>
</sdk:DataGrid>
```

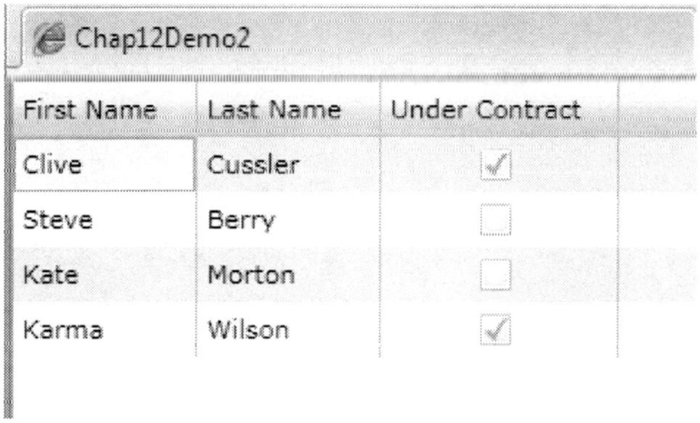

Figure 12-6. *Page displaying author data in a DataGrid*

In the following activity, you will build a page with controls bound to a collection of Author objects. You will also use TwoWay binding to update author data.

ACTIVITY 12-2. WORKING WITH DATA BOUND CONTROLS

In this activity, you will become familiar with the following:

- Binding controls to a collection.
- Updating data using TwoWay binding.

Binding Controls to a Collection

To bind controls to a collection, follow these steps:

1. Start Visual Studio. Select File ➤ New ➤ Project.
2. Choose a Silverlight Application. Rename the project to Act12_2 and click the OK button.
3. The next screen asks if you want to host the Silverlight application in a new web site. It also asks you what version of Silverlight you want to use. Accept the defaults and click OK.
4. Right-click on the Act12_2 project node in Solution Explorer and choose Add ➤ Class. Name the class Author.
5. At the top of the class file, add the following using statement:

```
using System.ComponentModel;
```

6. In the Author class, implement the INotifyPropertyChanged interface. This is needed to facilitate binding.

```
public class Author : INotifyPropertyChanged
{

    public event PropertyChangedEventHandler PropertyChanged;

    void RaisePropertyChanged(string propertyName)
    {
        var handler = PropertyChanged;
        if (handler != null)
        {
            handler(this, new PropertyChangedEventArgs(propertyName));
        }
    }
}
```

7. Add the following properties. Note that when the values are changed, the PropertyChanged event is raised.

```
string _firstName;
public string FirstName
{
    get { return _firstName; }
    set
    {
        if (_firstName != value)
        {
            _firstName = value;
            RaisePropertyChanged("FirstName");
        }
    }
}
string _lastName;
public string LastName
{
    get { return _lastName; }
    set
    {
        if (_lastName != value)
        {
            _lastName = value;
            RaisePropertyChanged("LastName");
        }
    }
}
Boolean _underContract;
public Boolean UnderContract
{
    get { return _underContract; }
    set
    {
        if (_underContract != value)
        {
            _underContract = value;
            RaisePropertyChanged("UnderContract");
        }
    }
}
double _royalty;
public double Royalty
{
    get { return _royalty; }
    set
    {
        if (_royalty != value)
        {
            _royalty = value;
            RaisePropertyChanged("Royalty");
        }
    }
}
```

8. Add the following constructor to the Author class:

```
public Author(string firstName, string lastName,
             Boolean underContract, double royalty)
{
    this.FirstName = firstName;
    this.LastName = lastName;
    this.UnderContract = underContract;
    this.Royalty = royalty;
}
```

9. Build the project and make sure there are no errors. If there are, fix them and rebuild.

10. Add the following XAML markup to the MainPage.xaml file to create the user interface:

```
<Grid x:Name="LayoutRoot" Background="White" >
    <Grid Name="AuthorList" DataContext="{Binding}" HorizontalAlignment="Center">
        <Grid.ColumnDefinitions>
            <ColumnDefinition Width="Auto" />
            <ColumnDefinition Width="Auto" />
        </Grid.ColumnDefinitions>
        <Grid.RowDefinitions>
            <RowDefinition Height="Auto" />
            <RowDefinition Height="Auto" />
            <RowDefinition Height="Auto" />
            <RowDefinition Height="Auto" />
            <RowDefinition Height="Auto" />
            <RowDefinition Height="Auto" />
        </Grid.RowDefinitions>
        <sdk:Label Content="Author Info" Grid.Column="0" Grid.Row="0"
                Grid.ColumnSpan="2" HorizontalAlignment="Center"
                Margin="3" VerticalAlignment="Center" />
        <sdk:Label Content="First Name:" Grid.Column="0"
                Grid.Row="1" HorizontalAlignment="Left"
                Margin="3" VerticalAlignment="Center" />
        <TextBox Grid.Column="1" Grid.Row="1" Height="23" HorizontalAlignment="Left"
                Margin="3" Name="txtFirstName" Text="{Binding Path=FirstName}"
                VerticalAlignment="Center" Width="120" />
        <sdk:Label Content="Last Name:" Grid.Column="0" Grid.Row="2"
                HorizontalAlignment="Left" Margin="3" VerticalAlignment="Center" />
        <TextBox Grid.Column="1" Grid.Row="2" Height="23" HorizontalAlignment="Left"
                Margin="3" Name="txtLastName" Text="{Binding Path=LastName}"
                VerticalAlignment="Center"  Width="120" />
        <sdk:Label Content="Royalty:" Grid.Column="0" Grid.Row="3"
                HorizontalAlignment="Left" Margin="3" VerticalAlignment="Center" />
        <TextBox Grid.Column="1" Grid.Row="3" Height="23" HorizontalAlignment="Left"
                Margin="3" Name="txtRoyalty" Text="{Binding Path=Royalty}"
                VerticalAlignment="Center" Width="120" />
        <CheckBox Name="chkContract" Content="Under Contract"
                IsChecked="{Binding Path=UnderContract}"
                Grid.Row="4" Grid.ColumnSpan="2" FlowDirection="RightToLeft" />
```

```
    </Grid>
</Grid>
```

11. Launch the application in the debugger. You should see a page similar to the one shown in Figure 12-7. After testing, stop the debugger.

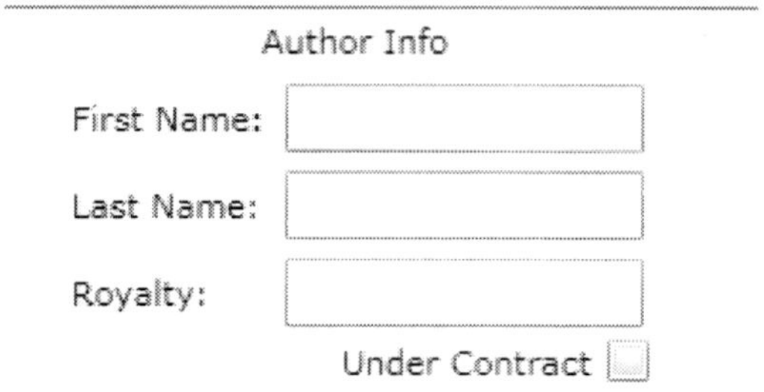

Author Info

First Name:

Last Name:

Royalty:

Under Contract

Figure 12-7. *Author info page*

Updating Data Using TwoWay Binding

1. Inside the MainPage UserControl tag, add a Loaded event handler attribute.

```
<UserControl xmlns:sdk="http://schemas.microsoft.com/winfx/2006/xaml/presentation/sdk"
    x:Class="Act12_2.MainPage"
    xmlns="http://schemas.microsoft.com/winfx/2006/xaml/presentation"
    xmlns:x="http://schemas.microsoft.com/winfx/2006/xaml"
    xmlns:d="http://schemas.microsoft.com/expression/blend/2008"
    xmlns:mc="http://schemas.openxmlformats.org/markup-compatibility/2006"
    mc:Ignorable="d"
    d:DesignHeight="300" d:DesignWidth="400" Loaded="UserControl_Loaded">
```

2. In the codebehind file MainPage.xaml.cs, add the following using statement to the top of the file:

```
using System.Windows.Data;
```

3. In the codebehind file, add the following code to the UserControl_Loaded event handler. This code creates a list of authors, adds it to a CollectionViewSource, and sets the DataContext of the AuthorList Grid control.

```
CollectionViewSource cvs;
private void UserControl_Loaded(object sender, RoutedEventArgs e)
{
    List<Author> authorList = new List<Author>();
    authorList.Add(new Author("Clive", "Cussler", true,.15));
    authorList.Add(new Author("Steve", "Berry", false,.20));
    authorList.Add(new Author("Kate", "Morton", false,.20));
```

```
        authorList.Add(new Author("Karma", "Wilson", true,.18));
        cvs = new CollectionViewSource();
        cvs.Source = authorList;
        this.AuthorList.DataContext = cvs;
        cvs.View.MoveCurrentToFirst();
    }
```

4. Launch the application in the debugger. Make sure the page is loaded with the first author's info. After testing, stop the debugger.

5. To enable moving through the records, add the following XAML after the Checkbox control in the MainPage.xaml file:

```
<StackPanel Grid.Column="1" Grid.Row="5" Grid.ColumnSpan="2"
      Orientation="Horizontal">
    <Button Name="btnPrev" Content="Prev" MinWidth="50"
            Click="btnPrev_Click"/>
    <Button Name="btnNext" Content="Next" MinWidth="50"
            Click="btnNext_Click" />
</StackPanel>
```

6. Add the following code to the btnPrev_Click event handler in the codebehind file. This code uses the CollectionViewSource to loop backward through the records.

```
private void btnPrev_Click(object sender, RoutedEventArgs e)
{
    cvs.View.MoveCurrentToPrevious();
    if (cvs.View.IsCurrentBeforeFirst)
    {
        cvs.View.MoveCurrentToLast();
    }
}
```

7. Add the following code to the btnNext_Click event handler in the codebehind file. This code uses the CollectionViewSource to loop forward through the records.

```
  private void btnNext_Click(object sender, RoutedEventArgs e)
  {
      cvs.View.MoveCurrentToNext();
      if (cvs.View.IsCurrentAfterLast)
      {
          cvs.View.MoveCurrentToFirst();
      }
}
```

8. Launch the application in the debugger. Test the buttons to make sure you can move through the authors list. After testing, stop the debugger.

9. Launch the application in the debugger. Update the royalty of the first author, move to the next author, and move back. You should see that your change was not kept. This is because the default binding mode is one way. Stop the debugger.

10. Update the txtRoyalty text box's XAML code make the binding TwoWay.

```
<TextBox Grid.Column="1" Grid.Row="3" Height="23"
         HorizontalAlignment="Left" Margin="3"
         Name="txtRoyalty" Text="{Binding Path=Royalty, Mode=TwoWay}"
         VerticalAlignment="Center" Width="120" />
```

11. Launch the application in the debugger. Update the royalty of the first author, move to the next author, and move back. You should now see that your change was kept. This is because the default binding mode is TwoWay.

12. After testing, stop the debugger and exit Visual Studio.

Validating and Converting Data

When you allow users to update data, it is very important to validate the data before it is saved back to the data store. For example, you don't want to allow a customer to order a negative amount of an item or set a birth date that occurs in the future. Silverlight supports error notification when exceptions are thrown by either the binding engine's type converter or the binding object's set accessor. If the ValidatesOnExceptions property and the NotifyOnExceptions property values are set to true, Silverlight will provide visual feedback that an error has occurred and will display the error message passed by the binding object. In this case, the Author class will throw an error if you try to set the Royalty property to a value less than zero. The following XAML markup shows the Binding setting of the textbox used to display the royalty. Figure 12-8 shows how the exception is displayed in the page.

```
Text="{Binding Path=Royalty,Mode=TwoWay, NotifyOnValidationError=True,
               ValidatesOnExceptions=True}"
```

Figure 12-8. *Displaying a validation error*

A common scenario in business applications is to convert data from the format used to store it to a more user-friendly format for display. For example, you may want to change the date format or display null values as user-friendly default values. Silverlight facilitates formatting string values using the

StringFormat property. The TargetNullValue property allows you to display a friendly default value instead of null values. You can also set a custom converter on the binding. You set the Converter property to a class that implements the IValueConverter interface.

The following XAML sets the StringFormat property to show the royalties in percent and the TargetNullValue to NA. Figure 12-9 shows the resulting display in the page.

```
Text="{Binding Path=Royalty, Mode=TwoWay, NotifyOnValidationError=True,
ValidatesOnExceptions=True, StringFormat=p, TargetNullValue=NA}"
```

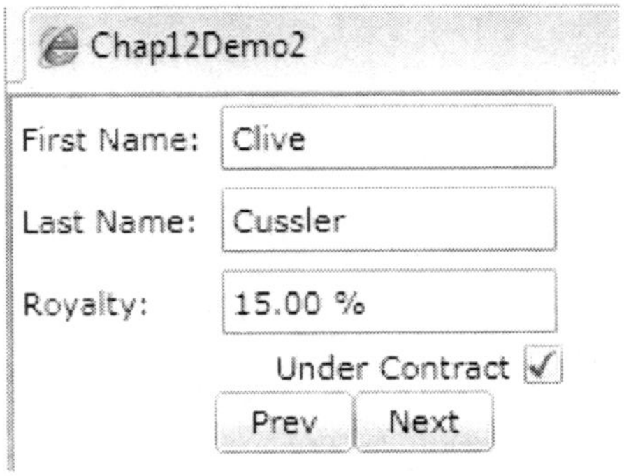

Figure 12-9. *Displaying royalties as percentages*

In the following activity you will implement some of the data validation and conversion capabilities of Silverlight controls described in this section.

ACTIVITY 12-3. VALIDATING AND CONVERTING DATA

In this activity, you will become familiar with the following:

- Data validation
- Data conversion

To implement data validation, follow these steps:

1. Start Visual Studio. Select File ➤ Open ➤ Project.
2. Navigate to the Act12_2 solution file and click the Open button.
3. Open the Author class file in the Code Editor and update the Royalty property to check to make sure it is not negative. If it is, throw an exception.

```
public double Royalty
{
    get { return _royalty; }
    set
    {
```

```
            if (_royalty != value)
            {
                if (value <= 0) throw new Exception
                    ("Amount must be greater than zero.");
                _royalty = value;
                RaisePropertyChanged("Royalty");
            }
        }
}
```

4. Right-click on the Act 12_2 project node in Solution Explorer and select Add ➤ New Item. Add a Silverlight UserControl and name it Page2.xaml.

5. Add the following code to display the author's info in a DataGrid. Note the binding of the Royalty column. The NotifyOnValidationError and ValidatesOnExceptions attributes are set to true.

```
<Grid x:Name="LayoutRoot" Background="White">
    <sdk:DataGrid Name="AuthorDataGrid" AutoGenerateColumns="False"
                  HorizontalAlignment="Center">
        <sdk:DataGrid.Columns>
            <sdk:DataGridTextColumn
                Header="First Name"
                Width="SizeToHeader"
                Binding="{Binding FirstName}" />
            <sdk:DataGridTextColumn
                Header="Last Name"
                Width="SizeToHeader"
                Binding="{Binding LastName}" />
            <sdk:DataGridTextColumn
                Header="Royalty"
                Width="SizeToHeader"
                Binding="{Binding Royalty,Mode=TwoWay,
                          NotifyOnValidationError=True,
                          ValidatesOnExceptions=True}" />
            <sdk:DataGridCheckBoxColumn
                 Header="Under Contract"
                Width="SizeToHeader"
                Binding="{Binding UnderContract}" />
        </sdk:DataGrid.Columns>
    </sdk:DataGrid>
</Grid>
```

6. Inside the MainPage UserControl tag, add a Loaded event handler attribute.

```
<UserControl xmlns:sdk="http://schemas.microsoft.com/winfx/2006/xaml/presentation/sdk"
x:Class="Act12_2.Page2"
    xmlns="http://schemas.microsoft.com/winfx/2006/xaml/presentation"
    xmlns:x="http://schemas.microsoft.com/winfx/2006/xaml"
    xmlns:d="http://schemas.microsoft.com/expression/blend/2008"
    xmlns:mc="http://schemas.openxmlformats.org/markup-compatibility/2006"
    mc:Ignorable="d"
    d:DesignHeight="300" d:DesignWidth="400" Loaded="UserControl_Loaded">
```

7. In the UserControl_Loaded event handler, add the following code to load the author list and bind it to the DataGrid:

```
private void UserControl_Loaded(object sender, RoutedEventArgs e)
{
    List<Author> authorList = new List<Author>();
    authorList.Add(new Author("Clive", "Cussler", true, .15));
    authorList.Add(new Author("Steve", "Berry", false, .20));
    authorList.Add(new Author("Kate", "Morton", false, .20));
    authorList.Add(new Author("Karma", "Wilson", true, .18));
    this.AuthorDataGrid.ItemsSource = authorList;
}
```

8. To make Page2 the startup page, open the App.xaml.cs code in the code editor. Change the Application_Startup event handler to use Page2.

```
private void Application_Startup(object sender, StartupEventArgs e)
{
     this.RootVisual = new Page2();
}
```

9. Launch the application in the debugger. You should see the grid showing the author's info.

10. Change one of the royalties to a negative value and click on another row. When the value tries to update, the debugger will stop on the error. Select Continue under the Debug menu. You should see the grid with the error message stating the amount must be greater than zero.

11. Stop the debugger.

12. In the Page2.xaml, update the Royalty column XAML to include formatting to display it as a percentage and change null values to NA.

```
<sdk:DataGridTextColumn
     Header="Royalty"
     Width="SizeToHeader"
     Binding="{Binding Royalty,Mode=TwoWay,
     NotifyOnValidationError=True,
     ValidatesOnExceptions=True,
     StringFormat=p, TargetNullValue=NA}" />
```

13. Update the Royalty property in the Author class so it can be set to null. The double? makes it a nullable type.

```
double? _royalty;
public double? Royalty
{
    get { return _royalty; }
    set
    {
        if (_royalty != value)
        {
            if (value <= 0) throw new Exception("Amount must be greater than zero.");
```

```
                _royalty = value;
                RaisePropertyChanged("Royalty");
            }
        }
}
```

14. Update the Author class constructor to accept null values.

```
public Author(string firstName, string lastName,
              Boolean underContract, double? royalty)
{
    this.FirstName = firstName;
    this.LastName = lastName;
    this.UnderContract = underContract;
    this.Royalty = royalty;
}
```

15. In the UserControl_Loaded event handler, include some null royalty values.

```
private void UserControl_Loaded(object sender, RoutedEventArgs e)
{
    List<Author> authorList = new List<Author>();
    authorList.Add(new Author("Clive", "Cussler", true, .15));
    authorList.Add(new Author("Steve", "Berry", false, null));
    authorList.Add(new Author("Kate", "Morton", false, null));
    authorList.Add(new Author("Karma", "Wilson", true, .18));
    this.AuthorDataGrid.ItemsSource = authorList;
}
```

16. Select Debug ➤ Start. You should see the royalties as percentages and the null values as NA. When you're done testing, stop the debugger and exit Visual Studio.

Summary

In this chapter, you took a second look at implementing the interface tier of an application, this time using the web-based Silverlight framework. Along the way, you took a close look at how to implement rich web-based user interfaces. You saw how to use XAML syntax to define Silverlight controls and their layout on a Silverlight page. You also saw how easy it is to bind the controls to the data and present it to the users. What's still missing from the story is information on how to retrieve data from a relational database on a server. In order to provide serverside data to a Silverlight application, you need to utilize a web service.

In the next chapter, you will look at creating web services using the Windows Communication Framework (WCF). You will also look at the fundamentals of implementing web services. As an exercise, you will create web services that will be consumed by a Silverlight application and databound to controls of the user interface.

CHAPTER 13

■ ■ ■

Developing and Consuming WCF Services

In the previous two chapters, you examined the steps required to create the graphical user interface of an application. Graphical user interfaces created with WPF and Silverlight provide users a way to interact with your applications and employ the services the application provides. This chapter shows you how to build another type of interface, one that is implemented using the Windows Communication Foundation (WCF) and is meant to be consumed by an application. Such a WCF service provides an application with a programmatic interface with which to access its functions, without the need for human interaction.

After reading this chapter, you will have a clearer understanding of the following:

- What WCF services are and how they came about.
- How WCF processes service requests.
- How to create a WCF service.
- How to consume a WCF service.
- How to use a WCF Data Services in a Silverlight Application.

What Are Services?

Microsoft first introduced the concept of services with its inclusion of web services support in .NET Framework 1.0. A web service provides a way for an application to request a service and receive a reply. This is essentially the same as a client object requesting a service (method) from a server object within the boundaries of your application. The difference is the location of the client objects and server objects. If they reside in the same application, then they can issue and receive binary messages and inherently understand each other because they are speaking the same "language." As the applications you build grow more complex, it is common to split the application up into distinct components. When you segment an application into components, each designed to perform a distinct specialized service, you greatly enhance code maintenance, reusability, and reliability. Additionally, separate servers can host the client components and server components for increased performance, better maintenance, and security.

Prior to the introduction of web services, the clients and servers of an application relied on distributed technologies such as DCOM and CORBA, which are based on proprietary standards. This is fine if the client and server applications utilize the same technologies, but when the client and server utilize disparate technologies, this becomes very problematic. The power of web services lies in the fact that they use a set of open XML-based messaging and HTTP-based transport protocols. This means that client and server components utilizing different technologies can communicate in a standard way. For example, a Java-based application running on an Apache web server can request a service from a .NET-based application running on an IIS server. In addition, since they communicate via HTTP, they can be located virtually anywhere in the world that has an Internet connection.

With the release of the .NET Framework 3.0, Microsoft introduced a new way to create web services in the form of Windows Communication Foundation services (WCF). Before WCF, Microsoft had a robust but confusing set of messaging technologies including ASP.NET Web services, MSMQ, Enterprise services, and .NET Remoting. Microsoft decided to roll all these technologies into a single framework for developing service-oriented applications. This made developing service-oriented applications more consistent and less confusing for developers.

Creating a WCF Web Service

A WCF service is made up of three parts: the service, an end point, and a hosting environment. The service is a class that contains methods you want to expose to clients of the service. An end point is a definition of how clients can communicate with the service. It's worth noting that a service can have more than one endpoint defined. An endpoint consists of the base *address* of the service, its *binding* information, and its *contract* information (the three are often referred to as the ABCs of WCF). The hosting environment refers to the application hosting the service. For your purposes, this will be a web server, but there are other options that exist depending on the type of WCF service you implement.

Creating and consuming WCF services using Visual Studio 2010 is a fairly easy process. If you use the templates Visual Studio provides, much of the plumbing work is done for you. Figure 13-1 shows the available templates. To create a WCF web service, you use the WCF Service Application template.

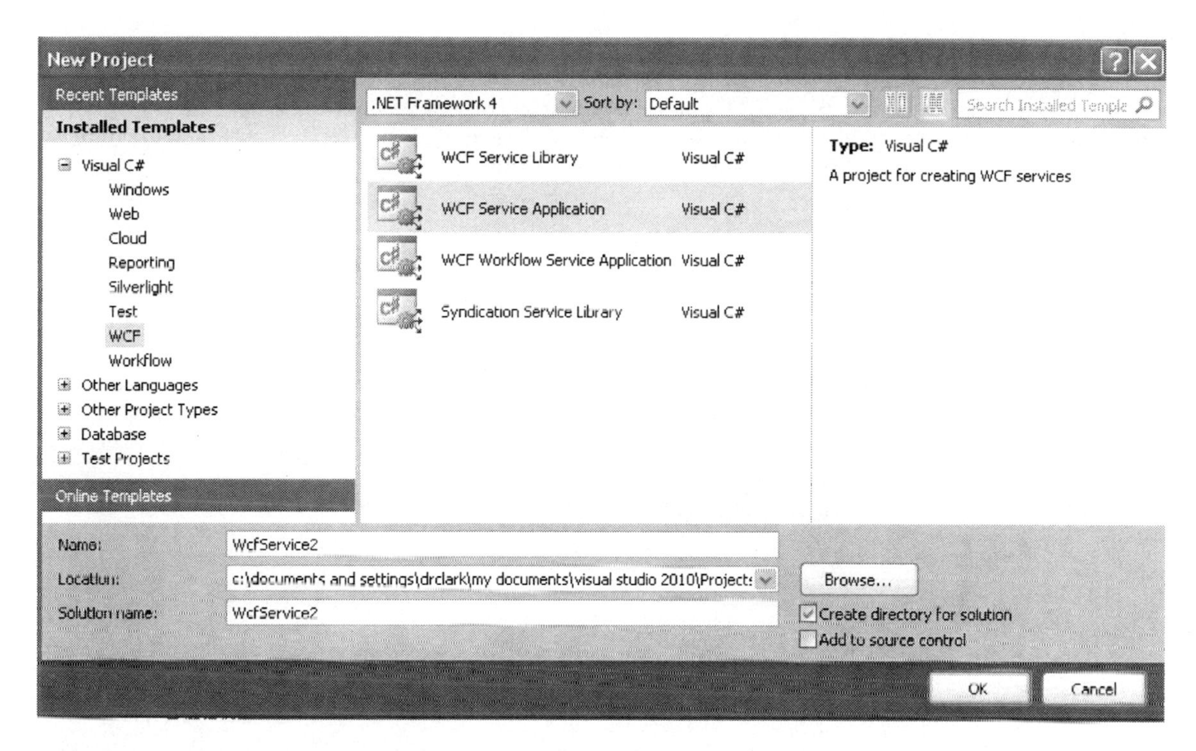

Figure 13-1. *WCF templates provided by Visual Studio*

Selecting a template adds two important files to the project: one defines the service contract using an interface and one is a class file that contains the service implementation code. In Figure 13-2, the IService1.cs file defines the interface and the Service1.svc.cs contains the class implementation for the service.

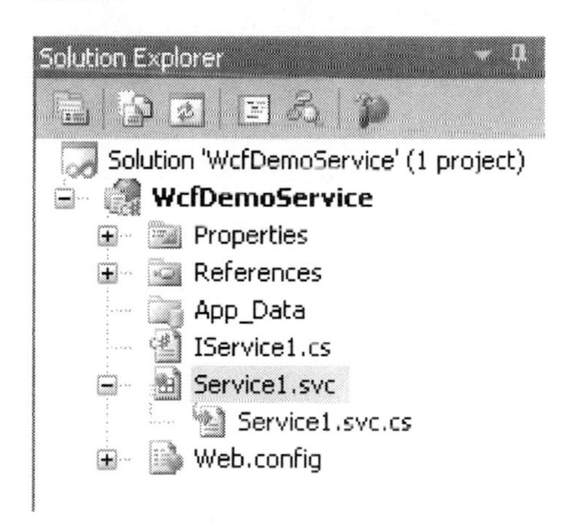

Figure 13-2. *WCF interface and class files*

When you create a service, you need to define the service contract. The contract is defined by an interface definition. The interface defines the methods exposed by the service, any input parameters expected by the methods, and any output parameters passed back by the methods. The following code shows the interface code for a tax service. The interface is marked with the [ServiceContract] attribute and any exposed methods are marked with the [OperationContract].

```
[ServiceContract]
public interface ITax
{
    [OperationContract]
    double GetSalesTax(string statecode);
}
```

Once the interface is defined, the next step is to define the class that implements the interface. The following code implements the ITax interface and provides the code to implement its exposed methods.

```
public class Tax : ITax
{
    public double GetSalesTax(string stateCode)
    {
        if (stateCode == "PA")
        {
            return .06;
        }
        else
        {
            return .05;
        }
    }
}
```

Once the interface and class are defined, compiling and running the application produce the web page shown in Figure 13-3. This page provides information on how you can create a test client for the service and a link to the WSDL file for the service. The WSDL (Web Services Description Language) file is an XML document that specifies the location of the service and the operations it exposes. Figure 13-4 shows a portion of the Tax Service's WSDL file as it appears when displayed by a browser.

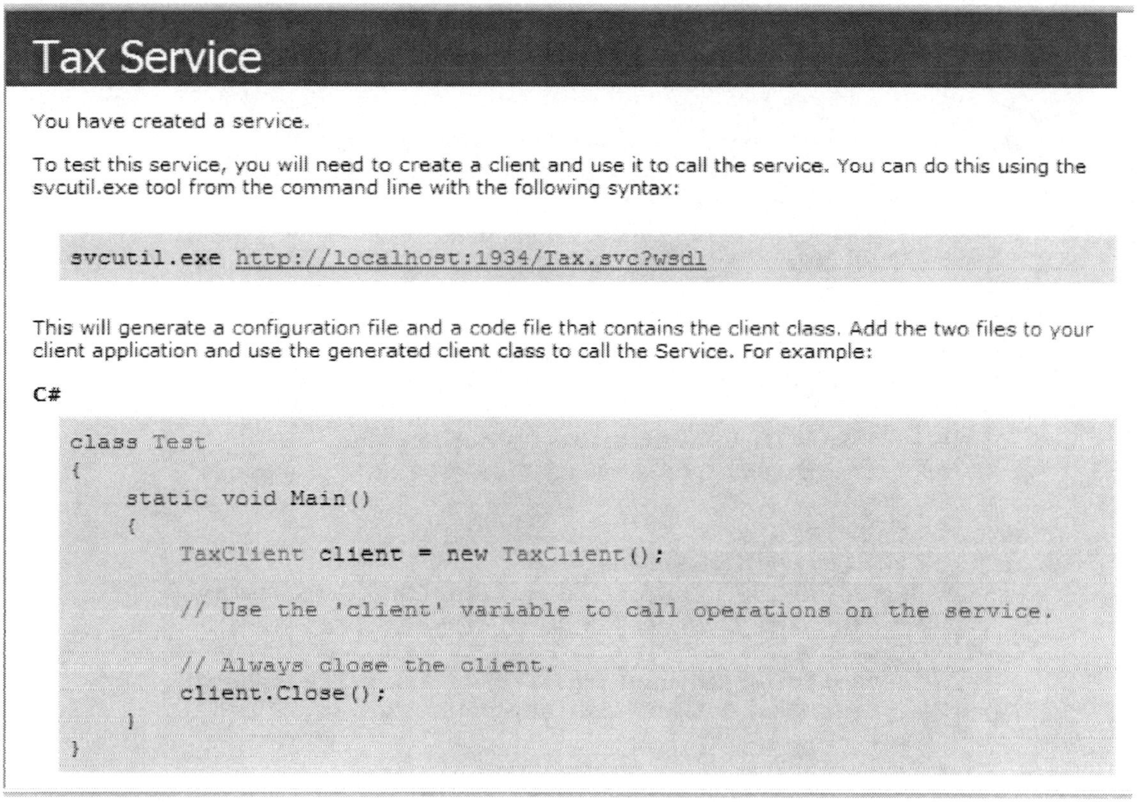

Tax Service

You have created a service.

To test this service, you will need to create a client and use it to call the service. You can do this using the svcutil.exe tool from the command line with the following syntax:

```
svcutil.exe http://localhost:1934/Tax.svc?wsdl
```

This will generate a configuration file and a code file that contains the client class. Add the two files to your client application and use the generated client class to call the Service. For example:

C#

```
class Test
{
    static void Main()
    {
        TaxClient client = new TaxClient();

        // Use the 'client' variable to call operations on the service.

        // Always close the client.
        client.Close();
    }
}
```

Figure 13-3. *Output of the service file*

```
    xmlns:wsa10="http://www.w3.org/2005/08/addressing"
    xmlns:wsx="http://schemas.xmlsoap.org/ws/2004/09/mex"
    xmlns:wsam="http://www.w3.org/2007/05/addressing/metadata">
- <wsdl:types>
  - <xsd:schema targetNamespace="http://tempuri.org/Imports">
      <xsd:import schemaLocation="http://localhost:1934/Tax.svc?xsd=xsd0"
        namespace="http://tempuri.org/" />
      <xsd:import schemaLocation="http://localhost:1934/Tax.svc?xsd=xsd1"
        namespace="http://schemas.microsoft.com/2003/10/Serialization/" />
    </xsd:schema>
  </wsdl:types>
- <wsdl:message name="ITax_GetSalesTax_InputMessage">
    <wsdl:part name="parameters" element="tns:GetSalesTax" />
  </wsdl:message>
- <wsdl:message name="ITax_GetSalesTax_OutputMessage">
    <wsdl:part name="parameters" element="tns:GetSalesTaxResponse" />
  </wsdl:message>
- <wsdl:portType name="ITax">
  - <wsdl:operation name="GetSalesTax">
      <wsdl:input wsaw:Action="http://tempuri.org/ITax/GetSalesTax"
        message="tns:ITax_GetSalesTax_InputMessage" />
      <wsdl:output
        wsaw:Action="http://tempuri.org/ITax/GetSalesTaxResponse"
        message="tns:ITax_GetSalesTax_OutputMessage" />
    </wsdl:operation>
  </wsdl:portType>
```

Figure 13-4. *The WSDL file, as displayed in a browser*

Consuming a WCF Web Service

To consume a WCF service in a .NET client, you must add a service reference to the project. When you add a service reference in Visual Studio 2010, you are presented with an Add Reference window (see Figure 13-5). This window allows you to discover the services available and the operations they expose. You can also change the namespace that you use to program against the service.

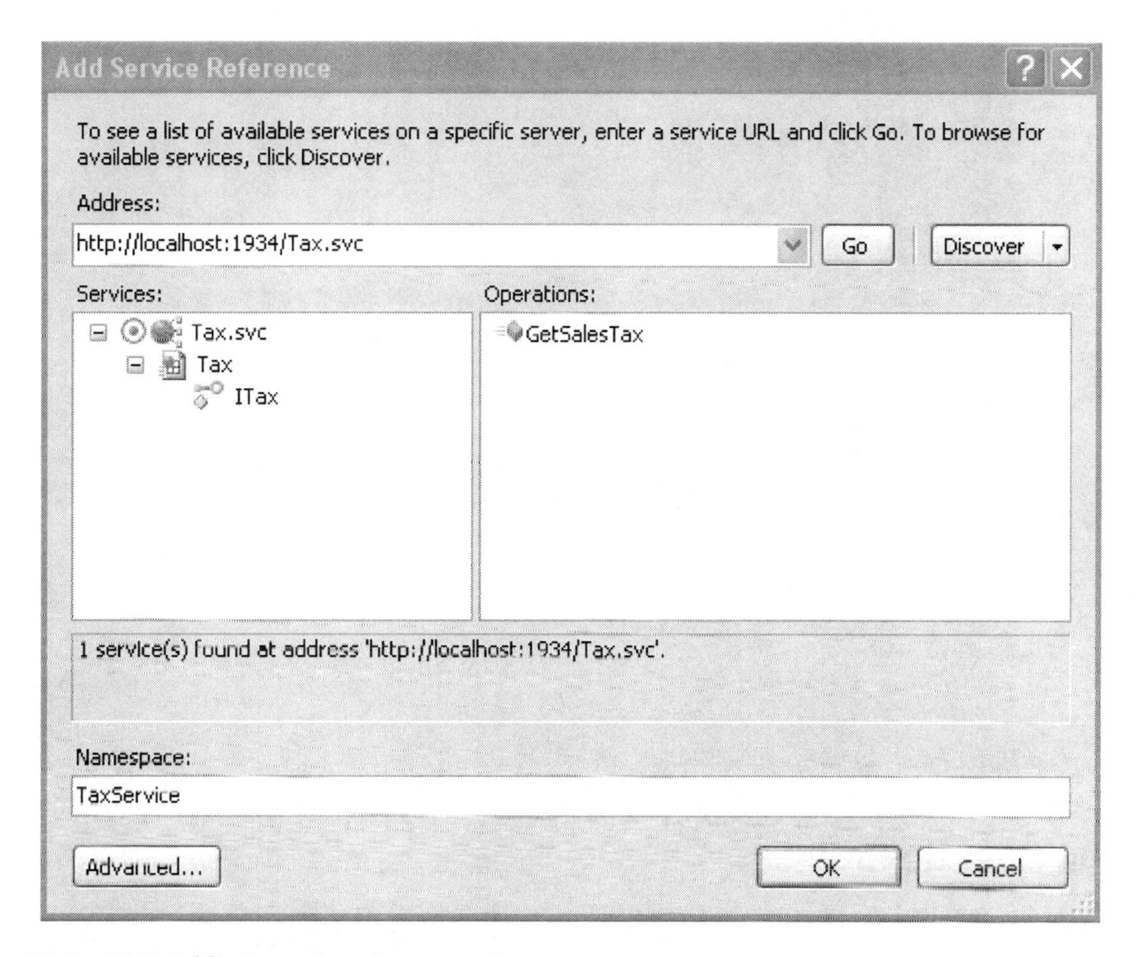

Figure 13-5. *Adding a service reference*

Once the service reference is added to the project, Visual Studio updates the application configuration file with the information needed to call the service. This includes the endpoint configuration with the address, binding, and contract information.

```
<endpoint address="http://localhost:1934/Tax.svc" binding="basicHttpBinding"
          bindingConfiguration="BasicHttpBinding_ITax"
          contract="TaxServiceReference.ITax"
          name="BasicHttpBinding_ITax" />
```

A client proxy is also added to the client application. The client application uses this proxy to interact with the service. The following code shows a client console application calling the service using the TaxClient proxy and writing the results out to the console window. Figure 13-6 shows the output in console window.

```
TaxServiceReference.TaxClient webService = new TaxServiceReference.TaxClient();
string state1 = "PA";
double salesTax1 = webService.GetSalesTax(state1);
Console.WriteLine("The sales tax for {0} is {1}", state1, salesTax1);
string state2 = "NJ";
double salesTax2 = webService.GetSalesTax(state2);
Console.WriteLine("The sales tax for {0} is {1}", state2, salesTax2);
webService.Close();
Console.ReadLine();
```

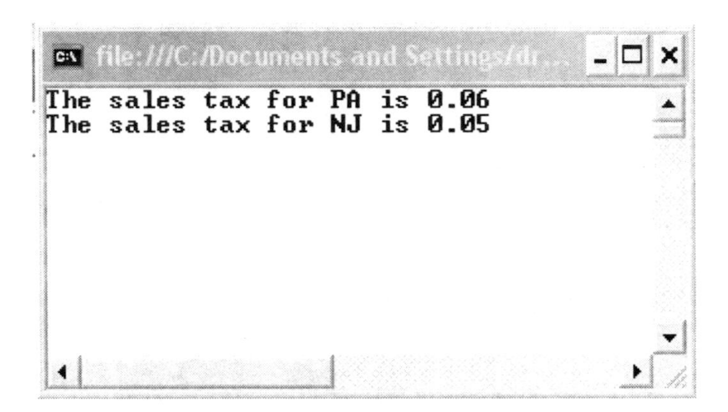

Figure 13-6. *Output from calling the TaxService*

Using Data Contracts

In the previous example, the WCF web service used only simple types to pass data back and forth between the service and the client. Simple types such as integer, double, and string do not require any special encoding to pass them between the client and server. There are times when you want to pass complex types between the client and server. Complex types are comprised of simple types. For example, you may have a service that takes an address type made up of street, city, state, and zip code and returns a location type made up of longitude and latitude. To facilitate the exchange of complex types, the WCF service uses data contracts. You create your data class normally then mark it with the [DataContract] attribute. The properties of the class that you want exposed are marked with the [DataMember] attribute. The following code exposes the Location class to clients of the service:

```
[DataContract]
public class Location
{
    double _longitude;
    double _latitude;
    [DataMember]
    public double Latitude
    {
        get { return _latitude; }
        set { _latitude = value; }
```

```
    }
    [DataMember]
    public double Longitude
    {
        get { return _longitude; }
        set { _longitude = value; }
    }
}
```

By marking the classes with the [DataContract] and [DataMember] attributes, an XSD file is created describing the complex types. Clients use this file to determine what to supply the service and what to expect as a return type. Figure 13-7 shows the portion of the XSD file created for the Location type returned by the service.

```
- <xs:complexType name="Location">
  - <xs:sequence>
      <xs:element minOccurs="0" name="Latitude" type="xs:double" />
      <xs:element minOccurs="0" name="Longitude" type="xs:double" />
    </xs:sequence>
  </xs:complexType>
  <xs:element name="Location" nillable="true" type="tns:Location" />
</xs:schema>
```

Figure 13-7. *XSD file defining the Location type, as displayed in a browser*

Let's put what you've learned so far to work by building a simple service that supplies a list of stores from the Pubs database. The service will then be consumed in a Silverlight client to display a list of stores.

ACTIVITY 13-1. CREATING AND CONSUMING A WCF SERVICE

In this activity, you will become familiar with the following:

- Creating a WCF Service.
- Consuming a WCF Service in a Silverlight client.

Creating a WCF Service

To create the WCF Service, follow these steps:

1. Start Visual Studio. Select File ➤ New ➤ Project.

2. Choose a Silverlight Application under the C# Projects folder. Rename the project to Act13_1 and click the OK button.
3. The next screen asks if you want to host the Silverlight application in a new web site. It also asks you what version of Silverlight you want to use. Accept the defaults and click OK.
4. Right-click on the Act13_1.Web project node in the Solution Explorer window and select Add ➤ New Item.
5. In the Add New Item window, click on the Web node in the Installed Templates section. Select the WCF Service template, rename it to PubsService, and click the Add button (see Figure 13-8).

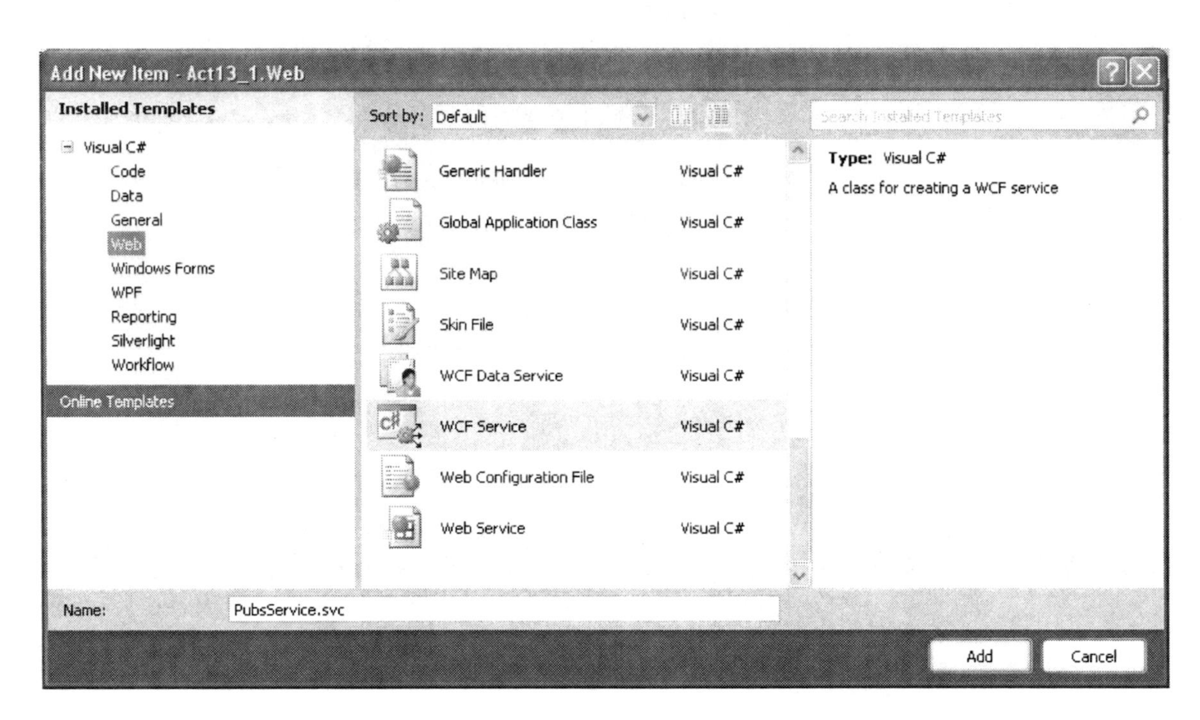

Figure 13-8. *Adding the WCF Service*

6. Right-click the PubsService.svc node in the Solution Explorer and select View Code. After the PubsService class definition, add a Store class definition. Add the [DataContract] attribute to the Store class and the [DataMember] attributes to the ID and name properties.

```
namespace Act13_1.Web
{

    public class PubsService : IPubsService
    {
        //ubsService class code
    }
    [DataContract]
    public class Store
    {
        string _id;
        [DataMember]
        public string Id
        {
            get { return _id; }
            set { _id = value; }
        }
        string _name;
        [DataMember]
        public string Name
        {
            get { return _name; }
            set { _name = value; }
        }
    }
}
```

7. At the top of the file, add a using System.Data.SqlClient statement. In the body of the PubsService class, add a GetStores method that returns a list of stores. This method uses the SQLDataReader to retrieve the data from the Pubs database. (Using the SqlDataReader class was covered in Chapter 10.)

```
public class PubsService : IPubsService
{
    public List<Store> GetStores()
    {
        SqlConnection con = new SqlConnection(@"Data Source=.\SQLEXPRESS;
                Initial Catalog=pubs;Integrated Security=True");
        SqlCommand cmd = new
                SqlCommand("Select stor_id, stor_name from stores", con);
        List<Store> stores = new List<Store>();
        con.Open();
        SqlDataReader dr = cmd.ExecuteReader();
        while (dr.Read())
        {
            Store store = new Store();
            store.Id = (string)dr[0];
```

```
                store.Name = (string)dr[1];
                stores.Add(store);
            }
            return stores;
        }
    }
```

8. Open the IPubsService.cs file in the Code Editor window. Update the code to define the GetStores method.

```
[ServiceContract]
public interface IPubsService
{
    [OperationContract]
    List<Store> GetStores();
}
```

9. In the Solution Explorer, right-click on the Act13_1.Web node and select Build. If there are any errors, fix them, and then rebuild.

Creating the Silverlight Client

1. In the Solution Explorer, right-click the Act13_1 project node and select Add Service Reference. In the Add Service Reference dialog, click the Discover button. You should see the PubsService.svc as shown in Figure 13-9. Click the OK button to add the reference.

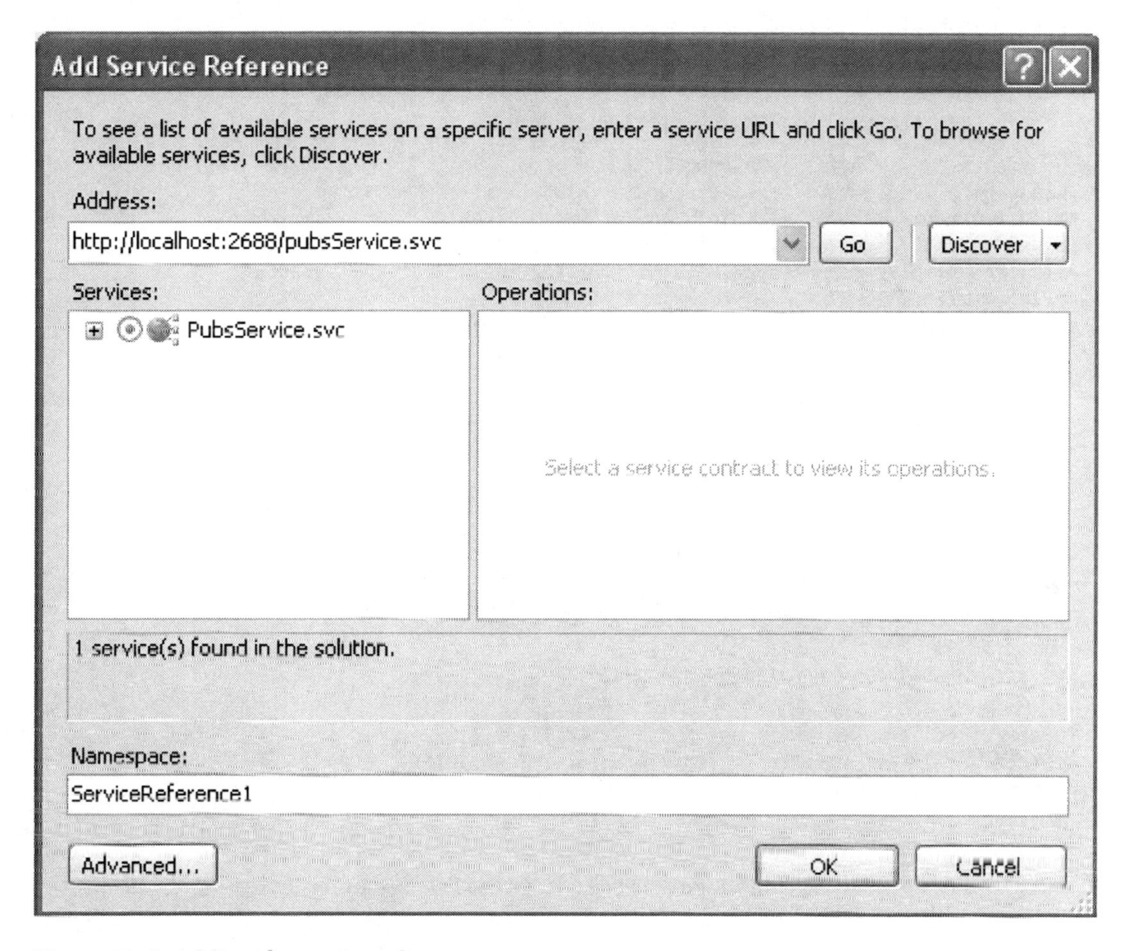

Figure 13-9. Adding the service reference

■ **Note** The port number of your service address may change when you develop it locally.

---

2. Open the MainPage.xaml file in the XAML Editor. Add the following XAML markup to add a Label and a ListBox control:

```
<Grid x:Name="LayoutRoot" Background="White">
    <Grid.RowDefinitions>
        <RowDefinition Height="Auto"/>
        <RowDefinition Height="Auto"/>
    </Grid.RowDefinitions>
    <sdk:Label Content="Stores:" HorizontalAlignment="Center"/>
    <ListBox Name="StoreList" Width="200" Height="200"
               HorizontalAlignment="Center" Grid.Row="1"/>
```

```
</Grid>
```

Add a Loaded event handler to the user control.

```
<UserControl x:Class="Act13_1.MainPage"
    xmlns="http://schemas.microsoft.com/winfx/2006/xaml/presentation"
    xmlns:x="http://schemas.microsoft.com/winfx/2006/xaml"
    xmlns:d="http://schemas.microsoft.com/expression/blend/2008"
    xmlns:mc="http://schemas.openxmlformats.org/markup-compatibility/2006"
    mc:Ignorable="d"
    d:DesignHeight="300" d:DesignWidth="400" Loaded="UserControl_Loaded">
```

At the top of the MainPage.xaml.cs codebehind file, add a namespace reference to the service you added in Step 1.

```
using Act13_1.ServiceReference1;
```

In the UserControl_Loaded event handler, call the service through the PubsServiceClient proxy. Since the Silverlight client calls the service asynchronously, you need to provide a callback event handler for when the call completes.

```
private void UserControl_Loaded(object sender, RoutedEventArgs e)
{
    PubsServiceClient context = new PubsServiceClient();
    context.GetStoresCompleted += context_GetStoresCompleted;
    context.GetStoresAsync();
}
```

Add the following callback event handler. In the handler, load the ListBox control with the store info returned by the service.

```
private void context_GetStoresCompleted(object sender,
                 GetStoresCompletedEventArgs e)
{
    foreach (var store in e.Result)
    {
        this.StoreList.Items.Add(store.Id + ", " + store.Name);
    }
}
```

Run the application in the debugger. You should see a web page with the list of stores, as shown in Figure 13-10. When you're satisfied with your testing, stop the debugger and exit Visual Studio.

Stores:

6380, Eric the Read Books
7066, Barnum's
7067, News & Brews
7131, Doc-U-Mat: Quality Laundry
7896, Fricative Bookshop
8042, Bookbeat

Figure 13-10. *List of store information*

WCF Data Services

Most business applications must work with data contained in a database. Clients need to be able to perform CRUD (create, read, update, and delete) operations on the data. While you can support these operations using the HTTP SOAP based WCF services discussed thus far, you need to write a lot of code to hook up the database layer and expose it through the operations exposed by the WCF service. This is where WCF Data Services can help. WCF Data Services is a framework that enables you to easily create services to expose and consume data over the Web.

WCF Data Services uses the Open Data (OData) protocol for addressing and updating resources. It exposes data in a text-based data exchange format an application can address with URIs. Data is accessed and changed by using the standard HTTP verbs GET, PUT, POST, and DELETE. WCF Data Services also includes a client library specifically for Silverlight-based applications that provides an object based programming model to access an OData feed.

Visual Studio 2010 provides the templates to easily create a WCF Data Service. First you create a web application to host the service. Once the web application is created, add an ADO.NET Entity Data Model. As explained in Chapter 10, the ADO.NET Entity Data Model creates an entity-to-relational mapping layer. This allows you to develop against the object-oriented data model, which then gets converted into the relational model of the database for you. Once the entity data model is created, add a WCF Data Service to the project. The Data Service class provides the functionality necessary to process request messages, interact with the entity data model, and generate response messages. This class inherits from a base Data Service class of the data entity type defined by the Entity Data Model. The following code shows a WCF Data Service class set up to interact with an Entity Data Model created for the Pubs database:

```
public class pubsDataService : DataService<PubsEntities >
```

The DataServiceConfiguration class defines the behaviors of the data service. This class is supplied by the InitializeService method of the data service. It can be used to set behaviors such as access to the entities by clients of the service. The following code shows the PubsDataService class limiting the access to the entities of the data model:

```
public static void InitializeService(DataServiceConfiguration config)
{
    config.SetEntitySetAccessRule("stores", EntitySetRights.AllRead);
    config.SetEntitySetAccessRule("sales", EntitySetRights.None);
    config.SetEntitySetAccessRule("titles", EntitySetRights.All);
    // config.SetServiceOperationAccessRule("MyServiceOperation", ServiceOperationRights.All);
    config.DataServiceBehavior.MaxProtocolVersion = DataServiceProtocolVersion.V2;
}
```

To consume a WCF Data Service in a client application developed in Visual Studio 2010, you simply create a service reference to it using the Add Service Reference dialog. Using this dialog will request the service metadata document from the data service. By using this metadata document, client side proxies are created to interact with the data service. The WCF Data Services client library enables you to execute language integrated querys (LINQ) against a data service. The client library translates a query into an HTTP GET request message.

The following code shows how to instantiate an instance of the data service proxy and use it to execute a LINQ query to return all the records from the titles table in the Pubs database. The result of the query can then be bound to the client UI controls.

```
svcPubs = new pubsEntities (new Uri("http://localhost:1396/pubsDataService.svc"));
var q = from t in svcPubs.titles
            select t;
```

In the following activity, you'll create a WCF Data Service that supplies data from the Pubs database. After creating the service, you will use it to load a DataGrid with title (book) information.

ACTIVITY 13-2. CREATING AND CONSUMING A WCF DATA SERVICE

In this activity, you will become familiar with the following:

- Creating a WCF Data Service.
- Consuming a WCF Data Service in a Silverlight client.

Creating a WCF Data Service

To create a WCF Data Service, follow these steps:

1. Start Visual Studio. Select File ➤ New ➤ Project.
2. Choose a Silverlight Application. Rename the project to Act13_2 and click the OK button.
3. The next screen asks if you want to host the Silverlight application in a new web site. It also asks you what version of Silverlight you want to use. Accept the defaults and click OK.

4. Right-click on the Act13_2.Web project node in the solution explorer window and select Add ➤ New Item.
5. Under the Data node in the Add New Item window, select an ADO.NET Entity Data Model. Name the model Pubs.emdx and click Add.
6. In the Choose Model Contents screen, select the Generate from database option and click Next.
7. In the Choose Your Data Connection screen, choose an existing connection or create a new connection to the Pubs database and choose Next.
8. In the Choose Your Database Objects screen, expand the tables node; select the sales, stores, and titles tables; and then click Finish.
9. Right-click on the Act13_2.Web project node in the Solution Explorer window and select Add ➤ New Item.
10. In the Add New Item window, click on the web node in the Installed Templates. Select the WCF Data Service template, rename it to PubsDataService, and click the Add button.
11. Open the PubsDataService.svc.cs file in the Code Editor. Update the code so that the PubsDataService class implements a DataService of type pubEntities.

```
public class PubsDataService : DataService< pubsEntities >
{
```

12. In the InitializeService method, update the code to set the entity access rules for the store, sale, and title entities created in the Entity Data Model.

```
public static void InitializeService(DataServiceConfiguration config)
{
    config.SetEntitySetAccessRule("stores", EntitySetRights.AllRead);
    config.SetEntitySetAccessRule("sales", EntitySetRights.All);
    config.SetEntitySetAccessRule("titles", EntitySetRights.All);
    // config.SetServiceOperationAccessRule("MyServiceOperation",
    ServiceOperationRights.All);
    config.DataServiceBehavior.MaxProtocolVersion = DataServiceProtocolVersion.V2;
}
```

13. In the Solution Explorer, right-click on the Act13_2.Web node and select Build. If there are any errors, fix them and rebuild.
14. In the Solution Explorer, right-click on the PubsDataService.svc node and select View in Browser. You should see the entities listed as in Figure 13-11. Note the URI for setting the service reference later.

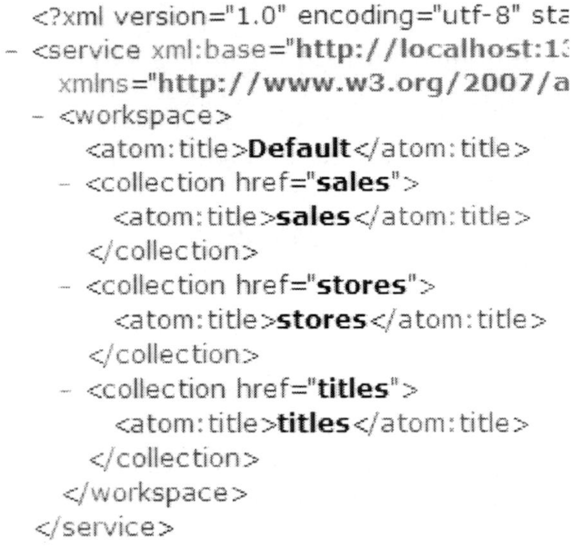

```
<?xml version="1.0" encoding="utf-8" sta
- <service xml:base="http://localhost:1
  xmlns="http://www.w3.org/2007/a
- <workspace>
    <atom:title>Default</atom:title>
  - <collection href="sales">
      <atom:title>sales</atom:title>
    </collection>
  - <collection href="stores">
      <atom:title>stores</atom:title>
    </collection>
  - <collection href="titles">
      <atom:title>titles</atom:title>
    </collection>
  </workspace>
</service>
```

Figure 13-11. *Viewing the PubsDataService.svc in the browser*

Consuming a WCF Data Service in a Silverlight Client

To consume the WCF Data Service, follow these steps:

1. Add the following XAML markup to the MainPage.xaml file to create the user interface. Note that you are using a cell editing template for the PubDate column. It will display a DatePicker control when edited.

```
<Grid x:Name="LayoutRoot" Background="White" DataContext="{Binding}">
        <Grid.RowDefinitions>
            <RowDefinition Height="Auto"/>
            <RowDefinition Height="Auto"/>
        </Grid.RowDefinitions>
        <Button Name="btnSave" Content="Save" Width="80" />
        <sdk:DataGrid AutoGenerateColumns="False"
                HorizontalAlignment="Center"
                ItemsSource="{Binding}" Name="titlesDataGrid"
                VerticalAlignment="Top" Grid.Row="1" >
            <sdk:DataGrid.Columns>
                <sdk:DataGridTemplateColumn x:Name="pubdateColumn"
                        Header="Pubdate" Width="SizeToCells">
                    <sdk:DataGridTemplateColumn.CellEditingTemplate>
                        <DataTemplate>
                            <sdk:DatePicker
                                SelectedDate="{Binding Path=pubdate,
                                    Mode=TwoWay,
                                    ValidatesOnExceptions=true,
```

```
                                NotifyOnValidationError=true}" />
                        </DataTemplate>
                    </sdk:DataGridTemplateColumn.CellEditingTemplate>
                    <sdk:DataGridTemplateColumn.CellTemplate>
                        <DataTemplate>
                            <TextBlock Text="{Binding Path=pubdate,
                                       StringFormat=\{0:d\}}" />
                        </DataTemplate>
                    </sdk:DataGridTemplateColumn.CellTemplate>
                </sdk:DataGridTemplateColumn>
                <sdk:DataGridTextColumn x:Name="title_idColumn"
                                Binding="{Binding Path=title_id}"
                                Header="Title id"
                                Width="SizeToCells"
                                Visibility="Collapsed"/>
                <sdk:DataGridTextColumn x:Name="title1Column"
                                Binding="{Binding Path=title1}"
                                Header="Title" Width="SizeToCells" />
                <sdk:DataGridTextColumn x:Name="typeColumn"
                                Binding="{Binding Path=type}"
                                Header="Type" Width="SizeToCells" />
                <sdk:DataGridTextColumn x:Name="ytd_salesColumn"
                               Binding="{Binding Path=ytd_sales,
                                        StringFormat=c}"
                               Header="Ytd sales" Width="SizeToCells" />
            </sdk:DataGrid.Columns>
        </sdk:DataGrid>
    </Grid>
```

2. Inside the MainPage UserControl tag, add a Loaded event handler attribute.

```
<UserControl xmlns:sdk="http://schemas.microsoft.com/winfx/2006/xaml/presentation/sdk"
    x:Class="Act13_2.MainPage"
    xmlns="http://schemas.microsoft.com/winfx/2006/xaml/presentation"
    xmlns:x="http://schemas.microsoft.com/winfx/2006/xaml"
    xmlns:d="http://schemas.microsoft.com/expression/blend/2008"
    xmlns:mc="http://schemas.openxmlformats.org/markup-compatibility/2006"
    mc:Ignorable="d"
    d:DesignHeight="300" d:DesignWidth="400" Loaded="UserControl_Loaded">
```

3. In the Solution Explorer window, right-click the Act13_2 project node and select Add Service Reference. In the Add Service Reference dialog, click the Discover button. You should see the PubsService.svc in the list, Click the OK button to add the service reference.

4. In the MainPage.xaml.cs codebehind file, add the following using statements to the top of the file:

```
using Act13_2.ServiceReference1;
using System.Data.Services.Client;
```

5. In the codebehind file, add the following class level variables:

```
public partial class MainPage : UserControl
    {
        pubsEntities svcPubs;
        DataServiceCollection<title> dscTitles;
```

6. In the codebehind file, add the following code to the UserControl_Loaded event handler. Use the URI noted in step 14 of the previous section. This code instantiates an instance of the data service that svcPubs uses it to load data from a LINQ query. The DataServiceCollection (dscTitles) is loaded from the result of the query and is used as the DataContext for the LayoutRoot grid.

```
private void UserControl_Loaded(object sender, RoutedEventArgs e)
   {
     //Do not load your data at design time.
     if (!System.ComponentModel.DesignerProperties.GetIsInDesignMode(this))
     {
         svcPubs = new pubsEntities
            (new Uri("http://localhost:1396/pubsDataService.svc"));
         dscTitles = new DataServiceCollection<title>();
         var q = from t in svcPubs.titles
                     select t;
         dscTitles.LoadAsync(q);
         this.LayoutRoot.DataContext = dscTitles;
     }
}
```

7. Launch the application in the debugger. Make sure the page is loaded with the title info loaded in the grid. After testing, stop the debugger.

8. To enable updating records, add a Click event handler to the XAML of the Save button in the MainPage.xaml file.

```
<Button Name="btnSave" Content="Save" Width="80" Click="btnSave_Click" />
```

9. Add the following code to the btnSave_Click event handler in the codebehind file. This code uses the data service proxy to call the save changes method of the data service. This is an asynchronous call so a callback method is passed in as well as a message to pass back indicating the changes saved.

```
private void btnSave_Click(object sender, RoutedEventArgs e)
{
    svcPubs.BeginSaveChanges(OnChangesSaved,"Data Saved");
}
```

10. Add the following call back event handler, which will fire when the data service completes the save changes method:

```
private void OnChangesSaved(IAsyncResult result)
{
    MessageBox.Show((string)result.AsyncState);
}
```

11. Launch the application in the debugger. Test updating the data and saving the changes. Refresh the page after saving the data to verify it was saved back to the database. After testing, stop the debugger and exit Visual Studio.

Summary

In this chapter, you were introduced to the fundamentals of implementing web services. In particular, you saw how to create web services using the Windows Communication Framework (WCF). You also built a Silverlight client application that consumes the WCF service and updates data back to the database through the service.

This was the final chapter in a series aimed at exposing you to the various technologies and .NET Framework classes used to build .NET applications. The goal of these chapters has been to give you the information necessary to start building .NET applications. These chapters only scratched the surface of these technologies. As you gain experience developing .NET applications, you will need to look more deeply into each of these technologies.

Thus far in your journey you have studied UML design, object-oriented programming, the C# language, the .NET Framework, creating graphical user interfaces, and developing WCF Services. You are now ready to put the pieces together and develop a working application. In the next chapter, you will revisit the UML models you developed for the case study introduced in Chapter 4. You will transform these models into a fully functional application.

CHAPTER 14

Developing the OSO Application

In the previous chapters, you looked at two ways to develop the graphical user interface of an application. Graphical user interfaces created with WPF and Silverlight provide human users a way to interact with your applications and use the services they provide. You also saw how services create programmatic interfaces that other programs can call to use the services of the application without any user interaction.

In this chapter you come full circle, back to the office supply ordering application (called OSO for short) that you designed in Chapter 4. This chapter is one big activity and a final exam of sorts. You will create a functional application incorporating the concepts you have learned in the previous chapters. As you work through creating the application, you should be able to identify these concepts and relate them back to the concepts covered previously. The application will contain a data access layer, a business logic layer, and a user interface layer.

After reading this chapter, you will understand why applications are split into different layers and how to construct them.

Revisiting Application Design

When you design an application, you can typically proceed in three distinct phases. First, you complete a conceptual design, then a logical design, and then a physical design.

The *conceptual design*, as explained in Chapter 4, constitutes the discovery phase of the process. The conceptual design phase involves a considerable amount of collaboration and communication between the users of the system and the system designers. The system designers must gain a complete understanding of the business processes that the proposed system will encompass. Using scenarios and use cases, the designers define the functional requirements of the system. A common understanding and agreement on system functionality and scope among the developers and users of the system is the required outcome of this phase.

The second phase of the design process is the *logical design*. During the logical design phase, you work out the details about the structure and organization of the system. This phase consists of the development and identification of the business objects and classes that will compose the system. UML class diagrams identify the system objects for which you identify and document the attributes and behaviors. You also develop and document the structural interdependencies of these objects using the class diagrams. Using sequence and collaboration diagrams, you discover and identify the interactions and behavioral dependencies between the various system objects. The outcome of this phase, the application object model, is independent of any implementation-specific technology and deployment architecture.

The third phase of the design process is the *physical design*. During the physical design phase, you transform the application object model into an actual system. You evaluate and decide upon specific technologies and infrastructures, do cost analysis, and determine any constraints. Issues such as programmer experience and knowledge base, current implementation technologies, and legacy system integration will all influence your decisions during the physical design phase. You must also analyze security concerns, network infrastructure, and scalability requirements.

When designing a distributed application, you normally separate its logical architectural structure from its physical architectural structure. By separating the architectural structure in this way, you will find it much easier to maintain and update the application. You can make any physical architectural changes (to increase scalability, for example) with minimal impact. The logical architectural design typically separates the various parts of an application into tiers. Users interact with the *presentation tier*, which presents data to the user and gives the user ways to initiate business service requests. The *business logic tier* encapsulates and implements the business logic of an application. It is responsible for performing calculations, processing data, and controlling application logic and sequencing. The *data tier* is responsible for managing access to and storage of information that must be persisted and shared among various users and business processes. Figure 14-1 shows the different logical tiers of a typical 3-tier application.

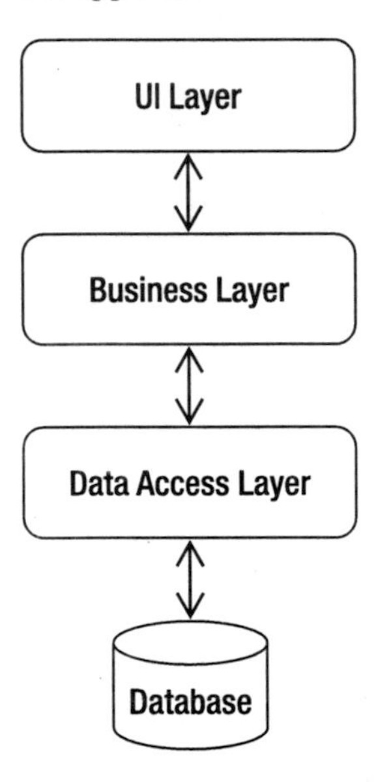

Figure 14-1. *Logical tiers of a 3-tiered application*

When you create the physical tiers of an application, each logical tier would ideally correspond to a distinct physical tier on its own dedicated server. In reality, the physical layers of the application are influenced by such factors as available hardware and network infrastructure. You may have all the logical tiers on one physical server or spread across a web and database server. What is important is that you create applications that implement clear separation of duties among the classes. Figure 14-2 shows the layout of the OSO application. The business logic classes and the data access classes are contained in the same assembly (BLL assembly), while the user interface layer is contained in its own assembly (UI assembly). Both assemblies are contained on the same server. Because there is a clear separation of duties between the business logic classes and the data access classes, as the application grows in features and users, it can easily be refactored into separate assemblies hosted on separate severs.

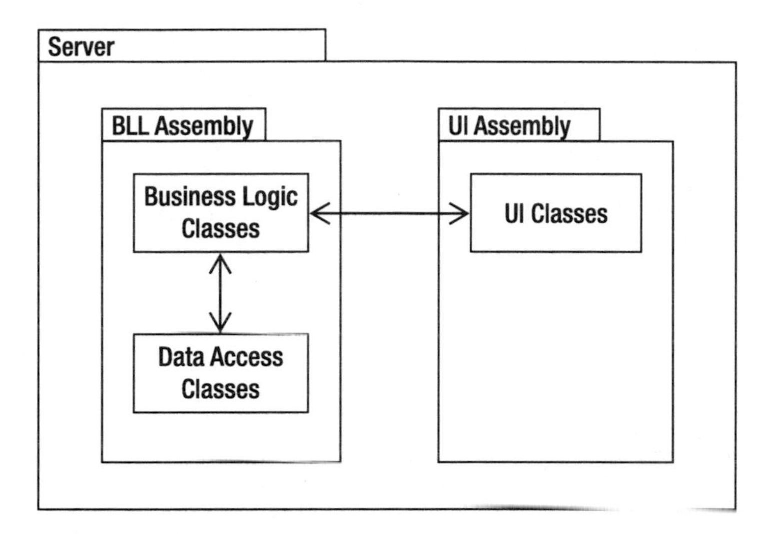

Figure 14-2. *Physical tiers of the OSO application*

Building the OSO Application's Data Access and Business Logic Layers

In order to develop the business logic and data access layers of the application, you need to review the OSO class diagram you created in Chapter 4 (shown in Figure 14-3).

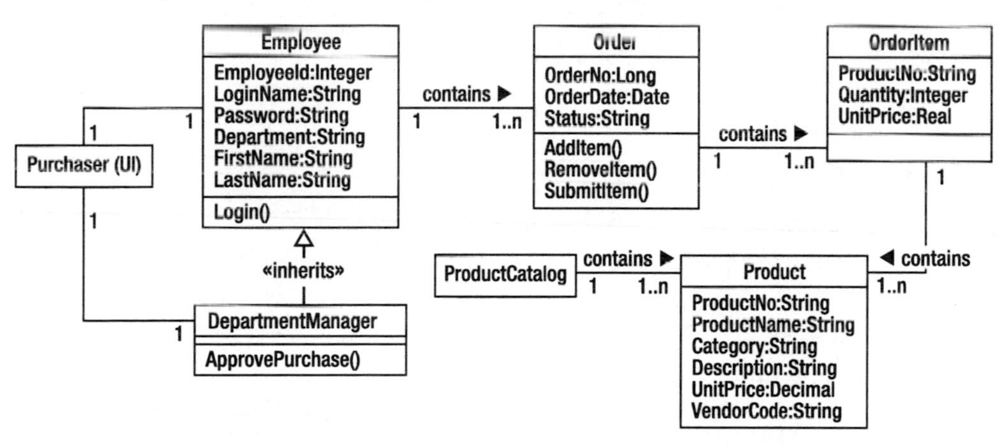

Figure 14-3. *OSO application class diagram*

As discussed in Chapter 4, you need to create an Employee class that implements a login method (Login()). The login method will interact with the database to verify login information. To accomplish this, you will create two employee classes: one for the business logic layer (Employee) and one for the data access layer (DALEmployee). The Employee class will pass the request to login from the User Interface (UI) to the DALEmployee class, which in turn will interact with the database to retrieve the requested information. Figure 14-4 is the database schema for the Office Supply database. This database is hosted in a SQL Server database.

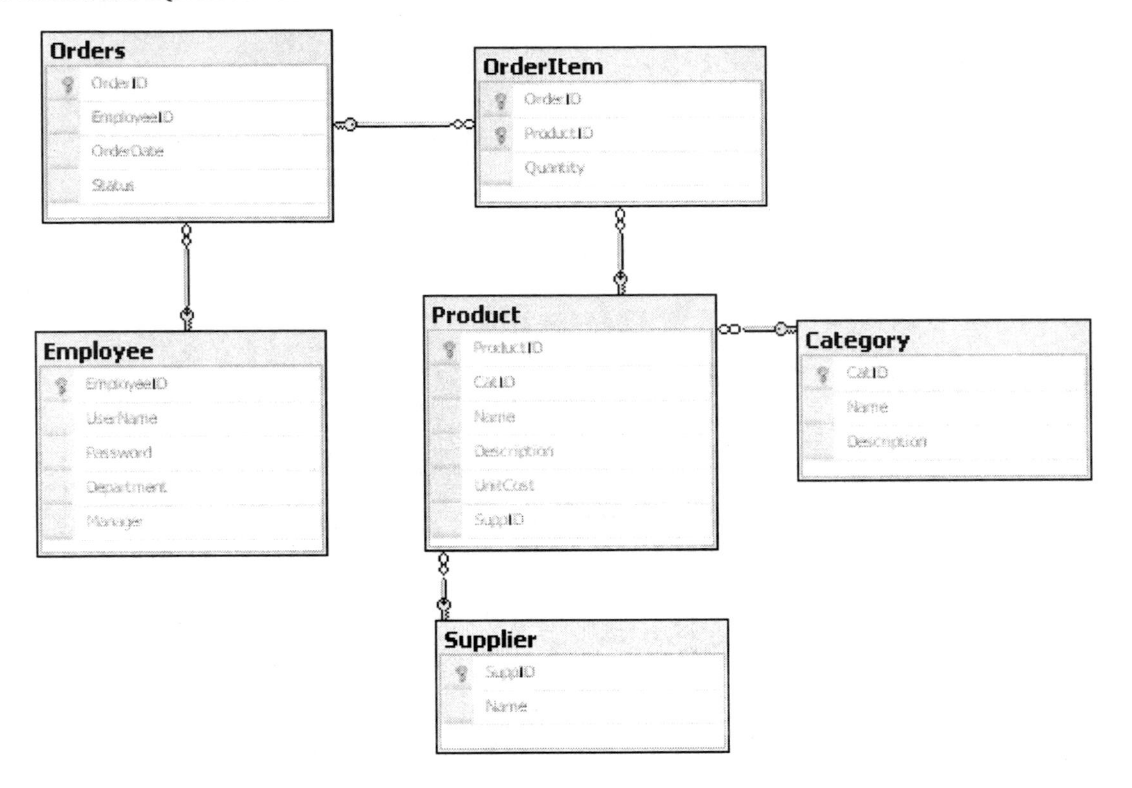

Figure 14-4. *Office Supply database diagram*

■ **Note** If you did not install the Office Supply database, see Appendix C for instructions.

Now, you'll begin with the data access layer and then implement the business logic layer.

1. In Visual Studio, create a Class Library application and name it `OSOBLL`; this application will contain the classes for the business logic layer and data access layer of the OSO application. If not already there, add the references shown in Figure 14-5. Figure 14-5 also shows the classes you will create to implement the data access and business logic of the application.

■ **Note** If you don't want to code the OSO application from scratch, you can download it from the Apress web site. See Appendix C for details.

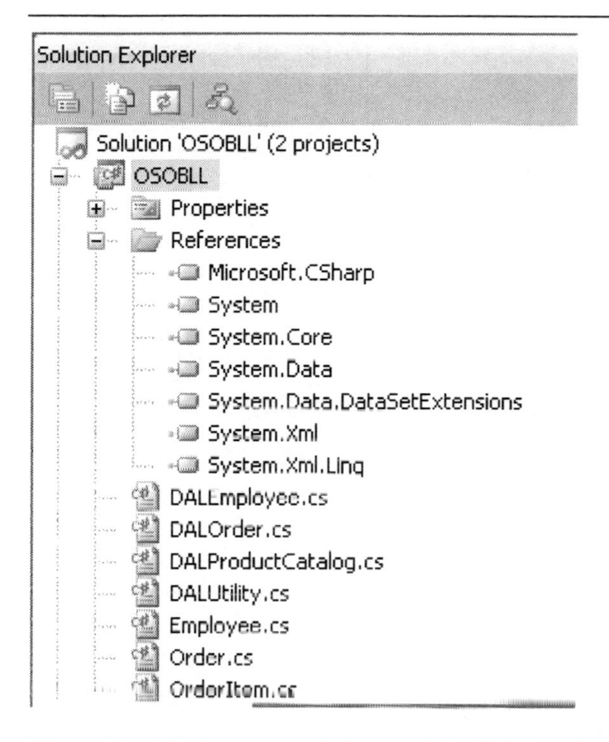

Figure 14-5. *References and classes of the OSOBLL class library*

Next, you'll create a static class (DALUtility) that implements the setting of the database connection string in one centralized location. The other classes will call its GetSQLConnection to retrieve the connection string.

2. Add a class to the application and name it `DALUtility`. Add the following code to the class file:

```
using System;
using System.Collections.Generic;
using System.Linq;
using System.Text;

namespace OSOBLL
{
    public static class DALUtility
    {
        public static string GetSQLConnection()
        {
```

```
            return @"Integrated Security=True;Data Source=.\SQLEXPRESS;" +
                "Initial Catalog=OfficeSupply";
        }
    }
}
```

3. The next class to add is the DALEmployee class. This class contains a Login method that checks the user name and password supplied to the values in the database. It uses a SQLCommand object to execute a SQL statement against the database. If a match is found, it returns the employee ID. If no match is found, it returns -1. Since a single value is returned by the SQL statement, you can use the ExecuteScalar method of the SQLCommand object. Add a class named DALEmployee and insert the following code into the class file:

```
using System;
using System.Collections.Generic;
using System.Linq;
using System.Text;
using System.Data.SqlClient;
using System.Diagnostics;
using System.Data;

namespace OSOBLL
{
    class DALEmployee
    {
        public int LogIn(string userName, string password)
        {
            string connString = DALUtility.GetSQLConnection();
            SqlConnection conn = new SqlConnection(connString);
            try
            {
                SqlCommand cmd = new SqlCommand();
                cmd.Connection = conn;
               cmd.CommandText = "Select EmployeeID from Employee where "
                    + " UserName = @UserName and Password = @Password ";
                cmd.Parameters.AddWithValue("@UserName", userName);
                cmd.Parameters.AddWithValue("@Password", password);
                int userId;
                conn.Open();
                userId = (int)cmd.ExecuteScalar();
                if (userId > 0)
                {
                    return userId;
                }
                else
                {
                    return -1;
                }
            }
```

```
            catch (Exception ex)
            {
                Debug.WriteLine(ex.ToString());
                return -1;
            }
            finally
            {
                if (conn.State == ConnectionState.Open)
                {
                    conn.Close();
                }
            }

        }
    }
}
```

4. The next class to construct is the DALProductCatalog class, the purpose of which is to encapsulate the functionality the application needs to retrieve and list the available products in the database. You also want to be able to view the products based on the category to which they belong. The information you need is in two database tables: the catalog table and the products table. These two tables are related through the CatID field.

   When a client requests the product catalog information, a dataset is created and returned to the client. This service is provided in the DALProductCatalog class's GetProductInfo method. The code for the DALProductCatalog class is shown in here:

```
using System;
using System.Collections.Generic;
using System.Linq;
using System.Text;
using System.Data.SqlClient;
using System.Data;
using System.Diagnostics;


namespace OSOBLL
{
    public class DALProductCatalog
    {
        SqlConnection _conn;
        DataSet _dsProducts;

        public DALProductCatalog()
        {
            string connString = DALUtility.GetSQLConnection();
            _conn = new SqlConnection(connString);
        }
        public DataSet GetProductInfo()
        {
```

```
            try
            {
                //Get category info
                String strSQL = "Select CatId, Name, Description from Category";
                SqlCommand cmdSelCategory = new SqlCommand(strSQL, _conn);
                SqlDataAdapter daCatagory = new SqlDataAdapter(cmdSelCategory);
                _dsProducts = new DataSet("Products");
                daCatagory.Fill(_dsProducts, "Category");
                //Get product info
                String strSQL2 = "Select ProductID, CatID, Name," +
                    "Description, UnitCost from Product";
                SqlCommand cmdSelProduct = new SqlCommand(strSQL2, _conn);
                SqlDataAdapter daProduct = new SqlDataAdapter(cmdSelProduct);
                daProduct.Fill(_dsProducts, "Product");
                //Set up the table relation
                DataRelation drCat_Prod = new DataRelation("drCat_Prod",
                    _dsProducts.Tables["Category"].Columns["CatID"],
                    _dsProducts.Tables["Product"].Columns["CatID"],false);
                _dsProducts.Relations.Add(drCat_Prod);
            }
            catch(Exception ex)
            {
                Debug.WriteLine(ex.Message);
            }
            return _dsProducts;
        }

    }
}
```

5. When a client is ready to submit an order, it will call the PlaceOrder method of the `Order` class, which you will define shortly in the business logic classes. The client will pass the employee ID into the method and receive an order number as a return value. The PlaceOrder method of the `Order` class will pass the order information in the form of an XML string to the DALOrder class for processing. The DALOrder class contains the PlaceOrder method that receives an XML order string from the Order class and passes it into a stored procedure in the SQL Server database. The stored procedure updates the database and passes back the order number. This order number is then returned to the Order class, which in turn passes it back to the client.

   Add the following code to define the DALOrder class:

```
using System;
using System.Collections.Generic;
using System.Linq;
using System.Text;
using System.Data.SqlClient;
using System.Data;
using System.Diagnostics;
```

```
namespace OSOBLL
{
    class DALOrder
    {
        public int PlaceOrder(string xmlOrder)
        {
            string connString = DALUtility.GetSQLConnection();
            SqlConnection cn = new SqlConnection(connString);
            try
            {
                SqlCommand cmd = cn.CreateCommand();
                cmd.CommandType = CommandType.StoredProcedure;
                cmd.CommandText = "up_PlaceOrder";
                SqlParameter inParameter = new SqlParameter();
                inParameter.ParameterName = "@xmlOrder";
                inParameter.Value = xmlOrder;
                inParameter.DbType = DbType.String;
                inParameter.Direction = ParameterDirection.Input;
                cmd.Parameters.Add(inParameter);
                SqlParameter ReturnParameter = new SqlParameter();
                ReturnParameter.ParameterName = "@OrderID";
                ReturnParameter.Direction = ParameterDirection.ReturnValue;
                cmd.Parameters.Add(ReturnParameter);
                int intOrderNo;
                cn.Open();
                cmd.ExecuteNonQuery();
                cn.Close();
                intOrderNo = (int)cmd.Parameters["@OrderID"].Value;
                return intOrderNo;
            }
            catch (Exception ex)
            {
                Debug.WriteLine(ex.ToString());
                return 0;
            }
            finally
            {
                if (cn.State == ConnectionState.Open)
                {
                    cn.Close();
                }
            }
        }
    }
}
```

Now that you have constructed the data access layer classes, you are ready to construct the business logic layer set of classes.

6. Add a class named Employee to the application. This class will encapsulate employee information used by the UI and pass a login request to the data access layer. Add the following code to the `Employee.cs` file:

```
using System;
using System.Collections.Generic;
using System.Linq;
using System.Text;

namespace OSOBLL
{
    public class Employee
    {
        int _employeeID;

        public int EmployeeID
        {
            get { return _employeeID; }
            set { _employeeID = value; }
        }
        string _loginName;

        public string LoginName
        {
            get { return _loginName; }
            set { _loginName = value; }
        }
        string _password;

        public string Password
        {
            get { return _password; }
            set { _password = value; }
        }
        Boolean _loggedIn = false;

        public Boolean LoggedIn
        {
            get { return _loggedIn; }
        }

        public Boolean LogIn()
        {
            DALEmployee dbEmp = new DALEmployee();
            int empId;
            empId = dbEmp.LogIn(this.LoginName, this.Password);
            if (empId > 0)
            {
                this.EmployeeID = empId;
                this._loggedIn = true;
                return true;
            }
            else
            {
                this._loggedIn = false;
                return false;
```

```
            }

        }
    }
}
```

7. The ProductCatalog class provides the Product dataset to the UI. It retrieves the dataset from the DALProductCatalog class. You could perform any business logic on the DataSet before passing it to the UI. Add the following code to a class file for the ProductCatalog class:

```
using System;
using System.Collections.Generic;
using System.Linq;
using System.Text;
using System.Data;

namespace OSOBLL
{
    public class ProductCatalog
    {
        public DataSet GetProductInfo()
        {
            //perform any business logic befor passing to client.
            // None needed at this time.
            DALProductCatalog prodCatalog = new DALProductCatalog();
            return prodCatalog.GetProductInfo();
        }
    }
}
```

8. When a user adds items to an order, the order item information is encapsulated in an OrderItem class. This class implements the INotifyPropertyChanged interface. This interface is necessary to notify the UI that a property changed so that it can update any controls bound to the class. It also overrides the ToString method to provide an XML string containing the item information. This string will get passed to the DAL when an order is placed. Add the following code to implement the OrderItem class:

```
using System;
using System.Collections.Generic;
using System.Linq;
using System.Text;
using System.ComponentModel;

namespace OSOBLL
{
    public class OrderItem : INotifyPropertyChanged
    {
        #region INotifyPropertyChanged Members
        public event PropertyChangedEventHandler PropertyChanged;
        protected void Notify(string propName)
        {
```

```
            if (this.PropertyChanged != null)
            {
                PropertyChanged(this, new PropertyChangedEventArgs(propName));
            }
        }
        #endregion
        string _ProdID;
        int _Quantity;
        double _UnitPrice;
        double _SubTotal;
        public string ProdID
        {
            get { return _ProdID; }
            set { _ProdID = value; }
        }
        public int Quantity
        {
            get { return _Quantity; }
            set {
                _Quantity = value;
                Notify("Quantity");
                }
        }
        public double UnitPrice
        {
            get { return _UnitPrice; }
            set { _UnitPrice = value; }
        }
        public double SubTotal
        {
            get { return _SubTotal; }
        }
        public OrderItem(String productID,double unitPrice,int quantity)
        {
            _ProdID = productID;
            _UnitPrice = unitPrice;
            _Quantity = quantity;
            _SubTotal = _UnitPrice * _Quantity;
        }
        public override string ToString()
        {
            string xml = "<OrderItem";
            xml += " ProductID='" + _ProdID + "'";
            xml += " Quantity='" + _Quantity + "'";
            xml += " />";
            return xml;
        }
    }
}
```

9. The final class of the business logic layer is the Order class. This class is responsible for maintaining a collection of order items. It has methods for adding and deleting items as well as passing the items to the DALOrder class when an order is placed. The following code implements the Order class:

```
using System;
using System.Collections.Generic;
using System.Linq;
using System.Text;
using System.Collections.ObjectModel;
using System.ComponentModel;

namespace OSOBLL
{
    public class Order
    {

        ObservableCollection<OrderItem> _orderItemList = new
            ObservableCollection<OrderItem>();

        public ObservableCollection<OrderItem> OrderItemList
        {
            get { return _orderItemList; }
        }
        public void AddItem(OrderItem orderItem)
        {
            foreach (var item in _orderItemList)
            {
                if (item.ProdID == orderItem.ProdID)
                {
                    item.Quantity += orderItem.Quantity;

                    return;
                }
            }
            _orderItemList.Add(orderItem);
        }
        public void RemoveItem(string productID)
        {
            foreach (var item in _orderItemList)
            {
                if (item.ProdID == productID)
                {
                    _orderItemList.Remove(item);
                    return;
                }
            }
        }
        public double GetOrderTotal()
        {
            if (_orderItemList.Count == 0)
            {
```

```
                return 0.00;
            }
            else
            {
                double total = 0;
                foreach (var item in _orderItemList)
                {
                    total += item.SubTotal;
                }
                return total;
            }
        }
        public int PlaceOrder(int employeeID)
        {
            string xmlOrder;
            xmlOrder = "<Order EmployeeID='" + employeeID.ToString() + "'>";
            foreach (var item in _orderItemList)
            {
                xmlOrder += item.ToString();
            }
            xmlOrder += "</Order>";
            DALOrder dbOrder = new DALOrder();
            return dbOrder.PlaceOrder(xmlOrder);
        }

    }
}
```

Now that you have constructed the data access and business logic layers of the OSO application, you are ready to construct the UI. In the next section you will construct a WPF application users will use to place office supply orders.

Creating the OSO Application UI

In order to create the ordering system's WPF interface, you'll need to add a WPF project to the solution containing the OSOBLL project.

1. In Visual Studio, add a WPF project to the solution and name it OSOWPFUI. Figure 14-6 shows the Solution Explorer with both projects added. Make sure you add the references shown in Figure 14-6 for the OSOWPFUI application. Notice a reference to the OSOBLL class library is included.

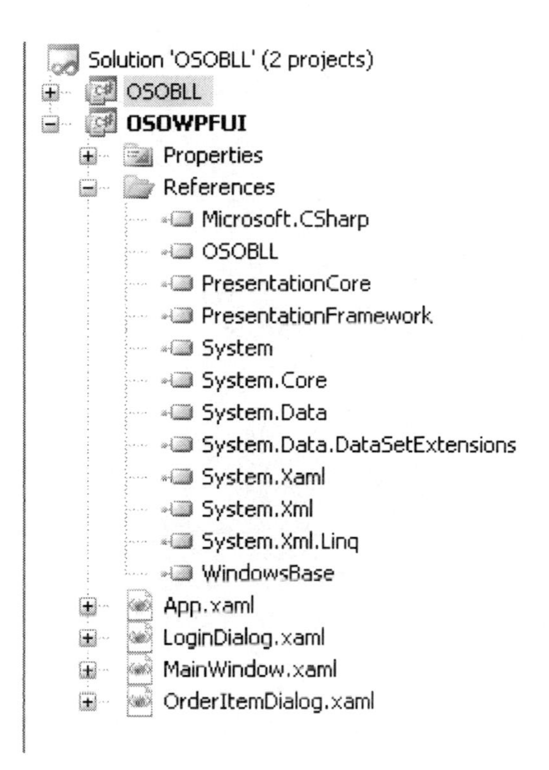

Figure 14-6. *References and classes of the OSOWPFUI application*

The first goal of the user interface is to present information about the products that can be ordered. The product information is presented in a DataGrid control. The user will view products in a particular category by selecting the category in a ComboBox control. Once products are listed, users can add products to an order. When a product is added to an order, it's displayed in a ListView below the DataGrid. Figure 14-7 shows the OSO order form with the items added to an order.

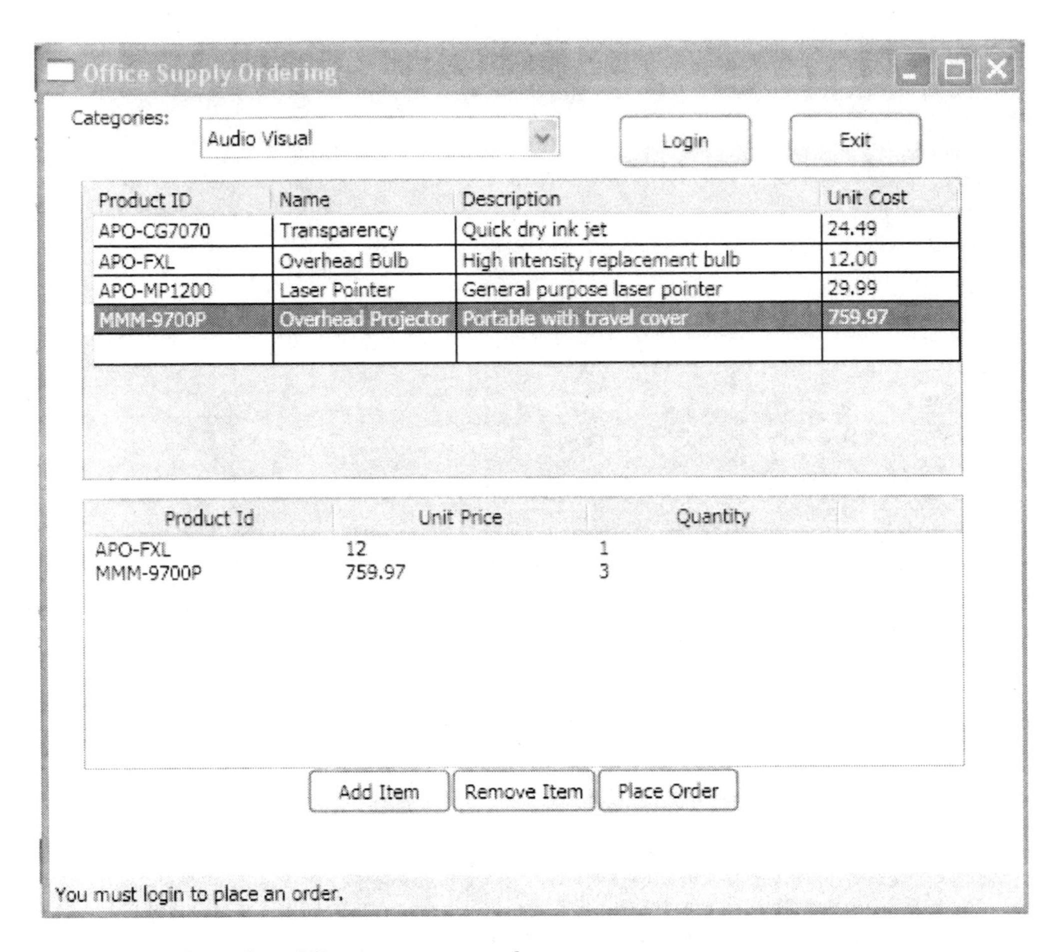

Figure 14-7. *Form for adding items to an order*

2. Add the following XAML code to the `MainWindow.xaml` file to create the OSO order form. Notice the use of data binding for the various controls.

```
<Window x:Class="OSOWPFUI.MainWindow"
        xmlns="http://schemas.microsoft.com/winfx/2006/xaml/presentation"
        xmlns:x="http://schemas.microsoft.com/winfx/2006/xaml"
        Title="Office Supply Ordering" Height="484" Width="550" Loaded="Window_Loaded">
    <Grid>
        <StackPanel Name="LayoutRoot" DataContext="{Binding}"
                Orientation="Vertical" HorizontalAlignment="Left" Height="auto" Width="auto">
            <StackPanel Orientation="Horizontal" HorizontalAlignment="Left">
                <Label Content="Categories:" Margin="10,0,0,0"/>
                <ComboBox ItemsSource="{Binding}" Name="categoriesComboBox"
                          IsSynchronizedWithCurrentItem="True"
                      DisplayMemberPath="Name" Height="23" Margin="12" Width="200" >
                <ComboBox.ItemsPanel>
```

```
                <ItemsPanelTemplate>
                    <VirtualizingStackPanel />
                </ItemsPanelTemplate>
            </ComboBox.ItemsPanel>
        </ComboBox>
        <Button Content="Login" Height="30" Name="loginButton"
                Width="75" Margin="20,5,0,0" Click="loginButton_Click" />
        <Button Content="Exit" Height="30" Name="exitButton"
                Width="75" Margin="20,5,0,0" Click="exitButton_Click" />
    </StackPanel>
    <DataGrid AutoGenerateColumns="False" Height="165"
              ItemsSource="{Binding drCat_Prod}"
              Name="ProductsDataGrid" RowDetailsVisibilityMode="VisibleWhenSelected"
              Width="490" HorizontalAlignment="Left" Margin="20,0,20,10"
              SelectionMode="Single">
        <DataGrid.Columns>
            <DataGridTextColumn
            x:Name="productIDColumn" Binding="{Binding Path=ProductID}"
            Header="Product ID" Width="40*" />
            <DataGridTextColumn
            x:Name="nameColumn" Binding="{Binding Path=Name}"
            Header="Name" Width="40*" />
            <DataGridTextColumn
            x:Name="descriptColumn" Binding="{Binding Path=Description}"
            Header="Description" Width="80*" />
            <DataGridTextColumn
            x:Name="unitCostColumn" Binding="{Binding Path=UnitCost}"
            Header="Unit Cost" Width="30*" />
        </DataGrid.Columns>
    </DataGrid>

    <StackPanel Orientation="Vertical">
        <ListView Name="orderListView" MinHeight="150" Width="490"
                  ItemsSource="{Binding}" SelectionMode="Single">
            <ListView.View>
                <GridView>
                    <GridViewColumn Width="140" Header="Product Id"
                                    DisplayMemberBinding="{Binding ProdID}" />
                    <GridViewColumn Width="140" Header="Unit Price"
                                    DisplayMemberBinding="{Binding UnitPrice}" />
                    <GridViewColumn Width="140" Header="Quantity"
                                    DisplayMemberBinding="{Binding Quantity}" />
                </GridView>
            </ListView.View>
        </ListView>

    </StackPanel>
    <StackPanel Orientation="Horizontal" HorizontalAlignment="Center">
        <Button Name="addButton" MinHeight="25" MinWidth="80"
                Content="Add Item" Click="addButton_Click" />
        <Button Name="removeButton" MinHeight="25" MinWidth="80"
                Content="Remove Item" Click="removeButton_Click"/>
```

```
                <Button Name="placeOrderButton" MinHeight="25" MinWidth="80"
                        Content="Place Order" Click="placeOrderButton_Click"/>
            </StackPanel>
        </StackPanel>
        <StatusBar VerticalAlignment="Bottom" HorizontalAlignment="Stretch">
            <TextBlock Name="statusTextBlock">You must login to place an order.</TextBlock>
        </StatusBar>
    </Grid>
</Window>
```

To add an order item, the user first selects a row in the DataGrid and then selects the Add Item button. The Add Item button displays a dialog box the user uses to enter a quantity and add the item. Figure 14-8 shows the Order Item Dialog.

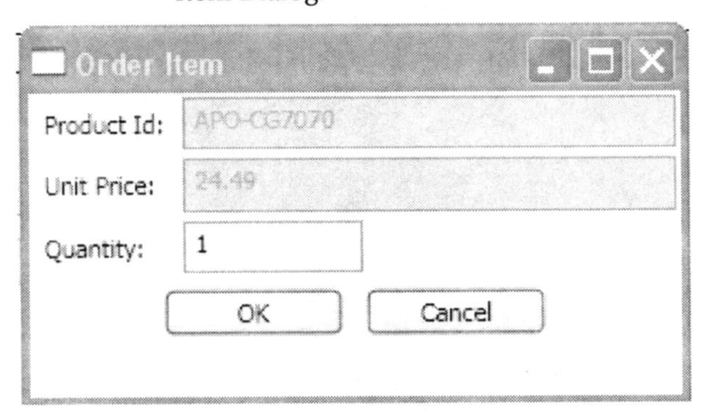

Figure 14-8. *The Order Item dialog*

3. Add a new Window to the project named `OrderItemDialog.xaml`. Add the following XAML code to create the OrderItemDialog form:

```
<Window x:Class="OSOWPFUI.OrderItemDialog"
        xmlns="http://schemas.microsoft.com/winfx/2006/xaml/presentation"
        xmlns:x="http://schemas.microsoft.com/winfx/2006/xaml"
        WindowStartupLocation="CenterOwner"
        Title="Order Item" Height="169" Width="300">
    <Grid>
        <Grid.ColumnDefinitions>
            <ColumnDefinition Width="Auto" />
            <ColumnDefinition Width="Auto" />
            <ColumnDefinition />
        </Grid.ColumnDefinitions>

        <Grid.RowDefinitions>
            <RowDefinition Height="Auto" />
            <RowDefinition Height="Auto" />
            <RowDefinition Height="Auto" />
            <RowDefinition Height="Auto" />
            <RowDefinition />
        </Grid.RowDefinitions>
```

```
        <Label Grid.Column="0" Grid.Row="0" Margin="2">Product Id:</Label>
        <TextBox Name="productIdTextBox" Grid.Column="1"
                 Grid.Row="0" Margin="2" Grid.ColumnSpan="2" IsEnabled="False"/>
        <Label Grid.Column="0" Grid.Row="1" Margin="2">Unit Price:</Label>
        <TextBox Name="unitPriceTextBox" Grid.Column="1"
                 Grid.Row="1" Margin="2" Grid.ColumnSpan="2" IsEnabled="False"/>
        <Label Grid.Column="0" Grid.Row="2" Margin="2" >Quantity:</Label>
        <TextBox Name="quantityTextBox" Grid.Column="1"
                 Grid.Row="2" Margin="2" MinWidth="80" Text="1"/>
        <StackPanel Grid.Column="0" Grid.ColumnSpan="3"
                    Grid.Row="3" Orientation="Horizontal"
                    HorizontalAlignment="Center">
            <Button Name="okButton" Click="okButton_Click" IsDefault="True"
                    MinWidth="80" Margin="5">OK</Button>
            <Button Name="cancelButton" Click="cancelButton_Click" IsCancel="True"
                    MinWidth="80" Margin="5">Cancel</Button>
        </StackPanel>
    </Grid>
</Window>
```

Before users can submit an order, they must log in. When they click on the Login button, they are presented with a Login Dialog window, shown in Figure 14-9.

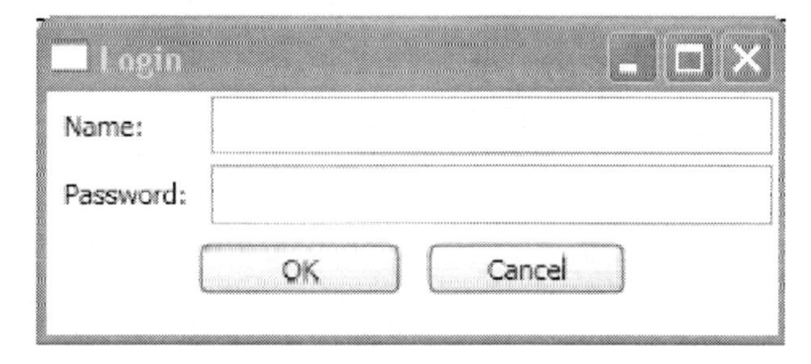

Figure 14-9. *The Login dialog*

4. Add a new Window to the project named `LoginDialog.xaml`. Add the following XAML code to create the LoginDialog form.

```
<Window x:Class="OSOWPFUI.LoginDialog"
        xmlns="http://schemas.microsoft.com/winfx/2006/xaml/presentation"
        xmlns:x="http://schemas.microsoft.com/winfx/2006/xaml"
        Title="Login" Height="131" Width="300"
        WindowStartupLocation="CenterOwner"
        FocusManager.FocusedElement="{Binding ElementName=nameTextBox}">
    <Grid>
        <Grid.ColumnDefinitions>
            <ColumnDefinition Width="Auto" />
            <ColumnDefinition />
        </Grid.ColumnDefinitions>

        <Grid.RowDefinitions>
```

```
            <RowDefinition Height="Auto" />
            <RowDefinition Height="Auto" />
            <RowDefinition Height="Auto" />
            <RowDefinition />
        </Grid.RowDefinitions>
        <Label Grid.Column="0" Grid.Row="0" Margin="2">Name:</Label>
        <TextBox Name="nameTextBox" Grid.Column="1" Grid.Row="0" Margin="2"/>
        <Label Grid.Column="0" Grid.Row="1" Margin="2">Password:</Label>
        <PasswordBox Name="passwordTextBox" Grid.Column="1" Grid.Row="1" Margin="2"/>

        <StackPanel Grid.Column="0" Grid.ColumnSpan="2" Grid.Row="2"
                    Orientation="Horizontal" HorizontalAlignment="Center">
            <Button Name="okButton" Click="okButton_Click" IsDefault="True"
                    MinWidth="80" Margin="5">OK</Button>
            <Button Name="cancelButton" Click="cancelButton_Click" IsCancel="True"
                    MinWidth="80" Margin="5">Cancel</Button>
        </StackPanel>
    </Grid>
</Window>
```

Now that you have created the windows that make up the UI, you are ready to add the implementation to the window's codebehind files.

5. Add the following code to the `MainWindow.xaml.cs` codebehind file:

```
using System;
using System.Collections.Generic;
using System.Linq;
using System.Text;
using System.Windows;
using System.Windows.Controls;
using System.Windows.Data;
using System.Windows.Documents;
using System.Windows.Input;
using System.Windows.Media;
using System.Windows.Media.Imaging;
using System.Windows.Navigation;
using System.Windows.Shapes;
using System.Data;
using OSOBLL;
using System.Collections.ObjectModel;

namespace OSOWPFUI
{
    /// <summary>
    /// Interaction logic for MainWindow.xaml
    /// </summary>
    public partial class MainWindow : Window
    {

        DataSet _dsProdCat;
        Employee _employee;
        Order _order;
```

```
public MainWindow()
{
    InitializeComponent();

}

private void Window_Loaded(object sender, RoutedEventArgs e)
{
    ProductCatalog prodCat = new ProductCatalog();
    _dsProdCat = prodCat.GetProductInfo();
    this.DataContext = _dsProdCat.Tables["Category"];
    _order = new  Order();
    _employee = new Employee();
    this.orderListView.ItemsSource = _order.OrderItemList;
}

private void loginButton_Click(object sender, RoutedEventArgs e)
{

    LoginDialog dlg = new LoginDialog();
    dlg.Owner = this;
    dlg.ShowDialog();
    // Process data entered by user if dialog box is accepted
    if (dlg.DialogResult == true)
    {
        _employee.LoginName = dlg.nameTextBox.Text;
        _employee.Password = dlg.passwordTextBox.Password;
        if (_employee.LogIn() == true)
        {
      this.statusTextBlock.Text = "You are logged in as employee number " +
        _employee.EmployeeID.ToString();
        }
        else
        {
            MessageBox.Show("You could not be verified. Please try again.");
        }
    }
}

private void exitButton_Click(object sender, RoutedEventArgs e)
{
    this.Close();
}



private void addButton_Click(object sender, RoutedEventArgs e)
{

    OrderItemDialog orderItemDialog = new OrderItemDialog();
```

```
            DataRowView selectedRow;
            selectedRow = (DataRowView)this.ProductsDataGrid.SelectedItems[0];
            orderItemDialog.productIdTextBox.Text = selectedRow.Row.ItemArray[0].ToString();
            orderItemDialog.unitPriceTextBox.Text = selectedRow.Row.ItemArray[4].ToString();
            orderItemDialog.Owner = this;
            orderItemDialog.ShowDialog();
            if (orderItemDialog.DialogResult == true )
            {
                string productId = orderItemDialog.productIdTextBox.Text;
                double unitPrice = double.Parse(orderItemDialog.unitPriceTextBox.Text);
                int quantity = int.Parse(orderItemDialog.quantityTextBox.Text);
                _order.AddItem(new OrderItem(productId,unitPrice,quantity));
            }
        }

        private void removeButton_Click(object sender, RoutedEventArgs e)
        {
            if (this.orderListView.SelectedItem != null)
            {
                var selectedOrderItem = this.orderListView.SelectedItem as OrderItem;
                _order.RemoveItem(selectedOrderItem.ProdID);
            }
        }

        private void placeOrderButton_Click(object sender, RoutedEventArgs e)
        {
            if (_employee.LoggedIn == true)
            {
                //place order
                int orderId;
               orderId = _order.PlaceOrder(_employee.EmployeeID);
               MessageBox.Show("Your order has been placed. Your order id is " +
                    orderId.ToString());
            }
            else
            {
                MessageBox.Show("You must be logged in to place an order.");
            }
        }
    }
}
```

A look at the preceding code reveals that when the window loads, the Window_Loaded event retrieves the ProdCat DataSet and sets it equal to the DataContext of the window so that the ComboBox and GridView controls can bind to it. An Order object is created and the ListView control is bound to its OrderItem collection. This code segment is repeated here for your review:

```
private void Window_Loaded(object sender, RoutedEventArgs e)
{
    ProductCatalog prodCat = new ProductCatalog();
```

```
        _dsProdCat = prodCat.GetProductInfo();
        this.DataContext = _dsProdCat.Tables["Category"];
        _order = new  Order();
        _employee = new Employee();
        this.orderListView.ItemsSource = _order.OrderItemList;
    }
```

The loginButton_Click event launches an instance of the LoginDialog window and checks the Dialog result. If it comes back as true, the _employee object's values are set to the values entered in the dialog and the Login method of the Employee class is called. If the Login method returns true, the user is notified that they are logged in.

```
    private void loginButton_Click(object sender, RoutedEventArgs e)
    {

        LoginDialog dlg = new LoginDialog();
        dlg.Owner = this;
        dlg.ShowDialog();
        // Process data entered by user if dialog box is accepted
        if (dlg.DialogResult == true)
        {
            _employee.LoginName = dlg.nameTextBox.Text;
            _employee.Password = dlg.passwordTextBox.Password;
            if (_employee.LogIn() == true)
            {
          this.statusTextBlock.Text = "You are logged in as employee number " +
              _employee.EmployeeID.ToString();
            }
            else
            {
                MessageBox.Show("You could not be verified. Please try again.");
            }
        }
    }
```

The addButton_Click event launches an instance of the OrderItemDialog window and fills the textboxes with information from the selected row of the ProductsDataGrid. If the DialogResult returns true, the information entered in the dialog is used to create an OrderItem object and add it to the Order's OrderItem collection.

```
private void addButton_Click(object sender, RoutedEventArgs e)
{

    OrderItemDialog orderItemDialog = new OrderItemDialog();

    DataRowView selectedRow;
    selectedRow = (DataRowView)this.ProductsDataGrid.SelectedItems[0];
    orderItemDialog.productIdTextBox.Text = selectedRow.Row.ItemArray[0].ToString();
    orderItemDialog.unitPriceTextBox.Text = selectedRow.Row.ItemArray[4].ToString();
    orderItemDialog.Owner = this;
    orderItemDialog.ShowDialog();
```

```
        if (orderItemDialog.DialogResult == true )
        {
            string productId = orderItemDialog.productIdTextBox.Text;
            double unitPrice = double.Parse(orderItemDialog.unitPriceTextBox.Text);
            int quantity = int.Parse(orderItemDialog.quantityTextBox.Text);
            _order.AddItem(new OrderItem(productId,unitPrice,quantity));
        }
    }
```

The removeButton_Click event checks to see if an item is selected in the orderList view and removes it from the order.

```
    private void removeButton_Click(object sender, RoutedEventArgs e)
    {
        if (this.orderListView.SelectedItem != null)
        {
            var selectedOrderItem = this.orderListView.SelectedItem as OrderItem;
            _order.RemoveItem(selectedOrderItem.ProdID);
        }
    }
```

The placeOrderButton_Click event checks to see if the user is logged in and places the order if they are.

```
    private void placeOrderButton_Click(object sender, RoutedEventArgs e)
    {
        if (_employee.LoggedIn == true)
        {
            //place order
            int orderId;
           orderId = _order.PlaceOrder(_employee.EmployeeID);
           MessageBox.Show("Your order has been placed. Your order id is " + orderId.ToString());
        }
        else
        {
            MessageBox.Show("You must be logged in to place an order.");
        }
    }
```

Now that the MainWindow's codebehind is implemented, you are ready to add the code behind for the dialog widows.

6. Add the following code to the `OrderItemDialog.xaml.cs` codebehind file. If the user clicks the OK button, the DialogResult is set to `true`. If the user clicks cancel, the DialogResult is set to `false`.

```
using System;
using System.Collections.Generic;
using System.Linq;
using System.Text;
using System.Windows;
using System.Windows.Controls;
```

```
using System.Windows.Data;
using System.Windows.Documents;
using System.Windows.Input;
using System.Windows.Media;
using System.Windows.Media.Imaging;
using System.Windows.Shapes;

namespace OSOWPFUI
{
    /// <summary>
    /// Interaction logic for OrderItemDialog.xaml
    /// </summary>
    public partial class OrderItemDialog : Window
    {
        public OrderItemDialog()
        {
            InitializeComponent();
        }

        private void okButton_Click(object sender, RoutedEventArgs e)
        {
            this.DialogResult = true;
        }

        private void cancelButton_Click(object sender, RoutedEventArgs e)
        {
            this.DialogResult = false;
        }
    }
}
```

7. Add the following code to the `LoginDialog.xaml.cs` codebehind file. It is similar to OrderItemDialog code.

```
using System;
using System.Collections.Generic;
using System.Linq;
using System.Text;
using System.Windows;
using System.Windows.Controls;
using System.Windows.Data;
using System.Windows.Documents;
using System.Windows.Input;
using System.Windows.Media;
using System.Windows.Media.Imaging;
using System.Windows.Shapes;

namespace OSOWPFUI
{
    /// <summary>
    /// Interaction logic for LoginDialog.xaml
    /// </summary>
```

```
    public partial class LoginDialog : Window
    {
        public LoginDialog()
        {
            InitializeComponent();
        }

        private void okButton_Click(object sender, RoutedEventArgs e)
        {
            this.DialogResult = true;
        }

        private void cancelButton_Click(object sender, RoutedEventArgs e)
        {
            this.DialogResult = false;
        }
    }
}
```

Now that you have added the implementation code to the UI, you are ready to test the application.

8. Launch the application in debug mode. You are presented with the order form (see Figure 14-7). Using the category drop-down, switch between the different categories and verify that the products are updated in the product grid. Select an item in the product grid and click the Add Item button. You are presented with the Order Item dialog (see Figure 14-8). Add some items to the order and test removing some items from the order. To test placing an order, click the Login button. You are presented with the Login dialog (see Figure 14-9). Enter a value of JSmith for the user and a value of js for the password. You should receive confirmation you are logged in. Click the Place Order button. You should receive confirmation the order was placed. When you've finished testing, click the Exit button to stop the program.

■ **Note** Although this is a functional application, it's for demonstration purposes only and is not production ready.

Summary

In this chapter, you revisited the office supply ordering (OSO) application designed in Chapter 4. You created a functional application incorporating the concepts you learned in the previous chapters. The application contains a data access layer, a business logic layer, and a user interface layer. You learned why applications are split into different layers and how to construct a working application comprised of the various layers. Although you didn't create a web-based user interface application layer, because you created the application in distinct tiers, you could easily replace the Windows-based WPF UI with a web-based Silverlight UI.

CHAPTER 15

Wrapping Up

If you've made it this far, take a moment and pat yourself on the back. You've come a long way since the day you first cracked open the cover of this book; you've gained valuable skills and learned concepts you can use to successfully program using the .NET Framework, C#, and the Visual Studio IDE. These include, but are not limited to, the following:

- The importance of the application design cycle.
- The Unified Modeling Language and how it can help facilitate the analysis and design of object-oriented programs.
- The Common Language Runtime (CLR).
- The structure of the .NET Framework.
- How to create and use class structures and hierarchies.
- How to implement inheritance, polymorphism, and interfaces.
- Object interaction and collaboration.
- Event-driven programming.
- Structured error handling.
- How to work with data structures and data sources using ADO.NET.
- Using the Entity Framework to create object relational mappings to a SQL Server database.
- How to use the features of the Visual Studio IDE to increase productivity and facilitate debugging.
- How to implement a Windows-based graphical user interface using the Windows Presentation Framework.
- How to implement a web-based graphical user interface using Silverlight.
- How to create and consume services using Windows Communication Framework.

Congratulations! You can now call yourself a C# programmer (albeit a neophyte). However, don't get too high on yourself. If your goal is to become a *professional* C# programmer, your journey has just begun. The next stage of your development is to gain experience. In other words, design and code, and then design and code some more. If you are designing and coding C# at work, this will be easy. (Although it will be stressful if you are expected to be an expert after that three-day course they sent you to!)

If you are learning on your own, you will have to find the time and projects on which to work. This is easier than you might think. Commit to an hour a day and come up with an idea for a program. For example, you could design a program that converts recipes into Extensible Markup Language (XML) data. The XML data could then generate a shopping list. Heck, if you really want to go all out, incorporate an inventory tracking system that tracks ingredients you have in stock. However you go about gaining experience, remember the important adage: use it or lose it!

The following sections highlight some other important things to consider as you develop your programming skills.

Improve Your Object-Oriented Design Skills

Object-oriented analysis and design is one of the hardest tasks you will perform as a programmer. This is not a skill that comes easily for most programmers. It is, however, one of the most important skills you should strive to master. It is what separates what I call a *programmer* from a *coder*. If you talk to most CIOs and programming managers, finding coders is easy; it is the programmer they are after.

Remember that there is no one "true" methodology, rather several that are equally valid.

Investigate the .NET Framework Namespaces

The .NET Framework contains a vast number of classes, interfaces, and other types aimed at optimizing and expediting your development efforts. The various namespaces that make up the .NET Framework Class Library are organized by functionality. It's important you take the time to become familiar with the capabilities provided by these namespaces.

Start out with the namespaces that incorporate functionality you will use most often, such as the root namespace System and the System.Data.EntityClient, which contains the .NET Framework Data Provider for the Entity Framework.

After you become familiar with the more common namespaces, explore some of the more obscure ones. For example, System.Security.Cryptography provides cryptographic services such as data encoding, hashing, and message authentication. You will be amazed at the extent of the support provided by the framework. You can find a wealth of information on the members of the various namespaces in Visual Studio's integrated documentation.

Become Familiar with ADO.NET and the Entity Framework

Data is fundamental to programming. You store, retrieve, and manipulate data in every program you write. The data structure a program works with during execution is *nondurable* data—it is held in RAM. When the application terminates, this data is lost and has to be re-created the next time the application runs. *Durable data* is data that is maintained in a permanent data structure such as a file system or a database. Most programs need to retrieve data from and persist data to some sort of durable data storage. This is where ADO.NET steps in. ADO.NET refers to the namespaces that contain the functionality for working with durable data. (It also contains functionality for organizing and working with nondurable data in a familiar relational database or XML-type structure.) Although I have introduced you to ADO.NET and the Entity Framework, this is such an important topic that it deserves a book devoted solely to these data access technologies. (Don't worry—there are many!) This is definitely an area where you need to devote further study. To learn more about these technologies, visit the Data Developer Center site at `http://msdn.microsoft.com/en-us/data`. A good book on the Entity Framework is *Entity Framework 4.0 Recipes* by Larry Tenny and Zeeshan Hirani (Apress, 2010).

Learn More About WPF and Silverlight

Although you were introduced to WPF and Silverlight in Chapters 11 and 12, I only scratched the surface of these powerful technologies. Silverlight and WPF are packed full of features for developing engaging, interactive user experiences on the web, desktop, and mobile devices. For more information on programming WPF, visit the Windows Client development center at `http://windowsclient.net`. For more information about programming in Silverlight visit the Silverlight developer center at `www.silverlight.net`. Both these sites are full of learning materials and demo applications showcasing the power of these technologies. A good book on WPF is *Applied WPF 4 in Context* by Raffaele Garofalo (Apress, 2011). A good book for further study into Silverlight is *Pro Silverlight 4 in C# 3rd Edition* by Matthew MacDonald (Apress, 2010).

Move Toward Component-Based Development

After you have mastered object-oriented development and the encapsulation of your programming logic in a class system, you are ready to move toward component-based development. *Components* are assemblies that further encapsulate the functionality of your programming logic. Although the OSO application's business logic tier is logically isolated from the data access tier, physically they reside in the same assembly. You can increase code maintenance and reuse by compiling each into its own assembly. You should start moving to a Lego approach of application development. This is where your application is comprised of a set of independent pieces (assemblies) that can be snapped together and work in conjunction to perform the necessary services. For more information on this and other best practices, go to the Microsoft's patterns & practices web site at `http://msdn.microsoft.com/en-us/practices/`.

Find Help

An enormous amount of information is available on the .NET Framework and the C# programming language. The help system provided with Visual Studio is an excellent resource for programmers. Get in the habit of using this resource religiously. Another extremely important resource is `http://msdn.microsoft.com`. This web site, provided by Microsoft for developers, contains a wealth of information including white papers, tutorials, and webcast seminars; quite honestly, it's one of the most informative sites in the industry. If you are developing using Microsoft technologies, visiting this site should be as routine as reading the daily paper. There are also a number of independent web sites dedicated to the various .NET programming languages. One good site is C# Corner (`www.c-sharpcorner.com/`), which contains tons of articles on all aspects of programming in C#. You can use your favorite search engine to discover other good sites on the web dedicated to C# programming.

Join a User Group

Microsoft is investing a lot of support for the development of local .NET user groups. The user groups consist of members with an interest in .NET programming. These groups provide a great avenue for learning, mentoring, and networking. There is a listing of .NET user groups available at http://msdn.microsoft.com. The International .NET Association (INETA) also provides support for .NET user groups; you can find a listing of INETA affiliated user groups at www.ineta.org.

If you can't find a .NET user group in your area, heck, why not start one?

Please Provide Feedback

Although every effort has been made to provide you with an error-free text, it is inevitable that some mistakes will make it through the editing process. I am committed to providing updated errata at the Apress Web site (www.apress.com), but I can't do this without your help. If you have come across any mistakes while reading this text, please report them to me through the Apress site.

Thank You and Good Luck

I sincerely hope you found working your way through this text an enjoyable and worthwhile experience. I want to thank you for allowing me to be your guide on this journey. Just as your skills as a developer increased as a result of reading this book, my skills as a developer have increased immensely as a result of writing it. My experience of teaching and training for the past two decades has been that you really don't fully comprehend a subject until you can teach it to someone else. So, again, thank you and good luck!

APPENDIX A

Fundamental Programming Concepts

The following information is for readers who are new to programming and need a primer on some fundamental programming concepts. If you have programmed in another language, chances are the concepts presented in this appendix are not new to you. You should, however, review the material briefly to become familiar with the C# syntax.

Working with Variables and Data Types

Variables in programming languages store values that can change while the program executes. For example, if you wanted to count the number of times a user tries to log in to an application, you could use a variable to track the number of attempts. The variable is a memory location where the value is stored. Using the variable, your program can read or alter the value stored in memory. Before you use a variable in your program, however, you must declare it. When you declare a variable, the compiler also needs to know what kind of data will be stored at the memory location. For example, will it be numbers or letters? If the variable will store numbers, how large can a number be? Will the variable store decimals or only whole numbers? You answer these questions by assigning a data type to the variable. A login counter, for example, only needs to hold positive whole numbers. The following code demonstrates how you declare a variable named counter in C# with an Integer data type:

```
int counter;
```

Specifying the data type is referred to as *strong typing*. Strong typing results in more efficient memory management, faster execution, and compiler type checking, all of which reduces runtime errors.

Once you declare the variable, you can assign it an initial value, either in a separate statement or within the declaration statement itself. For instance, the following code

```
int counter = 1;
```

is equivalent to this

```
int counter;
counter = 1;
```

If you do not explicitly assign an initial value to a variable at the time you declare it, the compiler will do so implicitly, assigning numeric data types to `0`, Boolean data types to `false`, character data types to empty (" "), date data types to `1/1/0001`, and object data types to `null` (which is an empty reference pointer). The following sections further describe these various data types.

Understanding Elementary Data Types

C# supports elementary data types such as numeric, character, and date.

Integral Data Types

Integral data types represent whole numbers only. Table A-1 summarizes the integral data types used in C#.

Table A-1. *Integral Data Types*

Data Type	Storage Size	Value Range
`Byte`	8-bit	0 through 255
`Short`	16-bit	–32,768 through 32,767
`Integer`	32-bit	–2,147,483,648 through 2,147,483,647
`Long`	64-bit	–9,223,372,036,854,775,808 through 9,223,372,036,854,775,807

Obviously, memory size is important when choosing a data type for a variable. A less obvious consideration is how easily the compiler works with the data type. The compiler performs arithmetic operations with integers more efficiently than the other types. Often, it's better to use integers as counter variables even though a byte or short type could easily manage the maximum value reached.

Non-Integral Data Types

If a variable will store numbers that include decimal parts, then you must use a non-integral data type. C# supports the non-integral data types listed in Table A-2.

Table A-2. *Non-Integral Data Types*

Data Type	Storage Size	Value Range
`Single`	32-bit	–3.4028235E+38 through –1.401298E–45 for negative values; 1.401298E–45 through 3.4028235E+38 for positive values
`Double`	64-bit	1.79769313486231570E+308 through –4.94065645841246544E–324 for negative values; 4.94065645841246544E–324 through 1.79769313486231570E+308 for positive values
`Decimal`	128-bit	0 through +/–79,228,162,514,264,337,593,543,950,335 with no decimal point; 0 through +/–7.9228162514264337593543950335 with 28 places to the right of the decimal

The decimal data type holds a larger number of significant digits than either the single or the double data types and it is not subject to rounding errors. Decimal data types are usually reserved for financial or scientific calculations that require a higher degree of precision.

Character Data Types

Character data types are for variables that hold characters used in the human language. For example, a character data type holds letters such as a or numbers used for display and printing such as "2 apples." The character data types in C# are based on Unicode, which defines a character set that can represent the characters found in every language from English to Arabic and Mandarin Chinese. C# supports two character data types: `char` and `string`. The char data type holds single (16-bit) Unicode character values such as `a` or `B`. The string data type holds a sequence of Unicode characters. It can range from zero up to about two billion characters.

Boolean Data Type

The Boolean data type holds a 16-bit value that is interpreted as true or false. It's used for variables that can be one of only two values, such as yes or no, or on or off.

Date Data Type

Dates are held as 64-bit integers where each increment represents a period of elapsed time from the start of the Gregorian calendar (1/1/0001 at 12:00 a.m.).

Object Data Type

An object data type is a 32-bit address that points to the memory location of another data type. It is commonly used to declare variables where the actual data type they refer to can't be determined until runtime. Although the object data type can be a catch-all to refer to the other data types, it is the most inefficient data type when it comes to performance and should be avoided unless absolutely necessary.

Nullable Types

By default, value types such as the Boolean, integer, and double data types can't be assigned a null value. This can become problematic when retrieving data from data structures such as a database that does allow nulls. When declaring a value type variable that may be assigned a null, you make it a nullable type by placing a question mark symbol (?) after the type name, like so:

```
double salary = null; // Not allowed.
double? salary = null; // allowed.
```

Introducing Composite Data Types

Combining elementary data types creates composite data types. Structures, arrays, and classes are examples of composite data types.

Structures

A structure data type is useful when you want to organize and work with information that is mostly just a piece of data and does not need the overhead of class methods and constructors. It's well suited for representing lightweight objects such as the coordinates of a point or rectangle. A single variable of type structure can store such the information. You declare a structure with the struct keyword. For example, the following code creates a structure named Point to store the coordinates of a point in a two-dimensional surface:

```
public struct Point
{
   public int _x, _y;

        public Point(int x, int y)
        {
            _x = x;
            _y = y;
        }
}
```

Once you define the structure, you can declare a variable of the structure type and create a new instance of the type, like so:

```
Point p1 = new Point(10,20);
```

Arrays

Arrays are often used to organize and work with groups of the same data type; for example, you may need to work with a group of names, so you declare an array data type by placing square brackets ([]) immediately following the variable name, like so:

```
string[] name;
```

The new operator is used to create the array and initialize its elements to their default values. Because the elements of the array are referenced by a zero-based index, the following array holds five elements:

```
string[] name = new string[4];
```

To initialize the elements of an array when the array is declared, you use curly brackets ({}) to list the values. Since the size of the array can be inferred, you do not have to state it.

```
string[] name = {"Bob","Bill","Jane","Judy"};
```

C# supports multidimensional arrays. When you declare the array, you separate the size of the dimensions by commas. The following declaration creates a two-dimensional array of integers with five rows and four columns:

```
string[,] name = new string[4,3];
```

To initialize the elements of a two dimensional array when the array is declared, you use curly brackets inside curly brackets to list the array elements.

```
int[,] intArray = {{1,2}, {3,4}, {5,6}, {7,8}};
```

You access elements of the array using its name followed by the index of the element in brackets. For example, name[2] references the third element of the names array declared previously and has a value of Jane.

Classes

Classes are used extensively in object-oriented programming languages. Most of this book is devoted to their creation and use. At this point, it suffices to say that classes define a complex data type definition for an object. They contain information about how an object should behave, including its name, methods, properties, and events. The .NET Framework contains many predefined classes with which you can work. You can also create your own class type definitions. A variable defined as a class type contains a 32-bit address pointer to the memory location of the object. The following code declares an object instance of the StringBuilder class defined in the .NET Framework:

```
StringBuilder sb = new StringBuilder();
```

Looking at Literals, Constants, and Enumerations

Although the values of variables change during program execution, literals and constants contain items of data that do not change.

Literals

Literals are fixed values implicitly assigned a data type and are often used to initialize variables. The following code uses a literal to add the value of 2 to an integer value:

```
Count = Count + 2
```

By inspecting the literal, the compiler assigns a data type to the literal. Numeric literals without decimal values are assigned the integer data type; those with a decimal value are assigned as double data type. The keywords `true` and `false` are assigned the Boolean data type. If the literal is contained in quotes, it is assigned as a string data type. In the following line of code, the two string literals are combined and assigned to a string variable:

```
FullName = "Bob" + "Smith"
```

It's possible to override the default data type assignment of the literal by appending a type character to the literal. For example, a value of `12.25` will be assigned the double data type but a value of `12.25f` will cause the compiler to assign it a single data type.

Constants

Many times you have to use the same constant value repeatedly in your code. For example, a series of geometric calculations may need to use the value of pi. Instead of repeating the literal 3.14 in your code, you can make your code more readable and maintainable by using a declared constant. You declare a constant using the const keyword followed by the constant name and the data type:

```
const Single pi = 3.14159265358979323846f;
```

The constant is assigned a value when it is declared and this value can't be altered or reassigned.

Enumerations

You often need to assign the value of a variable to one of several related predefined constants. In these instances, you can create an enumeration type to group together the values. Enumerations associate a set of integer constants to names that can be used in code. For example, the following code creates an enum type of Manager used to define three related manager constants with names of DeptManager, GeneralManager, and AssistantManager with values of 0, 1, and 2, respectively:

```
enum Manager
{
    DeptManager,
    GeneralManager,
    AssistantManager,
}
```

A variable of the enum type can be declared and set to one of the Enum constants.

```
Manager managerLevel = Manager.DeptManager;
```

■ **Note** The .NET Framework provides a variety of intrinsic constants and enumerations designed to make your coding more intuitive and readable. For example, the StringAlignment enumeration specifies the alignment of a text string relative to its layout rectangle.

Exploring Variable Scope

Two important aspects of a variable are its scope and lifetime. The scope of a variable refers to how the variable can be accessed from other code. The lifetime of a variable is the period of time when the variable is valid and available for use. A variable's scope and lifetime are determined by where it is declared and the access modifier used to declare it.

Block-Level Scope

A code block is a set of grouped code statements. Examples of code blocks include code organized in if-else, do-loop, or for-next statements. Block-level scope is the narrowest scope a variable can have. A variable declared within a block of code is available only within the block it is declared. In the following code, the variable blockCount can only be accessed from inside the if block. Any attempt to access the variable outside the block will generate a compiler error.

```
if (icount > 10)
{
    int blockCount;
    blockCount = icount;
}
```

Although the scope of blockCount is limited to the if block, the lifetime of the variable is for the entire procedure where the block exists. You will probably find block-level scope to be too restrictive in most cases and will instead use procedure scope.

Procedure Scope

Procedures are blocks of code that can be called and executed from other code. There are two types of procedures supported in C#: method and property. Variables declared outside of a code block but within a procedure have procedure-level scope. Variables with procedure scope can be accessed by code within the same procedure. In the following code, the counter iCount is declared with procedure scope and can be referenced from anywhere within the procedure block of the Counter method:

```
void Counter()
{
    int iCount = 0;
    do
    {
        iCount = iCount + 2;
    }
    while (iCount < 10);
}
```

The lifetime of a procedure scope variable is limited to the duration of the execution of the procedure.

Module Scope

Variables with module scope are available to any code within the class or structure. To have module scope, the variable is declared in the general declaration section (outside of any procedure blocks) of the class or structure. To limit the accessibility to the module where it is declared, you use the private access modifier keyword. In the following code, the iCount variable can be accessed by both procedures defined in the class:

```
public class Class1
{
    private int _iCount;
    public void IncrementCount()
    {
        int iCount = 0;
        do
        {
            iCount = iCount + 2;
        }
        while (iCount < 10);
    }
    public void ReadCount()
    {
        Console.WriteLine(_iCount.ToString());
    }
}
```

The lifetime of the variable declared with module scope is the same as the lifetime of the object instance of the class or structure in which it is declared.

■ **Note** There are several additional variations of scope addressed in the main body of the book.

Understanding Data Type Conversion

During program execution there are many times when a value must be converted from one data type to another. The process of converting between data types is referred to as *casting* or *conversion.*

Implicit Conversion

The C# compiler will perform some data type conversions for you automatically. For numeric types, an implicit conversion can be made when the value to be stored can fit into the variable without being truncated or rounded off. For example, in the following code, an integer data type is implicitly converted to a long data type:

```
int i1 = 373737373;
long l1 = i1;
l1 *= l1;
```

Explicit Conversion

Explicit conversion is referred to as *casting*. To perform a cast, you specify the type that you are casting to in parentheses in front of the value or variable to be converted. The following code uses a cast to explicitly convert the double type n1 to an integer type:

```
double n1 = 3.73737373;
int i1 = (int)n1;
```

Widening and Narrowing Conversions

Widening conversions occur when the data type being converted to can accommodate all the possible values contained in the original data type. For example, an integer data type can be converted to a double data type without any data loss or overflow. Data loss occurs when the number gets truncated. For example, 2.54 gets truncated to 2 if it is converted to an integer data type. Overflow occurs when a number is too large to fit in the new data type. For example, if the number 50000 is converted to a short data type, the maximum capacity of the short data type is exceeded, causing the overflow error. Narrowing conversions, on the other hand, occur when the data type being converted to can't accommodate all the values that can be contained in the original data type. For example, when the value of a double data type is converted to a short data type, any decimal values contained in the original value will be lost. In addition, if the original value is more than the limit of the short data type, a runtime exception will occur. You should be particularly careful to trap for these situations when implementing narrowing conversions in your code.

Working with Operators

An operator is a code symbol that tells the compiler to perform an operation on a value. The operation can be arithmetic, comparative, or logical.

Arithmetic Operators

Arithmetic operators perform mathematical manipulation to numeric types. Table A-3 lists the commonly used arithmetic operators available in C#.

Table A-3. *Arithmetic Operators*

Operator	Description
=	Assignment
*	Multiplication
/	Division
+	Addition
-	Subtraction

The following code increments the value of an integer data type by the number one:

```
Count = Count + 1
```

C# also supports shorthand assignment operators that combine the assignment with the operation. The following code is equivalent to the previous code:

```
Count += 1
```

If you are going to increment by one, you can also use the shorthand assignment `++`. The following code is equivalent to the previous code:

```
Count ++
```

Comparison Operators

A comparison operator compares two values and returns a Boolean value of `true` or `false`. Table A-4 lists the common comparison operators used in C#.

Table A-4. *Comparison Operators*

Operator	Description
<	Less than
<=	Less than or equal to
>	Greater than
>=	Greater than or equal to
==	Equal to
!=	Not equal to

You use comparison operators in condition statements to decide when to execute a block of code. The following if block checks to see if the number of invalid login attempts is greater than three before throwing an exception:

```
if (_loginAttemps > 3)
{
    throw new Exception("Invalid login.");
}
```

Logical Operators

Logical operators combine the results of conditional operators. The three most commonly used logical operators are the And, Or, and Not operators. The And operator (&&) combines two expressions and returns `true` if both expressions are true. The Or operator (||) combines two expressions and returns `true` if either one is true. The Not operator (!) switches the result of the comparison: a value of `true` returns `false` and a value of `false` returns `true`. The following code checks to see whether the logged-in user is a department manager or assistant manager before running a method:

```
if (currentUserLevel == Manager.AssistantManager ||
    currentUserLevel == Manager.DeptManager)
{
    ReadLog();
}
```

Ternary Operator

The ternary operator evaluates a Boolean expression and returns one of two values depending on the result of the expression. The following shows the syntax of the ternary operator:

```
condition ? first_expression : second_expression;
```

If the condition evaluates to true, the result of the first expression is returned. If the condition evaluates to false, the result of the second expression is returned. The following code checks to see if the value of x is zero. If it is, it returns 0; if not, it divides y by x and returns the result.

```
return x == 0.0 ? 0 : y/x;
```

Introducing Decision Structures

Decision structures allow conditional execution of code blocks depending on the evaluation of a condition statement. The if statement evaluates a Boolean expression and executes the code block if the result is true. The switch statement checks the same expression for several different values and conditionally executes a code block depending on the results.

If Statements

To execute a code block if a condition is true, use the following structure:

```
if (condition1)
{
     //code
}
```

To execute a code block if a condition is true and an alternate code block if it is false, add an else block.

```
if (condition1)
{
    //code
}
else
{
    //code
}
```

To test additional conditions if the first evaluates to `false`, add an else-if block:

```
if (condition1)
{
    //code
}
else if (condition2)
{
    //code
}
```

```
else
{
    //code
}
```

An if statement can have multiple else-if blocks. If a condition evaluates to `true`, the corresponding code statements are executed, after which execution jumps to the end of the statements. If a condition evaluates to `false`, the next else-if condition is checked. The else block is optional, but if included, it must be the last. The else block has no condition check and executes only if all other condition checks have evaluated to `false`. The following code demonstrates using the if statement to evaluate a series of conditions. It checks a performance rating to determine what bonus to use and includes a check to see if the employee is a manager to determine the minimum bonus.

```
if (performance ==1)
{
    bonus = salary * 0.1;
}
else if (performance == 2)
{
    bonus = salary * 0.08;
}
else if (employeeLevel == Manager.DeptManager)
{
    bonus = salary * 0.05;
}
else
{
    bonus = salary * 0.03;
}
```

Switch Statements

Although the switch statement is similar to the if-else statement, it's used to test a single expression for a series of values. The structure of the switch statement is as follows:

```
switch (expression)
{
case 1:
    Console.WriteLine("Case 1");
    break;
case 2:
    Console.WriteLine("Case 2");
    break;
default:
    Console.WriteLine("Default case");
    break;
}
```

A switch statement can have multiple case blocks. If the test expression value matches the case expression, the code statements in the case block execute. After the case block executes, you need a break statement to bypass the rest of the case statements. If the test expression doesn't match the case expression, execution jumps to the next case block. The default block doesn't have an expression. It executes if no other case blocks are executed. The default block is optional, but if used, it must be last. The following example uses a `switch` to evaluate a performance rating to set the appropriate bonus rate:

```
switch(performance)
{
    case 1:
         bonus = salary * 0.1;
         break;
    case 2:
         bonus = salary * 0.08;
         break;
    case 3:
         bonus = salary * 0.03;
         break;
    default:
         bonus = salary * 0.01;
         break;
 }
```

Using Loop Structures

Looping structures repeat a block of code until a condition is met. C# supports the following looping structures.

While Statement

The while statement repeats the execution of code while a Boolean expression remains `true`. The expression gets evaluated at the beginning of the loop. The following code executes until a valid login variable evaluates to `true`:

```
while (validLogin = false)
{
    //code statements...
}
```

Do-While Statement

The do-while loop is similar to the while loop except the expression is evaluated at the end of the loop. The following code will loop until the maximum login attempts are met:

```
do
{
    //code statements...
}
while (iCount < maxLoginAttempts);
```

For Statement

A for statement loops through a code block a specific number of times based on the value stored in a counter. For statements are a better choice when you know the number of times a loop needs to execute at design time. In the parenthesis that follow a for statement, you initialize a counter, define the evaluation expression, and define the counter increment amount.

```
for (int i = 0; i < 10; i++)
{
    //Code statments...
}
```

For Each Statement

The for-each statement loops through code for each item in a collection. A *collection* is a group of ordered items; for example, the controls placed on a Windows Form are organized into a Controls collection. To use the for-each statement, you first declare a variable of the type of items contained in the collection. This variable is set to the current item in the collection. The following for-each statement loops through the employees in an employee list collection:

```
foreach (Employee e in employeeList)
{
    //Code statements
}
```

If you need to conditionally exit a looping code block, you can use the break statement. The following code shows breaking out of the for-each loop:

```
foreach (Employee e in employeeList)
{
    //Code statements
    if (e.Name == "Bob")
    {
        break;
    }
}
```

Introducing Methods

Methods are blocks of code that can be called and executed from other code. Breaking an application up into discrete logical blocks of code greatly enhances code maintenance and reuse. C# supports methods that return values and methods that do not. When you declare a method, you specify an access modifier, a return type, and a name for the method. The following code declares a method with no return type (designated by the keyword void) used to record logins to the event log:

```
public void RecordLogin(string userName)
{
    EventLog appLog = new EventLog();
     appLog.Source = "OSO App";
     appLog.WriteEntry(userName + " has logged in.");
}
```

You can declare methods with a parameter list that defines arguments that must be passed to the method when it is called. The following code defines a method that encapsulates the assignment of a bonus rate. The calling code passes an integer type value to the method and receives a double type value back.

```
public double GetBonusRate(int performanceRating)
{
    double bonusRate;
    switch (performanceRating)
    {
        case 1:
            bonusRate = 0.1;
            break;
        case 2:
            bonusRate = 0.08;
            break;
        case 3:
            bonusRate = 0.03;
            break;
        default:
            bonusRate = 0.01;
            break;
    }
    return bonusRate;
}
```

The following code demonstrates how the method is called:

```
double salary;
int performance;
double bonus;
// Get salary and performance data from data base...
bonus = GetBonusRate(performance) * salary;
```

If the access modifier of the method is private, it is only accessible from code within the same class. If the method needs to be accessed by code in other classes, then the public access modifier is used.

APPENDIX B

Exception Handling in C#

The topics discussed here extend the discussion of exception handling found in Chapter 8, so this discussion assumes that you have first thoroughly reviewed Chapter 8. The purpose of this appendix is to review Microsoft's recommendations for exception management and present a few of the exception classes provided by the .NET Framework.

Managing Exceptions

Exceptions are generated when the implicit assumptions made by your programming logic are violated. For example, when a program attempts to connect to a database, it assumes that the database server is up and running on the network. If the server can't be located, an exception is generated. It's important that your application gracefully handles any exceptions that may occur. If an exception is not handled, your application will terminate.

You should incorporate a systematic exception handling process in your methods. To facilitate this process, the .NET Framework makes use of structured exception handling through the Try, Catch, and Finally code blocks. The first step is to detect any exceptions that may be thrown as your code executes. To detect any exceptions thrown, place the code within the Try block. When an exception is thrown in the Try block, execution transfers to the Catch block. You can use more than one Catch block to filter for specific types of exceptions that may be thrown. The Finally block performs any cleanup code that you wish to execute. The code in the Finally block executes regardless of whether an exception is thrown. The following code demonstrates reading a list of names from a file using the appropriate exception handling structure:

```
public ArrayList GetNames(string file)
{
    StreamReader stream = new StreamReader();
    ArrayList names = new ArrayList();
    try
    {
        stream = File.OpenText(file);
        while (stream.Peek() > -1)
        {
            names.Add(stream.ReadLine());
        }
    }
    catch (FileNotFoundException e)
    {
        //Could not find file
    }
```

```
        catch (FileLoadException e)
        {
            //Could not open file
        }
        catch (Exception e)
        {
            //Some kind of error occurred. Report error.
        }
        finally
        {
            stream.Close();
        }
        return names;
    }
```

After an exception is caught, the next step in the process is to determine how to respond to it. You basically have two options: either recover from the exception or pass the exception to the calling procedure. The following code demonstrates how to recover from a DivideByZeroException by setting the result to zero:

```
 ...
try
{
    Z = x / y
}
catch (DivideByZeroException e)
{
    Z = 0
}
 ...
```

An exception is passed to the calling procedure using the Throw statement. The following code demonstrates throwing an exception to the calling procedure where it can be caught and handled:

```
catch (FileNotFoundException e)
{
    throw e;
}
```

As exceptions are thrown up the calling chain, the relevance of the original exception can become less obvious. To maintain relevance, you can wrap the exception in a new exception containing additional information that adds relevancy to the exception. The following code shows how to wrap a caught exception in a new one and then pass it up the calling chain:

```
catch (FileLoadException e)
{
    throw new Exception("GetNames function could not open file", e);
}
```

You preserve the original exception by using the InnerException property of the Exception class.

Implementing this exception management policy consistently throughout the various methods in your application will greatly enhance your ability to build highly maintainable, flexible, and successful applications.

Using the .NET Framework Exception Classes

The Common Language Runtime (CLR) has a set of built-in exception classes. The CLR will throw an object instance of the appropriate exception type if an error occurs while executing code instructions. All .NET Framework exception classes derive from the SystemException class, which in turn derives from the Exception class. These base classes provide functionality needed by all exception classes.

Each namespace in the framework contains a set of exception classes that derive from the SystemException class. These exception classes handle common exceptions that may occur while implementing the functionality contained in the namespace. To implement robust exception handling, it's important for you to be familiar with the exception classes provided by the various namespaces. For example, Table B-1 summarizes the exception classes in the System.IO namespace.

Table B-1. *Exception Classes in the System.IO Namespace*

Exception	Description
`IOException`	The base class for exceptions thrown while accessing information using streams, files, and directories
`DirectoryNotFoundException`	Thrown when part of a file or directory can't be found.
`EndOfStreamException`	Thrown when reading is attempted past the end of a stream.
`FileLoadException`	Thrown when a file is found but can't be loaded.
`FileNotFoundException`	Thrown when an attempt to access a file that does not exist on disk fails.
`PathTooLongException`	Thrown when a path or filename is longer than the system-defined maximum length.

Every exception class in the .Net Framework contains the properties listed in Table B-2. These properties help identify where the exception occurred and its cause.

Table B-2. *Exception Class Properties*

Property	Description
`Message`	Gets a message that describes the current exception.
`Source`	Gets or sets the name of the application or the object that causes the error.
`StackTrace`	Gets a string representation of the frames on the call stack at the time the current exception was thrown.
`InnerException`	Gets the exception instance that caused the current exception.
`HelpLink`	Gets or sets a link to the help file associated with this exception.

In addition, the ToString method of the exception classes provides summary information about the current exception. It combines the name of the class that threw the current exception, the message, the result of calling the ToString method of the inner exception, and the stack trace information of the current exception.

You will find that the exception classes in the .NET Framework provide you with the capabilities to handle most exceptions that may occur in your applications. In cases where you may need to implement custom error handling, you can create your own exception classes. These classes need to inherit from System.ApplicationException, which in turn inherits from System.Exception. The topic of creating custom exception classes is an advanced one and thus beyond the scope of this text; for more information, consult the .NET Framework documentation at `http://msdn.microsoft.com/en-us/library/`.

APPENDIX C

Installing the Required Software

I have included many learning activities throughout this book. In order to get the most out of the topics I discuss, you should complete these activities. This is where the theory becomes concrete. It is my hope that you will take these activities seriously and work through them thoroughly and even repeatedly.

The UML modeling activities in Part 1 are meant for someone using UMLet. I chose this program because it is a good diagraming tool to learn on. It enables you to create UML diagrams without adding a lot of advanced features. UMLet is a free open source tool and can be downloaded from `www.umlet.com`. But you don't need a tool to complete these activities; a paper and pencil will work just fine.

The activities in Part 2 require Visual Studio 2010 with C# installed. You can use either the free version, Visual Studio 2010 Express, or a trial version of Visual Studio 2010 Professional. These versions are available at `http://msdn.microsoft.com/en-us/vstudio/`. I encourage you to install the help files and make abundant use of them while you're completing the activities.

The activities in Part 3 require Microsoft SQL Server 2008 R2. You can use either the free version SQL Server 2008 R2 Express or a trial version of SQL Server 2008 R2 available at `http://msdn.microsoft.com/en-us/sqlserver/`. When you install SQL Server, be sure you add yourself as an administrator.

Installing the Sample Databases

The scripts to install the sample database used in this book are available at `www.apress.com`. In order to install the scripts, follow these steps:

1. Open a command prompt window.
2. From the command prompt, use the cd command to navigate to the folder containing the sample database scripts.

```
cd c:\SampleDatabases
```

3. Run `SQLCmd.exe` specifying `instOSODB.sql` as the input file.
4. To install the database on a default instance, use

```
SQLCmd.exe -E -i instOSODB.sql
```

5. To install the database on a named instance, use

```
SQLCmd.exe -E -S ComputerName\InstanceName -i instOSODB.sql
```

6. Repeat the procedure for the `instpubs.sql` and `instnwnd.sql` files.

Verifying the Database Installs

To verify the database installs:

1. Start Visual Studio. If you don't see the Database Explorer window shown in Figure C-1, open it by choosing Server Explore on the View menu.

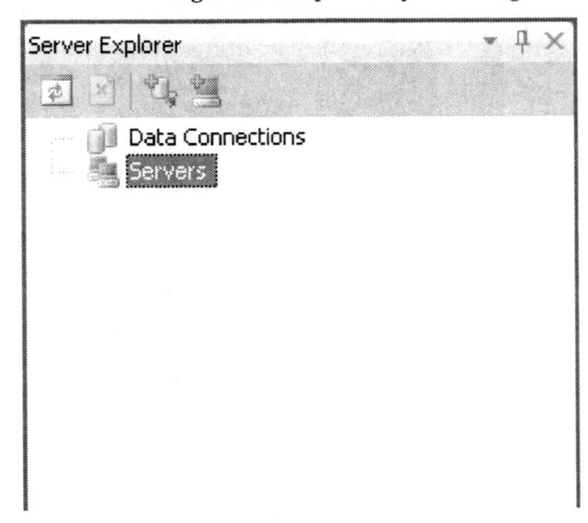

Figure C-1. *The Database Explorer window*

2. In the Database Explorer window, right-click the Data Connections node and select Add Connection. In the Add Connections dialog box shown in Figure C-2, fill in the name of your server, select the Northwind database, and click OK.

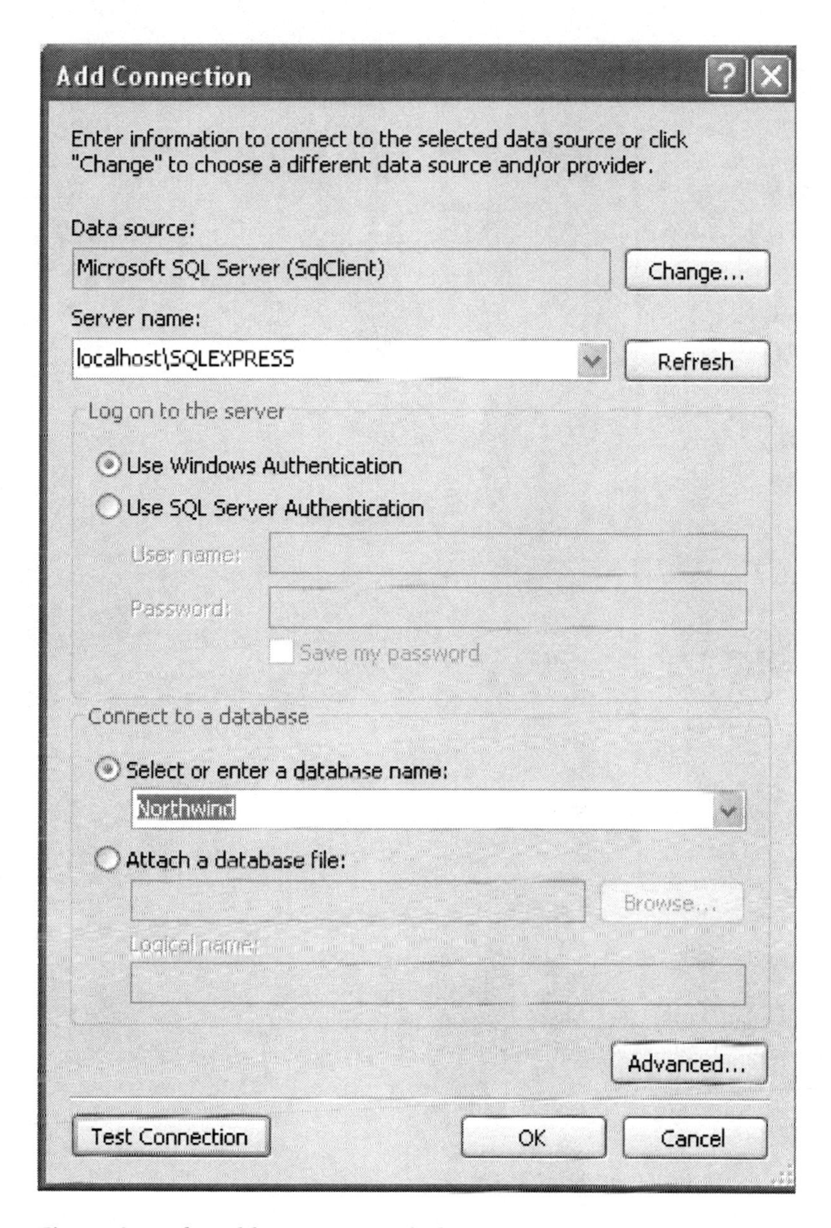

Figure C-2. *The Add Connections dialog box*

3. Expand the Northwind database node and the Tables node in the Database Explorer window, as shown in Figure C-3.

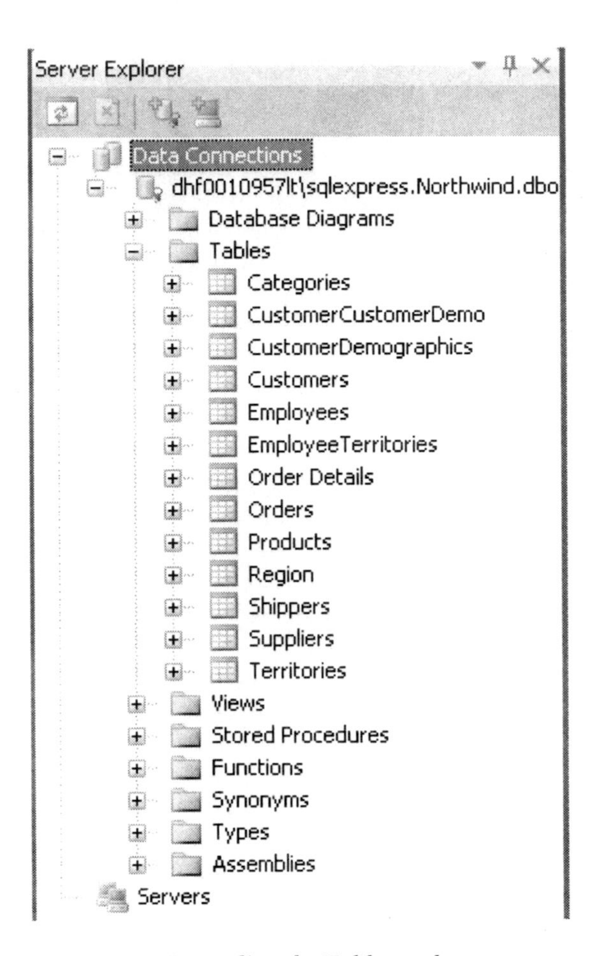

Figure C-3. *Expanding the Tables node*

4. Right-click the Suppliers table node and select Show Table Data. The Suppliers table data should display as shown in Figure C-4.

Suppliers: Query(dhf...qlexpress.Northwind) × Start Page

SupplierID	CompanyName	ContactName	ContactTitle	Address	City
1	Exotic Liquids	Charlotte Cooper	Purchasing Man...	49 Gilbert St.	Londo
2	New Orleans Caj...	Shelley Burke	Order Administr...	P.O. Box 78934	New C
3	Grandma Kelly's ...	Regina Murphy	Sales Represent...	707 Oxford Rd.	Ann A
4	Tokyo Traders	Yoshi Nagase	Marketing Manager	9-8 Sekimai Mus...	Tokyo
5	Cooperativa de ...	Antonio del Valle...	Export Administr...	Calle del Rosal 4	Ovied
6	Mayumi's	Mayumi Ohno	Marketing Repre...	92 Setsuko Chu...	Osaka
7	Pavlova, Ltd.	Ian Devling	Marketing Manager	74 Rose St. Moo...	Melbo
8	Specialty Biscuit...	Peter Wilson	Sales Represent...	29 King's Way	Manch
9	PB Knäckebröd AB	Lars Peterson	Sales Agent	Kaloadagatan 13	Göteb
10	Refrescos Ameri...	Carlos Diaz	Marketing Manager	Av. das America...	Sao P
11	Heli Süßwaren G...	Petra Winkler	Sales Manager	Tiergartenstraße 5	Berlin
12	Plutzer Lebensmi...	Martin Bein	International Ma...	Bogenallee 51	Frankf
13	Nord-Ost-Fisch ...	Sven Petersen	Coordinator For...	Frahmredder 112a	Cuxha
14	Formaggi Fortini ...	Elio Rossi	Sales Represent...	Viale Dante, 75	Raven
15	Norske Meierier	Beate Vileid	Marketing Manager	Hatlevegen 5	Sandv
16	Bigfoot Breweries	Cheryl Saylor	Regional Accoun...	3400 - 8th Aven...	Bend
17	Svensk Sjöföda AB	Michael Björn	Sales Represent...	Brovallavägen 231	Stockh

1 of 29 | Cell is Read Only.

Figure C 4. *Viewing the table data*

5. Repeat these steps to test the pubs and the `OfficeSupply` databases. After testing, exit Visual Studio.

Index

B

D

E

H

I

J

K

N

O

P

Q

R

S

T

U

V

W

X

CPSIA information can be obtained at www.ICGtesting.com
230885LV00006B/79-260/P

9 781430 235309